the Baby Gizmo™ buying guide

From Pacifiers to Potties . . .
Why, When, and What to Buy
For Pregnancy through Preschool

Heather Maclean with Hollie Schultz

THOMAS NELSON
Since 1798

NASHVILLE   DALLAS   MEXICO CITY   RIO DE JANEIRO   BEIJING

Published in Nashville, Tennessee, by Thomas Nelson. Thomas Nelson is a registered trademark of Thomas Nelson, Inc.

Thomas Nelson, Inc. titles may be purchased in bulk for educational, business, fund-raising, or sales promotional use. For information, please e-mail SpecialMarkets@ThomasNelson.com.

The contents of this book are for informational and entertainment purposes only and should not replace medical or professional advice from a doctor or other experts in the field of child safety and welfare. You should always make your own choices regarding your baby's safety, based on the advice of your chosen professionals.

Illustrations by Art-Builders

Library of Congress Cataloging-in-Publication Data

Maclean, Heather, 1972–
   The baby gizmo buying guide / Heather Maclean.
   p. cm.
   Includes index.
   ISBN 978-1-4016-0354-0
   1. Infants—Care. 2. Infants' supplies—Catalogs. I. Title.
RJ61.M304 2008
649'.1220284—dc22   2007027900

Printed in the United States of America

08 09 10 11 12 — 5 4 3 2 1

For our children, because they made us mothers.

For our husbands, because they had a small,
   rather fun role in making us mothers,
   but their constant love and support helped make
   us great mothers.

Do you know how many people there are
   in the whole universe?
That's how much we love you.

Contents

vii

Smoke Signals from the Stroller Aisle

My husband and I have an arrangement. If I've been gone for hours and it's getting late, I send him a modern-day distress signal via cell phone.

He'll answer immediately. "Are you lost?"

"Yes," I'll moan, barely coherent.

"Where are you?" he'll respond, car keys already in hand.

"The store. . ."

It's fairly well known that casinos in Vegas have no windows, no clocks, and are purposely built like confusing labyrinths to keep you walking in circles and spending your money. What is less well known is that most major retailers employ similar tactics.

The neon-lit slot machines and brightly patterned carpets are replaced by shiny end cap displays and tantalizing trial sizes, but the sentiment is the same. They'll keep you there, you'll be happy while you're spending, but somehow $200 and two hours will slip through your fingers and you won't know what happened.

Moms, of course, are especially vulnerable. What is jokingly referred to as "mom brain" during pregnancy—the forgetfulness and inability to do simple math or remember most of one's vocabulary—can, sadly, by the third or fourth kid, become a permanent affliction.

As a mom of three well-spaced children, I've been shopping for baby products for ten years. You'd think I'd be good at it by now. Or at least faster.

Yet time and again, I still find myself at the store aimlessly walking in circles for *hours*, completely ignorant of why I came in and what I was looking for.

Sure I have a list. Somewhere. Provided I haven't already lost it or absent-mindedly set it down on a shelf. I have literally gone to the lost and found to report my missing list.

"Um, ma'am, you say you lost a *list*?"

"Yes, that's right. My list! I need it. Otherwise, I don't know what I'm doing here!"

"So, um, what did it look like?"

"It's very small—I ripped a Post-it note in thirds. It's probably scrunched up because it was in my pocket. I think. And it's written in pencil."

"All right, ma'am, we don't have any 'lists' back here. But we'll keep our eyes out."

"Can I look in your trash can?"

Yet even my precious list is useless when I get to the baby gear aisle. While items such as "toilet paper" and "trash bags" are easily fetched, the words "baby swing" or "toddler booster" can strike fear into the heart of even the most seasoned shopper. No matter how prepared you were, no matter how much you read about this product or that model, once you approach the baby section, the number of products and product variations—wait, *that* one wasn't on the Internet!—is at once overwhelming and mind-numbing.

And then there's the money.

According to a government study, the average mom spends a whopping $8,200 on baby products the first year. Sound like a lot? If your annual household income is over $40,000, that number jumps to $11,500. Husband got a raise? Thank goodness, because families that make over $67,000 a year spend $17,000. The first year. On the first kid. Subsequent kids may be cheaper, but with product advancements and just as many recalls, not significantly so.

With five children under the age of 7 between us (plus seven siblings, eight nieces and nephews, and 19 first cousins!), my sister Hollie and I did the math and discovered we've spent over $75,000 on baby stuff. Regular baby stuff. Rest assured, we shop at discount stores, not Petite Trésor.

We're middle class moms from Middle America and don't part with that much money easily. So we've been extremely choosy, almost obsessive, about our purchases. We're the moms who take the strollers off the shelf, take products out of the box; we buy, try, and aren't afraid to return. We've been known to take a box of batteries to the store so we could see a product in action, and we even lick the merchandise. (Yes, that's right, lick the merchandise. We want to know if the industrial plastic our baby is supposed to gum tastes nasty.)

Like most wired mamas, we used the Web for much of our preliminary product research. And discovered that unlike the modern miracle it's supposed to be, the Web is really a black hole for all things baby.

Online baby magazines feature only a handful of products and must toe the line with their product manufacturer advertisers. Online retailers routinely delete negative product reviews so they can sell more stuff. And while online reviews are great, most reviewers are passing judgment based on their experience with just one or two models, not all two hundred available. Worst of all, we could never find information about new products.

Sick of reading about car seats from three years ago, we decided that necessity dictated we be mothers of invention. So in 2005, Hollie and I created our own perfect baby product website: BabyGizmo.com.

Of course, we're biased, but we believe that we have created the Web's most comprehensive product resource site dedicated exclusively to baby gear. Featuring editor reviews, everyday mom reviews, Top Five picks, price comparisons, message boards, video clips, audio samples, and industry news, BabyGizmo.com aims to be the most up-to-date baby product site on the planet.

The Baby Gizmo Company is now a product testing and research coalition of moms, pediatricians, and child development experts. We leave the crash testing and safety ratings to the government and consumer organizations like *Consumer Reports*. We love the information packed into testing reports, but found their reviews didn't speak to other important issues, like if the music is annoying or if you'll ever get dried green beans out of the cracks.

Our product testing is real-world testing. We built a stroller obstacle course. We weigh products. We throw food on them. We run through parking lots carrying them, two other kids, and our diaper bags.

And in our quest to publish information about what's actually on the store shelves right now, we of course, make almost daily visits to the nation's major retailers.

And still find ourselves walking in circles.

Master multitaskers with a chronic shortage of time, moms don't venture into the store for only one thing (that's a dad's specialty). So we arrive, armed and ready to look at double jogging strollers (or possibly a double bicycle trailer), an umbrella stroller for our upcoming vacation, and a travel swing. We're confident we know just what we want.

Until the questions begin.

There's no basket on the jogging stroller—do I need one? Should the front wheel pivot or be stuck like that? Is side-by-side or stadium seating better? Is my kid really supposed to sit underneath like that? What's the difference between a "lightweight" and an "umbrella" stroller? The stroller weight maximum is 35 pounds, but what does the average 4-year-old weigh? Is there a difference between one-hand and one-step fold? What the heck is stand-up fold? Is a sun canopy important or a waste of space? How about a rain cover? A peekaboo window? A cup holder? A snack tray?

Head throbbing, we head to the swings aisle for a break. But there are portable swings, cradle swings, bouncers, rockers, and gliders . . . We stare blankly as we contemplate never shopping again. Surely our babies can just play in a laundry basket and sleep in a sock drawer . . .

Aside from printing pages and pages off the Internet (many of which won't print correctly anyway) or lugging around a giant book full of product reviews that were outdated before the book was even published, there seemed no hope for the modern in-store mom. Until now.

The Baby Gizmo Buying Guide is our conspiratorial and collective knowledge of the secrets to successful baby gear shopping. How do we know so much? Because, unlike other baby book authors whose youngest kids are *teenagers*, we're still having babies. Right now. Well, not this second, but little Sawyer was born just four weeks ago, making the third baby under the age of 2 between us. We've been there, and we're back again, straddling every stage from breastfeeding to potty training. We agonize over new, monumentally important purchases daily. We feel your pain.

But we also interview manufacturers, attend industry trade shows, talk to government experts, call pediatricians, take safety certification classes, troll message boards, ask our friends, and do everything under the sun to find the answers. And these, we happily share.

The Baby Gizmo Buying Guide was designed to help you be a smarter, more efficient baby product shopper: to keep your thoughts and research organized, to get you in and out of the store in record time, to no longer fear the baby section.

Because if we're going to walk around in circles, we'd much rather do it in Vegas.

A Best Friend for Your Pocket

The Baby Gizmo Buying Guide is just that: a guide to help you buy baby gizmos. It's filled with buying guides for every major baby gear purchase you'll ever make: definitions; product history; key features to look for; how most moms use or don't use it; and our advice on whether you really need it, when you should buy it, and how long your baby will use it. We'll also tell you, bottom line, why we love or don't love a product, unless of course it's a product you have to have (like a car seat), or a tiny purchase (like a bottle nipple).

We designed *The Baby Gizmo Buying Guide* to go to the store with you. To help you ask the right questions, look for the right accessories, and remind you what makes a particular product good or bad. It's like having your best friend (the one with four kids who knows exactly what makes a good high chair, not the one with no kids that still gets to spend all of her paycheck on shoes) in your back pocket.

To keep from being outdated before it even hits the shelf (and from being too big to be practical), this book does not include reviews of specific brands. For detailed product reviews, our Top Five picks, and the opinions of thousands of moms across the nation, you can visit BabyGizmo.com. But to save you from printing pages and pages off the Internet, we've included a Notes section after each product category. In it, you can list which specific models you are seeking before you leave the house, and then take notes when you actually see them in the store. We even give you room to grade them yourself, so you can easily rank different products from different stores against one another.

The book begins with a concise guide to product safety and developmental stages—critical information you need to know before you hit the mall. The 25 major product categories—such as "car seats" and "strollers"—are then listed by chapter, in alphabetical order. We conclude with indispensable lists, such as products to include (and not include) on your baby registry, and items to store in the perfectly packed diaper bag. So you don't become overwhelmed in the store, the appendix features In-Store Buying Guide Reminders: these handy checklists for the major product categories will keep you focused on the most important features as you make your selections.

Because we don't want you to ever see a product in the store and wish you knew what it was and if you needed it (belt tightener? harness buddy? snack trap?), we've also created a glossary called Every Baby Product on the Planet. Here you'll find an alphabetical listing of every single type of baby gadget and gizmo on the market with a quick definition and some valuable mom feedback. There's also an index in the back to help you locate information quickly.

A Best Friend for Your Pocketbook

Millionaire or middle class, all moms love a good deal. And while this book is not technically one of those baby bargain books (we might love a bargain, but sticking mutilated maxipads in our bras instead of buying nursing pads is not our idea of fun), *The Baby Gizmo Buying Guide* can save you money.

We'll teach you to shop smarter. There is no greater torture than the bad baby product cycle: you buy an item, take it home, assemble it, use it for a few weeks—then decide you can't stand the music, your baby is afraid of it, and it clashes horribly with your décor. So you take it back (assuming you have the original packaging and receipt and it shows no signs of wear and tear) and start over with another item. Or, even worse, you keep it, but seethe with hatred every time you look at it.

The Baby Gizmo Buying Guide will help you make the right purchase the first time to match your unique lifestyle and needs, so you can bask in the bliss of a perfect purchase, stroll with confidence, and know your neighbors have diaper bag envy.

We also offer tips and tricks on the best time of year to buy certain items, which products make good secondhand purchases, and what you really need versus what's just nice-to-have.

That said, if you want the nice-to-haves, we pass no judgment here. While other books shame you for considering unnecessary or luxury items, we say, if you want it and can afford it, why not? Even when we're on the strictest budget, sometimes we moms just can't resist the tiny leather baby shoes or the expensive soft-as-heaven blankets. Nor should we.

One

The Three Most Important Things to Consider When Buying a Baby Product: Safety, Safety, and Safety

I remember very clearly where I was when I was first shamed into rethinking my whole philosophy on baby gear. My driveway. I was bemoaning the cost of a new car seat for my daughter and scheming about buying a cheap one on eBay, when my neighbor lost it on me.

"You mean to tell me you drive a $40,000 SUV, but you only want to spend $40 on a car seat to protect your *baby*?!?" she shrieked, howler-monkey style.

It was true. I had traded in my previous car at a financial loss because I was so concerned about getting a safer vehicle, yet I wouldn't dream of spending $200 on one of those "fancy" car seats.

Why was I so cheap when it came to baby gear? I would never buy used pillows, sleep on an old mattress, or wear hand-me-down underwear. I would never pick up a smoke alarm at a secondhand store or get a fire extinguisher at a garage sale.

Sure, babies are expensive. But when it comes to your baby's well-being, you should never, ever settle. Buy toys at an outlet. Accept hand-me-down clothes. But don't skimp on baby gear. It's just too dangerous.

I'm a convert. And I hope you will be too.

1

What You Don't Know Can Hurt Your Baby

You would think that products made for use by the tiniest, most helpless (and most adorable) of creatures would be put through rigorous tests by the government before they hit the stores. You would *think*. And you would be wrong.

Believe it or not, companies are not required to test most children's products for safety before they are sold. In fact, the government sets safety standards for only four types of children's products: car seats, pacifiers, toys, and cribs. Everything else—high chairs, strollers, monitors, and so forth—can be placed on the market with no safety testing at all.

The juvenile products industry does issue voluntary safety standards, but they are indeed voluntary. And while most manufacturers do test their own products, many times the tests take place in a controlled laboratory environment. (And we all know a toy-strewn family room with a rambunctious toddler and a distracted mom making dinner is hardly the same as a controlled laboratory environment.) Safety issues or product defects frequently aren't discovered until children actually begin using the products.

During the 1990s alone, *more than a million* portable cribs and playpens were recalled. In 2000, two children's products were recalled every week, resulting in the recall of *37 million individual items*. And sadly, every year, over 200,000 children are treated for injuries resulting from unsafe children's products.

So what's a mother to do?

Keep on Top of Recalls

We know it's a pain, and yes, we too figure if it's a biggie, eventually we'll hear about it. But then we look at our tiny angels and remember that we'd never forgive ourselves if we had the power to keep them out of harm's way and didn't use it.

Here are some tips on how to be diligent:

1. Check Your Inventory for Recalled Products

Make a list of every product your baby uses or you're considering buying, and verify that it hasn't been recalled. For the most complete and up-to-date list, visit www.recalls.gov.

2. Check Products Your Baby Uses Outside Your House

You know your playpen is safe, but what about the one at your day care center? Babysitter's? Grandma's house? Hotel? Gym? Write down and research all products your baby uses at every location. Don't assume because it's a licensed or respectable facility that it's on top of recalls. It's ultimately your job to protect your baby.

3. Sign Up for Recall E-mail Alerts

We know your inbox is full, but there's no better way to be in the know immediately. It's super simple to sign up at the government's recall website: www.recalls.gov. They won't send you junk or ads— just one to two messages a week as recalls are announced. When you hear news, share the love and tell your friends.

4. Use Common Sense

If the buckle frequently comes undone or the handle seems shaky, don't wait for an accident to report or retire your product. If it seems unsafe, it probably is.

5. Maintain Your Products

Young children are masters of perpetual and repetitive motion. Their constant use can compromise even the safest product. Check your baby gear regularly for loose screws, rickety rails, fraying cords, and so forth. Better yet, put your husband on the task. He gives regular maintenance love to his car. Have him give some of that concern to your helpless newborn. Every time he gets the oil changed, have him inspect everything your children use.

6. Don't Blindly Trust Brand Names

As brand conscious as we all are, even the most well-respected companies shouldn't be blindly trusted. It's easy to distrust a cheap-looking toy from overseas, but be aware that almost every brand-name manufacturer has had multiple recalls. Don't give blind trust to any brand.

7. Don't Assume More Expensive Means Safer

Many times more expensive products are better made and could be safer, but that is hardly the rule. One of the most popular and expensive brands of baby carriers has recalled its famous product three times in the last six years for a variety of reasons that resulted in babies falling and fracturing their skulls. Keep on top of all your products, even the expensive, designer ones.

Go for the New

Many parents mistakenly believe that baby gear that's purchased second-hand or handed down, especially from an older sibling, is safer than a new product because it was "kid tested." Your older daughter used it and was just fine, so it must be safe. Not true.

Not only do the mechanical parts of baby products, like all products, deteriorate over time, but safety standards are raised each year, more stringent policies are constantly being put into place, and manufacturers do actually learn from their mistakes on past design flaws.

And just because you see a secondhand product for sale, doesn't mean it hasn't been recalled. The Consumer Product Safety Commission (CPSC) estimates that currently *69 million recalled products are still on the shelves, mostly at thrift and resale shops.*

While new products do get recalled, with a new version you have a much better chance of hearing about the safety problem and getting a retrofit, refund, or replacement.

Because of the vast number of historical recalls and frequency with which you will use (and abuse!) certain products, we highly suggest you buy the following baby products new.

Car Seats

Because a safe and correctly installed car seat can cut the risk of injury to a child in an automobile accident by over 60 percent, you should pick the best possible seat for your child. And to reduce your chances of getting a product that has been recalled—over the last 10 years, mil-  lions of car seats and boosters from every major manufacturer have been recalled—your best bet is a new seat.

Used car seats are also dangerous because they have unknown histories. If a car seat is in even a minor crash, its structural integrity is forever compromised.

By the time our kids grew out of their car seat, it was usually ready for the trash anyway, thanks to holes in the fabric and permanent juice box damage. But if you drive a disciplined car, have your kids close enough in age, and stay on top of maintenance and recall information, you may be able to reuse some car seats and boosters for your subsequent children. But know that car seats are only tested when brand new, and everything wears out eventually. No one has ever officially tested used car seats to find out how old is too old. While nobody wants to state an exact age of expiration, most car seat manufacturers themselves recommend not keeping a car seat more than five or six years from the date of manufacture (which you can find on the car seat itself), not the date of purchase.

Cribs

Cribs cause more infant deaths than any other nursery product. Every year, nearly 12,000 children are hospitalized with crib-related injuries, and an average of 35 children die in unsafe cribs. Most of those deaths and injuries occur in sec-  ondhand or hand-me-down cribs. Cribs made before 1990 should never be used because they have slats that are wide enough to injure children, or were built too wide to snugly fit a standard baby mattress. Antique cribs are not recommended for these same reasons, but also because of additional lead paint concerns.

How long can you use your first child's crib? Ten years is a good rule of thumb, provided the crib hasn't been recalled, isn't missing any hardware, and shows no sign of structural distress. It's a good idea to accept a used crib only from your own immediate family, so you are assured of its history. Say "no thanks" to the crib from your neighbor.

While it's easy to see how a 15-year-old crib might have a higher recall risk, cribs just a few years old are recalled at alarming rates. A record number of cribs were recalled in 2005. And in 2007, 40,000 cribs were recalled—cribs that had been made from 2005 to 2007. Current crib hazards include defective supports, rails that detach, and lead paint; in addition, even though manufacturers have known about crib mattress safety for years, thousands of cribs are still too wide for a standard baby mattress. Mattresses need to fit snugly into a crib: there should be less than two finger widths between the edge of the mattress and the crib.

Whatever the age of your crib, stay vigilant about its care, repair, and recall status. The CPSC estimates that 20,000,000 (*that's 20 million!*) unsafe cribs and play yards are still in use or waiting in storage.

Play Yards/Playpens

The granddaddy of potentially unsafe products, millions of portable cribs and mesh play yards have been recalled over the years—and caused a heartbreaking number of deaths— because of serious safety flaws. The main defect was in how the rails were constructed and how easily they could collapse on a child's neck. Other hazards included risks of choking or entanglement, head entrapment, suffocation, and injury when the product tipped over as legs loosened or separated.

What makes play yards especially dangerous is that they are easy to set up incorrectly, they are the ultimate store-and-use-years-later product, and recalled models are hard to spot. A large percentage of the recalled play yard population was never retired because they serve as a portable baby sleeping staple for people without kids (and cribs) in their house: folks who have no reason to routinely check for baby product recalls. Problematic play yards are particularly insidious because they were intended to provide a safe environment for your baby, so parents automatically trust them, and they pop up in seemingly safe locations where you might bed your baby (like a hotel room or day care).

The sheer number of product recalls in this category and the seriousness of the injuries make this a poor hand-me-down choice.

Another reason to buy this product new is the advancements in convenience and safety features. Modern play yards include features such as floating bassinet sections, changing tables, night-lights, and music. And while 2001 models had solid sides in the bassinets, newer versions have mesh siding to allow babies better breathing conditions and hopefully cut down on SIDS risks.

Changing Tables

Changing tables result in thousands of serious injuries each year, because a baby literally can fall as quickly as you can turn your back. New changing tables are recommended because they have four side rails for safety and safety straps for your infant. Keep in mind that babies won't alert you the day they turn from a gelatinous glob into a rolling maniac. They will just roll. Hopefully you'll have the safety measures in place when they do.

P.S. No matter what the store is selling, never use an attachable mattress pad on a regular dresser. Velcro just doesn't cut it. If you don't want to invest in a proper changing table, use the floor (we won't tell).

Baby Carriers, Slings, and Backpacks

These products are recalled almost too frequently to count. Faulty products in this category are especially dangerous because you use the product to carry your baby high off the ground, and you trust that it's going to hold them. Common reasons for recall include leg openings that are too large, and faulty latches, buckles, and straps. All result in the same thing: babies plummeting to earth.

Because there are so many recalls, because the models look so alike year to year, and because the secondhand stores are chock-full of the recalled versions, we don't recommend buying them used. If you must, though, or want to use one from a family member, check the recall information thoroughly.

Baby Gates

Baby gates are frequently recalled, but they have also been completely redesigned in recent years to have smaller slat openings, be less kid-climbable, and have stronger latches. Most recalls are for larger slat openings that can cause entrapment or strangulation, gates that are easy for children to climb, and latches that break or can be easily opened, allowing children access to dangerous areas like stairs.

Baby gates made before 1985 with the diamond-shaped openings that closed accordion-style are especially dangerous and should never be used.

Seven Deadly Sinners:
Unsafe Baby Products You Should *Not* Buy

While the CPSC will recall defective products, for some insane reason, it will not ban some especially dangerous products outright, even though consumer organizations, the American Academy of Pediatrics, and masses of parents beg them to.

The following is our personal list of the seven most dangerous baby products you can buy, but shouldn't.

1. Baby Walkers

We have a personal reason for hating these things. When our brother Sean was 12 months old, he drove his baby walker down our basement stairs and ended up in a full body cast for eight weeks. But we're not the only ones who hate them. The American Academy of Pediatrics has long called for a ban on baby walkers, and Canada has already banned them. (And what a ban it was! On April 7, 2004, the Canadian government announced an immediate ban on the sale, importation, and even advertisement of baby walkers.)

More than 14,000 babies are sent to the hospital every year with baby walker injuries, and studies have found that they don't encourage walking and can actually delay development. In 1997, the walkers were widened to supposedly no longer fit through doorways, but babies can still zip around, tip themselves over, and reach dangerous things like stovetops and counters.

So why are manufacturers still making them? Because people are still buying them. The same people, we suspect, who let their 7-year-olds ride ATVs and their 10-year-olds ride power lawn mowers.

Let's put this dangerous product out of business before one more baby zooms into a space heater or fireplace. Please.

2. Baby Bath Seats

Most manufacturers have (wisely) quit making these, but you can still find them. Avoid them like the plague. Baby bath seats have little suction cups that are supposed to hold them down, but frequently, they fail. And babies fall over. And become trapped by the seat. And because a baby can drown (silently) in just an inch of water, the danger is clear.

Just as big a danger as faulty suction cups seems to be the false sense of security the seats give parents. Baby bath seats are not safety devices. They will not hold your child safely in the bath. Do not use them. (And of course, never, *ever* leave your baby alone in the bath. For even a second.)

3. Doorway Jumpers

Doorway jumpers are dangerous not just because they allow wild wee ones to bash their heads against door jambs, but because the springs and straps break just as frequently as parents are afraid they will. Manufacturers have been trying to perfect this product for over two decades, to no avail. In 2005, another 29,000 doorway jumpers were recalled for faulty springs. So bad is this problem that the CPSC, which has set safety standards for only four types of baby products, has banned most jumpers for design flaws because, according to its 2006 report, they cause "amputation, crushing, lacerations, fractures, hematomas, bruises, or other injuries to fingers, toes, or other parts of the anatomy of young children." We're convinced.

4. Wipe Warmers

Tens of thousands of wipe warmers were recalled recently because they posed a fire risk. You mean an electrical box that heats wet paper isn't a safe thing to plug into my baby's nursery? Yeah, that's what we're saying. God gave you two hands. If your baby needs a warm wipe, press one between your palms. Three seconds, and voilà!

5. Sleep Positioners

These wedges were invented during the dawn of the back-to-sleep campaign, and because they encouraged people to get infants off their stomachs, no one had a problem with them. Until babies started suffocating against them. The National SIDS Alliance does *not* recommend using sleep positioners. Even the ones designed with mesh sides or special airflow fabric are dangerous not just because of smothering risks, but because of the risk of a baby rebreathing its own carbon dioxide (a possible cause of SIDS).

6. Crib Bumpers and Plush Bedding

Since 1994, the rate of SIDS deaths in the United States has declined a glorious 50 percent. The idea that SIDS is frequently caused by infants smothering in their cribs or rebreathing their own air led not only to the back-to-sleep campaign, but to a new outlook on crib safety. A firm, bare crib is a safe crib. Soft bedding, blankets, pillows, and stuffed animals are not to be placed in a baby's crib. What most people don't know is this recommendation also extends to crib bumpers.

We know, we're sad, too. We hated to lose our crib bumpers, as they were a design highlight in our baby's nursery. However, they not only pose a breathing risk, but they also no longer serve a functional purpose. Crib bumpers were created to keep babies from knocking themselves unconscious on old iron cribs or from getting their limbs tangled in too-wide slats. New cribs eliminate both concerns. You should eliminate your crib bumpers too.

7. Baby Bicycle Seats

Yes, we know you rode on the back of your dad's bike in one. And you lived. We all did. Without helmets or seat belts too. Congratulations.

But baby bicycle seats mounted on the back of adult bikes are still extremely dangerous. Always were. Always will be. They cause a shift in weight and balance for the adult biker and can extend braking times. And as no one can predict uneven pavement or an ill-placed rock, if the adult should fall off the bike, the strapped-in baby is especially vulnerable to injury.

The best alternative is a bicycle trailer, right? Wrong! Babies shouldn't ride in those either. Bicycle trailers are often involved in collisions with motor vehicles, leading to more serious injuries and death, and the jarring motion from regular riding can lead to injuries similar to "shaken baby syndrome" that might not show up as developmental delays until years later.

The fact is bicycle accidents are the third most common cause of accidental death in children, behind automobile accidents and drowning. In many states, it's literally against the law to have a baby under the age of 1 on a bike or in a bike trailer.

Ever wonder why you couldn't find a teeny-tiny baby helmet in the store? Now you know. Until they're ready for preschool, you should not introduce baby to a bike. Period.

Ready, Set, Shop!

Now, no more serious, sad, safety talk. The rest of this book is about putting the fun back into baby shopping. We want to help you stop wasting time and money walking in aggravated circles, so you are free to revel in the joys of tiny overalls and anything with puppies on it. Because after the pregnancy/birth/colic, darn it, you deserve it.

The way we look at it: God gave us shopping to make up for stretch marks.

Two

Ages and Stages

his chapter is dedicated to the couple we saw in a baby superstore who registered for a bouncer they didn't really like because it was the only one with a weight limit of 40 pounds. *40 pounds?!?* By the time their kid is 40 pounds, he'll be able to throw the bouncer at them.

But of course, until you're at that stage, most people have no idea how big a baby typically is or what you can expect them to be doing. So we've included an Average Height and Weight Chart and an Ages and Stages Chart to help you see at a glance how big your bundle of joy will get, what your baby will likely be doing when, and the average use range of key baby gear purchases.

So now you can see at a glance that a monitor lasts three times as long as a mobile, and that by the time your child reaches the 80-pound weight limit on her car seat, she may be close to getting her own driver's license.

Average Height and Weight Chart

Age	Average Weight	Average Height
3 months	15 pounds	24½ inches
6 months	18 pounds	26½ inches
9 months	20 pounds	28½ inches
12 months	23 pounds	30 inches

Age	Average Weight	Average Height
18 months	25½ pounds	32½ inches
2 years	30 pounds	36 inches
3 years	33 pounds	38½ inches
4 years	42 pounds	40 inches
6 years	48 pounds	46 inches
8 years	60 pounds	51 inches

Ages and Stages Chart

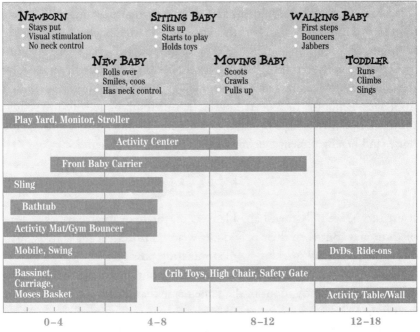

NEWBORN
- Stays put
- Visual stimulation
- No neck control

NEW BABY
- Rolls over
- Smiles, coos
- Has neck control

SITTING BABY
- Sits up
- Starts to play
- Holds toys

MOVING BABY
- Scoots
- Crawls
- Pulls up

WALKING BABY
- First steps
- Bouncers
- Jabbers

TODDLER
- Runs
- Climbs
- Sings

Play Yard, Monitor, Stroller

Activity Center

Front Baby Carrier

Sling

Bathtub

Activity Mat/Gym Bouncer

Mobile, Swing

DvDs. Ride-ons

Bassinet, Carriage, Moses Basket

Crib Toys, High Chair, Safety Gate

Activity Table/Wall

| 0–4 | 4–8 | 8–12 | 12–18 |

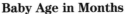

Baby Age in Months

Three

Activity Toy Systems:
Mats, Gyms, Centers, Tables, and Walls

For centuries, the way to entertain a baby was simple: baby + toys + blanket on the floor. Until someone got the bright idea to combine the toys with the blanket. And then things got complicated.

First came activity mats. Blankets with toys sewn onto and into them provided baby with squeaks, mirrors, and no more errant playthings. The mats soon turned into gyms, with bars that crisscrossed to the sky providing a place for more toys to be hung—toys that now sang, spun, and even spoke Spanish.

Activity centers, activity cubes, activity tables, and even activity walls took the stationary toy extravaganza to new heights for the older crowd. Children from ages 4 months to 3 years now have a plethora of activity toy system choices—from deluxe to downright spectacular. Fear not! We cut through the noise, and hereby present a definitive guide on all things activity.

Activity Mats

It used to be we only used baby blankets on the floor to give babes a clean place to play. But then their play quilts went gonzo. Meet the activity mat: a toy mecca literally sparkling with stimulating possibilities.

You can still find quaint and quiet play mats, but they're sold next to elaborate electronic contraptions of the same name that literally scream for your attention.

An activity mat is just that: a mat with activities. Although, in newborn speak, "activity" can mean anything from a single picture of a panda bear (visual

14

stimulation!) to an overwhelming array of multisensory toys.

There are two types of activity mats: traditional and tummy time.

TRADITIONAL ACTIVITY MATS

When you lay a baby on them backside down, traditional activity mats serve mostly as large blankets. (Granted, nice blankets with bits for baby to play with.) The feast of activities only opens for babies when you turn them over for tummy time, or when they are old enough to sit up, crawl, and play with things themselves.

Generally activity mats are brightly colored, themed, and chock-a-block with choice. Developmental delights, such as crinkly pockets and peekaboo flaps, teething rattles, and tiny mirrors, are sewn right in. Contrasting textures and patterns are meant to engage baby, but be warned, they can make for some pretty ugly room décor.

> *Why we love them:* Regular baby blankets and quilts aren't as big or as fun as activity mats.
>
> *Why we don't:* Regular baby blankets are far more comfortable. The quality of most activity mat fabric is bad. Criminally bad. And sometimes it smells. Like cheap bad fabric.

Activity Mat

Also Known As
Tummy time mat, play quilt

Age Range
Birth to 6 months

Total Usage
6 months

Recommendation
Nice to have

When to Buy
New patterns don't come out that often, and hot sellers are hard to find. So if you spot one you love, get it. Because most can be used from day one, this is a great item for your registry.

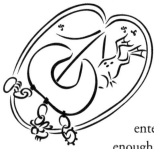

TUMMY TIME MATS

Tummy time mats are smaller than traditional activity mats, more rectangular, and specifically designed for tummy time only. Some sport a little underarm pillow for extra baby support. And all provide at-your-fingertips entertainment options that will hopefully give baby enough of a distraction that he might not scream bloody murder at having to lay in a new position for all of ten minutes.

Why we love them: The smaller size means tummy time mats can sport a more attractive design than their larger cousins. What's cuter than a lily pad or surfboard mat? Nothing, that's what.

Why we don't: Because activity mats offer face-down stimulation in a larger, more versatile package, tummy time mats are the least necessary activity system with the shortest life span. (But the superior styling makes us want one all the same!)

Activity Gyms

Once an activity mat goes three-dimensional, it becomes an activity gym. Despite what the name implies, babies do not crawl on, hang from, or engage in much physicality with an activity gym beyond batting at hanging objects. In fact, once baby is big enough to really touch the heights of the activity gym, in most cases, the product renders itself obsolete due to its own unstable nature or baby's newfound interest in other objects.

The primary benefit of an activity gym is that it gives back-lying babies who have nothing to do but stare at the ceiling an interesting vista full of stimulating shapes, colors, sounds, and even motion.

The first activity gyms consisted of activity mats with soft bars of fabric crisscrossing from their corners, providing a place to hang toys and other visual stimulation. However, now the term "activity gym" applies to any toy

Activity Gym

Also Known As
Baby gym, play gym

Age Range
Birth to 6 months

Total Usage
6 months

Recommendation
Nice to have

When to Buy
As with activity mats, new designs don't come out that often, so if you see one you like, buy it, even if you're not due for another five months. Also a great registry item.

apparatus that hangs over baby's head, with quilt or without.

Activity gyms today come in two flavors: soft and hard.

SOFT ACTIVITY GYMS

A soft activity gym is a traditional activity mat with soft fabric arches of toys overhead (although some manufacturers have replaced the fabric arches with ones made of soft plastic). Generally speaking, the toys within baby's reach are soft, sensory objects, although some models sport more sophisticated hanging diversions including lights, melodies, and even mobiles. Due to their architecture, the music and motion on soft activity gyms are usually parent-operated. Due to their size, the theme is very important. You need to really love fish if you buy an aquarium-themed one, as that will be all you and your visitors see when they enter your living room. Twenty-seven square feet of fish.

Why we love them: A soft fabric fairy dome with a mobile overhead? Heaven.

Why we don't: A licensed-character-covered behemoth? The opposite.

HARD ACTIVITY GYMS

A hard activity gym is a single molded plastic arch that baby lies under. Most come without a play mat, although some versatile models include a convertible play mat that works with or without the overhanging arch. Hard activity gyms are significantly less attractive than soft gyms, but they are also smaller and present baby with more cause-and-effect learning opportunities. The usual setup of a hard activity gym is a tilted, themed plastic scene, such as a piano keyboard or barnyard, overhead with three or four dangling easy-to-reach plastic targets. Once baby swats, kicks or otherwise moves a target, she is readily rewarded with lights, sounds, and music. Many hard activity gyms offer softer, sensory toys fastened to the legs as well.

Why we love them: We love watching our baby learn out loud.

Why we don't: The out loud part can get old quick. Really quick.

Convertible Mats and Gyms

The size, expense, and sheer volume of baby products available make versatility a key consideration, and activity mats and gyms offer hybrids galore. You can find hard activity gyms that turn into soft activity mats, soft activity mats that turn into crawl-through tunnels, and even hard activity mats that turn into toddler ride-ons!

Age Range

While manufacturers advertise a use range on convertible gyms that numbers into the years, our experience is that even the best activity gym or mat wears out, or wears out its welcome, well within the first 12 months.

Whatever the box might brag, once your baby can sit up, he will most likely lose all interest in any activity mat or gym. Even the gyms that later turn into baby pianos will pale in comparison to multilevel coffee tables, siblings' toys, and your potted plants.

The average age range for most activity mats or gyms is from birth to 6 months, although we've found the primary usage range to be between 2 and 4 months old.

While that range is rather short compared to other baby products, the amount of time a baby will use an activity gym at any given time is also very short. Unless you're using it as just a floor blanket, it's a 10-minute toy.

Even so, the options are extremely limited for engaging a baby at this age, and by our baby's sixth week, we were desperate for anything that might help us bond with our adorable blob. The manufacturers know this and charge accordingly. Activity mats and gyms are wildly overpriced for what they offer, although to the full-time, stay-at-home caregiver, they might be worth every penny.

While nice to have, activity gyms are not a necessity. You can live a full life with just a blanket and nonattached toys. Your baby will be more than happy to look at the ceiling fan. But if you have the means, the space, and the desire to give your baby a more stimulating view, here are some of the important features of activity mats and gyms.

Educational Benefits

No matter how much "tactile stimulation" and "developmental benefit" the products claim to offer, the truth is, we're talking about newborns. They get the same sensory learning experience from a bumpy toy butterfly wing as they do from a dishrag.

Because babies will learn gross motor skills and cause-and-effect from nearly everything in their surroundings, we recommend you ignore all educational claims on activity mat or gym packaging. Instead, use your common sense, and gear your purchase toward the most important benefit the activity mat can offer: bonding with your baby.

An activity mat can give you and your baby your first place to play together. It gives you things to talk about and describe, point to, wiggle, spin, and imitate, enhancing your baby's receptive language and bonding through compassionate touch.

Design

While sadly the lion's share of activity mats and gyms are clown-loud or cartoon-covered, don't feel obliged to pick a wildly contrasting patterned one. A pastel, garden-themed mat that gives you a starting point for telling stories is a much better bet because it encourages you to interact with your baby. Look for the design you like the best. The benefits will follow.

Toys

Variety is key with activity mat toys—variety of color, texture, sound, and motion. Rather than toys that all do the same thing, look for some that spin, some that bounce, some that rattle, and so on.

Mirrors and mobiles are most babies' favorite accessories. See if you like the mobile's music, because you'll be subjected to it the most, and look for a quality, but nonbreakable, mirror. A silver brushed piece of plastic won't reflect anything but your baby's frustration.

Height and Position of Toys

While at first baby will only look at the toys, eventually she will reach for them. Make sure that reach is not a lost cause. Incomprehensibly, some activity gyms position their hanging toys—toys meant to be touched some-day—so far above baby's head, they'd need octopus arms to ever reach them.

Look at the placement of the toys offered on the activity gym and determine if your baby will ever be able to adequately operate them. Toys tethered too tightly to side legs or arches aren't much better. Babies should be able to actually hold, squeeze, and manipulate at least some of the toys, rather than just bat at them.

Size

Activity mats and gyms are some of the larger baby products, and they can take up a pretty good chunk of family room real estate, but ideally, you do want a mat or gym that's large enough to accommodate baby's squirming, scooting, and rotating. A baby that rolls and gets a face full of plastic product leg is not a happy baby.

Portability

While all mats claim to fold, roll, or disassemble for easy storage and portability, the fact is they're not all easy. Check the set-up and take-down instructions before you buy to confirm it's not too complicated.

Versatility

Because we assume only a life expectancy of six months on any activity mat or gym, we don't care for future uses that extend into toddlerhood. But to get the most for your money, to change your toy landscape up a bit, and to keep both you and your baby from getting bored, you might want to consider one that offers versatility within the first six months, for instance, an electronic, baby-operated activity gym with lights and music that can also be used as an unplugged activity mat.

Baby Comfort

Newborns have extremely sensitive and delicate skin; the tiniest tag can leave a scratch, a rash, or worse. If the product has a mat, make sure the fabric is at least slightly padded, relatively soft, and scratch-free. No baby deserves rug burn on his chubby little cheeks from a shoddy product. We highly recommend washing any fabric quilt in a baby-safe detergent before you place your baby on it. If it's not washable now, it's not salvageable later, as we guarantee baby will baptize it with at least three different bodily fluids.

Check all angles and aspects of activity mats and gyms, especially plastic molded ones, for protruding bits, errant tags, or anything even slightly sharp that might nick your little one. File it down, cut it off, or return it for a better quality model.

Price

The price variance of activity mats and gyms is almost $100. The cheapest ones are $20; the most expensive $120. You'll pay more for extra features such as lights and motion (possibly worth it), and for products covered in licensed characters (not so worth it).

Summary of Features

☆ Interesting, pleasing design

☆ Variety of toys

☆ Position of toys

☆ Size

☆ Portability

☆ Baby-soft fabric and features

NOTES: *Activity Mats and Gyms*			
Model Name / Manufacturer	Store/Price	My Impressions	Grade

Activity Centers

ACTIVITY CENTERS

You bought your infant every single baby gadget made. You did gangbusters at your baby shower. You've got the bouncer, a rocker, and two swings (oh my!). A bassinet, the playpen, the gyms, even the tummy time mats. But you swore off the activity center as a too-expensive, too-big, too-garish nonnecessity. Reconsider! (Although you're right about the "too garish" part.)

Once your baby hits 4 months and starts squawking, squirming, and screaming in frustration because he wants to play but can't, the activity center may be the answer to your prayers.

The 4- to 5-month-old baby is a peculiar being, with all the willpower and none of the dexterity of an older child. No longer content to just sit in a bouncer or smile tranquilly from a swing, they want to move. They *can* roll over . . . which makes their activity gym mat totally useless as they roll off it or into the bars and squawk even louder. They *do* have good head control and the ability to swat at things, but the hit-mom-in-the-face game gets old quick (for moms, anyway). They can't sit up yet, can't crawl, can't grab toys, catch balls, sort blocks, stack rings, or even fetch their own binky.

Enter the activity center. With a miraculous seat that keeps them safely in a standing position and allows their strong little legs to kick, bounce, and spin their entire body in endless circles. With a veritable smorgasbord of toys they can actually activate, just by banging, smacking, and gumming. Featuring teething toys, lights, music, and more, the activity center is expensive, but by this age, you'd pay triple for the privilege.

History of the Activity Center

Activity centers were born out of the biggest design flaw in baby walkers: baby-propelled wheels. The idea of putting babies into a sling seat so they could build leg muscles, stretch their bodies, play with secured toys within reach, and get off the floor was a good one. Giving them madcap mobility and the ability to cruise down stairs wasn't.

Activity centers are almost exactly like baby walkers, without the wheels. The thrill of crashing into fireplaces now gone, activity centers are built with extra toys to keep baby entertained from all angles.

Because activity centers offer babies the first fixed toys they can actually reach—believe it or not, they won't be able to touch the toys on their swing or bouncer seat until they are too big for the entire product!—they are one of the first sources of independent play for your child. And after four months of nonstop mommy-activated attention, you'll be more than happy for any sign of independence.

Activity centers are also thought to be one of the safest places for baby to play. Not plagued by historical, deadly recalls (although they are still recalled for small parts choking hazards), their giant size and sturdy design makes them almost impossible to tip over—even for your large dog or larger children. The plastic ring of toys surrounding baby also provides a barrier of protection, for in the activity center, babies have a limited reach for dangerous objects nearby.

Obviously, as with any product, you should never leave baby unattended or in an activity center for too long, but most babies—bless their hearts!—are content to play in their activity center for ages.

Why we love them: For the amount of usefulness, safety, and stimulation they provide, for as often and long as they provide it, we are big, big fans of activity centers.

Why we don't: Please, please, someone make a pretty one! Or how about just a non-ugly one? Perhaps even a modern one that comes even remotely close to matching our décor?

Age Range

Babies are ready for activity centers as soon as they can hold their head up and steady, usually at 4 or 5 months of age. Once they can crawl and pull up, around 9 or 10 months, they need to be removed from the center, as they might try to climb out. (And once they can move on their own, we dare you to try to stick them back into an activity center.)

Size and Portability

Yes, most activity centers are large, but some are bigger than others. If space is a concern, look for a more compact model. Even the smallest centers will delight a baby for months. Some activity centers also collapse or fold for easy portability. And some are just plain easier to drag from room to room (rounded bases are the key).

Flat Head Corrector

Does your baby have a flat spot on her head? Activity centers keep baby upright and can help reverse the positional molding common since babies now sleep on their backs. Especially great for babies who hate tummy time!

The Seat

Almost all seats are the same: a sling of (hideously patterned) fabric with two big holes for baby's legs. The crucial difference is in how the seat moves. Most seats allow baby to bounce in one place, while a few let baby slide along a track (hint: most babies prefer to bounce). Almost all allow baby to spin in 360-degree circles, but some seats are easier to move than others. You want to find a seat that your 4-month-old can move easily (or what's the point?).

Convertibility

Believe it or not, manufacturers finally got smart and made some of these behemoths actually convertible into other toys for future play. Two of our favorite activity centers can be turned into a freestanding activity table and a racetrack. (How cool is that?)

Height and Reach

Because all babies are different sizes, choose an activity center with a height adjustment feature so your baby can enjoy it at any age. Also take a look at how the toys are positioned in relation to your baby. Most are set up well, but some inexplicably place the toys too far away for young arms to reach. Toys baby can't reach equals baby frustration. And we know who pays for that.

The Toys

Unfortunately, many activity centers are overloaded with toys that are too hard, too sharp, not age appropriate, and frankly, quite ugly. You want to keep babies busy, but not overwhelm or overstimulate them. And—repeat after me—more electronics does not mean a smarter baby.

Let's be honest, your baby isn't going to learn the color "orange" at age 4 months (and certainly not in French!). But an activity that encourages fine motor control, such as a tiny sliding lever that must be grasped between forefinger and thumb, is worth worlds to your developing child. We actually prefer the more low-tech activity centers because they encourage concentration and repetition rather than rewarding an unintentional hand jerk with a parade of effects.

Chew Friendliness

It seems obvious, but make sure everything can be safely chewed and is (relatively) soft. Believe it or not, some activity centers include toys that are not chew-friendly. At this age, babies gum and bite everything, not just to teethe, but to learn about the world with the most easily stimulated part of their bodies. They also have limited motor control and bang things into their face on the way to their mouth. The best activity centers have teething toys attached (we like crinkly the best), but watch out for hard plastic toys with sharp, poorly molded edges that can rip up tender lips and gums. We routinely sand down the odd plastic rough spot with our nail files.

Also, as weird as this may sound, be the first to taste test all the toys on your baby's activity center. Some industrial plastic and fabric tastes awful and can leave a nasty sting on your tongue. Disinfect everything before baby plays for the first time, but just to be sure, give it a good lick yourself first too. Can't stand the taste? Take it back!

Music and Lights

Make sure the music isn't too loud or the sound effects too startling. And by all means pick a musical selection you don't mind hearing over and over . . . and over and over and over. You're not a bad mom if you select an entire activity center based solely on the music you can (or cannot) stand.

We like music that is allowed to run its course, rather than songs and noises that start over every time baby touches a certain button, because the resulting cacophony will do more harm than good to everyone's aural sensibilities.

Lights? We like 'em.

Unnecessary Extras

Babies usually become disinterested in activity centers (and the confinement they represent) once they can crawl, so accessories designed for the older child, such as cup holders or snack trays, are unnecessary.

Price

Prepare to pay! Activity centers range in price from $49 to $129. A lot for a five-month toy, but still very, very worth it.

Activity Jumpers

Because doorway jumpers are out (see our Seven Deadly Sinners in Chapter 1, Safety) but babies love to jump, a couple of manufacturers have added springs to activity centers. An activity jumper is a round plastic chair with a sling seat and built-in toys that hangs from a large metal frame by four, long, covered springs. It almost looks like a cross between an activity center and a giant swing.

We've seen them in action, delighting baby jumping beans, but we still pass on this product. You can't lock them in place and stop the bouncing, which means babies can get seasick trying to play with their toys. Overuse of jumping products can stunt walking development because it teaches babies to stay on tiptoe. And these jumpers are just so darn big. Really big. And expensive.

Our babies might be deprived of giant, uncontrolled leaps, but they seem happy enough bouncing in their stationary activity centers.

Features to Consider

☆ Size

☆ Portability

☆ Toys, lights, and music

☆ Bounce versus slide

☆ Height adjustment

NOTES: *Activity Centers*

Model Name / Manufacturer	Store/Price	My Impressions	Grade
_____	_____	_____	_____
_____	_____	_____	_____
_____	_____	_____	_____

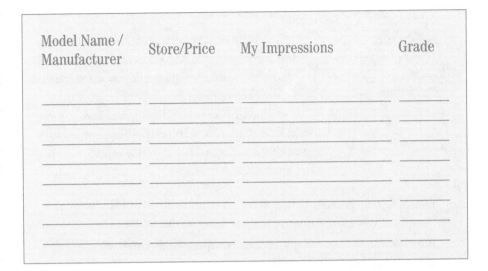

Model Name / Manufacturer	Store/Price	My Impressions	Grade

Toddler Activity Stations

We'll shamelessly admit it: even before they were born, our children had too many toys. But we'd trade them all for a good toddler activity station. Your children will play with these three times as long as anything else in their toy box.

A toddler activity station is a small, toddler-size table, cube, or wall made of plastic or wood that includes interesting activities meant for beginning walkers to age 3. It is compact and portable and provides endless hours of entertainment for otherwise busy walkers.

Toddler Activity Station

Also Known As
Activity table, play table, learning table, activity cube, baby playground, play wall

Age Range
12 to 36 months

Total Usage
2 years

Recommendation
Nice to have

When to Buy
Once baby can walk. These make a great first birthday present.

ACTIVITY TABLES

Typically made of plastic, activity tables often feature either a removable top or detachable legs that allow babies to enjoy the toy on the floor before they can stand.

While all offer motor development skills, some are geared more toward play—like simple block stacking and page turning—while others provide a full kindergarten curriculum.

Why we love them: Anything that gets a toddler to stand still in one place for more than a minute is a good buy in our book!

Why we don't: They are not all created equal. Grandma bought our kids a flimsy one with horrible music that is still the soundtrack of our nightmares.

ACTIVITY CUBES

A favorite of waiting rooms everywhere, activity cubes are heavy, hollow wooden boxes that offer five sides of fun. This nostalgic classic delivers the old-fashioned awe of wooden mazes, loopy bead roller coasters, and all manner of things that can be slid, spun, and slapped. We love no-frills fun, but activity cubes are heavy, hard to move, and also especially rough on top-heavy little heads.

Why we love them: The colored wire roller coaster gets us every time.

Why we don't: Unfortunately, nice as they look, they can be quite dangerous. Aside from sharp corners, activity cubes are frequently recalled for major problems like poisonous lead paint and small choking hazards.

ACTIVITY WALLS

The king of activity toys, activity walls are basically giant, freestanding, molded plastic structures that present their embedded entertainment vertically. Although meant for early walkers, most have activities that floor-bound babies can reach as well. Activity walls are mammoth sized and mammoth fun, but what stands up can come down. Choose an activity wall with a wide, solid base that isn't easily toppled by unsteady toddlers.

Why we love them: We bow to the toy with the two-year life span. Worth every penny.

Why we don't: They take up a lot of room for a long, long time.

Educational Benefits

Even though we know deep down our babies are geniuses, there was no way they were learning the alphabet at 4 months of age. Fourteen months, however, is an entirely different story. A number of activity tables and walls offer a wealth of educational lessons—introducing your child to colors, shapes, letters, numbers, rhyming words, musical creativity, and our favorite, manners. Did we teach our kids to say "thank you" or was it the talking mailbox? We'll never know.

Talking Tables

For a fistful of batteries, an electronic table will sing, recite the alphabet, light up, play music, and generally dazzle all . . . all who don't have to listen to it five million times, that is. As the person who already knows the ABCs and will be subjected to the repetition relentlessly, you should pick a product that has sound effects you can stand. That it has music you like, whether it's classical or calypso, is as important a factor as any. Believe us when we tell you two years is far too long to hear an adult woman singing nonsensical songs in a baby voice: "When I ride on a unicorn . . ."

Also look for products with volume control (if only we could super glue them into the quietest setting).

Product Stability

Because they are designed for wobbly but wild wee ones, choose a product stable enough for inevitable bumps, shoves, and tackles. Look for a product made of sturdy material with a wide, stable base. You shouldn't be able to easily tip it over.

Baby Stability

Many products advertise their usefulness for pre-walkers, suggesting that encouraging a baby to stand builds leg muscles and allowing baby to pull up builds dexterity. We're not buying it. When small legs buckle with no warning, babies can end up with a face full of pain. And most tables are not nearly sturdy enough for a baby to pull up on. There are plenty of toys for crawlers. Wait until baby can walk before buying this one.

Safety

This product category is plagued by recalls, so do your own safety testing by regularly checking for loose parts, choking hazards, and spaces that can trap small limbs or pinch tiny fingers. For more information on how to spot a toy hazard, see Chapter 27, Toys.

Price

The bigger and fancier the product, the more you'll pay, although wood products will cost three times as much as plastic, regardless of size. The sheer length of play they deliver make them worthwhile investments. Toddler activity stations range in price from $30 to $90. Most are in the $50 range.

P.S. The Other "Activity Table"

Another breed of product also called an "activity table" is nothing like the above choices and is completely devoid of built-in toys. Previously referred to as "train tables" (manufacturers re-christened them to demonstrate their versatility for other building sets), they are large but low, furniture-quality wooden tables meant for bigger kids to use with their train sets, LEGO blocks, and the like. The main features include storage drawers and optional play mats, and your main buying decision is probably price (they start at $200) and if it matches your décor. We've found that even though toddlers can't build train sets, they enjoy standing at a large, waist-high table and playing with anything on it.

Features to Consider

☆ Style

☆ Electronic or not

☆ Price

☆ Size

☆ Educational content

☆ Durability

☆ Music

NOTES: *Toddler Activity Stations*

Model Name / Manufacturer	Store/Price	My Impressions	Grade

Four

Baby Carriers

Perhaps the world's oldest baby product, baby carriers have been used since the dawn of civilization as a way to keep infants close but allow parents the freedom to continue working and caring for their family.

Long associated with outdoor living—think Indian papooses and baby backpack–wearing hikers— "babywearing" has become a full-blown modern phenomenon both indoors and out. Why? Perhaps because it fosters parent-child bonding and we're all more in touch with our feelings. Perhaps because we're multitasking maniacs who refuse to slow down, even when we have a baby.

Baby Carrier

Age Range
Birth to 36 months

Total Usage
Sling: 6 months
Soft carrier: 12 months
Backpack: 24 months

Recommendation
Nice to have

When to Buy
Great registry item, but get a gift receipt!

By definition, baby carriers are contraptions made of fabric reinforced with plastic or metal buckles and bindings that secure a baby to an adult's torso, allowing for hands-free carrying. There are three basic types of baby carriers: slings, front carriers, and backpacks.

SLINGS

A sling, the most organic baby carrier, is simply a long piece of fabric that wraps around an adult's body and fastens at one shoulder. The youngest babies curl up in an almost horizontal, fetal position around the wearer's body and eventually graduate to more vertical riding. How the sling fastens depends on its type. Ring slings use fabric threaded through two rings; pouch slings are a continuous loop of fabric that make a pouch seat for baby; Asian-style slings have straps that tie; and wraps are a single piece wrapped around the body and tied in place. Slings can be adjusted to allow babies to lie in the fetal position, face outward, or even straddle their parent's hip. Slings can be used from birth to about 6 months, but are not appropriate for active pursuits like hiking. The privacy and easy access they offer make them very popular with breastfeeding moms.

Why we love them: We feel like the very epitome of Mother Earth when we're wearing our baby in a sling. Mother Earth with a sparkly cell phone, but Mother Earth just the same.

Why we don't: They take some getting used to. It was a few tries before we felt like the baby wasn't going to fall out and actually stopped carrying the baby with our hands over the sling.

SOFT FRAME CARRIERS

Soft carriers are little fabric seats with leg openings for babies and two shoulder straps for the adult wearer that fasten in the back for safety. More structured than slings, they resemble mini, open backpacks you wear on your front. Most soft baby carriers are for front carrying, although some are designed for hip riders. Babies can face in toward their parent's chest, or out toward the world. Soft carriers allow babies to hang only in a vertical position, requiring tiny riders to have at least some neck control, so they are not recommended for newborns. Many soft carriers come with small pockets for baby accessories, various hooks and loops for baby toys, and removable, washable bibs for baby spit-up.

Why we love them: We'd never get any housework done if not for our soft carriers.

Why we don't: We'd never get any housework done if not for our soft carriers.

BABY BACKPACKS

Baby backpacks, also called "frame carriers" and "hikers," are larger carriers designed for prolonged baby-carrying outings and provide a seat for babies to ride on your back. Like a hiking backpack, they usually have lightweight metal frames and extensive padded straps to help comfortably distribute baby's weight. Suitable only for older babies who can sit up on their own, backpacks are made of tougher, often waterproof material and frequently come with sun canopies. Many include enough pockets that you can leave the diaper bag at home and reflective strips for outdoor, nighttime safety. Some even have kickstands that allow you to set baby on the ground, still seated like a tiny, vertical camping chair.

Why we love them: With our baby backpacks, we can go where our strollers fear to tread: the beach, the mountains, the woods, the boardwalk, the subway.

Why we don't: We don't get to have wonderful outdoor adventures nearly as often as we'd like anymore, so the fancy baby backpack we bought was not used more than twice. As our friends and family are in the same homebound boat, this is an item we pass around and share.

Age Range

Slings are best for newborn to 5 or 6 months; soft carriers are great for 2 to 12 months; backpacks are perfect for 6 to 24 months. Check with each product's manufacturers for specific minimum and maximum age limits, but also use your common sense. If your baby lunges toward the ground screaming "No, no, not the sling!" he is probably too old for it.

Weight Limits

Pay close attention to each model's weight limits, regardless of your baby's age. Slings generally have a weight limit of around 20 pounds, soft carriers 30 pounds, and backpacks 40 pounds—although any kid that big in our family is walking!

Sizing

Many baby slings offer different sizes, from petite to plus, that give you more or less fabric, but soft carriers and backpacks come in "one size fits all." That's not to say you are always going to be that size. Not all carriers fit all body shapes, so if something feels off on you because you're short-waisted, very tall, or have a supermodel body, look for a different model. (And know that we hate you—if you are the supermodel body, that is. Short-waisted? You are our sister friend.)

Also, if you plan on sharing baby-carrying duty with someone else, know that that person might not fit the same size product you do. You may need two different sizes if it's an equal partnership. We usually took the early babywearing shifts because we didn't trust anyone else carrying our babies, but right around backpack age, we were over our bad selves and passed the kid quickly off to Dad.

Comfort of Carrier

Once you saddle up, you will probably be carrying your baby for more than a few hours, so a comfortable carrier is key. But it's hard to tell in the store if an empty carrier is going to be comfortable after two hours. The best test is to borrow a friend's, or buy a bunch, have a home carrier fashion show, select a winner, and take the rest back.

Instructions

Unlike a baby stroller that you basically snap open and push, a baby carrier can require Zen-like patience to master; each model has a unique and complicated fastening system. Especially with baby slings, which have quite a lot of room for user error, study the instructions thoroughly. We put our first baby sling on completely upside down. It's easier to do than you think.

Almost every baby carrier virgin feels awkward the first couple of times, but you will get used to it and most likely learn to love it.

Working It Solo

You should be able to adjust, load, and unload a baby carrier by yourself without anyone's help, because we all don't always have someone nearby. You don't want to be glued to your baby or, worse, injure her trying to free yourselves from the straitjacket you accidentally purchased. Not all models are easy for everyone to manipulate solo, so keep looking until you find one that is.

Carriers with a side entry option for baby are usually the easiest to maneuver, especially when trying to unload but not wake a sleeping baby.

And to avoid turning your baby into a crash test dummy, practice with a doll or stuffed animal first, until you've perfected it.

Structure and Durability

When looking at baby carriers, look for a durable design with strong material; tight, well-sewn seams; solid straps and snaps; and good head support for a sleeping baby.

Safety Straps

Most soft baby carriers and all baby backpacks have safety straps to secure baby. The best safety straps slip over baby's shoulders and buckle at the chest. Check for strong, secure, baby-proof clasps.

Think the model you like could do with some safety straps? You're probably right. Pick another one that has 'em.

Support and Padding

Some carriers come with more padding than others, which can make for a more comfortable carry, but does bulk the product up a bit. We prefer models with shoulder padding and waist belts, as they help distribute baby's weight more evenly.

On baby backpacks, check that the metal frames around baby are sufficiently padded, because walking across a jagged terrain will bump them around and into the frame.

Leg Openings

Soft carriers and backpacks have leg openings for babies that allow their little legs to hang down (and kick dad in just the right spot as they get older). Make sure the leg openings are not too large, as a very well-known soft carrier was recently recalled after several babies fell through the too-wide leg openings and were seriously injured. Also make sure they aren't too small and cut off baby's circulation. Many carriers offer adjustable leg hole openings, but the adjustments should be strong, secure, and baby proof.

Material

Baby carriers and slings are made from every fabric under the sun. Baby will be riding pressed up next to you and you'll generate quite a bit of body heat, so look for a breathable fabric. Babies can get overheated very easily in baby carriers, especially dark ones in the sun.

Look for a fabric with some stretch in it, which will make it easier to load and unload baby and provide a more comfortable ride for both of you.

Finally, machine washable fabric is a requirement, as babies spit up quite a bit at this age, especially when in motion. We've seen the silk baby carriers and while they are gorgeous, we think that is a crazy, crazy fabric to use. Not only is it slippery, it's just begging for a projectile vomit covering. Call us party poopers, but we don't let anyone touch our wedding china, we save the good towels for company, and we don't carry our babies anywhere near silk. Maybe someday when we're filthy rich, we'll change our tune. And maybe we'll also wipe our butts with dollar bills. But we don't think so.

Breathing

Check that your baby can breathe adequately, no matter how old she is or what carrier you're using. Just because everyone else has their baby all smothered against their bosom doesn't mean it's safe for your baby. Use your common sense and provide enough space around your baby's nose and mouth so that fresh air can easily circulate around them.

Accessories

Many baby carriers come with accessories, either included or for separate purchase: sun shades, rain protection, carrier covers, head and neck supports, drink holders, storage compartments, and more. All good. Newer models sport music for baby, a vibrating massage option for parents, and even rearview mirrors. Nice, but not necessary.

Some front carriers come with attached backpacks for actual stuff, not babies. There are even diaper bags that convert into carriers.

Price

Slings range anywhere from $29 to $400, depending on fabric and the designer. You can get a good, very attractive sling in the $50 range. Soft front carriers will cost between $15 and $150. You will ache if you choose anything less than $75. Baby backpacks are the most expensive models, costing between $40 and $250. The best ones start at $100.

Got sticker shock? Remember, God gave you two arms for free. And your husband's make four.

Safety Precautions

Be on the lookout for snaps and hinges that might pinch baby's tiny fingers or legs.

Baby carriers should never be worn when you are doing anything but walking on your own two legs; this includes riding a bicycle, rollerblading, skating, driving, even jogging. And walk carefully. If you lose your balance and fall, you fall on your baby.

When wearing your baby carrier, don't reach for items overhead that could fall on your baby. Never cook with a carrier on. Don't climb ladders or stand on anything tall. And when bending, bend at the knees so baby can't fall out.

Features to Consider

☆ Age and weight limits
☆ Size

☆ Comfort and padding

☆ Solo loading and unloading

☆ Durability

☆ Safety straps

☆ Leg openings

☆ Fabric

☆ Breathable material

☆ Accessories

☆ Price

NOTES: *Baby Carriers*

Model Name / Manufacturer	Store/Price	My Impressions	Grade

Five

Bassinets, Cradles, and Co-sleepers

Cradles and bassinets are steeped in history. We all know about Moses and his basket, but there are hundreds of other romantic portraits of babies and their cradles. Literally, there are portraits. Museums are stuffed with tons of paintings that show mothers lovingly gazing at cherubic infants in gauzy bassinets and beautiful babes in beautiful cradles—even the milkmaid's baby looks like she has a pretty sweet crib.

Alas, those images are fairy tales. The truth is that stand-alone bassinets and cradles aren't a great option for most modern parents because they present serious safety hazards and a very limited life span. Before we get into the whys, let's look at the whats.

Bassinet, Cradle, and Co-sleeper

Age Range
Birth to 3 months

Total Usage
3 months

Recommendation
Don't need

When to Buy
Before baby is born.

Despite the interchangeability of terms for different products, technically bassinets and cradles are sleeping spaces that are raised on legs. Moses baskets and carry-cots are sleeping spots that stay on the floor. Bassinets and cradles are used as sleeping alternatives to cribs. Moses baskets and carry-cots are for naps only.

BASSINETS

A bassinet is essentially a small oval bed meant to give wombsick newborn babies a confined but snuggly sleeping space. Bassinets are made of wood, metal, or plastic. Some convert to changing tables or co-sleepers. Many come with soft storage bins on the bottom. Bassinets are generally stationary, although some have wheels (look for ones with strong locks). Many bassinets have hoods to help darken baby's lair (look for ones that retract). And some models are equipped with battery-operated vibration features (look for these, period).

Why we love them: We do think the full-size crib is kind of cavernous for a tiny newborn, and having baby sleep in our room the first few weeks helps our paranoia and our breastfeeding.

Why we don't: We prefer our bassinets to have a wider, more useful base, such as those on a play yard. (See Chapter 21, Play Yards and Playpens.)

CRADLES

Cradles are small, usually rectangular beds similar to bassinets, except that they include a movement mechanism for soothing baby. Cradles either rock on rockers, glide on gliding mechanisms, or swing from big, giant metal hooks set in the side of the frame. You need a way to stop the cradle from rocking, gliding, or swinging for those times when you would prefer baby's movements not to shake her awake. Cradles are generally made of wood, wood laminate, or metal.

Why we love them: We love the way the fancy "Old World" ones look. We also love fantasizing about the fancy house we'd have if we could afford those $7,000 Old World cradles. Perhaps someplace sunny on the French Riviera?

Why we don't: No matter what the price, they're not the safest, their usefulness expires after just a few months, and the cheaper models are nothing to fantasize about.

Moses Baskets

Moses baskets have changed little over the past several thousand years. They are still simple oval baskets that provide a low-tech sleeping station for baby. Most are made of woven natural fibers, such as sea grass, and lined with fabric. The inside should be smooth, with no naughty sticks poking in toward your baby. Moses baskets usually have two side handles for transporting the basket, but never use the handles unless the basket is empty.

Why we love them: We're girls, and there's no more girly mom product than a frilly Moses basket. They're gorgeous. We loved ours and used it . . .

Why we don't: . . . for all of two weeks. We're kidding. It was more like two months. It seemed like two weeks though.

Carry-Cots

Like a Moses basket, a carry-cot is an oval-shaped bed for baby lined with fabric. However, a carry-cot is made entirely of fabric; the sides are supported by an inner, lightweight plastic frame. Carry-cots have handles and most come with sunshades. Carry-cots are sold separately, but are usually found as part of a luxury stroller package. Stroller carry-cots, frequently called bassinets, can clip onto the stroller frame and clip off for transport into the house. Most are sturdy enough to tote a sleeping baby, but this is entirely dependent upon the specific model, so check the manufacturer's instructions (and we still wouldn't trust the handles enough to use them when fully loaded).

Why we love them: We're suckers for the plush carry-cots that come with luxury strollers. What's more fun than walking over to a friend's house and bringing your posh baby bed along?

Why we don't: For all its finery, it's a short-lived product. More useful than a Moses basket, but still only good for a couple of months.

Age of Use

Due to their size, construction, and lack of safety measures, bassinets, cradles, and Moses baskets should only be used for the first couple months of baby's life. As soon as babies can roll over, usually by 2½ to 3 months, they should graduate to a more secure sleeping place. Also check the product's specific weight limits, as some are as low as 15 pounds.

As the lifespan is so short, and you can find alternative, multiple-use products, this is a "don't need" for most moms. Full-size cribs can be used from birth. Most bassinet-loving moms prefer bassinets attached to a convertible, sturdier product that can be used later, such as a play yard. But if you decide to go the freestanding bassinet or cradle route, use extra care and keep the following safety suggestions in mind.

Government Safety Standards

There are none. Zero national safety standards for cradles, bassinets, or Moses baskets. No one dictates to the manufacturers how wide the base should be, how much weight they should be able to hold, how resistant they should be to tipping over, or what kind of bedding gives babies the best breathing environment.

Cribs do have government safety requirements, and you can use some of these measures to test a cradle or bassinet product yourself. The space between slats or openings should be less than two and three-eighths inches. How can you easily measure that? It's almost the exact diameter of a soda can. Take a can of Diet Coke with you to the store, and if you can fit it between the slats, they are too wide. Walk away.

There also shouldn't be a height differential between the sides at the corners or any protruding posts or knobs higher than one-sixteenth of an inch because babies can get their clothes caught on them and strangle. Amazingly, the fanciest, most expensive sculpted iron bassinets on the planet usually have insanely dangerous decorative posts protruding from all sides. Avoid these.

Stability

Most baby injuries associated with these products occur when babies fall out of them, either because the bottom of the cradle or bassinet broke, a support piece failed, or the unit tipped over. When shopping, look for a sturdy, well-constructed model made of quality materials. Also look for a wide base that is not easily tipped over.

The wider something is, the harder it is to tip over. The opposite, of course, is true. Some smaller bassinets and cradles are more prone to tipping over than others because of their design. Remember too that your baby will move around; some bassinets and cradles have been tipped over by the active infants inside them.

For cradles and bassinets, a simple shake in the store isn't enough to gauge how easy it is to tip. Especially if you have other children or pets, imagine how the product will react when a 4-year-old leans on it to peek inside, or a large dog puts its paws on the edge.

Incidentally, babies can be left unattended in full-size cribs, but should not be left alone in cradles or bassinets. For our money, it's not worth it, because we do enjoy the few hours a day we don't have to attend to one end or the other of our babies. Oh, do we enjoy those hours . . .

Suffocation Risks

Two things make bassinets and cradles bigger suffocation risks than other baby products. The first is the narrow design. When babies roll in a full-size crib, in most cases, they are simply on their stomach. When babies roll in a bassinet or cradle, many times they end up face first into the side, where a heartbreaking number have suffocated. Rocking cradles pose an extra risk because a baby can roll and cause the bed unit to tip. The angle of the tipped cradle bed can then cause babies to roll further into the side, where their weight traps them against the rail and possibly creates too much pressure on their chest to allow them to breathe.

Bedding

The second inherent suffocation risk comes from soft bedding. Because full-size cribs are all the same standard size, their bedding is too. Bassinets and cradles come in all shapes and sizes. Bedding is usually either customized and included, or homemade to match. This type of bedding is not regulated and tends to be frillier, less breathable, and softer than crib bedding.

You know how some bassinets—like the round ones with cushy pillows and pretty scalloped skirts—look like giant pet beds? Your cat thinks so too. If you have animals, you might consider passing on the cradle or bassinet, as the low profile makes it super easy for Mr. Whiskers to jump up and curl around your tiny baby's face.

You know how some bassinets—like the ones with frothy canopy confections dripping with gauzy fabric and gorgeous bows—look like the life-size doll bed of your childhood dreams? The retailers think so too. Those amazing billowy displays wreak havoc on our princess psyches. However, dolls don't die of SIDS. Babies do. The day your baby is born, you have to strip that bassinet down to its bare bones. No flowing canopy, no eyelet lace pillows, no dreamy quilt. Not so pretty now, is it?

Mattresses

If the product uses a mattress, it should fit snugly to decrease suffocation and entrapment risks. You should not be able to fit more than one finger between the mattress and any side of the cradle or bassinet. And the mattress or sleeping surface should be very firm for an infant. So firm it seems uncomfortable. (For more on shopping for a safe mattress, see Chapter 12, Crib Mattresses.)

Safe sleeping environment recommendations for babies are the same regardless of where they're resting: no large or bulky blankets, no pillows, no plush toys or stuffed animals, no sleep positioners or wedges, and no hanging fabric or ties. And of course, babies should always be put to sleep on their backs.

Placement

Place your cradle or bassinet in a safe location, not near window blind cords or other hanging hazards, and where it's not easily tipped over. Possible bad locations: near the top of the stairs, super close to doorways and entrances, by heating elements, anywhere near the alarm clock the morning after the Oscars or the Super Bowl.

Price

Cheap bassinets start at $35. More sturdy varieties usually cost around $100 to $150. Deluxe brands will run you up to $1,000 and beyond. The cheapest cradles start at around $100 and run into the thousands. You can get a no-frills Moses basket for around $70. Most cost around $100. Super deluxe baskets can cost up to $450.

No Homemade Sleepers

Moms are born crafty. We can MacGyver our way out of any crisis. Snowsuit made out of garbage bags? Done. Dinner party hors d'oeuvres made from grilled cheese crusts and last week's pot roast? Voilà. But we have to draw the line at homemade baby sleepers. Yes, we know you can weave a Moses basket from the weeds in your common area. We can too. But the experts tell us we're not supposed to. And just in case it needs saying, you should never put your baby to sleep in any kind of homemade contraption. This includes laundry baskets, sock drawers, and big spaghetti pots.

Co-sleeping

We know many people who advocate co-sleeping. We also know people who breastfed their kids until they were 6. We're not either of those people.

Like sex in the shower, co-sleeping sounds good on paper, but is not so fun in practice. It can also be very dangerous. So dangerous that the American Academy of Pediatrics and the CPSC advocate very strongly against it. National statistics show that almost one baby a week dies by suffocating in an adult bed. The Center for Disease Control (CDC) reports that more babies die of accidental suffocation and strangulation in adult beds than die in car crashes.

Co-sleeping proponents argue that it promotes bonding. We argue that it certainly doesn't promote the kind of bonding we usually like to do in our beds, and we generally bond with people and babies when they are awake. When we are asleep, we toss, turn, hit, cry out, kick, throw the covers around, and sometimes even sleepwalk.

We know most people believe they would never roll over on their babies. We're super light sleepers too, and wake up at the slightest squeak. Except when we have newborns. And then we're so sleep deprived, we are hallucinating zombies.

But you don't have to ever touch a co-sleeping baby to suffocate him. The biggest risk comes from the bedding. Everything we've ever read suggests soft bedding is a possible cause of SIDS. Babies now aren't even allowed to use blankets or crib bumpers and must be zipped into little sleeping bags for warmth. I don't know about you, but my bed is a soft, soft wonderland, with no less than six king-size pillows, a feather top mattress pad, and a dreamy down duvet. A simple tug of the sheet or shift of a pillow could cover your baby's face.

P.S. Your husband does not want your baby in the bed with you two, anyway. We promise. Sure, he told you he's fine with it, as long as you're happy, but you're hormonal, and he's smart. Men love their children, yes, but make no mistake, if he thought he'd get more sex, he'd let the baby sleep in the garage.

Co-sleepers

If you must co-sleep with your newborn, several nest-like products are available. Most look like little padded rectangles with tiny raised sides. Some even come with a night-light. The bumpers can help wake you, should you roll toward your infant, but they are soft, and won't stop you. They also won't stop the thudding arm my husband likes to drop on me in his sleep sometimes. To make your adult bed as safe as possible, we would recommend removing all extra bedding and pillows while baby is on board. Slip into your long johns for warmth.

Some portable bassinets and play yards come with a co-sleeping option that essentially removes one side of the crib and allows it to saddle up to the side of your bed. While this setup does eliminate most rollover risk, there are still safety concerns about how securely the crib is attached to your bed. Most attach under the adult mattress with safety straps, but because this is an unregulated product, there is a risk of misuse or malfunction that could lead to a baby trapped between the crib unit and the adult bed. Also, there is nothing to stop an adult pillow from tumbling into the attached co-sleeper, so again, strip your bed down to its bare minimum.

Why we love them: If you must touch your baby in the night, the bedside co-sleepers are better than the in-bed ones.

Why we don't: We don't love anything baby in bed with us.

Features to Consider

- ☆ Sturdy, well constructed
- ☆ Wide base, difficult to tip
- ☆ Small spacing between slats
- ☆ Firm sleeping surface
- ☆ No permanently attached plush bedding
- ☆ Locks for rocking
- ☆ Retractable canopy

NOTES: *Bassinets, Cradles, and Co-sleepers*

Model Name / Manufacturer	Store/Price	My Impressions	Grade

Six

Bathtubs and Accessories

Any parent of a newborn worries endlessly about somehow, unwittingly, breaking their fragile new child. The anxiety from ridiculous imagined situations—forgetting what your baby looks like in the nursery, not knowing how to hold her, setting your baby on top of the car like a cup of coffee and accidentally driving away—eventually subsides as you pass each day successfully.

Until baby's first bath. And then all your nightmares seem to come true.

Don't know how you're going to manage a squirmy, slippery newborn in a slippery, plastic tub? We don't either. After five kids, we've never been able to figure it out. It's a total disaster from start to finish.

Here's how it works: you buy a giant plastic, oval shaped tub. You try to set it in your sink, but discover it doesn't fit. (The sinks in pictures

Bathtub

Also Known As
Baby tub, bath center, bath cradle, bath sling, baby bather, bath shower, bath sponge, bath hammock

Age Range
2 weeks to 6 months

Total Usage
5 months

Recommendation
Don't need

When to Buy
The week before baby is born. You won't know if the bathtub you have is the one for you until you use with your baby, and babies usually can't have that first bath until 2 weeks old. Save your receipts and make sure you are within the purchasing store's return period! Most people try two to four bathtubs before they settle on one they like.

on the box must be in Godzilla's kitchen. There's no other explanation.) You contemplate putting it on a counter, but you can't find a counter big enough in an area you don't mind getting waterlogged. You worry (rightfully so) about the entire tub slipping around on the soon-to-be-wet countertop and have no idea how you're going to empty the thing without causing a flood.

You end up setting the baby tub in the bottom of your bathtub, straining your back reaching over, and finally climbing into the tub yourself to get a better washing angle on your baby. You wonder why you didn't just take a bath with your baby in the first place, because you're wet now anyway, he would have been warmer on your lap, and you wouldn't have to deal with filling, emptying, and storing a tub the size of a sixth grader.

We've tried every tub on the market for the last 10 years. They all present a variation of the above scenario. One of us finally settled on the fancy one-piece European baby tub and teeth-clenched her way through each bathing. The other gave up completely and discovered the joy of bathing with her babies.

The Hot New Trend: Co-bathing

Terrified of bathing your newborn? Consider the no-frills, no-cost, low-stress alternative to baby tubs: co-bathing with your little one.

Unlike the cold, startling, hurried, parent-panicked, countertop experience of plastic tubs, co-bathing recreates a womb experience, with skin-to-skin contact, warm water submersion and bonding through the power of touch.

It might seem weird at first (I wore a bikini the first time—why, I have no idea), but every mom I know who's ever bathed with her baby counts it as some of the most precious time they ever spent together.

Of course, for safety, be sure to always have an adult helper on hand to transport baby to and from your arms.

Should you wish to embark on the Perfect Baby Bathtub Quest (brave soul!), here's the lowdown on the rub-a-dub world.

PLASTIC BATHTUBS

The most common bathing accessory is the plastic bathtub: a giant, elongated bucket with a sloping seat for baby and a drainage plug. Look for a tub that is nice and sturdy, made of a thick plastic that won't buckle or break under the weight of a wet baby and all that water. Nonslip material on the baby seat is nice, unless of course, it becomes slippery when wet (which, believe it or not, many of them do). We're big fans of nonslip material on the bottom of the entire tub as well.

Why we love them: They wipe dry easily.

Why we don't: They're a POUS (product of unusual size) that's hard to fill, hard to empty, and hard to store.

INFLATABLE BATHTUBS

Inflatable baby baths are made of vinyl or other soft fabric and resemble mini wading pools. Most are designed to fit in your regular bathtub to give older babies who can already sit up a smaller, soft-walled bath experience, and shouldn't be used for babies less than 6 months old. However, some smaller inflatable models with a slanted but slippery incline are made for newborns.

Why we love them: We like the idea of sectioning off the big bathtub for our bigger babies, especially to keep them away from the faucet.

Why we don't: They usually smell horrible at first, many have hard seams that scratch baby's skin, cracks and crevices are hard to dry and invite mildew, and seriously, who's going to deflate and re-blow this thing up every two days for a bath? Not us.

BATH HAMMOCKS/BATH SLINGS

A sling of mesh fabric that hooks over the opening of a specially designed plastic baby bathtub, the bath hammock allows just enough give for newborns to be slightly submerged in water, but provide some support. Bath hammocks are sold with a plastic tub and generally only fit the tub they came with. While we do like the hammock, it's a short-lived product, as baby will outgrow it quickly. And the plastic tubs that come in the set are generally subpar.

Why we love them: The best of both worlds for a newborn: a snug, less-slippery seat slightly in the water with a giant basin beneath for overflow.

Why we don't: The hammocks are hard to fully dry, especially if they have cushioned headrests, and eventually mildew.

BATH CRADLES/BABY BATHERS

A sling of mesh-like fabric stretched on a metal frame, the bath cradle resembles a small baby bouncer and is meant to be set in a (very large) sink or in a larger bathtub. Unlike a bouncer, the bath cradle doesn't have straps, so we found our babies constantly slipping off it. Material will mildew eventually, and parts of the metal frame will, sadly, rust.

Why we love them: We really don't.

Why we don't: They only accommodate small babies for a short time, and not very securely.

BATH CENTERS

When manufacturers bundle several of their products or add accessories to the basic plastic bathtub, they call it a "bath center." Bath centers can refer to a combination bath product gift set—a tub with a hammock, bath sponge, and matching pitcher—or a tricked-out plastic bathtub, with storage compartments or a showerhead, for instance. Generally the gift sets are hiding inferior plastic tubs and are overly themed, although baby whales are cute no matter what you say.

Why we love them: Bath centers usually have the cutest accessories. Who wouldn't like an animal-shaped bath sponge and cute coordinating pitcher?

Why we don't: We like the accessories far more than the tub they come in and wish we could just buy them separately.

How Much Water?

The CPSC studied the circumstances of baby drownings over the last decade and concluded that parents are putting babies in too much water. They found that the average level of water in the tubs where babies drown was seven inches, with the lowest recorded amount being three inches deep.

While acknowledging there is "no safe level of water for an infant," CPSC Commissioner Thomas Moore suggests that *three-fourths of an inch of water* would provide all the washing and splashing a baby needs, while dramatically increasing safety.

BATH PILLOWS/SUPPORTS

Bath supports are big, water-resistant pillows meant to sit in the sink or a tub. Molded with a hollow in the middle for baby's body, they do a great job of supporting a newborn softly. While not as slippery as a bath cradle, they are best when used as flat as possible. Some come with Velcro adjustments allowing for bigger babies, but it is a strictly newborn bath aid.

Why we love them: While it doesn't allow for the easy mesh warm water submersion of a hammock, it does seem to cradle our baby better.

Why we don't: Because it is a large, stuffed foam pillow, it's not easy to dry out completely and will—*say it with me*—eventually mildew.

BATH SPONGES

It's hard to believe, but the most ingenious baby bathing solution has been around for centuries and costs less than $10! The baby bath sponge is a large, thick, rounded sponge with a contour for baby's body that you can set just about anywhere: on the counter, in a baby tub, in the bath, or in the sink. The bath sponge does a great job of cradling baby and soaking up excess water. And with a simple twist of the wrist, it will dry out completely.

Why we love them: It feels like the safest, least fussy, most logical solution to our newborn bath time hassles. It's low-tech, super cheap, and practically foolproof.

Why we don't: Yes, mildew will catch up with this product too, but for $5, you can just toss it and buy a new one.

BATH SEATS

As you will know from our safety chapter, the baby bath seat is one of the Seven Deadly Sinners—a baby product you should *not, repeat, not* buy. Want to help stop the hundreds of drowning deaths and near-drowning accidents involving baby bath seats? Stop buying them. And pass the word on.

Why we love them: Are you kidding? We hate them.

Why we don't: They give parents a false sense of security, they come undone unexpectedly, and tiny, helpless babies drown.

Price

We suspect not much fuss is made about the disastrous lack of good baby bathing products because the products are so cheap. Most baby bath sets are under $30; many are well under $20. But the key word is cheap: you will get what you pay for.

Accessories

To differentiate their large oval plastic tub from the other large oval plastic tubs on the market, manufacturers will stop at nothing to wow you with exciting features and accessories. Some, such as attached teething toys to distract baby, are great. Others, such as battery-operated showerheads, are not. If it seems too good to be true, in baby bath world, it probably is. We haven't met a showerhead yet that provides more than a messy, leaky dribble. And if you were wondering how they made the nifty folding bathtubs leakproof, the answer is, they didn't.

Safety Products

Dozens of safety products are designed to protect your baby from the three most common bath mishaps: slipping, scalding, and touching (or smashing into) the faucet. A nonslip surface is a must for any baby's bottom. If your older baby sits in the regular bathtub, it should be on a nonslip mat or on bath appliqués. Bath water temperature should ideally be between 90° and 100° F, which is just about lukewarm. Plenty of bath thermometers are available, from color changing dots to floating rubber duckies, or you can use your own elbow for free. Finally, keeping your kid away from the faucet is important because of burning and severe bonking injuries. Choices range from spout covers to retractable bath gates. We favor covering the faucet as our little Hulks can bust through just about anything with suction cups, but why they design faucet covers with funny animals is beyond us, as our kids are then drawn to the dangerous side of the tub like moths to the flame. Our favorite bath spout cover is a sleek, modern, non-animal design that not only cushions the faucet, but sprays water out 12 inches into a gentle waterfall, perfect for rinsing older kids' hair.

Baby Comfort

Before you try a baby bath product on your delicate newborn, road test it on yourself first. Rub your cheek along the edges to see if they're nice and smooth. Slide your soap-covered hand along the slanted seat back to see if it slips. Using a hammock attached to a tub? Use your hand to push the hammock down as far as you can to discover if the weight of your baby might bring his bum into close contact with any nasty contours or humps on the tub bottom. On any tub, pay special attention to the incline of the seat in relation to any baby bottom bumpers. Little boys especially might not appreciate the squish a protruding plastic hill presents to their private parts. Would you?

Parental Supervision

No matter what baby bathing product you choose (although it better not be a bath seat!), realize that no hands-free product exists. You always, always need at least one hand on your baby, and you always, always need to be with her in the bathroom, period. Because babies can drown silently in just an inch of water, they cannot be left alone near sinks, toilets, and especially bathtubs with water for even 10 seconds. Let the doorbell ring. Let your voicemail pick up. Gather all towels, washcloths, and baby shampoos ahead of time. Because the minute your baby goes in the water, all eyes—and at least one hand—should be on your child.

Location

Finally, a word about location. Our mom has told us many times she bathed us in the kitchen sink with nary a tub or accessory in sight. Today, many bathtubs are specifically designed for kitchen sink use. And our kitchen sink is the largest sink in our house, with plenty of counter space to boot. So we tried it. Twice. And herewith, our findings:

Seven Reasons to Never Bathe Your Baby in the Kitchen

1. We barely have time to bathe our baby at all. To make us have to wash the dishes first is just cruel.

2. Dragging all your bath accessories into the kitchen every time doesn't seem like fun to us.

3. Water and hardwood floors don't play well together.

4. In your sleep-deprived state, you may accidentally soap up your baby with Dawn rather than baby soap.

5. Where do you dry your baby off? On the kitchen counter next to the defrosting chicken?

6. A clean baby and crusty food from lunch don't mix.

7. As soon as a baby boy catches a draft, he will pee on the wall, the dishrag, and anything else he manages to hit on your kitchen counter.

Bath Accessories

As an added bonus, here's the lowdown on the most popular bath extras, along with our advice on which you should have and which you should skip.

☆ **Bath appliqués:** Textured, nonslip surface decals for the bottom of the bathtub to prevent slipping. Some tubs have nonslip surfaces built right in. If yours doesn't, get bath appliqués or a nonslip bath mat since even babies that can sit up on their own are slippery.

☆ **Bath mats (cushioned):** Cushioned mats for the bottom of the bathtub to prevent baby from slipping around. How do they compare to bath appliqués? Bath appliqués tend to be rougher on small bums, but bath mats have a tendency to slip around themselves. We vote appliqués.

☆ **Bath thermometers:** While there are simple water thermometers like you use in a swimming pool, most meant for baby baths combine the thermometer with a fun, floating toy. They help safely gauge and monitor the temperature of bath water. Nice to have.

☆ **Bath splash guards:** Heavy-duty clear vinyl shields that protect your bathroom floor from messy spills and splashes during bath time and help prevent dangerous slips or water damage. Baby splashes, we can live with. Preschool tidal waves? Get a bath splash guard.

☆ **Bath toys:** Special waterproof toys designed for bath time play; bath toys usually float, if baby is lucky, they squirt. We love bath toys (how else would we distract a baby during hair washes?), but we hate how they all hold water indefinitely and then grow mold quite definitely.

☆ **Bath toy organizers:** Containers made of mesh or plastic that attach to the bathtub/shower wall or hook over the side of the bathtub, designed to organize bath toys and accessories. Most organizers allow toys to dry out quickly with draining holes. A must-have if you have bath toys.

☆ **Bathtub rails:** Rails that securely attach to the side of the bathtub with no tools, designed to give your child a sure grip when getting in and out of the slippery bathtub. If they are installed correctly and have a solid suction, then bathtub rails are great. If they aren't or don't, they can contribute to even more accidents. We give this product a miss because we don't want our babies standing up in the tub at any time (and this product can encourage them to), and our older kids can manage just fine (thanks to those nonslip appliqués!).

☆ **Bathtub spout covers:** Soft, protective bathtub faucet covers designed to prevent bumps and bruises from babies and toddlers bumping into the spout. A must-have.

☆ **Bath drain valve covers:** Rounded covers that suction over the bath drain to prevent bumps and pinches from the drain valve. Useful product; nice to have.

☆ **Tub guard set:** A set of two foam, nonslip cushions for the parent; one for your elbows on the side of the tub and one for your knees on the floor, to make bathing your child more comfortable for you. Anything that helps alleviate our aching back during bath time gets an A+ in our book!

Features to Consider

☆ Size

☆ Nonslip surfaces

☆ Baby comfort

☆ Drying ease

☆ Smooth edges

☆ *Never* consider a bath seat

NOTES: *Baby Bathtubs*			
Model Name / Manufacturer	Store/Price	My Impressions	Grade

Seven

Bouncers, Rockers, and Infant Seats

Your baby has more furniture than you do: a crib, changing table, bassinet, swing, car seat, activity mat, and playpen. Do you really need an infant seat too? The short answer: *yes.*

No mom can hold her baby all day long; eventually you have to set babies down. And because couches, chairs, and the counter are out (seriously, in case no one told you, those are out because of safety issues), your choices for where to lay your baby are limited. As long as infant seats are placed in a safe location (read: on the floor), they offer a great place to soothe, entertain, lull to sleep, and just let your infant hang out.

Bouncers are the most popular infant seat, followed by rockers, and the newest entry into the market, the stationary infant seat. We're big fans

Bouncer and Rocker

Also Known As
Baby seat, bouncy seat, rocking seat, baby rocker, activity rocker, babysitter, Bouncenette®, Baby Papasan™

Age Range
Birth to age at which baby can sit unassisted (about 6 months)

Total Usage
6 months

Recommendation
Must have

When to Buy
Before baby is born. A perfect item for your registry.

of bouncers, think rockers rock, but stationary infant seats—well, the jury's still out. We hated them at first sight. We tried them out, tried to like them, and we just don't see the point. Why? Read on.

BOUNCERS

Bouncers are slings of fabric mounted on a metal frame that bounce at baby's slightest movement. Unlike baby swings, the motion of bouncers is manual and parent- or baby-propelled. However, most come equipped with battery-operated, multi-setting, nirvana-inducing vibration packs. Babies are strapped into place, and should always remain so while in this seat.

Why we love them: Our babies love them. And what baby loves, mama loves.

Why we don't: For some reason, bouncers tend to have much louder, uglier, and otherwise harder-to-swallow patterns than rockers. Why, *why*???

BABY ROCKERS

Baby rockers are close cousins to bouncers, but rockers rock instead of bounce. Most rockers have a nonrocking stabilizer that allows the seat to stay stationary. Some bouncers are convertible to rockers and vice versa.

Why we love them: Some of the world's top designers make rockers and they're beautiful!

Why we don't: Most rockers don't have as many music and motion features as bouncers. Rockers are harder for babies to move by themselves, but we do know bigger babies who have managed to rock themselves out. And because big, old-fashioned, adult rocking chairs still kind of scare us a little, we're a tiny bit afraid of these too. Irrational perhaps, but there you have it.

Stationary Infant Seats

New to the market, these seats resemble small, round restaurant boosters that allow babies to sit upright long before they can on their own. The secret is in the design of the high-back seat: babies are either folded in half with a sunken bum to keep them "upright" or snugly situated with their legs around a pommel that keeps them in place. Made of molded plastic, these seats are one-size-fits-all, and by "all" we mean most babies, but not those that are too big, too small, or have extra chubby legs. The seats do *not* have safety straps, either for the baby or the seat, and are meant for use on the floor only. Some have trays and toy attachments to keep baby occupied, which is nice, because once stuffed in these seats, babies can't reach anything. Because these seats should not be used until babies have good head control, at about 2 months, and expire when babies can sit up on their own, they have a much shorter life expectancy than bouncers or rockers and can't be used from day one.

Why we love them: "Love" is too strong a word. We like the portability, although it doesn't fold. It's nice for the park. Some of the ones with trays are super cute.

Why we don't: It doesn't rock or soothe. Baby can't sleep in it. No music or built-in stimulation. We're certainly not going to lie on the ground to feed our baby, so that's out. And we have a bouncer, so what's the point?

Age Appropriateness

While most bouncers and rockers are fit for an infant, some require their "riders" to have a decent amount of neck control first, so check the manufacturers' age recommendations, and chose appropriately. Because the bouncer seat is a lifesaver from the day you get home from the hospital, we highly recommend getting one that's suitable from birth. Some have special infant headrests, but in most cases, those aren't necessary. If you have one, make sure it doesn't obstruct baby's breathing in any way.

All infant seats—bouncers, rockers, and stationary seats—are no longer safe to use once a baby can sit up on his own or is active enough to try. If your baby is lurching and squirming to get out, it's time to retire the bouncer, as he could tip it over and injure himself.

Comfort

The design and comfort of baby bouncers and rockers vary greatly. Some are narrow; some are circular. Some seats are simple slings of fabric and some are soft slices of heaven. Choose one with a seat that offers some amount of comfort; no one deserves to sit on scratchy fabric, not even fussy babies who cry all day. Of course, make sure there isn't too much fabric or cushion near baby's face.

Portability

Many bouncers fold for easy travel; just as many do not. The large frame of those that don't will *not* fit into your average trunk, so if portability is your bag, get a product that folds.

Convertibility

Some bouncers and rockers convert by function, some by age range, and some by both. There are bouncers that also rock, rockers that also bounce, and some that even turn into toddler seats.

We usually like products that convert from infant to toddler, but in the case of infant seats, we don't. Generally seats that offer that big of an age range don't fit either end of the range particularly well. Infants get shortchanged on the fabric (we want our newborns cradled in the clouds!), and toddlers inherit a rickety, rather ugly chair they just don't need. By age 2, they'll have a whole lot of new fun furniture options, or more likely, prefer to climb up on the couch next to you anyway.

Vibration

Most bouncers come with a vibration effect that not only provides some physical soothing similar to a ride in the car, but also an audible hum that can give babies a sort of "white noise" calm. Some bouncers offer different levels of vibration, stronger for bigger babies.

Check to see how the vibration is put into motion. Some have automatic start-up settings, and baby's motion will start them up. However, we found that someone walking past a bouncer can set it off in the same way (even when empty!), so remember not to leave it in that setting or you'll burn through batteries.

Many also allow you to set the length of vibration and offer an auto-off setting. Auto-off is a nice feature—as long as it's longer than a few measly minutes—but we prefer our bouncers also have a "never off" setting that will allow them to run far, far into the night for our finally-she's-sleeping! bundles of joy.

Music and Sound Effects

We think music is a must; sound effects a maybe. It all depends on exactly what your seat is spewing. Nobody minds a good classical tune, but a five-note nursery rhyme will get old fast. Remember, the reggae ditty that was cute in the store won't be so cute the six millionth time you hear it. Babies like almost anything, so pick a melody you enjoy.

Sound effects are hit and miss, and unfortunately, until your baby uses the seat, you won't know which is which. Some babies are lulled by cricket noises, some are scared to death of them. In general, aside from muted nature sounds—key word: *muted*—we think sound effects are better suited to toys, not bouncers.

Because your infant is forced to lie on the seat's speakers, check that the volume isn't too loud for sensitive new ears. In fact, we recommend you stick your own head on the seat and listen to the music for yourself. You'll learn volumes about the product. (Pun intended.)

Finally, look at how the music and sound effects operate. Are there auto settings? What sets them off? How long will they play? Can you adjust the volume?

Toy Bars

Many bouncers and rockers come with toy bars, from simple hanging stuffed animals to mirrors, mobiles, and mini light shows. The trick is to look for a toy bar that strikes a healthy balance between useless and Vegas. Keep in mind that by the time babies can actually grab, pull, or play with a hanging toy, they are too old for a bouncer seat anyway. Yet a tiny teddy bear that just hangs in their face offers little more than a front row seat for dust.

We like toy bars that offer baby some visual stimulation but aren't too over the top. Little light and motion effects are cute. A song-and-dance, fireworks spectacular every time baby sneezes is too much.

The most important attribute of any toy bar is that it is detachable or swings out of the way, so you have easy access to baby, and she isn't forced to live a tiny Clockwork Orange existence.

Other Features

Most bouncers and rockers come with retractable fabric hoods. They aren't essential, but can be helpful if you have a well-windowed house and want to keep errant sunbeams out of your baby's eyes.

Remote controls are another much hyped feature, but we find them completely unnecessary. Manually restarting vibration or music is a simple maneuver that won't disturb your baby, and actually checking on your child frequently at this age, up close and in person, is a good thing. Besides, we have far too many remote controls as it is.

Safety

Now the common sense caveats. The following things are bad: letting your baby "veg" in an infant seat for hours and hours, placing the infant seat near danger such as a stairwell or fireplace, leaving your baby unattended at any time.

Always strap your baby into the seat, every time. And if your seat doesn't have straps, reconsider why your tiny, precious, oh-so-breakable baby is in it.

Don't Fall Victim to SPS!

What's the widely known syndrome that has pediatricians worried behind closed doors? SPS. Stupid Parent Syndrome. We're not sure why, but stationary infant seats seem to be causing rampant cases of SPS across the nation.

For decades it's been drilled into us: don't set the baby on the couch, even for a second, because they might roll off! That would be a safer alternative than the spots where helpless babies are being perched in their *strapless* stationary infant seats.

A quick search on YouTube confirms that somehow, despite the obvious lack of straps on the baby or the seat, these products are giving parents a false sense of security. Let us repeat it one more time: these seats are *strapless!* They don't attach to anything! They will not magically keep your baby safe on the dining room table, on the sofa, or heaven help us, on the kitchen counter! Please, do us a favor. Help stamp out SPS. Keep your stationary infant seat on the floor, where it belongs.

Price

In general, you'll pay more for more features, but also for the brand. Several top designers have released limited edition seats that are quite beautiful but quite bare. Bouncers and rockers range in price from $19 to $119. Most are in the $30 to $40 range. Stationary infant seats cost around $40.

Features to Consider

☆ Motion: bounce versus rock

☆ Age range

☆ Fabric

☆ Portability

☆ Vibration

☆ Music

☆ Toy bar

NOTES: *Bouncers, Rockers, and Infant Seats*

Model Name / Manufacturer	Store/Price	My Impressions	Grade
_____	_____	_____	_____
_____	_____	_____	_____
_____	_____	_____	_____
_____	_____	_____	_____
_____	_____	_____	_____
_____	_____	_____	_____
_____	_____	_____	_____
_____	_____	_____	_____
_____	_____	_____	_____
_____	_____	_____	_____

Eight

Breastfeeding Accessories, Bottles, and Feeding Accessories

I t seems a silly thing because we all must feed our babies, but how moms choose to do it is a hotly debated topic. God gave us a built-in feeding system for free. Science gave us some pretty convenient, healthy alternatives. Those in favor of breastfeeding are really, really in favor of it. Those who prefer bottle feeding see no difference in the two.

It's an interesting debate because most breastfeeding proponents have only breastfed, and most bottle feeders have never nursed. I'm going to go out on a limb and declare myself the ultimate expert because I have done it all.

I've breastfed for a full year, breastfed for just four months, and introduced formula as early as four weeks. I've pumped with manuals and with electrics and then figured out the best system of all: training your breasts not to produce when you don't want them to. I've used generic formula, gone broke on fancy DHA/ARA-enhanced formula, tried soy, organic, and lactose-free. I've used bottles with liners, natural flow wide-bottle systems, and $5 no-nonsense, multicolored bottles from the discount store.

I've been an 18-hour-a-day working mom who relied on day care, a full-time stay-at-home mom, and, my personal favorite, a work-at-home mom. Whatever your choice, it was my choice too.

Take it from me, all feeding options have pros and cons, trials and tribulations, and hidden costs. Here's one woman's humble rundown.

Breastfeeding Accessories

So you've decided to give breastfeeding a try. Good for you! It's the best gift you can give your new baby. But if you think you don't need any special baby products for nursing, think again. There are quite a few on the market for good reason.

Nursing Bras

Nursing bras are a necessity for easy access to the milk supply. Most are u-g-l-y and don't have an alibi, but for some serious cash you can find sexy, lacy nursing bras to cover up your new porn star–sized assets.

By definition, a nursing bra is a regular bra that allows you to unlatch and uncover the cups without taking the bra off. The important features to look for are

☆ **Comfort:** Because you'll be wearing it 24/7, you want the most comfortable one you can find. Also a too-tight or restrictive bra can cause milk flow or engorgement problems, so select one that is roomy enough, but gives some support.

☆ **One-hand release:** You need to be able to release the latch on the cup with one hand. Some are easier than others. Hooks are good; too-tight snaps are bad.

☆ **Breathable fabric:** Choose a breathable fabric, whether cotton or a breathable synthetic.

☆ **Underwire free:** It seems counterintuitive because you've never needed a metal infrastructure more, but underwires can obstruct milk

---

Breastfeeding Accessories

Age Range
Birth to 12-plus months

Total Usage
12-plus months

Recommendation
Must have

When to Buy
As you need them. Some items, such as pillows, are great for your registry.

ducts—milk-producing tissue runs all the way around your rib cage and into your armpits. A blocked milk duct means pain and suffering for all involved. Skip the underwire, no matter how pretty it is or comfortable it seems.

☆ **Not front split:** Instead of flaps over the cups, some nursing bras have hooks in the middle that allow you to basically split the entire bra open from the front. These are not a clever design. Think elastic bands springing open, two boobs on the loose, surprise, leakage, and embarrassment. No good.

Nursing bras are hit-or-miss; the one your sister loved will drive you crazy. Because you can't really return used undergarments, finding the perfect bra can be an expensive proposition, but one you need to invest in all the same. Once you find the bra you love, buy all they have in stock.

NURSING TANKS

Nursing tanks are tank tops with a nursing bra built in. They still allow you to unhook each side one-handed, and make for some darn convenient dressing. Nursing bras are great, if you're naked. But any other top you put over it, has to allow access. And sometimes unbuttoning to your belly can be a bit embarrassing. A nursing tank can be worn alone just like a regular tank in the summer, or easily layered under regular cardigans, sweaters, and button-down blouses. We always feel a little better with our belly covered when we're doing a public striptease, but that's just us.

NURSING SHIRTS

Nursing shirts are specially designed to have slits, hidden pockets, or flaps on the front to allow easy nursing bra access. They are not all very pretty or flattering, but if you hunt, you can find some. But buying more maternity-minded clothes after we've had our baby was always low on our list of fun. We prefer nursing tanks that allow us to wear more of our regular wardrobe.

Body Benefits of Breastfeeding

If you've always dreamed of breastfeeding, then you're way ahead of me. I was scared to death of it. But I know I'm tougher than Tori Spelling. And she, along with all those other celebrity moms—Katie Couric, Faith Hill, Madonna, Gwyneth Paltrow, and Sarah Jessica Parker, to name a few—can't stop talking about how much they love breastfeeding. These famous moms with nannies, private chefs, and trainers could hire a wet nurse as easily as a stunt double. However, they've embraced breastfeeding, and considering we've seen their nursing bra straps in more than one tabloid, we actually believe they're really doing it.

So what gives? Yes, they love their babies, but they also love their bodies. We all know breast is best for baby, but the body benefits of breastfeeding for mom are many. Not only does it help your uterus contract more quickly and release chemicals that make you feel better, but breastfeeding also helps you lose the baby weight faster than any diet on earth. It is also believed to cut your breast cancer risk in half. We're sold.

Oh, and all those worries? For naught. Once you get the hang of it, you won't believe you ever considered anything else. Take that, Donna Martin!

BREAST/BRA PADS

Bra pads are like little maxipads for your bra to help soak up the inevitable leaks. There are cloth ones you wash and disposable ones you pitch. Some have adhesive to help them stay in place, which we highly recommend. Having a breast pad fall onto the counter at the grocery store is one of the most embarrassing things ever. Actually, sporting a fresh, wet breast milk stain on your blouse in a meeting with your boss is the most embarrassing thing ever. Makes the old breast pad in the produce aisle pale in comparison.

Just like maxipads, there are varying thicknesses for varying flows. At first, you'll probably need thicker pads, but can graduate to thinner, and usually, eventually none.

Some have waterproof linings to protect your clothes, but make sure your breasts can breathe. Sealing them behind plastic bags will allow them to retain moisture and can lead to sore nipples, bacteria growth, and possible infection.

Nipple/Nursing Shields

Nipple shields, also called "nursing shields," look like a hollow breast cast in silicone with a hole in the nipple. Like a naughty Halloween accessory, but not. You wear them over your own breast and nipple to aid in breastfeeding

Shield Confusion?

The only product without "shield" in the name is the one you actually use to shield sore nipples. Huh? Here's a quick primer.

- **Nipple shields:** A fake breast with a hole in the nipple worn over the breast during feeding.

- **Breast shields:** The flexible, plastic cup you press your breast against on a breast pump.

- **Breast shells:** A plastic shell you wear in your bra between feedings to protect your nipple from rubbing against your bra or to help correct inverted nipples.

while your baby is actually sucking. They are used to help babies with breast-feeding problems latch on, as well as to help mothers with inverted, flat, or super sore nipples. They are usually made of silicone, although you can find them in rubber or latex.

Nipple shields have been used since the 1500s, although back then they were made of silver, pewter, glass, ivory, or wood and had a rubber teat. Nipple shields are readily available today, but the lactation community by and large hates them because they do cut down on milk production and the baby only learns to use suction instead of a mouth massaging technique critical to successful breastfeeding.

If you are told to wear nipple shields, try them, but try to wean yourself and your baby off them as soon as possible. If you are using them to help block pain, consider trying to treat the pain instead, because nipple shields will only mask it. Try different breastfeeding holds or doctor-approved creams or pain relievers.

Breast Shells

Unlike nipple shields that are used during feeding, breast shells are worn in the bra between feedings. Breast shells are actually little shields for the breast to protect the sore nipple and areola from the mean, mean chafing of the nursing bra. Breast shells are plastic cups with a roomy, ventilated spot for your nipple that allow for air ventilation but not for moving surface contact.

Breast shells are also used to help inverted nipples. This variety of breast shell has a small hole that lies close to the nipple base, exerting pressure that stretches the areola and allows the nipple to pop out.

Breast shells are used to alleviate discomfort, so if yours are causing pain, you may be using them incorrectly, or may need a bigger size or different brand.

Nipple Creams and Ointments

Sore and cracked nipples have been the downfall of more than one earnest breastfeeder. The store shelves are full of nipple creams and ointments promising salvation, but you should be very wary because what goes on your breast goes directly into baby's mouth. Some creams require you to rub them off before you breastfeed. Um, come again? If we were able to scrub cream off our nipples, we wouldn't need the cream in the first place. Avoid these. And maybe consider a voodoo curse on the manufacturers who would trick the unsuspecting mom into such a painful pain relief venture.

Even though many creams claim they are good for breastfeeding nipples, the only cream you should use contains just one thing: 100 percent lanolin. Any cream with any other ingredient, including Vitamin E or any other natural ingredients, should be avoided.

Be warned that lanolin cream is sticky. Honey sticky. Don't-quite-know-what-to-do-now-that-it's-on sticky. Can't-even-wash-it-off-your-fingers sticky. But it does work.

The best treatment for dry, sore, or cracked nipples is prevention, and God, our favorite pharmacist, gave you the magic serum for free. Breast milk itself is full of emollient, moisturizing goodness that will help keep your nipples happy. The best course of action: after each feeding, express a little milk onto your fingertips and rub it all over your nipples and areolas. Then allow your breasts to breathe, nudist style, for 10 to 15 minutes. Not suitable for most public places, but guaranteed to make your husband happy.

NURSING PILLOWS

Nursing pillows are little C-shaped cushions designed to be worn around a mother's middle when breastfeeding. They raise a baby up and give mom a chance to concentrate on proper baby latch position rather than full-body support.

Nursing pillows are also frequently used for babies when they are learning to sit up, to give them extra, cushy support.

Some nursing pillows come with removable, washable covers. Still others have straps that fasten them completely around a mother's body. We're suckers for the pretty ones.

Nursing Stools

A nursing stool is a little footstool designed to give moms, especially short moms like us, better, more ergonomic posture during feedings. Having used a bathroom stool with limited success, we think nursing stools are genius. Just remember to move it out of the way when you're done. They are nasty buggers to kick or fall over in the dark.

Breast Pumps

The most loved and most feared of all nursing products, the breast pump is a staple for most moms. If you plan on being with your child full-time, you can certainly live without it, and you can express by hand (although this is a *slooooooow* process). Or if you want to supplement with formula during the times you won't be around your baby, like when you're at work, but still want to breastfeed when you are, you can train your breasts and avoid the pump.

Many moms swear by breast pumps, and use them to provide milk for other caregivers to feed, boost milk supply, and even relieve engorgement. Heck, some moms have even toted their breast pumps to the Oscars.

There are three kinds of breast pumps: hospital grade, electric, and manual.

Hospital-Grade Breast Pumps

Hospital-grade breast pumps are super giant, expensive, and usually noisy, but they get the job done quickly, efficiently and quite painlessly. They aren't very portable, (some weigh up to 18 pounds!), and are quite costly (a new one can run over $1,000). But because they work so well and you can rent them for as little as $1 to $3 a day, they are a great way to start your pumping adventure. (Note: If you're renting a pump, you'll still need to purchase a personal collection kit, although many hospitals now hand them out for free.)

Why we love them: There's no messing around with a hospital-grade pump. They get the job done, in record time.

Why we don't: They are big, noisy, and expensive. No good for our anniversary trip to the Bahamas.

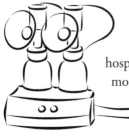

PERSONAL ELECTRIC BREAST PUMPS

While they are a step down in performance from hospital grade, personal electric breast pumps are much more portable and much more affordable. Some models are fairly quiet for more discreet pumping. Some come with carrying bags, backup battery power, and even car adapters.

Why we love them: Because we're pros by the second month but more mobile, we're willing to trade a bit of power for portability.

Why we don't: All models are not created equally. Some literally suck more than others. And because you can't tell just by the box, and you can't return a pump once you've "broken the seal," finding the right one is not a cheap endeavor.

MANUAL BREAST PUMPS

Manual pumps are the smallest, lightest, quietest, and cheapest type of pump. A single handle is squeezed or pulled by the mom to activate the sucking or massaging motion. They are easy to transport, but they are slower. Many moms prefer this simple method because it's quiet and peaceful, and they can control the sucking.

Why we love them: We're one of those moms who prefer to control the suction.

Why we don't: We grow old waiting for the bottle to fill with milk when we use a manual pump. And our hands get so, so tired.

Comfort

As with most baby products, especially those we have to stick our nipples into, comfort is king. No pump is better than any other pump. Pick the system you're most comfortable with that gives you the most personal comfort.

Adjustable Suction Control

Being able to control the amount of suction is another critical feature of any breast pump. Some moms prefer a stronger suck that leads to a quicker completion, but some like to take it slow. Even manual pumps should offer a few different suction settings.

Don't Share Your Electric Pump

Because they are expensive and when you're done with it, you're done, personal electric pumps seem like a great item to pass down to friends and family. However, it's not recommended, because even if you buy new collection pieces such as breast shields and tubing, droplets of milk can get sucked into the machinery of personal electric pumps and stay there (hospital-grade pumps are sealed against this risk).

The Food and Drug Administration (FDA) warns that breast milk can carry bacteria and viruses, including HIV and hepatitis that might not show up for years. A virus left behind in a used breast pump, even from a good friend, can be potentially very harmful to your baby because everyone's body reacts to illness differently, and the original user might not know she was a carrier.

Save your money somewhere else, and always buy your breast pump new. It might seem expensive, but compared to the $1,800 to $2,800 a year that formula costs, it's a small investment for a healthy baby.

Massaging versus Sucking

Some pumps use a straight vacuum suck, while others employ a more massaging method that better mimics a baby's mouth. Some also include automatic cycling, which varies the speed and frequency of the sucking like a baby does naturally. We prefer any pump that's less like plugging into a vacuum hose and more like actually feeding our babies.

Efficiency

In case no one told you—and no one told us!—pumping is not a fast activity. While we can sate our babies in seven minutes flat on each side, some pumps take more than half an hour to use. But not all breast pumps deliver the same efficiency, and more expensive models are generally quicker.

The measurement to look for is how many times the pump can suck per minute. Hospital-grade machines can deliver 60 sucks per minute, while lower-end electrics will give you 12. We recommend at least a 48 suck per minute capability.

Double Pumping

Many pumps offer the ability to empty both breasts at once. It can take a little coordination effort at first, but the payoff is huge: half the time spent pumping! We love anything that cuts our pumping time in half. Especially when we're hiding under our desks, frantic because we're already 10 minutes late for the board meeting and our employers frown upon pumping at the table.

Ease of Use

Some pumps are more complicated than others. Some you just flip a switch, grab a boob, and go. Others require a degree in rocket science. We prefer the former.

Easy to Clean

Look for a pump that is easy to clean. If you have to unscrew 153 pieces, we don't consider it easy. Dishwasher safe? We're in love.

If you need to dry inner parts in a hurry, or live in a humid climate where things don't dry out well, run your hair dryer over the pump to help speed the process along.

Breast-Pumping Accessories

BREAST SHIELDS/FLANGES

Breast shields, also called "flanges," are the cup or collar that you place your breast over to funnel the milk through some tubes to the bottle or collection container. While most new breast pumps come with breast shields, they are not one-size-fits-all. You can purchase alternative sizes separately, so get the size you need. Breast shields should be comfortable and cover you adequately.

COLLECTION KITS

A breast milk collection kit is a personal kit that you purchase for use with an electric pump. Most personal electric pumps come with collection kits, but you might need extra pieces, and you do need to purchase your own for rental pumps (although many hospitals include a new collection kit with their rental pumps).

Collection kits usually include breast shields, tubes, gaskets, rings, disks, filters, bottles, and caps. Collection kits are made to specifically fit a certain model, so be careful to buy the correct one. Don't ever buy a used collection kit. Verify that a new kit is sealed before you open it.

STORAGE BAGS AND BOTTLES

This is a crucial component of the breast pumping experience, as you need to package your end product for delivery. Some collection containers are more foolproof than others. Look for very foolproof ones with wide openings and tight seals. Wanna know who cries over spilled milk? Breast-pumping moms do. We cry and cry and cry.

The type of container you'll need depends on how long you need to store your milk. If you're a part-time pumper, you can use bottles. Some pumps empty right into a bottle, which is fabulous. If you're going to store your milk a while, or even freeze it, you will need bags. There are microwavable bags that allow for self-sterilization, insulated bags, and freezer packs.

Carrying Cases

Some breast pumps are more travel-friendly than others. Most come with a carrying case, but a mesh bag isn't our idea of a great one. We like the ones that zip neatly into tiny backpacks or little briefcases. A carrying case is useless if it doesn't have room for all your extra accessories, and you end up stuffing them, quite unsanitarily, into your purse.

Hands-Free Pumping Bras and Bands

If you've perfected the art of pumping and wish to use your hands for other activities, you're in luck. Special nursing bras and elastic band contraptions hold the breast shields in place for you while you pump. We're not brave enough to try this (see why breastfeeding moms cry, above), but if you are, know that some moms even jury-rig their own pumping bands out of ponytail holders. An all-too-quick search on the Internet, and you'll have pictures, diagrams, and step-by-step instructions.

Price

Breast pumps are quite expensive, but a cheap alternative to formula. Manual pumps range from $15 to $65. Personal electric pumps cost anywhere from $50 to $350. The more expensive pumps will do a much better job. We'd recommend looking at manual pumps in the $35 range, and electric pumps in the $150 range.

Features to Consider

☆ Hospital grade, personal electric, or manual

☆ Adjustable suction control

☆ Sucking methods

☆ Efficiency

☆ Double pumping

☆ Ease of use

☆ Easy to clean

☆ Storage containers
☆ Carrying case
☆ Price

NOTES: *Breastfeeding Accessories*

Model Name / Manufacturer	Store/Price	My Impressions	Grade

Bottles and Feeding Accessories

Bottles and Feeding Accessories

Age Range
Birth to 12 months

Total Usage
12 months

Recommendation
Must have

When to Buy
Buy a couple just before you need to use them.

Whether you're going the formula route, or don't plan on always being the one to personally deliver your breast milk, you're going to need more than a few bottles. To make life easier, most moms choose a style and stick with it.

Did we say moms choose? Actually, we moms more suggest. Our babies do all the choosing. The best bottle is the one your baby likes. That's not to say we can't influence our babies, and hopefully have them love the first one we present because we loved it too.

Tempting as it is, don't stock up on baby bottles and accessories in advance. You won't know what your baby likes until he actually tries it, so we recommend buying one of each of the major bottles on the market and doing your own product testing.

STANDARD BOTTLES

The standard baby bottle hasn't changed much in the last 30 years. It's still made of see-through plastic, still has a collar ring, nipple, and cap. Standard bottles are the cheapest and easiest to find, and work quite well for most babies. Glass baby bottles are still available, for those nervous about plastics. We're worried about the reports concerning the safety of plastic, but we're personally a little more worried about broken glass everywhere.

WIDE-NECK BOTTLES

Wide-neck bottles are just like standard bottles, only shorter and fatter. (Is it any wonder we love them?) We're big fans of wide bottles. Babies still breastfeeding, making the transition from breastfeeding, or using bottles in addition to breastfeeding usually prefer the nipples on wide-mouth bottles because the large nipple rests on their face more like mom's. The bigger opening on wide bottles makes for easier filling and much easier cleaning. And the larger base makes them less likely to tip over. The only drawback: the wider size means they won't fit as easily in some diaper bag bottle pockets.

ANGLE-NECK BOTTLES

Some bottles have a 45-degree angle near the top to help cut down on air. Angle-neck bottles also allow a baby to be more upright during feeding, which can help with digestion.

BOTTLE SYSTEMS

There are standard bottles and then there are the bottle "systems." Bottle systems come with extra gadgets and accessories, levers, and liners to create a more natural flow of milk and eliminate air. They do this in a number of patented ways: with collapsible, disposable liners; anti-vacuum nipples; bottom bottle vents; internal vent systems; and built-in burpers. Bottle systems usually consist of several small, separate pieces that can be a pain in the butt when washing, when traveling, and when making a dozen bottles a day. They are also far more expensive than your average bottle. But the bottle systems do an amazing job of what they promise: eliminating bubbles, turning gassy babies into happy babies, and helping combat colic. And if you have a fussy baby, they are worth triple the price! And then some.

NIPPLES

The most important part of the bottle is the nipple. If the baby doesn't like the nipple, nothing else about the bottle matters. Most bottles have several different nipple choices, so buy one of each nipple, too, until you find the perfect match.

Nipple Material

Today's nipples are either made of latex (the brownish-yellow ones) or silicone (clear colored). Latex nipples are softer than silicone, and many babies prefer them for this reason. However, latex nipples will degrade over time, eventually breaking down and breaking up, resulting in a choking hazard for babies. Check your nipples frequently and avoid cheap, no-name brand versions that are made overseas with no testing. Keep in mind that, while it's rare, some babies are allergic to latex, or can develop a later latex allergy from early exposure to latex. If your baby ever acts extra fussy on the nipple or shows signs of swelling or redness, consult your doctor immediately.

Silicone nipples are harder, but the firmness means they won't collapse in baby's mouth. They are also more resistant to rips or tears, and won't discolor or hold odors.

Nipple Shape

Choices include standard shape nipples with an elongated, rounded top; squared-off nipples meant to mimic a mother's shape; flat orthodontic nipples to promote baby's oral development; and nipples with a wide, cushy base to remind babies of breastfeeding.

The best shape is the one your baby prefers. Some like a normal nipple. Some gag on the thinness of them. Some prefer to have their cheeks smashed into a fat-based nipple, while others can't quite figure out how to breathe around them. We've tried them all, had babies who liked everything, and babies who liked nothing. Good luck to you.

Nipple Flow

Cheaper bottles won't give you a choice or distinction, but most bottles offer nipples with varying flow: smaller holes for tinier babies and larger holes for older ones. There are even cross-cut nipples for those who prefer to put cereal straight into their baby's bottle (although pediatricians do not recommend this).

Nipples with flow have age suggestions on the packaging, but they are just suggestions, not rules. The flow your baby needs has less to do with her age and more to do with her dexterity, drive, and hunger. Match flow according to her skills. If she's sputtering and gagging, get her a slower flow. If she's working hard for the money and coming up short, get one with a faster flow.

Safety Scares and Plastic Bottles

New reports are scaring the heck out of parents concerning the safety of plastic baby bottles. The same frightening studies seem to crop up every few years in various forms, warning against certain types of plastic over others. As soon as a report comes out, everyone freaks out, the phone lines light up, the blogs go crazy, the media milks it until the bottle manufacturers readjust and offer bad-chemical-of-the-month-free bottles, and everyone goes back to business. Until a new report surfaces that the newest bottles are bad too. Lather, rinse, repeat.

We buy into the panic every time, until we realize we're surrounded by plastics, chemicals, and all manner of things certain to kill us. Short of moving to Mars, what's a mom to do?

The common theme in the plastic warnings seems to be problems resulting from heat causing chemicals to leach into the milk. So here are the safety precautions we take that seem to make the most sense without making us crazy.

☆ Don't heat your plastic baby bottles for prolonged periods of time. A quick dip every so often in boiling water will sterilize them just fine (especially after an illness). Let them sit for a few minutes to cool to room temperature before you fill them with milk or formula.

☆ Never heat plastic bottles in the microwave. Don't heat plastic anything in the microwave, actually.

☆ Don't let milk or formula sit around in plastic baby bottles. This particular rule causes us to have to throw away quite a few bottles we forgot about. The car likes to hide them from us. So does the couch.

BOTTLE WARMERS

Bottle warmers are electrical devices that warm your bottles. Some even work in your car. Look for one that fits your bottle and has an auto-shutoff. There are also models with night-lights, attached cooling sections that keep bottles on ice until you want them to warm up, and even baby food warming capabilities. However convenient it might be, we'd still keep them out of the nursery though. Electrical appliances are safest in the kitchen.

BOTTLE STERILIZERS

We hate germs, so we're all for sterilizing, but then we remember you're not supposed to overheat plastic bottles. And while some bottle sterilizers are freestanding electrical appliances, others have you place your plastic bottles in the microwave. I thought we agreed we weren't going to do that.

This is another appliance we skip because we can. A pot of boiling water on the stove will sterilize bottles just fine. Most dishwashers also have sterilization settings now.

The whole idea of sterilizing a bottle came about before tap water was as safe as it is now anyway. If your baby is healthy and your tap water is drinkable, regular soapy washes will do just fine. (Unless, of course, you find a bottle of curdled milk under the couch. Those you have our permission to just toss.)

BOTTLE BRUSHES

A bottle brush is a specially shaped brush for reaching all the way inside bottles when you clean them by hand. An absolute necessity. Some come with smaller nipple brushes in the handle. Absolute genius.

BOTTLE DRYING RACKS/TREES

Bottle drying racks and trees are plastic contraptions that hold bottles, nipples, training cups, and accessories. Some even have drain reservoirs. If you have loads of extra counter space and money to spend, have at it. We just use the regular dish drainer in our sink.

BOTTLE AND FEEDING ORGANIZERS

The proper amount of organization is something we have lacked since the day our firstborns came into this world, and no place more so than our kitchen. We have eagerly bought every organizer on the market, but sadly, have yet to find the perfect solution.

The problem lies in the size. No organizer out there, no matter how monstrous, is large enough to hold all the baby-feeding gadgets and gizmos we use.

The best bottle organizers we've found have drawers for nipples and tops, a pull-out lazy Susan to accommodate even wide-neck bottles, and our favorite feature, a sliding door to hide everything so we don't have to look at it. Unfortunately, some of the longer pieces of bottle systems don't fit in any organizer.

Our favorite baby food organizers hold not just the little round glass jars, but the new rectangular plastic baby food containers as well. None of them, however, hold as many baby food containers as we have on hand. All baby food organizers are made of pretty flimsy plastic and aren't nearly attractive enough for the counter, but they do help save some space in the pantry.

All in all, both baby bottle and baby food organizers fall way short of the modern mom's needs. Why is it so hard to design an attractive, space-saving device that matches our kitchens and yet is big enough to hide everything? Lucky moms in dream kitchens can co-opt their appliance garages for baby gear. We personally bit the bullet and cleaned out a drawer and shelf. We passed on the baby bottle organizer entirely (well, truthfully, we bought, it, tried to use it, hated it, glared at it for a few months, and then gave it away), but because of the simple fact that unlike soup cans, you can't stack slippery glass jars on top of one another, we do have a baby food organizer. It still doesn't hold all of our baby jars, but it comes close.

Features to Consider

☆ Standard or wide neck bottles

☆ Bottle systems

☆ Easy to clean

☆ Latex or silicone nipples

NOTES: *Bottles and Feeding Accessories*

Model Name / Manufacturer	Store/Price	My Impressions	Grade

Nine

Car Seats

We admit, we didn't take this purchase as seriously as we should have with our firstborns. In fact, we didn't take it seriously until about three car seats in.

We knew that all car seats were required to meet federal guidelines for safety, so we assumed they were all just as safe as each other, and chose the one with the pattern that best matched our stroller or car interior. It's crazy to think that we spent weeks researching the safest car on the market, but chose a car seat with hardly a second thought.

Meet one mom who's lost a child or had a child injured when a car seat failed, and you'll never take this purchase lightly again.

We count ourselves extremely lucky that we were never in an accident all those years our kids were in unsafe, incorrectly installed, or just plain wrong car seats. But we've repented, researched our hearts out, and even gotten Child Passenger Safety (CPS) certified. And we're here to tell you, this is a critically important purchase that deserves your very last dime.

The Truth about Car Seat Safety Ratings

You understand a safe car seat is paramount. You know that every single car seat sold in the United States must meet strict federal safety regulations. So where do you find those official safety ratings? The mind-boggling answer is "nowhere."

The government doesn't actually publish crash test results. Perhaps because they don't rate or rank the seats' safety with a scale of stars or letters, but just give a "pass" or "fail" grade. Perhaps because they don't even test for side impact collisions. Perhaps because they don't want you to know that the U.S. safety standards are far lower than those in Europe and Japan.

The National Highway Traffic Safety Administration does publish "ease of use" ratings, but they don't test all seats, they publish the lists a year after the seats are on the store shelves, and they give almost everyone an A.

Independent consumer advocate Consumer Reports does its own independent testing—actually it hires an outside lab to do it—but not on all models and not very often. And it actually had to retract some of its recent car seat safety ratings after the tests were found to be flawed.

And in case you were wondering, or hoping as we were, the manufacturers themselves don't release their own test ratings.

So how is anyone supposed to pick a safe car seat?

What Is a CPS Tech?

CPS tech is shorthand for a Child Passenger Safety technician, someone who has completed a standardized 32- to 40-hour course that includes hands-on training.

CPS techs are the most well-versed people on the planet in terms of how to safely transport children in automobiles. While many police officers and firefighters are required to become CPS certified as part of their jobs, many well-meaning moms also seek the certification so they can help spread the gospel of child car safety.

While the CPS training costs a couple hundred dollars, techs (who are certified for two years) volunteer their services at community car seat checks just for the joy of knowing they are helping children stay alive.

The CPS certification program was started in 1997 by Safe Kids Worldwide, a nonprofit organization dedicated to the prevention of childhood injuries, and the National Highway Traffic Safety Administration (NHTSA).

Manufacturer Reputation

Because companies literally take their reputation to the bank, most are quite interested in maintaining a good one. When shopping for a car seat, look for a reputable manufacturer. Search all top brands on the Internet and you'll quickly learn who is known for quality car seats and whose get recalled en masse every couple of years.

And as Europe has stricter safety standards, do European companies develop and manufacture safer car seats? Our vote is yes.

Latest Safety Features

The automobile and juvenile products industries have every interest in making car seats safer for children, and they develop new and better safety features every year. The best car seat companies are early adopters of these safety features. The not-so-good car seat companies wait several years until the features become standard and are thrust upon them.

For each particular kind of car seat, we'll tell you how to look for the latest and greatest safety innovations.

Price

While books about finding bargains will tell you that all car seats are safe and extra money only buys you luxury conveniences such as fancier fabric, we disagree. Yes, you will get nicer fabric (which can help keep your car seat looking nicer longer, which in the long run, could save you money if you don't have to buy a new seat for the next-in-line, closely aged sibling) and fancy foot muffs. But thanks to higher prices, which help fund product development, the more expensive car seat brands have historically been ahead of the curve in offering extra safety features (such as side impact protection) that go above and beyond government requirements.

That's not to say you can't get a mid-range seat and still do fine by your baby, but the cheapest seats are the cheapest for a reason. They use cheaper materials and have fewer safety features.

The good news is the price range between cheap and top-of-the-line isn't so horrible you'll be emptying your 401(k). Unlike strollers, which can have a

$2,500 differential between the top and the bottom, the cheapest car seats are in the $50 range, while good solid ones are in the $100 range. The top, top, top of the line seats are only around $200 (although the new full-size car seats for grade-schoolers can top out at $400, they are in use for two to three times as long as other seats). Not the price of a trip to McDonalds, but not St. Tropez either.

Can't afford the best car seat? Sell something on Craigslist. Raise the money. We did—literally. I just sold some old Disney memorabilia on eBay to finance my 6-year-old's new $300 car seat. Painful purchase of course, but every time I see her smile, it's more than worth it.

Material

We don't care if every seat gets a passing grade, but there's no way a seat made of the same plastic as a Happy Meal toy is as strong as a seat made from aerospace-grade aluminum. Sure, they all have padding, but is it just a cushy pillow or true energy-absorbing foam?

Think all padding is the same? The parents of children who died from head injuries in seats with insufficient padding will tell you differently.

The best seats have the best material inside and out. Take a peek under the fabric covers. Cheap seats just glue pieces of foam in certain spots. Great seats are completely lined in EPS (expanded polystyrene) foam.

Look for shiny hardware, the more the better. Bases, handles, and key joints reinforced with metal hardware are much safer than plastic, plastic everywhere.

Side Impact Protection

The government doesn't make manufacturers offer side impact protection yet, but because more children are seriously injured in side impact crashes than in frontal or rear impacts, many car seat manufacturers have stepped up and voluntarily developed wonderful side protection properties. While some seats just added extra padding around the head, others offer stronger material along the entire car seat, higher sides, and actual protective wings around the head.

Of course, because there are no government regulations, there are no side impact standards, so anyone can paste a little foam near the top and call it side impact protection (SIP, for short). To differentiate themselves, many upscale manufacturers now claim they have "true" SIP. While it's impossible to judge true effectiveness from the manufacturer's claims alone, you can get a pretty good idea of how safe it is by studying the design and construction, especially compared to other models on the market. We highly recommend a seat stuffed with as much SIP as possible.

Search the Internet

The Web has given "word-of-mouth" new, superhuman meaning. Chances are someone has tried the car seat before you and written to tell about it. Besides checking BabyGizmo.com (we list comprehensive, up-to-date car seat reviews from our senior editors and moms from around the country), do a few Google searches. Type in the name of the specific car seat you're considering, along with the words "bad seat" and "death." You will find out which seats have macabre nicknames and should be recalled, and which are praised for saving small tots.

Vehicular Fit

Safety features matter very little, however, if the car seat doesn't fit into your car properly. With hundreds of cars, trucks, SUVs, and vans on the market, all with different sized, sloped, and structured back seats, car seat manufacturers are hard pressed to make a seat that fits every car.

Choose a seat that fits your car as perfectly as possible. A good fit is a snug fit that doesn't slide, easily accesses all the necessary belts and tethers, and sits at the correct angle. Some seats are too tall, some too wide, and others just too pitched for some cars.

The only way to tell is to fit the seat into your car. Or better yet, buy the seat (saving the receipt of course), take it to a car seat safety check, and have an expert help you install it. For a listing of car seat inspection locations near you, visit www.seatcheck.org.

Child Fit

Just as all seats don't fit all cars, all babies don't fit all seats. Some babies are tall, some are wide, some are long, some have broad shoulders. Choose a seat that fits your baby adequately and comfortably. Check that your baby is within the height and weight limits. And if something looks off, it probably is. A popular convertible seat fit one 12-month-old perfectly, but made her same-aged cousin look as if he was slumping forward. She got the seat; he got a different one better suited to his body.

Obviously, you're going to be doing a bit of guessing when purchasing the first seat before your baby is born, but for every seat after that, take your child with you to the safety check to not only have the experts check the fit, but to have them teach you about proper child belting maneuvers.

Bad Car Seat Accessories

While the world is full of gizmos to make our lives with baby easier, there are actually some dangerous car seat accessory products you should avoid.

- **Belt tighteners:** These devices are supposed to help you tighten seat belts for a safer installation, but they can compromise the actual seat belt and fly off in an accident, causing injury.

- **Anything that could become a projectile:** In an accident, anything not securely tied down can become a flying missile that can seriously injure your baby. This includes car seat mobiles, toy bars, and even special babyview mirrors. We know, we loved 'em too, but we love our cute little babies more.

- **Extra car seat cushions and belt pillows:** Car seat belts can be sharp, and car seats themselves aren't always very padded. But adding extra strap covers and head pillows can compromise the entire seat's safety in a collision. They can compress and give extra room around a baby, which means slacker straps and an unsafe restraint. Car seats that come with these features included are OK (and we actually highly recommend them) because they are tested with the accessories and must pass to be sold with the seat.

Correct Installation

You can have all the degrees you please, but it still doesn't mean you can guess how to correctly install your kid's new car seat. Each car is different and each seat requires a unique installation.

Think you've got it down? Think again! The National Highway Traffic Safety Administration (NHTSA) estimates that 8 out of 10 children riding in car seats are incorrectly buckled in.

Get out your vehicle's user manual. Get out the car seat installation instructions. And actually read them. A correctly installed seat should have less than one inch of movement when pushed from side to side or front to back.

We highly recommend stopping by a child passenger safety seat inspection location to check your seat.

Car seats are safest installed in the middle or back row of an automobile. You should avoid installing one in the front seat at all costs. We know it's a pain when you have a two-door, or worse, two-seater car, but seriously consider getting a new car then. Believe me, it's not a recommendation I make lightly. I know how tough (and expensive) this can be. I personally got rid of

What Is LATCH?

LATCH stands for Lower Anchors and Tethers for Children and refers to squared-off metal rings soldered into automobiles at the factory on the seat base, usually hidden a bit under the seat cushions.

Because the rings are standard and since 2001 required in all automobiles sold in the United States, they are supposed to make installing a car seat easier. LATCH isn't intended as a stronger tether for a car seat than seat belts, just a more convenient, more standard, and easier-to-use system. In most cases, you are not supposed to use both LATCH and your car's seat belts to fasten a seat; check with both your car seat and car manufacturer.

Check your vehicle owner's manual for information about how many LATCH anchors your car has, where they are located, and how much weight they can bear.

the very first car I ever owned, my beloved British racing green Mazda Miata convertible, when I became pregnant with my first child. I loved that car! But I love my daughter more.

If you must use a car seat in the front seat, turn off any air bags and push the front passenger seat as far back from the dashboard as you can.

In the middle and rear seat rows, the seat in the very middle is the very safest because it offers the most distance between the edges of a crashed-in car and your young rider. The youngest passenger should ride in the middle-most seat, provided it has the correct seat belt or LATCH configuration. (For an explanation of LATCH, see page 97.)

More Safety References

To ensure that you're picking the very best seat and installing it correctly, check out these fabulous resources:

☆ American Academy of Pediatrics Car Seat Safety Guide: www.aap.org/family/carseatguide.htm

☆ Safe Kids Child Passenger Safety: www.usa.safekids.org/skbu/cps/index.html

☆ National Highway Traffic Safety Administration "Ease of Use" Ratings: www.nhtsa.dot.gov/CPS/CSSRating/Index.cfm

Infant Car Seat Carriers

Unless you plan on using a convertible car seat from birth—which can't be easily removed from the car and toted into the grocery store—the infant car seat carrier is your baby's first (of many) car seats. Infant car seat carriers have a handle that allows you to carry baby like a (very heavy) purse, transporting baby from house to car to mall and back again with (relative) ease.

Infant car seat carriers are made of hard, molded plastic and feature two parts: the actual seat and the base. Most infant car seats can be used alone in a car or with their base, although a few require the use of their base at all times. Used alone, you simply strap the car seat into your car using the car's seat belts. The downside is you must safely restrap the seat each time you remove it. (Incorrect installation is the cause of most infant car accident injuries.) Or you can strap the car seat base into your car (using seat belts or LATCH), leave it attached, and snap your car seat on and off its base every time you leave the car.

> ## Infant Car Seat Carrier
>
> **Age Range**
> *Birth to 8 months*
>
> **Total Usage**
> *8 months*
>
> **Recommendation**
> *Nice to have (you must have a car seat, but you can use a convertible seat from birth)*
>
> **When to Buy**
> *Before baby is born.*

While using the car seat base is the most foolproof and convenient method, some models snapped off their bases during accidents in crash tests when the baby rider was near the weight limit. While those seats were recalled, we highly recommend you pay close attention to the weight and height limits on infant car seats, as they differ among manufacturers.

So, aside from safety, installation ease, and vehicular fit, what features should you look for?

Side Impact Protection

The NHTSA reports that 42 percent of fatalities for children ages 0 to 8 years involved in automobile accidents occur in side-impact collisions. In our book, this makes side impact protection a critical feature on car seats.

The more side impact protection, the better, especially for newborns, especially around their heads. This comes in various forms on infant car seats, including EPS foam, inflatable wings, and deeply recessed seats. Whichever version you choose, make sure baby still has adequate breathing room.

Anti-rebound Bar

In a collision, an infant car seat is very likely to flip up toward the seat back. An anti-rebound bar reduces the rebounding of the seat. Another good idea. Another feature hard to find. Another feature we look for.

Weight and Height Limits

Most infant car seats have a weight limit of 20 to 22 pounds and height limit of 26 to 29 inches. Some new seats have raised the limits to 30 pounds and 32 inches, but the seats got much larger and heavier. In our opinion, the extra weight and height limits are not worth a seat that is three or four pounds heavier. We prefer carrying a lighter seat and moving our big babies into rear-facing convertible seats earlier if need be, rather than lugging around an extra heavy seat the first couple of months. By 6 to 8 months, no matter what their weight, most babies will struggle to escape their infant car seat carriers and prefer to sit upright in strollers and shopping carts anyway.

Weight of Seat

The weight of the infant car seat carrier is infinitely important to the mom who must lug it around 80 times a day, especially when she's recovering from

Shopping Cart Dangers

Perching your infant car seat carrier over a shopping cart seat is a really bad idea. Really, really bad. We'd like to say we've never done it, but then we'd be big liars. We had no idea how dangerous this was, or we'd never have done it. Honest.

In fact, because thousands of babies are treated every year in hospitals after they fall from this precarious perch, the American Academy of Pediatrics now officially recommends against it.

Suggested alternatives include front carriers, strollers, and just staying home and feeding your Internet shopping addiction.

labor. Do you complain about how heavy your 7-pound laptop is? Try carrying a 10-pound infant seat with a 15-pound infant!

Infant car seats range from 7 to a whopping 12 pounds. If you've found two seats you love and you need a tiebreaker, go with the lighter seat.

Carrying Comfort

Because carrying infant car seats causes more repetitive strain injuries to new moms than any other activity, choose a model that's easy and comfortable for you to carry. Experts recommend you carry the seats in front of you using both hands, rather than over your forearm like a purse, but be warned, the awkward positioning takes some getting used to.

The Handle

For supreme carrying comfort, look for an ergonomic handle with some nice padding. Pure plastic with scratchy seams is mean, mean, mean.

Handles that break and collapse unexpectedly have been the reason for more than one recall, so look for a solid handle. The more metal, the better, especially where the handle meets the seat. Aluminum handles offer both superior strength and a lighter load.

Sophisticated Reinforcements

Because infant car seat carriers are taken in and out of cars, snapped into and out of strollers, and toted around, a big window for user error exists; your baby is at risk if things are not solidly connected each and every time.

The best infant car seats have foolproof connections that leave little doubt in your mind whether they are securely attached. Key parts reinforced with metal are much better than all-plastic pieces. Look for metal in the seat-to-base attachments and metal handle hub hardware.

Five-Point Harness

Check the harness type: three-point harnesses are available, but five-point harnesses are considered much safer because they hold a baby in place more securely and cut down on the ability to wiggle free.

Solid Straps

Some straps are thicker, wider, and more twist-resistant than others. You want those straps. You can tell right away in the store with a little stroking and tugging which straps are going to stay in place and which will slip off baby's shoulders more easily.

Because thick straps can literally cut into a baby's neck, choose ones with protective covers attached.

Chest Clip

Look for a chest clip that actually snaps together rather than just loops around the straps like a giant paper clip, as babies have been known to free their arms from the latter. Chest clips should always be worn at armpit level, not near the baby's stomach, to properly position the straps over the baby's shoulders.

Front Harness Adjustment

The easier it is to loosen or tighten the harnesses, the more likely you will be to fasten your babies up snugly every time you put them in their seat, no matter what they are wearing. The best fit is a tight fit. The best seats have an easy-to-operate front harness adjustment.

Because bulky clothes can make safety harnesses less effective, experts are now recommending you don't load up your winter coat–wearing baby into a car seat. Layer your child with multiple, thin outfits for warmth, strap him in, and then cover him with a blanket or all-weather boot (a fancy, attached blanket that comes with some seats).

Height-Adjustment Dial

A height-adjustment dial is a knob on the base that allows you to raise or lower the base at one end to accommodate the slope of your specific vehicle's seat, forever banishing the rolled-up towel we've been sticking under our car seat base to achieve a perfect fit.

Level Indicator

Many infant car seats come with level indicators—usually in the form of a little ball that rolls in a little tunnel—to let you know when the car seat is set at the correct angle for safe newborn sitting. Sadly, they are frequently wrong (mounted in the factory at the wrong angle, for example). Don't depend solely on them. To make sure your seat is installed correctly so that your child will be sitting at a 45-angle, you can use the fancy tool they use at CPS certification classes: a single piece of letter-sized paper. Fold a bottom corner up so that it meets the opposite edge, forming a perfect right triangle. Now cut off the extra rectangle at the top and discard it (so you're left with a perfect square of paper, folded in half into a right triangle). Now hold the longest side of the triangle (the hypotenuse) against the part of the car seat where your baby would rest her back. Right in the cushiony bit where she sits, with one of the points where her bottom would be. The top side of the triangle should be straight across, running parallel to the floor at 180 degrees. If that top edge is tilted, your seat is at the wrong angle. Fix it until you get a straight top edge.

Newborn Headrests and Cushions

Because most newborns are tiny blobs that look weird buckled into a car seat, special headrests and even full-body positioning cushions can be great, but are only recommended if they come with the seat. These are generally only good for kids under 10 pounds, so if you have small babies, definitely look for them. If you, like us, give birth to linebackers, you won't need them at all.

Canopies

Almost every infant car seat comes with a sun canopy, but some are better than others. Better means bigger and with a peekaboo window. Sun canopies are essential for shielding a baby's eyes from the glaring sun, both in and out of the car.

Fabric

Of course, pattern is important to us. Sadly, most car seats are still pretty awful looking. We personally prefer the solid colors over the cartoon covered things, but still we end up with a car seat that doesn't match our stroller.

Because the car seat is much more important to our baby's safety than having everything match, in this instance we turn a blind eye to the ugly and get the best seat regardless of its garishness.

Look for a fabric that isn't scratchy, is easily removed for the wash, and is breathable. Some car seats are made with fabric that turns innocent little babies into sweathogs. A quick check on BabyGizmo.com will tell you which ones.

Color

While light-colored fabrics do show stains more easily, dark-colored fabrics tend to get hot in the sun. Especially in the sun in the summer in the car. We try to choose middle-of-the-road grays and cooler blues and greens (although if you have a girl, who can resist pink?).

Car Seat Covers

We're not the only ones who think most car seat fabric covers are ugly. Plenty of other parents out there do too, and many of them offer their own, homemade car seat covers for sale online. While we're more than happy to transform an ugly seat into a hip, fashion-forward pleasure, we can't recommend a car seat cover that didn't come directly from the manufacturer of the seat itself. As we learned in CPS training, if it came in the box, it's been tested. If it's available after-market by a separate company, it's not a safe purchase.

The good news is there are a couple of car seat manufacturers that do offer additional, extra purchase car seat cover choices, including collegiate logos and animal prints, but make sure to only buy those offered by the seat manufacturers themselves. Anything, no matter how nice it seems, marked "custom made" is not from a car seat manufacturer.

All-Weather Covers

If you live anywhere near Jack Frost, seriously consider an all-weather boot for your infant car seat. The attached blanket keeps your baby snug and warm.

Some car seats come with them, but you can buy them separately: several really amazing ones are available, ranging from thin windshields to thick and fleecy snow barriers. The ones from the manufacturer are the safest bet, but if you need to buy one separately, look for one that only covers the top of the car seat, the part that baby doesn't sit on. Anything you add between the seat, your baby, and the car seat's safety harness could possibly compromise the seat's safety.

Extra Bases

Almost every manufacturer offers extra bases, which can be great if you plan on using more than one car and you don't want to constantly transfer the belted-in base.

Price

Infant car seat carriers range from $39 to just over $200. The best ones start in the $70 range.

A Special Safety Note

The advent of travel stroller systems and even swing bases that use an infant car seat inside have led parents to believe that a baby can safely hang out all day in an infant car seat, anywhere, anytime. In fact, infant car seat carriers cause over 13,000 injuries and 5 deaths every year—*outside the car.*

The dangers of infant cars seats when used outside the car include

- ☆ Strangulation and entanglement in restraining straps

- ☆ Suffocation and breathing difficulties due to padded fabric and permanent incline of seat back

- ☆ Injuries caused by seats toppling over when the curved bottom is placed on a soft surface or when baby kicks

Repeated use outside the car also compromises safe installation and adds excessive wear and tear to the car seat.

Recent studies warn that small infants in car seat carriers are not positioned for optimum breathing, due mostly to the incline of the seat, especially when it is out of its in-car base. Experts are now recommending that parents leave car seats in the car, as they were designed as car seats and should not be compromised by being used any other way; such uses only compromise the safety of their tiny passengers.

While we used our infant car seat carriers as baby purses pretty much full-time with our firstborns, even letting them nap unattended in the seat whenever we could, no one ever told us any better. In fact, we were (wrongly) convinced that the infant car seat carrier was one of the safest places for baby, both in and out of the car.

One of our good friends thought so too, and she happily dropped her baby off at the sitter's strapped into his infant car seat carrier. When his rocking motion overturned his seat, he suffocated in his carrier because he was too strapped down to free himself.

We're all about convenience, but we're much more about seeing our baby graduate from college or get married someday. Yes, you might have to actually wake sleeping babies when you transfer them from car seat into a stroller or pram or infant carrier, but the world won't stop turning. And you'll have a better chance of hearing their sweet little cries again tomorrow.

Features to Consider

- ☆ Safety reputation
- ☆ Vehicular fit
- ☆ Side impact protection
- ☆ Top tether
- ☆ Anti-rebound bar
- ☆ Weight of seat
- ☆ Size of seat
- ☆ Weight and height limit
- ☆ Ease of installation
- ☆ Handle
- ☆ Harness type
- ☆ Seat straps
- ☆ Chest clip
- ☆ Height adjustment and level indicator
- ☆ Carrying comfort
- ☆ Canopy
- ☆ Fabric

NOTES: *Infant Car Seat Carriers*

Model Name / Manufacturer	Store/Price	My Impressions	Grade

CONVERTIBLE CAR SEATS

Convertible car seats are so christened because they convert from an infant seat to a toddler seat. Many parents prefer an infant car seat carrier for newborns and then switch to a convertible seat once baby has outgrown the carrier seat, but just as many opt for the convertible seat right out of the gate.

Convertible car seats are strapped into your car via either your vehicle's seat belts or the LATCH system. Convertible car seats have a deep recline for smaller babies that adjusts to a straighter back for older children.

Most convertible car seats are suitable for infants from birth. And the newest seats have raised weight and height limits considerably, so you can use the seat in a safer position for longer than ever, making the investment of a good seat wiser than ever.

Rear Facing

The old rule of thumb was to keep babies rear facing until they reach 20 pounds or 1 year old, but new research suggests that keeping a child reversed as long as possible can greatly decrease the chance of injury in an accident. Babies have immature, still developing bones and connective tissue; the longer you give their neck muscles to strengthen, the better!

Many parents mistakenly turn their babies forward facing too early because their baby's legs start to get scrunched up against the back of the seat, but there are no reports that a baby with bent knees is any less safe than a baby with straight legs. In fact, we found so much more evidence of the increased safety of the rear-facing position that we tend to agree with the fellow CPS tech that told us "better a broken leg than a broken neck!"

The American Academy of Pediatrics cites the 20 pounds/1 year mark as a minimum, but states "it is best for baby to ride rear-facing until he reaches the highest weight or height limit allowed by the car safety seat."

The weight and height limits for convertible seats differ dramatically, so check with the manufacturer directly or the owner's manual for the last word on a particular model. But consider investing in a seat with higher rear-facing weight limits so that your child can ride safer longer.

Weight Limit

Convertible car seats have two different weight limits: rear facing and forward facing. The rear-facing limit is lower because of the design of the seat,

---

Convertible Car Seat

Age Range
Birth to 4-plus years

Total Usage
4-plus years

Recommendation
Must have

When to Buy
Before your baby outgrows his infant car seat, or before birth, if you plan on using it from birth.

but while they used to all top out at 30 pounds, many can now accommodate children all the way to 40 pounds (a typical 4-year-old!). Great for keeping your child rear facing as long as possible.

Forward-facing weight limits used to be around 40 pounds, but those have increased on many models dramatically as well, to up to 65 pounds. Every new model has new weight limits, so they are changing all the time. Check the particular seat you're interested in carefully. You can also find regularly updated, easy-to-use comparison charts at BabyGizmo.com that show both the rear-facing and forward-facing weight limit for all current models.

Height Limit and Height of Seat

Most convertible seats have a height limit of 40 inches, although some go all the way to 52 inches. None of this matters if your child is particularly tall and thin (something we simply cannot relate to personally) and outgrows the tallest shoulder strap position or tops out over the top of the seat, regardless of how tall she actually is standing on the ground.

When rear facing, there should be an inch of room between the top of the seat and the top of the child's head. Once a child passes that, you need to reverse the seat to face forward for added protection. Once forward facing, the top of the child's ear should be below the top of the shell. Once a child has passed that, he's outgrown the seat entirely.

The height of the car seat back varies considerably among models. Some are shorter and rounder, which is fine for a newborn, but your child will outgrow these seats height-wise quicker than you think.

The top position of the shoulder straps varies among different seats as well. And because a front-facing child's shoulders should always be below the highest strap slots to minimize slack in the harness, some children will outgrow a convertible seat this way as well.

Vehicular Fit

Sadly, some parents are denied the seat of their dreams because it doesn't fit into their car. The higher weight and height limits on some convertible seats makes them so large you can't actually fit them in your car when rear facing. (You can only push your own seat forward so far before you're driving with your nose, or the front passenger seat forward so far before the front rider is bent in half, which isn't safe for anyone.) Some convertible seats are also extra wide, which is good for firstborns and only children, but not so good if you have to fit other siblings and their car seats side by side.

Verify that the seat you want fits the car you drive.

Side Impact Protection

According to the NHSTA, 42 percent of children ages 0 to 8 who die in automobile accidents were involved in side impact collisions, so we look long and hard for car seats with side impact protection. And because convertible seats hold kids up to preschool age—kids who usually get moved to the side of the car while baby brother takes the coveted middle seat—we're all in favor of as much side impact protection as anyone will offer us.

Other good safety features: EPS, energy-absorbing foam, and any extra protection around the head.

Top Tether for Forward-Facing Use

Most newer convertible car seats have a top tether—an extra strap on the top of the seat that allows you to secure the seat to the top tether anchors that are standard inclusions in all automobiles manufactured since 2001. These top tethers are for use when a convertible car seat is forward facing; they help keep the seat, especially the top of the seat, more securely fastened into the car. Top tethers may be used with either regular seat belt installation or LATCH. Check your car seat manual for top tether use instructions and your automobile owner's manual for tether anchor locations (as they are sometimes hard to find or hidden under plastic caps).

A top tether is an extremely important safety feature, and we highly recommend purchasing a seat that has one.

Top Tether for Rear-Facing Use

When you install a rear-facing convertible car seat into a vehicle, you fasten the seat at the base, but not at the top. And since convertible seats are taller than infant seats, almost like tall, backward-facing chairs, the top of the seat is free to flop backward toward the back seat. This always bothered us.

Why not use a top tether to strap the top of the seat to a piece of the automobile, say under the front driver's seat?

Well, it turns out they do that frequently in Sweden and Australia, and their kids are much, much safer for it. Studies in Sweden show very low vehicle accident fatality rates among children, mostly due to the fact that they keep their small riders backward facing until preschool age, and they tether the top of rear-facing seats.

That said, you can *only* use the top tether on a convertible car seat when it is rear-facing if the car seat manufacturer specifically states this use is OK. Otherwise, believe it or not, the top restraint might compromise the entire seat. (We say, you probably don't want to use that seat at all then, if it's not strong enough for the safest tethering around.)

And while only a few car seat manufacturers in the United States offer rear-facing top tethers, we bought a seat that does include this feature, and we're happier for it.

Five-Point Harness

While three-point harnesses are available, as well as the three-point harness with an overhead shield that basically looks like a padded tray in front of the child, five-point harnesses are considered the safest bet.

Harness Strap Slot Safety Warning

Some convertible car seats require you to use the topmost shoulder strap slot when the seat is used forward facing because that is the only slot specially reinforced to withstand a collision in that position. The other slots, regardless of the height of your child, should not be used because they are not reinforced and the harness can rip free.

This is a nonissue for several car seat models because they are designed with reinforcements at every slot and can safely hold the harness at any height. Those are the car seat models we buy.

Chest Clips

The best chest clips are two separate pieces that snap into each other, rather than just hooking around the straps. Be on the lookout for chest clips that are too easily undone by naughty little kids. We had a child that loved to undo himself and climb entirely out of his car seat, inevitably while we were on the highway, going 70 miles per hour, with nary an exit in sight. Try clipping a crazy child back into her seat with one hand while you're driving, and you'll see why we stress the importance of hard-to-open chest clips.

Chest clips should always be fastened at a child's chest, not their stomach. Every time. No matter how much they whine.

Wide, Twist-Resistant Straps

Especially on convertible car seats that will hold older kids, many of whom like to buckle themselves, twist-free straps are key. A twisted strap doesn't deliver the same strength and safety as an untwisted strap and can actually cause more injury. But because the straps are longer, they tend to twist more easily on convertible seats.

We purchased an otherwise great convertible car seat that we were warned had a strap-twisting problem that we thought we could overcome. Sadly, we could not and our garbage man hauled away that otherwise great seat.

Front-Adjustable Straps

As your child grows taller, you'll be moving the straps up to accommodate his growth. Some seats force you to adjust the straps from the back, meaning you have to unhook your perfectly installed, snug car seat and start all over with a new installation. Seats that allow you to adjust the belts from the front are much better.

Crotch Strap Adjustments

Most convertible car seats offer a couple of different adjustments for the strap that goes between your child's legs, which is important for a comfortable fit, especially for little boys. It depends on your child of course, but some seats are tighter and less forgiving than others about where that crotch strap is placed. Look for a seat with multiple slots.

Fabric

Because you'll use this seat the longest, picking a good, quality fabric is paramount. We've failed miserably at this task. Somehow our kids manage to rub, pick, and then rip apart the fabric at their fingertips, at least on the cheaper seats we used to buy. We've tried denim, velvet, and just plain polyester. They all tore, wore down, and faded in the sun. And if that didn't ruin them, juice boxes did.

We recommend getting a nice, sturdy, washable fabric so you aren't embarrassed to have the seat in your car for a few years, but don't hold any high hopes that you'll be passing this seat down to a sibling. Its first owner will most likely break it in and then break it down.

As with infant seats, although now your child is more likely to curse you out for it, dark-colored seats do get hot in the summer sun, so beware the black and navy blue seats.

Comfort

Some convertible car seats are more comfortable than others due to softer fabric, more padding, and built-in pillows. Because your child will be strapped into it like a straitjacket for years and years, be a nice mom and get them a nice seat.

Extras

Convertible car seats have no canopies (even though the sun still beats through the window into their little eyes), but you can get cup holders. Cup holders are fun, providing the child strapped into the seat can actually reach them. It would seem like an obvious thing, and maybe our children have super short arms, but we've had more than one seat with an impossible-to-access cup holder.

Price

Convertible car seats range in price from $50 to $300. We're not going to lie: the best seats are over $200. And well worth it.

Features to Consider

☆ Safety reputation

☆ Vehicular fit

☆ Side impact protection

☆ Top tether

☆ Size of seat

☆ Weight and height limits

☆ Harness type

☆ Seat straps

☆ Crotch strap adjustment

☆ Chest clip

☆ Fabric

NOTES: *Convertible Car Seats*

Model Name / Manufacturer	Store/Price	My Impressions	Grade

FULL-SIZE CAR SEATS

In May 2005, a mom in Texas named Christine Miller lost her precious 3-year-old son, Kyle, in a car accident. Because he had outgrown a convertible seat, he, like millions of other preschoolers, was riding in a booster seat strapped in with a regular car seat belt that failed him. As if her tragedy weren't bad enough, Christine learned afterward that a better car seat she'd not even known existed might have saved his life.

Determined to spare as many other children as she could, Christine created the most beautiful, shocking, informative little tribute video you've ever seen, and put in on YouTube. (We sobbed at our computers for 20 minutes straight when we first saw it.) In just a few weeks, her e-mail traveled around the world to more than two million moms!

Other moms who suffered similar losses have joined the awareness campaign to let parents know that there is a crucial car seat stage between the convertible and booster seat: a full-size car seat with a five-point harness. Little Isabelle Broadhead and Toni Perry, ages 3 and 4, both died after slow speed car accidents due to the injuries they suffered from their belt positioning boosters; one had her liver cut in half by the seat belt, the other had a major heart artery severed. Their older siblings, strapped in the same way, walked away from the

Full-Size Car Seat

Also Known As
Youth car seat, toddler car seat

Age Range
1 to 8-plus years

Total Usage
7-plus years

Recommendation
Must have

When to Buy
Before your child outgrows his convertible seat.

crashes unharmed. Isabelle's and Toni's parents, like most, were unaware that a vehicle's seat belt can be a deadly restraint for small bodies.

Booster seats simply elevate a child's rear, allowing for apparently better placement of a regular car seat belt across a small body. But for tiny riders—ages 2 to 6—the use of the regular car seat belt is not ideal for many reasons. To provide restraint, regular car seat belts must catch in a crash—and with lighter weight riders or slower speed impacts, they often do not. To provide optimal protection, regular car seat belts must also be placed in exactly the right position, flat across the chest, not twisted or looped under the arm. Hoping a wriggly 4-year-old keeps her seat belt in exactly the right position 100 percent of the time is not our idea of the safest ride. (Especially for our naughty kids who, as we explained in the last section, know how to push our buttons by escaping from their car seats entirely. Surely we're not the only parents with naughty kids. Right? Anyone?) Perhaps most importantly, regular car seat belts can cause irreparable internal damage to little bodies.

Many experts believe a five-point harness is the key to a safe ride for minor passengers as it tightly restrains the body at both shoulders at any speed, cannot be repositioned by the child, and can cause less stress on small bodies. Professor Lynne Bilston of the Prince of Wales Medical Research Institute, an international car seat collision expert, explains this is because a five-point harness evenly distributes crash forces across the body in a way that is better for younger skeletons.

Don't get us wrong—seat belts are great and should be used by everyone for every car trip. But they were designed for adults. Dr. Arthur Croft, director of the Spine Research Institute in San Diego, explains that the lap portion of the seat belt is designed to distribute force across the bony pelvis of an adult; in children, the lap belt rides up over the pelvic brim and delivers all the force to the soft abdomen. On adults, the shoulder sash crosses over the middle of the collarbone; in children, it crosses dangerously across the neck.

Until very recently, children who outgrew their convertible car seat by weight, height, or comfort were forced to graduate to a belt-positioning booster because there were no seats with five-point harnesses with a weight limit over

40 pounds. Moms worried that their little preschoolers suddenly seemed too free and floppy in a regular car seat belt, and rightly so. We hated the day our kids moved into a big kid booster, but we had no other option.

Thankfully, we now can get a full-size car seat with a five-point harness that can hold kids all the way to 80 pounds!

The day we learned about this new car seat species, we took our 6-year-old out of her much-loved, but barely there, big girl booster and strapped her back into a five-point harness. She was mad to be forced back into a "baby chair," but we're happy to be safety trendsetters. We consider Kyle, Isabelle, and Toni guardian angels for getting the message out there, and we want to help them. Allow us to introduce you to the wonders of the full-size car seat.

Size

It's meant for big kids to be sure, and the full-size car seat is the biggest car seat you've ever seen. Like La-Z-Boy big. It's so big, once installed in our SUV, we can no longer fold the seat next to it down and our kids have to climb through the trunk. No matter. That giant size is giant goodness in our opinion.

If a full-size car seat doesn't fit in your car, look for a booster car seat with a five-point harness that has the highest weight limit you can find, so you can safely secure your child the longest.

LATCH Benefits

Full-size car seats are forward facing only and can be attached to your car via seat belts or LATCH. Even though some booster seats do have five-point harnesses, we don't believe they are quite as good as a full-size seat because most boosters don't offer LATCH.

We're big fans of LATCH for its ease of use and the fact that it's much harder to accidentally come unclipped, whether by accident or older sibling. Most vehicles' LATCH anchors have a 48-pound weight limit, however. Check with your auto manufacturer to be sure, but if your child is over 48 pounds, it is recommended you use the seat belt attachment rather than LATCH. But for the years before the 48-pound limit, you've got the LATCH option should you want it.

Weight and Height Limits

The weight and height limits for full-size seats differ wildly, so check with the manufacturer directly or the owner's manual for the last word on particular models.

Most full-size seats worth their salt have a weight limit of 65 pounds and a height limit of 52 to 59 inches.

While some advertise weight limits up to 80 pounds, most kids will grow past the height limit long before that. A 65-pound seat weight limit will see most children through age 6 and beyond quite easily. For easier reference (because frankly, once we stopped putting stickers in their baby books, we had no idea how much an average kid was supposed to weigh either), here are average child heights and weights for ages 2, 4, 6, and 8 years:

Age	Average Weight	Average Height
2 years	30 pounds	36 inches
4 years	42 pounds	40 inches
6 years	48 pounds	46 inches
8 years	60 pounds	51 inches

As you can see, kids' growth slows down, so you can keep them in a good full-size car seat almost until junior high! (We're kidding.) Older kids might balk that it's not cool, but bicycle helmets weren't either until everyone started wearing them. If everyone starts using full-size, five-point harness seats now, by the time our babies are 6, it won't even be an issue (we found calling the full-size seat an "astronaut chair" or a "seat just like the NASCAR guys use" helped our little doubters tremendously).

Five-Point Harness Weight Limits

Many booster seats and larger car seats come with five-point harness options and advertise high weight limits, but they are in fact touting the weight limit of the seat when used with a regular seat belt, not the lower-weight harness limit. Check the weight limit for use of the five-point harness. You want your child to be safely strapped into a five-point harness as long as possible. Don't let clever packaging tricks fool you into picking the wrong seat. (To make your life easier, BabyGizmo.com has a handy comparison chart that shows all height, weight, and five-point harness weight limits for all types of car seats.)

Side Impact Protection

While some boosters also offer side impact protection, the sheer size of a full-size car seat means you're getting more protection on all sides. Look for a full-size seat with side impact protection, head protection, and EPS foam.

Top Tether

Another great aspect of the full-size car seat is the addition of the top tether. Booster seats are free floating in a car, which means they can travel with a child in an accident, adding to their velocity, and become dangerous projectiles on their own. Good full-size car seats have a top tether that clips them more securely to the vehicle's seat, adding to their safety.

Harness Adjustment

You will be moving the straps up as your child grows taller. Some seats make this easy. Some require you to have an engineering degree. At least make sure you can tighten and release the straps from the front rather easily.

Twist-Resistant Straps

The less the straps tend to twist and tangle, the better.

Chest Clip

As on all seats, a two-piece set that snaps together is safer than a simple loop.

Fabric

Because full-size seats are so big and securely installed, you'll most likely be spot cleaning it (or, if you're like us, never cleaning it and should someone happen to see it, claiming your child just messed it up that very afternoon). Machine washable fabric is nice, but at this size, you'll never remove it.

As always, a dark color might look cool, especially in your fancy car, but will get scalding hot in the summer sun.

Price

Full-size car seats range from $200 to a whopping $450. But if you average it out by years of usefulness, it's really only about $75 a year, or $6 a month. A small price to pay for our children's safety. Skip a couple of lattes or one movie a month, and you've paid for your seat, no problem!

Features to Consider

☆ Safety reputation

☆ Vehicular fit

☆ Side impact protection

☆ Top tether

☆ Size of seat

☆ Weight and height limit

☆ Five-point harness weight limit

☆ Chest clip

☆ Fabric

NOTES: *Full-Size Car Seats*

Model Name / Manufacturer	Store/Price	My Impressions	Grade

BOOSTER CAR SEATS

If your child has outgrown a convertible car seat and you're considering moving to a booster, stop, go back, read the previous section, and consider if what you really need is a full-size car seat.

However, while we believe children should be in five-point harnesses as long as possible and that boosters are generally introduced too early, they are still very necessary for older children.

Booster Car Seat

Age Range
6 to 10 years

Total Usage
4 years

Recommendation
Must have

When to Buy
After your child outgrows his five-point harnessed full-size seat.

The Importance of a Booster

The last car seat you'll ever need—and thankfully the cheapest!—booster car seats give big kids (generally ages 7 to 9) a boost in the car, raising their bums so the vehicle's seat belts cross their chest at the correct place.

Studies show, however, that 33 percent of parents don't use boosters and another 33 percent use them incorrectly. Having a mouthy 8-year-old in the house, we can probably guess why. They are inconvenient for kids on the go, for after-school activities, and they sure muck up carpool. Our kids beg us to ditch them, and after all, we barely wore seat belts when we were that age. All true. Also true: a lot fewer of us survived car accidents back then; the actual number of crashes is on the rise because more cars are on the road; kids spend more time than ever in the car; car accidents are the number one cause of death for kids ages 3 to 18; and (here's the good news) the odds of serious injury are 59 percent lower for children in belt-positioning boosters than those who use a seat belt alone.

Scary Math

As if math weren't scary enough, consider this: Newton's Law of Motion can turn an 8-year-old child into a small elephant. When? When the child is not wearing a seat belt. Since Force = Mass × Acceleration, an unrestrained 8-year-old child (weighing an average of 60 pounds) in a car accident at just 35 miles per hour will fly forward with a force of 2,100 pounds, or about the weight of a small elephant.

Because more than 60 percent of accidents happen on streets where the speed limit is under 40 miles per hour, it's important to buckle up everybody, every time, even on quick trips to the grocery store.

Who Needs a Booster?

We personally wouldn't introduce a car's regular seat belt system to a child under the age of 6, but after that, children do need a boost to correctly position those belts. In fact, in 38 states, a booster is required by law. Each state has different requirements (some require booster use until age 9!); you can find the specific laws for your state at www.boosterseat.gov.

The NHTSA recommends that children use boosters until they are at least 8 years old, 80 pounds, and 4 feet 9 inches (57 inches) tall. Experts also say that height and age shouldn't be the only indicators. If children cannot sit all the way back in a seat and bend their knees over the edge, they should sit in a booster. Also, if a vehicle seat belt rides up over a child's abdomen or cuts into the neck, that child needs to stay in a booster.

There are two types of booster seats: those with backs and those without.

Backless Booster Seats

Backless booster seats look much like a booster chair you'd use in a restaurant. Free floating, they are small padded seats that kids sit upon while using the regular seat belts.

While backless boosters are the cheapest, smallest, and easiest to use, they are not the safest choice. They raise the child up, but don't lower the seat belt down for better chest placement. More importantly, they don't provide good head or body protection in a collision.

A study published in 2001 by the Department of Pediatrics at the Children's Hospital of Philadelphia concluded that while high-back boosters reduced the risk of injury for 4- to 8-year-olds by 70 percent, backless boosters did not lower injury risk at all.

Many experts are calling for parents to ditch "useless, backless boosters" and use only high-backed models.

HIGH-BACK BOOSTER SEATS

High-back booster seats are high-back chairs that raise a child up but also sport a guide through which you thread the vehicle's seat belt to lower it for your little guy. They provide head support and protection, as well as side impact protection and EPS energy-absorbing foam in some cases.

Five-Point Harnesses

Some boosters do offer a five-point harness for younger riders, but check the weight limit for their use—sometimes it's so low, your child has already graduated out of it before you've even bought the seat. You can use a five-point harness on most boosters with or without LATCH. And when your child has outgrown the five-point harness, it can be removed completely from the car seat, allowing your child to use solely the automobile seat belts.

Lack of LATCH

We were surprised too, but booster seats are the first car seat you'll buy without LATCH. Because they are really just boosts that you use with your car's own safety belts, most booster seats are free-floating in your car. This can make transporting older kids easier because they can move their own seat around. However, always remove the booster seat entirely from your car when not in use (or put it in your trunk), as it can become a dangerous projectile to other car occupants in a collision.

Side Impact Protection

You know by now, we're big fans. The more EPS foam in the more places, the better. If they could build bodysuits out of bicycle helmet foam, we'd make our kids wear them.

Comfortable Fit

Choose a booster that positions your vehicle's seat belt correctly and comfortably on your child's body. Every child is different and not every booster will correctly accommodate your child. The shoulder sash of the seat belt should cross the middle of a child's shoulder, and not ride up on the neck. The lap sash should sit on the child's thighs or hips, not cross over the belly.

Easy to Use

Because you're going to be asking your pre-tween to buckle into a booster, choose a seat that is easy for your child to use. Neither of you will appreciate Mom's having to buckle the biggest kid in every time (although you should still watch for correct placement and nontwisted straps).

Armrests

Most boosters do include armrests, which are much appreciated by their riders. Look for armrests that fold up out of the way when you want them to, as they can get in the way when a child tries to buckle herself in.

Foldable Boosters

Because you should take your child's car seat with you when you travel, some manufacturers are making it easier by making seats that actually fold.

Fabric

Letting your children choose the color of their seat can help make them an active advocate of using a booster. You can find just about every pattern, from pink flowers to green camouflage.

Cup Holders

Most booster seats have retractable cup holders, but by now, your kid can probably reach the ones in the side door. They can be nice, however, if you plan on installing the booster in the middle seat. Sadly, the cup holders still don't fit juice boxes very well.

Extra Features

Manufacturers know you're taking your kid with you to the store for this purchase, and they're hoping to woo your child with a range of kid-friendly accessories. Our kids went crazy for little reading lights. We expect iPod speakers any day now.

Price

Backless boosters cost from $13 to $40. High-back boosters are priced from $49 to $350, with most in the $100 range.

Features to Consider

☆ Safety reputation

☆ Side impact protection

☆ Backless or high back

☆ Comfort

☆ Ease of use

☆ Armrests

☆ Cup holders

NOTES: *Booster Car Seats*

Model Name / Manufacturer	Store/Price	My Impressions	Grade

Ten

Changing Tables and Diapering Accessories

An interesting tidbit: "diaper" spelled backwards is "repaid." And are we ever repaid by our babies! More than 7,000 times the first two years of their lives, in fact. We've been told that changing tables are not a necessity. We've lived those numbers, and we disagree.

That's not to say that you can't live without a full-size, furniture-style changing table. You can change your baby on the floor, and you most definitely will. You'll even stop using a changing pad underneath every single time, and eventually just change them right on the carpet.

(We used to think that was gross and were horrified when people changed their kids anywhere in public besides on a changing table. But right around diaper change #1,735, we changed our tune.)

What about Changing Tables on Portable Play Yards?

We love 'em, but they are not replacements for a full-size changing table because they are only meant for small babies. Most changing stations on portable play yards and bassinets have weight limits of around 20 pounds, and your kid will be nowhere near potty trained by then.

There are, however, enough changing table options that we think it's a worthy investment. A raised changing surface can not only save your back in the long run, but stop you from popping your stitches the first few weeks you're home from the hospital. In fact, we recommend one on each floor of your house—at least for the first few months—to save you from the stairs.

There are two kinds of changing tables: freestanding and dresser attachments. Which you choose depends on your budget, space, and personal preference.

FREESTANDING CHANGING TABLES

Freestanding changing tables serve one purpose only: to bring tiny soiled babies up to mom's waist height. They are an extra piece of furniture not everyone has room for, but they aren't very big. Most have storage for diaper paraphernalia built right in, although you can buy hanging baskets, trays, and diaper storage sacks separately. Freestanding changing tables come in a variety of styles, colors, and finishes.

Why we love them: While some believe it's a waste of money for a short-lived product, we don't think two years is short-lived. We love ours.

Why we don't: We couldn't find one to match our crib perfectly, but we hear matchy-matchy is out anyway.

DRESSER ATTACHMENT CHANGING TABLES

Some full-size juvenile dressers come with changing table attachments. A changing pad on the dresser's top can be removed when your youngster is out of diapers, leaving a regular dresser behind. Check that the pad is securely attached; one strip of Velcro is not a safe attachment. Dressers offer plenty of storage, although not always the perfect storage for baby lotions and creams, and opening drawers to access things is more of a pain than having items on an open shelf.

Why we love them: We like the idea of a changing table that turns into a dresser.

Why we don't: We just don't usually like the dressers that are left behind. Because we hope our children's furniture will long outlast their diaper days, we look for dressers we're going to love forever, regardless of whether they have changing tabletops.

Make Your Own Changing Table

Yeah, don't. We've heard about people using a nonslip pad and a changing table mattress on a regular dresser or countertop. We've also heard that 1,800 babies are injured because of changing tables every year. Don't increase your baby's odds with a homemade product.

Folding Changing Tables

The very design of folding changing tables makes them recall magnets. Not only are they less stable and more easily toppled, but the fact that they have pieces that fold, usually in an X-shape, spells entrapment hazard.

Squirmy Baby Tip

A diaper change is a cruel blast of cold air that most babies do not appreciate. In fact, many downright hate it. On occasion, babies will try to kick, scream, spit, and krump their way out of it.

These twisting tyrants require two hands to hold them down, and you've still got to change their diapers.

We've found that hanging an object from the ceiling over the changing table can provide enough distraction to give us the precious few seconds we need to rip, wipe, throw, grab, open, lift, and secure a new diaper.

While there are special wall-hanging distractions designed just for this purpose, anything will do. A model airplane or tiny butterflies hanging from fishing wire can be spun with a fingertip, and add a delicious three-dimensional element to your nursery décor.

Of course, hang all items well out of your baby's reach but still within yours.

Slight, minimalist tables that look like fancy dinner trays appeal to our snob sensibilities, but use your common sense. If you think a piece of fabric slung over a thin wooden frame looks too flimsy to accommodate your newborn, you're probably right.

Stability

The single most important attribute of a changing table is that it is sturdy. Sturdy enough to withstand baby's weight. Sturdy enough to resist tipping over when brushed by a big dog or pushed by an angry sibling. Sturdy enough to stay standing when your toddler attempts to climb it. No matter how elegant it may appear—and the smaller ones are gorgeous—if the changing table can be easily tipped, it's not the table for you.

Durable Construction

You want a changing table that is solid from the ground up. Many, many cheap tables will eventually break down after enough shakes and shimmies from your change-resistant babe. Our first changing table was made of thin wood-composite boards that slipped into grooves in side rails. One day as I laid my baby on the top changing surface, the board snapped in two. Thankfully I still had hold of her and she didn't plummet four feet to the ground, but many other babies are not as lucky.

Add the changing table to the list of baby products you check monthly. Check for loose screws, sagging supports, and any structural compromises.

Guardrails

Guardrails are an important safety feature that can significantly reduce the risk of falls. Look for guardrails that are at least two inches high and surround baby on all four sides.

Safety Straps

All changing tables should have a safety strap that tethers baby to the table. If you see one that doesn't, keep walking. You should always use the safety strap when changing your baby's diaper, but also keep one hand on your child at all times. Be vigilant about never turning your back on your baby when on the changing table, strapped or not.

While we joke about "mom brain" preventing us from being able to balance a checkbook, many dads seem to have a blind spot on their brains when it comes to changing tables. Our husbands used to cross the room to fetch something, leaving our babies lying alone and us shrieking like harpies from the doorway. We don't know if they do it as a ploy to get out of changing dirty diapers, but you should instill in all members of your household the importance of never leaving a baby unattended.

Think a safety strap, a guardrail, and one hand on baby at all times is overkill? Picture a fish flopping violently on the ground. Now picture that fish weighing 20 pounds, hopped up on grape juice, and with a diaper rash vendetta. Nope, not overkill.

Changing Table Pads

Some changing tables come with a pad, others do not. If yours doesn't, a multitude of changing table pads is available for sale separately. Some are thin, flat pieces of foam, but better ones are contoured to provide extra little bumpers on baby's left and right. All pads should have a waterproof cover. If they don't, get a waterproof pad to lie between the mattress and cover.

Some changing table pads come with safety straps attached, but you want to use straps attached to your changing table, not its mattress.

Changing table pads require a separate cover, also purchased separately. Not all covers fit all pads, so check the packaging. Changing table pads come in every color and fabric imaginable to match any nursery room décor. Look for a soft one and buy two or three, as this is one item that gets dirty often. And we don't mean from actual dirt.

Placement

You can give your changing table extra stability and cut down baby's escape routes by placing it against the wall. In a corner is even better, as now you've blocked two sides.

Never place a changing table near a window because of drapery hazards and because a baby can actually roll off and right out the window. Screens have deceived more than one mom into thinking an open window was safe when in reality your baby will crash right through them.

Accessory Accessibility

Because you can't leave your baby unattended for even one moment, having all the ingredients at hand for a successful diaper change is crucial. Good changing tables allow you to easily reach extra diapers, wipes, and creams. Bad changing tables make you open a bottom drawer with one toe.

Numerous changing table accessory shelves available for separate purchase can make most changing tables into the good kind.

Height

We're not all the same height, and neither are changing tables. Look for one that is comfortable for you. You shouldn't have to strain upward or stoop down.

Price

Freestanding changing tables range in price from $80 to $450, with most in the $150 to $200 range. Dresser attachment changing tables are more expensive because they come with dressers; they can cost anywhere from $200 to $2,000 and beyond.

DIAPER ORGANIZERS/STACKERS

Diaper organizers, also called diaper stackers, are fabric bags that resemble clothes storage bags with a flat bottom and hanger or ties on the top. They are meant to be hung from the side of a changing table and store loads of diapers out of sight. You access the diapers through a slit in the fabric.

If your changing table has shelves, you probably don't need a separate diaper organizer, but they are included in many crib bedding sets.

DIAPER PAILS

Diaper disposal pails—the fancy plastic pails that individually wrap dirty diapers to help contain their smell—are one of those baby items that splits public opinion right down the middle. Half the moms we know swear by them and couldn't live without them. The other half hated theirs, thought it was a waste of money, and couldn't see the point. Before deciding to buy one, ask yourself how you are likely to handle diaper changes, and how much you like exercise.

First, a clarification: diaper pails are only meant for pee-pee diapers. While they might claim otherwise, no pail on earth can sufficiently contain the noxious smell of a pooper, and you will ruin your pail trying to force it to. Poopy diapers must be exiled from your house immediately, each and every time, on the spot, preferably double wrapped (although many people suggest you flush the solid contents first). Mercifully, this is only a few times a day. Pee diapers, on the other hand, can be a double-digit occurrence.

Your two choices for the pee diaper disposal: wrap the diaper in a leftover grocery bag and walk it to the trash can, or dispose of it in an odor-controlling diaper pail next to your changing station.

Maybe because we're inherently lazy, maybe because we're forgetful, we're diaper pail mamas . . . at least in the nursery. We have friends that have them in every corner of the house, but we can't keep track of that many. We do, however, appreciate the convenience of a diaper pail beside the changing table because most changes there happen in the early morning and late at night when we're half asleep.

The inherent dangers of not having a permanent catchall for dirty diapers is that the single diaper you forgot, the one that rolled off the dresser and into the closet, can ruin your reputation as a good housecleaner. The day the hidden treasure starts to stink up the whole house will be the precise day your book club is scheduled for your place.

However, diaper pails are not magic pails. They still need to be emptied every other day or so or they will unceremoniously announce their contents. They also need to be disinfected and cleaned every once in awhile. But we find the convenience of not having to run to the garage ten times a day well worth it.

While there are many choices, all with their own disposal system, much to our chagrin none of them actually grab the diaper from our outstretched fingers and automatically wrap it like the Jetson's robot machine we were dreaming of. They all have a simple manual operation involving pushing, pulling, and a couple of twists, and you will be wrist—if not elbow—deep into the pail each time.

One of the biggest decision-making factors for most people is whether the diaper pail uses regular kitchen bags or proprietary refills. From an odor standpoint, diapers are better contained by the special refills because these bags are specifically meant to work with the system, snaking around various seals, wrapping around each diaper individually, and locking in nasty smells. Pails using regular trash bags do tend to emit a pouf of smell when you open the lid because diapers are all just hanging out together in one big pile-on party.

Even though special refills are more expensive, trash bags aren't free. We did the math and the price difference isn't as great as that nosy lady in the diaper aisle would have you believe. On average, special refills will cost you about $7 a month; trash bags to fit the diaper pails will cost you $3.75. Yes, it is $3 more a month, but the refills are multilayered and have odor shield built in.

Emptying the diaper pails is never fun. The regular models using trash bags are a no-brainer, but the special refill versions spit out a weird tube of wrapped diapers that looks like a snake that had too many snacks. It can be clumsy and stinky to dispose of; we've dragged it down the stairs like a stretched out Slinky, wrapped it around our necks like a toxic boa, and even resorted to dumping it into a regular trash bag after all. And then we swore off emptying it entirely. If ever a job had "Dad" written all over it, it was this one.

PORTABLE CHANGING TABLES

Portable changing tables are like tiny cots that sit a couple of inches off the floor. They fold for portability, but we don't care. If we have to bend all the way down to the floor anyway, what do we care if our baby is on a changing pad on the carpet or lifted a couple of inches on a tiny cot? This product just presents a mess: babies can wriggle off it, fingers can get pinched, and why would we want to transport something bigger and more cumbersome than an easy, thin, light-as-a-feather changing pad?

Portable baby changers and pads that are fabric and lay on the floor are fine. Portable tables are—dare we say it?—just stupid.

Changing Stations

Many people, especially in multilevel houses, have mini diaper-changing stations around their house to make on-the-spot changes more convenient. We stashed a wicker basket with diapers, wipes, a changing pad, and rash cream under our family room coffee table. It's decorative, discreet, and always on hand.

Other Diapering Accessories You'll Need

- ☆ Washcloths
- ☆ Diaper rash cream
- ☆ Changing pads

Features to Consider

☆ Freestanding or dresser attachment

☆ Stability

☆ Durability

☆ Safety straps

☆ Guardrails

☆ Waterproof changing pad

☆ Easy access to storage

☆ Height

NOTES: *Changing Tables and Diapering Accessories*

Model Name / Manufacturer	Store/Price	My Impressions	Grade

Eleven

Cribs

If you're still in denial that you're having a baby, crib shopping will clear that right up. We've all bought baby accessories for friends and family, but a crib is usually our first permanent furniture purchase that drives home the fact that we'll be parents . . . soon and forever! Sounds scary. And it is. The parent part, not the crib shopping part. Thankfully, that's a relative breeze.

One of the things that makes crib shopping so fun is that one of your main decision-making factors is personal preference. Because cribs are

Crib

Age Range
Birth to 36 months

Total Usage
3 years

Recommendation
Must have

When to Buy
As soon as you tell people you're pregnant—get shopping!

one of the four categories of baby items with nationally mandated safety standards, when you are buying new you don't have to worry about measuring slats or looking for certification seals. All cribs sold in the United States and manufactured after 1991 must meet the government's safety requirements by law before they can be sold.

That's not to say cribs aren't still recalled, and you don't have to do your own safety checks. You do. But your first order of business is just picking one you like. How fun is that?

What Is a Jenny Lind Crib?

Because our entire childhood was brought to you by the Letter H and crisp, clean, refreshing tastes (C'mon, you know you wanted to be a Pepper too . . .), we have a certain built-in acceptance of corporate branding. So we just naturally assumed Jenny Lind was the name of a crib manufacturer. Imagine our surprise when we learned this is a generic term to refer to any crib with those knobby spindles.

In fact, Jenny Lind was a famous Swedish opera singer who became one of the first celebrity brand names, thanks to circus monger P. T. Barnum. Back in the mid-1800s, they named all sorts of things after her—ships, churches, and towns—but the one thing that stuck was cribs. It's crazy when you consider she supposedly only slept in a bed with turned spindles once while visiting America. And for this, we name an entire style of cribs after her? It's sort of like if two hundred years from now people referred to any especially springy couch as a "Tom Cruise Couch." Or not.

Happily, the choices are endless. Cribs come in as many different styles, colors, and finishes as all other bedroom furniture. There are sleek modern cribs, turned spindle cribs, sleigh bed cribs, canopies, hand-painted luxury cribs, and wrought iron cribs. You can find them in almost every color from natural to cherry, white to black, even chrome and rust colored. While the features vary slightly, most people choose a crib based on aesthetics, and coordinate their other nursery pieces accordingly.

Here are the four basic types of nursery cribs.

Standard Full-Size Cribs

The standard crib is rectangular in shape, but everything else varies from there. Some have a single drop side for easy baby access; some have double drop sides; some have none. Some have canopies; some wheels. Some cribs are convertible to toddler beds and beyond. Some cribs have attached dressers or changing tables. Some have storage drawers underneath. All have peekaboo slats running around at least two sides of their perimeter, but the slats might be solid, spindles, or slots. Styles of standard cribs include sleigh cribs and Jenny Lind cribs.

Why we love them: We're traditional, budget-minded girls. Standard cribs have the most color and feature choices. They match our furniture and fit in our rather small nursery the best.

Why we don't: We can always find one we do, no matter what our budget.

Round Cribs

Round cribs are exactly like standard cribs, except they are round. Many have canopies and at least one drop side. Touted by their makers as safer than standard cribs, there is little doubt that the round design means nobody puts baby in a corner. Round cribs look small in pictures, but they are actually three square inches bigger than standard cribs, usually 14 inches wider at their diameter. This can be helpful if you have a standing baby who likes to let go and fall backward like a little log. Round cribs do require custom mattresses and sheets, which are more expensive, harder to find, and available in fewer choices.

Why we love them: They're usually very beautiful.

Why we don't: They're usually very expensive.

Safe Crib Checklist

- Always place babies on their backs to sleep.
- Use a firm mattress.
- No extra bedding, bumpers, or pillows in the crib.
- No stuffed animals in the crib!
- Layer pajamas and use a sleeper sack rather than a blanket.
- Never cover baby's head in the crib (this means no cute little hats for sleeping!)
- Don't use a sleep positioner or wedge.
- Remove mobiles with hanging parts and canopy fabric when baby can sit up.
- As soon as baby can sit up, adjust the mattress support to its lowest setting, so baby cannot climb out.

MINI CRIBS

A mini crib is exactly like a standard crib, except smaller. It's not a foldable, portable thing. They are nice and sturdy. Quite attractive. But really, really small. A standard crib is 57 inches by 30 inches. A mini crib is 38 inches by 25 inches. That's not a lot of wiggle room, especially when baby is learning to sit and stand up. Most mini cribs have adjustable mattress height positions, and they are awfully cute. But baby won't last in "cute" for three years.

Why we love them: We love it . . . for Grandma's house.

Why we don't: Mini cribs need special mini mattresses and mini sheets. And for some crazy reason, they're not mini priced.

PORTABLE CRIBS

Unlike a portable playpen with mesh sides and multiple uses, a portable crib is a wooden or metal crib with slatted sides that resembles a standard rectangular crib, only slightly smaller and cheaper. Portable cribs have wheels for easy transport. Transport to where, we ask? Unless you're a day care center with a fire drill problem, you shouldn't need to roll your crib a whole lot of anywhere. We steer clear of portable cribs. They are generally much flimsier than a standard crib, they aren't substantial enough to qualify as permanent nursery furniture, and portable playpens are more easily transported and have more and better features.

Why we love them: We don't. Not even at day care.

Why we don't: They're cheap in every way.

Stability

While we normally enjoy shaking things in the store, crib floor models are likely to have been shaken quite a bit, so you may not be able to tell how sturdy they actually are. But you can certainly give them a few knocks, climb around and inspect the materials, and tell by the price tag if they're cheap quality.

It's easy to picture a peaceful newborn all tucked in his bed, but you must also imagine the 30-pound toddler jumping furiously and shaking the sides like a mad miniature Hulk. Because your child will be in his crib daily for almost three years, mostly unattended, we recommend getting the most durable crib you can possibly afford.

Crib Materials

Most cribs today are made of wood, but metal cribs are available, and even cribs made of injection molded plastic (the thick kind used in bulletproof glass, not the cheap kind used in toys). Wood cribs can be solid wood or made of wood laminates or veneers.

As long as no lead paint is involved (there shouldn't be by law, but we hear about lead paint recalls every day, so check), the choice of material is a personal preference. We personally prefer a softer surface for when baby bashes his head against the side in an epic tantrum when we abandon him in his crib, so we choose wood. Metal cribs probably work beautifully for beautiful people with calm kids, but ours would knock themselves unconscious.

Mattress Support

There are many ways for a mattress to be supported in a crib: spring frames, slats, lips, or even solid platforms. Because this is where most faulty cribs fail, choose a crib with a solid mattress support system. Thick steel joists? Good. Aluminum foil and rubber bands? Bad. We're exaggerating, but you get the idea.

Look at the way the mattress support is attached to the crib and ask yourself how safe it would be in the event of a hardware or material failure. How many screws would have to fail before a corner of the mattress support caved in? Just one or a dozen? If a single slat buckled, would that be enough to compromise the entire support? If so, look for a crib with a different bottom.

Historically, most recent crib recalls occurred in cribs with slat type supports, when the slats or hardware used on them failed. Spring frame mattress supports seem to be sturdier, but know that they will likely shred the underside of your crib mattress once your baby starts a-bouncin'.

Adjustable Mattress Height

To prolong their usefulness, most cribs have a height adjustment feature for the mattress. When baby is teeny tiny, you can have the mattress at its highest height, easing parental back pain. By the time a baby can sit up unassisted, you should move the mattress all the way down, eliminating the ability to escape. Just make sure the method of mattress height adjustment is something that requires adult action. A jumping toddler maniac should not be able to wiggle the mattress support into the next level.

Drop Sides

Many cribs come with one or even two lowering sides. This feature is a completely personal preference. Some moms find drop sides incredibly helpful when changing crib bedding. Other moms pop the entire mattress out every time and never lower a single side.

If you do choose a crib with a drop side, always keep the side fully raised when baby is in the crib and verify that the side is locked in place. Drop sides have several types of release mechanisms: metal rods with a little foot pedal on the bottom you tap in, trigger release buttons you depress or pull simultaneously with both hands, and notched tracks that require you to lift with your hands while pushing in with your knee. Look for a release that's solid and quiet.

Convertibility

Some convertible cribs promise two, three, and even four future furniture uses. Some turn into toddler beds, some day beds, and some full-size beds. Convertible beds are more expensive and usually require a separate purchase for the future bed's supports. These extra pieces can run you up to $100 per bed configuration, but buy them now because when you're ready to convert the crib, we can almost guarantee they won't make that model anymore. No use paying extra for a convertible crib if you can't actually convert it later.

If you plan on having more children, you probably won't be converting the crib for quite a few years, so select a design that you'll still like down the road.

Wheels

We never saw the point of cribs with wheels because even if we wanted to push it somewhere, a fully assembled, full-size crib won't fit through the bedroom door. The first time we changed baby's bed, wrestled with the insanely tight, firm crib mattress and obsessed over getting the crib sheets as fully around the mattress as possible without completely screwing up the bed skirt, we got it. Oh, we got it. Wheels would have made it much, much easier, because they allow you to push the crib away from the wall and have access to all sides.

Like the idea of wheels? Look for metal wheels, which are more durable than plastic ones.

Decorative Touches

While they might look sweet, you should avoid cribs with cutout designs and decorative knobs and short posts. Babies can get heads or little limbs trapped in the cutouts. Fancy decorations can break off and present a choking hazard. And knobs and posts can entangle children and strangle them in their own clothing. Keep the fancy touches on their walls, not their cribs.

Storage Drawers

Many cribs now come with long, shallow storage drawers underneath. If you like them, great, but we're not big fans. Here's why. They're smaller than you think, you can't access them if you're using a cute coordinating bed skirt, and now you've lost one of your greatest hiding spaces for large, odd-shaped things you'd rather not look at, such as a mega pack of diapers or that weird quilt your great aunt made.

Additional Attached Furniture

Some cribs come with attached furniture: changing tables, little dresser drawers, even nightstands. Again, we're not big fans. They make the crib extra long and bulky and our nursery rooms aren't that big to begin with (who doesn't give the baby the smallest room in the house?). If you like attached extras, make sure the attachment doesn't compromise the crib safety and is made of relatively durable construction.

Price

Because it is furniture, you will pay dearly for a crib. Because your baby will spend so much time in it, and possibly future baby siblings, we recommend getting the nicest crib you can afford. A good quality crib will run from $200 to $400, with convertible cribs costing a bit more. You can add hundreds more for even better quality or fancier brands. Round and luxury cribs will start at $750 and run all the way to $7,000-plus (most sit in the $2,000 range). Mini and portable cribs are both around $200.

Not excited about spending so much in one place? Do what we did. Convince your mom that the new tradition is for Grandma to buy the very first grandchild her very first crib. Tell her all the other grandmas are doing it. We'll back you up.

When to Order

Remember your wedding dress woes? How it took three times as long as they promised and as your big day approached with no dress in sight, your panic and your ulcers multiplied? It's kind of like that with cribs. Cribs can take anywhere from 8 to 18 weeks to arrive, even when ordered from a national chain retail store whose showroom is stuffed with display models. And just like wedding dress horror stories, we have friends who ordered a crib that was discontinued during the waiting period, the store never bothered to tell them, and their baby ended up sleeping in a drawer. OK, the last part is an exaggeration, but the potential headaches are true. Our advice: order early—super early! As soon as you're comfortable telling people you're pregnant, go crib shopping.

When It Arrives

Once the crib arrives, assemble it immediately so you can check for safety and stability, and if you have a problem, still have time to get a new part or a whole new crib. Be on the lookout for cracked, irregular, or buckled pieces; chipped corners; and missing bolts or screws. If any part looks suspect, return the whole crib!

When put together properly, your crib should be sturdy, all edges should be aligned pretty perfectly, and the crib should be level. If it's not, return it.

To test its strength, give it a good shake. Jostle the rails. Yank any moveable parts up and down a few times. It should feel sturdy, not as if it's going to wobble apart.

Continued Safety Checks

Because it is the only product meant for baby to be in unattended, and because babies spend 50 to 70 percent of their tiny lives in their cribs, you want to give your crib regular safety checks. Once a month, on your baby's birthday, inspect all joints, slats, and supports. Look for loose rails, loose bolts or screws, and any other potential hazards. Give it a good shake, and if need be, tighten everything up.

Because most crib recalls have involved mattress supports failing and causing the mattress to slip and trap baby, climb under your crib and check all parts of the mattress support. Note stretched-out springs, loose joists, and anything that wobbles at all.

Crib Placement

When deciding how to lay out your nursery, do not place your crib near window blinds or drapery. Do a two-foot perimeter check around the crib to see that wandering arms can't pull anything down on themselves, including clocks, pictures, and monitors.

CRIB BEDDING

You know soft bedding is out, as are crib bumpers, quilts, bulky blankets, and sleep positioners. And you should not use baby pillows. Fitted crib sheets, however, also pose their own safety risks. Should they pop off the corner of the crib mattress, they can pose a strangulation or suffocation hazard—it's rare, but we worry. Because all crib mattresses are not the same height, not all sheets will fit the same. The sheet you purchase should fit snugly on your mattress, but not so snugly that it might snap off. Long-term usage and repeated washings usually lead to shrinkage and broken-down elastic edges, so inspect the sheets every time you change your baby's bed.

Several wonderful crib sheet products are available to help reduce the pop-off risk. Wrap-around crib sheets have extra fabric around the bottom, and either slip over the crib mattress like a giant pillowcase or Velcro into place underneath. Crib sheet security clips are tiny suspenders that hold sheet corners together underneath the mattress and can be used with virtually any crib sheet.

And don't forget to wash any baby bedding before you use it to help avoid skin irritations. (And we recommend specially formulated baby detergent for the first year to protect baby's delicate skin.)

CRIB WEDGES

Crib wedges are triangular pieces of foam designed to give babies an elevated sleeping surface. Don't buy the hype that babies prefer this. This product is completely unnecessary in normal day-to-day life. If you have a sick baby or a baby with reflux or colic, check with your doctor for advice about crib wedges.

We're not fans of soft foam wedges that fit under the standard sheet because they present a softer surface for baby and will stretch your sheet into dangerous corner-ejection territory. You can find crib wedges for under the mattress, but they shouldn't lift the mattress enough to cause an unsafe gap between the mattress and any crib side. Finally, platforms made to raise the entire crib are available. We don't know about you, but we prefer our furniture flat on the floor. The possibility of the entire crib tipping over or the angle compromising the integrity of the crib's structure is enough to keep us away.

We've tested all the crib wedges, and even made our own, but our experience is that babies too sick to sleep flat are too sick to sleep still, and they end up sliding down off the incline anyway. Our sick babies always slept in a swing, but because you can't leave them unattended, the swing was placed in our room and we sat up next to them all night worrying. These are the nights we moms are securing our places in heaven.

Cribs, Lies, and Videotape

Purchasing a crib couldn't be easier, right? OK, maybe we lied. It's not all fun and games. But if we told you how complicated this category was, you would have abandoned us long before now. We will leave you with a happy thought, though. According to the Centers for Disease Control and Prevention, since 1990 the overall rate of SIDS in the United States has declined by more than 50 percent. That's a lot of parents, pediatricians, and product manufacturers doing things right and that's a lot more happy, smiling babies. And that makes all our SIDS prevention and safe nursery preparation well, well worth it.

Features to Consider

☆ Crib style, color, and material

☆ Sturdiness

☆ Quality of materials

☆ Mattress support

☆ Adjustable-height mattress

☆ Drop sides

☆ Convertibility

☆ Wheels

NOTES: *Cribs*

Model Name / Manufacturer	Store/Price	My Impressions	Grade

Twelve

Crib Mattresses

On the baby product shopping scale of fun, where tiny leather crib shoes are a big fat 10, crib mattresses are a 1. A low 1. A would-rather-be-at-the-used-car-lot 1.

Actually, as absurd as it sounds, the experiences of shopping for a crib mattress and a used car are unbelievably similar. Things are falsely advertised, you'll encounter confusing sales gimmicks, you can't really see under the hood, some salespeople use nasty scare tactics, and warranty claims are confusing.

To make matters worse, aside from a new flammability standard, there are no government safety requirements for crib mattresses, no industry standards, and no certification programs by anyone, not even the Juvenile Products Manufacturers Association (JPMA). As long as cribs burn within the government's new

Crib Mattress

Age Range
Birth to 36 months

Total Usage
3-plus years

Recommendation
Must have

When to Buy
Not until your crib arrives. You need to make sure it fits, but still be within the return period in case it doesn't.

149

performance standards—and companies achieve that any way they choose, from organic options draped on the outside to chemical cocktails sprayed on the inside—crib mattresses can be any height, any density, and made of anything. Literally anything.

It's crazy if you think about it. Cribs, which every parent needs, must meet dozens of federal safety mandates down to the sixteenth of an inch, or they can't be sold in the United States. Every single crib needs a mattress. Mattresses are what the babies actually sleep on in the cribs. Most experts believe there is a big link between soft bedding and SIDS. And yet, zero regulations exist on crib mattresses.

Crib mattresses are sold by many stores as a no-brainer accessory and purchased by many parents as an afterthought. Because standard full-size cribs are all the same size, crib mattresses claim to be as well, so you just grab a medium-priced one and call it a day.

We certainly did the first time we bought a crib. I think Hollie actually used a garage sale mattress from 1982. But there was no one to tell us differently. In fact, even today the government, the juvenile products industry, the American Academy of Pediatrics, and every baby book we ever read all either tiptoe around mattress recommendations, just saying to "buy the best you can find," or come out and recommend the cheapest as a perfectly acceptable choice.

Now that we're recall junkies and know that crib mattresses that are too soft can cause babies to slip under the crib, and mattresses that are too firm, too tall, and too slippery can cause a crib sheet corner catapult, we realize how profoundly lucky we are that our first poor mattress choices never came back to haunt us. We are reformed and ready to spread the word on how to buy a safe crib mattress.

We've tested every crib mattress on the market. We poured water on them, pulled at their seams, tested the firmness of their corners, and even jumped on them. We put them into full-size cribs and then attempted to change them, noting height, depth, and corner struggles. We placed newborns on them and watched diligently as the babies slept, noting their comfort, their ability to breathe, and the general noisiness of the mattresses. And we happily report our specific findings and you can find our Top Five picks, with pictures, videos, and the opinions of other moms on BabyGizmo.com.

But right here, right now, we'll tell you how we determine what makes a good mattress so you can perform your own in-store safety checks.

While technically you could fill a garbage bag with peanut butter and jelly and call it a crib mattress, most mattresses sold today claim to be stuffed with one of two things: foam or springs.

FOAM MATTRESSES

Foam has come a long way since we were kids. In the past, foam was soft when new and would age rather quickly, becoming hard and brittle and cracking easily. You can still find this kind of foam in cheap mattresses, but quality foam products offer firm support that doesn't degrade and makes for a pretty comfortable and convenient choice. A good foam mattress has three hallmarks: density, firmness, and resiliency. You want the densest mattress possible for a newborn, but of course most manufacturers don't list density on the packaging. Generally, the denser a foam mattress is, the heavier it is, so pick up the selections in the store to compare them. Pass on the ones that fly out of your hands or bend in the middle like a spaghetti noodle. You want a firm mattress, and a little later we talk about how to test for that. Finally, good foam mattresses have good resiliency, which means if you squish them, they pop back to shape quickly. A slow riser is a sign of bad foam. Foam mattresses come in varying thickness, and cheaper ones do tend to be thinner, but that doesn't mean thicker is automatically better. You can find super-thick cheap foam mattresses, but you can spot them because they are light, too soft, and slow to reform when you punch 'em. Another risk of foam mattresses is that if bacteria or mold gets into them, it's never coming out. Cheap foam is a big Barbie Dream House for nasty buggies. Good quality foam mattresses are treated inside to prevent bacteria growth, and sealed well to stop anything from getting there in the first place.

> *Why we love them:* They are more comfortable, especially for our older babies, and they are easier to change.
>
> *Why we don't:* We're not giant fans of chemicals, and cheap foam mattresses scare us for what they are potentially made of.

INNERSPRING MATTRESSES

Many people are more comfortable with innerspring mattresses because they are a more traditional filler, although if you're afraid of foam because it's a chemical creation, realize that innerspring mattresses use it as a cushion inside as well. Because they are packed with steel, innerspring mattresses are heavier than foam mattresses: much, much heavier. A typical foam mattress weighs six pounds to an innerspring's 30 pounds. However, innerspring mattresses are less likely to degrade over time. Quality innerspring mattresses can be spotted by the number of coils they contain—look for a minimum of 150 coils—but that number by itself can be deceiving. Quality is also marked by thicker steel and more turns in the springs. A mattress with fewer, higher quality coils is better than one with lots of cheap coils. Steel thickness is measured by gauge; the lower the gauge number, the thicker the steel. Also look for a mattress with a quality steel border rod.

Why we love them: They're safe, dependable, and durable.

Why we don't: They're soooo heavy! Innerspring mattresses are five times heavier than foam and five times harder to change.

Which Is Better? Foam or Innerspring?

If we had to say—which in the spirit of no more waffling, we will—we prefer foam mattresses, but only the top-of-the-line ones. If we didn't have the budget to go all out and had to settle for a mattress of average quality, we would choose innerspring. Cheap innerspring mattresses aren't going to be that comfortable and may eventually tear, but we think that's a safer alternative to cheap foam mattresses. The cheapest innerspring will still offer some support because it is steel. The cheapest foam mattresses offer the barely solid equivalent of toxic goo that can compromise your baby's breathing safety, collapse on the edges when your toddler stands up, invite mold and bacteria to take up permanent residence, and over time, break into dangerous chunks.

Good quality foam mattresses are modern marvels of comfort, safety, and convenience. They're light and hypoallergenic, and many are quite chemical free.

Crib Mattresses and Chemicals

We've read the same rumors on the Internet you have about noxious fumes from the chemicals used in crib mattresses being a possible link to SIDS, especially when used by a second baby (because leaks from the first baby mix with those chemicals, fester, and stew). And as we both have tiny infant boys who are currently reusing their big sisters' crib mattresses, we're as paranoid as anyone.

While corporate cover-up conspiracy theories abound, the fact is no one has been able to undoubtedly prove or disprove a crib mattress and SIDS link.

But we're moms and we reserve the right to worry. So if you're concerned about chemicals, mold growth, or germs, you might consider the following:

- Unwrap a new crib mattress, prop it against a wall in a well-ventilated area, and allow it to air out for several weeks before your baby uses it.
- Invest in a mattress with a quality, multilayer covering to prevent germs and mold from entering the inner mattress material.
- Use a separate mattress cover to prevent rips and tears to the mattress and help seal in fumes. Wash it before using it.
- Vinyl products smell bad for a reason: they are bad. Avoid covers made of PVC or vinyl (polyvinylchloride). Instead look for polyethylene (also called polythene).

Fit

No matter which mattress you choose, the most important feature—aside from firmness—is that it actually fits in your crib.

Because all standard cribs are the same size, crib mattresses should be too:

52 by 27 inches. So the rows and rows of crib mattresses you see in the store will all be the same width and height. No worries there. Mattress depth varies from four to six inches.

If you've chosen a nonstandard size crib, you'll need a special order mattress to fit, but you can usually find them from the same retailer, and many special cribs come with mattresses.

The size selection was easy, but of course, while everything standard is supposed to actually be standard, that's not always the case. Some crib mattresses are actually a little smaller than they should be and some cribs are roomier. Regardless of what size it says it is, you can't be sure a mattress fits well until you plop it into place.

A safe mattress is a snug mattress. You have a good fit if you can't fit more than one finger between the mattress and the crib side on any side. Two fingers is too much. If you have too big of a gap, try another mattress. If there's still a hole, your crib is probably too big and needs to be sent back.

Ever wonder why the mattresses made for rectangular cribs had rounded corners? Especially when the extra space at the vulnerable corners adds extra entrapment hazards? We did too. Thankfully, so did some of the new crib mattress manufacturers. They've introduced crib mattresses with squared-off corners that virtually eliminate the extra space risk and hold onto crib sheets better. Genius!

Firmness

The second most important factor in mattress selection is firmness. Because soft bedding is widely thought to be a SIDS risk, you don't want a mattress that could obstruct little airways. Experts repeatedly say, "Get a firm mattress," but how firm is firm enough? Unfortunately, because there's no safety standard for firmness or even a quantitative measure to use for comparison, parents are left to their own devices.

Here's how the experts suggest you test overall mattress firmness:

1. Stand mattress on its short side.
2. Place a flat palm on either side in the middle of the mattress.
3. Push in.

The harder you have to push, the firmer the mattress is. However, that little test doesn't speak to surface plushness. A good quality mattress might have a nice solid core, but too much memory foam or Tempur-Pedic goodness on its top to be safe for newborns. The best parent test seems to be to press on the middle with your index finger. If the surface indents too easily, the mattress is too soft. In our experience, even too soft mattress covers rebound pretty quickly, less than a second usually, so also eyeball the depth you can easily push. The best way to judge, of course, is to compare a really crappy mattress that's too soft to a nice firm mattress. Next time you're in a discount store, even if you don't plan on buying a crib mattress from them, wander on over to their mattress section and give everything a good poke.

Know that a crib mattress of the correct firmness might seem painfully hard to you and me, used to all our pillow-topped, featherbed glory, but babies sleep like, well, you know.

Convertible Crib Mattresses

Most people are fine with their tiny babies sleeping on a surface as hard as plywood, but worry about older toddlers not being comfortable later down the line. If you're concerned about how an older child will sleep on such a hard mattress, especially if you plan on using it for a toddler bed, look for a dual-sided crib mattress with a firmer side for infants and a softer side for bigger kids. Just be sure to put the right kid on the right side.

Internal Side Rails

One of the ways crib mattress makers construct a more solid mattress and discourage babies from sleeping at the edges is to include internal side rails. These come in the form of steel rods in innerspring mattresses, and harder, more uncomfortable foam in foam mattresses. The inclusion of extras such as internal side rails is a sign of a good mattress.

The Ticking

If we hadn't grown up with parents who listened to the singer John Denver, we might never have known that the "ticking" is the fabric that encases a mattress. Today, many people refer to it as the "mattress cover," but you can also buy separate mattress covers, which we cover below, so we're going to use the terminology from the song "Grandma's Feather Bed" and stick with the tick.

A surefire signal of a quality mattress can be found in the ticking: which fabric is used, how it is attached, and what type of binding is used around the edges. The first thing to look for is the type of fabric and number of layers. Good quality mattresses will give you multiple layers made of non-PVC materials, some even with hypoallergenic and antibacterial properties. Poor quality mattress will be covered in a single layer of vinyl. To keep it safe and germ free, you want the mattress to have a pretty thick shell. A single layer is more easily punctured, ripped, or cracked.

Cloth binding around the seams is a sign of quality; cheaper mattresses use vinyl. Also note the stitching. Tiny, tight, uniform stitching is best. Missing or torn seams in the store don't bode well for how the mattress will hold up over time and tyrannical toddlers.

The newest, premium mattresses don't have any binding at all. They are ultrasonically sealed. They are only a few years old, but from everything we've seen—and judging by the number of celebrity moms snapping them up—they do stay sealed. No binding means dirt and germs can't hide out under the cracks or sneak in through the needle holes.

Many mattresses tout their waterproof ticking as a sign of quality, but we disagree. The cheapest vinyl is quite waterproof, but covering a junky mattress in the equivalent of a camping tarp does not make it a better product. And while even the most expensive mattresses have special water-resistant covers, we don't put too much stock in them. Once bodily fluids leak into a mattress, the gig is up. We're big believers in adding separate waterproof mattress covers to any mattress, especially the more expensive ones, to protect our investment.

And one more thing, remember that the texture of the mattress surface is completely irrelevant because you're going to be using a crib sheet over it. We do look for quieter coverings with no PVC if we can find them, but don't get hung up on a soft suede your baby's cheek will never touch.

MATTRESS COVERS

While most quality mattresses are water resistant and spot cleanable, we don't care. We still cover them. Why? Imagine, if you will, a mattress covered in vomit. Would you rather gingerly grab the edges of a separate cover and toss the whole nightmare in the wash (or, if you're like us and have a problem dealing with throw-up, in the trash), or spend an hour scooping, scraping, and scrubbing yuck off the mattress itself? Behold the genius of the mattress cover!

Mattress covers are sold separately and resemble a large, fitted sheet. Some have slight, quilted padding for extra comfort, and some are giant sheets of vinyl. While our mom was a big fan back in 1978—she loved rubber pants too—we don't like the vinyl sheets because they smell bad and are extremely crunchy. Crunchy things sabotage our get-baby-to-sleep-through-the-night plans.

The best mattress covers are made of microfiber polyester with a waterproof backing that also keeps dust mites and other mattress allergens at bay. If asthma or lazy housekeeping runs in your family, you might even consider a mattress pad that zips over the entire mattress to completely seal in dust. Just be sure it fits snugly.

Whatever extra cover you choose, keep baby's sleeping surface as firm as possible. This means no shaggy wool, extra memory foam pads, or egg crate cushions.

Vents

Some mattresses are touted as "naturally breathable." Others have actual vents on the sides. Vented mattresses have pros and cons. Venting means you can air out any possible fumes and germs can circulate out. Vents also let little critters into your mattress.

Of course, because no tests have been done by anyone to support or protest the inclusion of vents, we have no answers on this one. We personally just ignore this feature. There are enough other, far more important things to look for. We find the mattress that we like best, and don't care if it has vents or not.

Crib and Crib Mattress Sets

Some cribs come with mattresses included. Beware, because a popular crib and mattress combo was just recalled because of the mattress. Crib manufacturers are by and large not also crib mattress manufacturers, so you're probably not going to get the best mattress if you purchase a set. If you love the crib anyway, by all means buy it. And remember you are allowed to throw out the included mattress and buy your own. Just because it's free, doesn't mean we have to eat it . . . I mean, keep it.

Have a unique-sized crib or cradle? Many smaller crib mattress companies will custom make a quality mattress in any size you need.

The Scary Mattress Salesperson

Before you send us hate mail, we don't think all mattress salespeople are scary. Just the commissioned ones. We don't know if they make more on the crib mattresses than the cribs themselves, but they sure do like to push you around. Push you around toward the most expensive models.

Now we're all for spending as much as you can on a quality crib mattress. But we don't want to be scared into it. The newest sales tactic making the rounds is salespeople telling unsuspecting parents that they must buy a new crib mattress for every single baby. We've read the reports about fumes and biological gases, but if it were such a big deal, why don't hospitals change their mattresses after every patient?

We recommend buying your own new crib mattress for your first baby so you know its history—the good, the bad, and the explosive—but with subsequent children close in age, and a mattress in good shape, we would keep it.

Before you reuse a crib mattress, check the entire outside for wear and tear, rips, cracks, holes, or an unusual amount of surface staining. Because you can't see what's going on inside the mattress, if the outside looks bad, buy a new one.

The Warranty Scam

A long warranty is not a sure sign of a quality mattress. In fact, some companies use this pitch as a sales gimmick. A good quality mattress should have quality materials and solid construction that last longer than you'll ever use the mattress. With an unusual defect in the workmanship, a good company will help you sort it out regardless of a warranty. We've found that many of the companies that relied on their "lifetime warranty" claims aren't even in business anymore. Also, any damage your child does to the mattress, such as stabbing it with scissors, voids your warranty anyway.

Crib Mattress Cheat Sheet

Here's a quick reference for how to spot a good quality and a great quality mattress. Good quality will meet most families' needs (and budgets). Great quality will get you extra luxury and fewer chemicals.

How to Spot a Good Quality Mattress

- Not too light
- Firm
- Bounces back quickly when punched
- Well made with tightly stitched edges
- Around $100

How to Spot a Great Quality Mattress

- Multilayered cover
- Cloth binding or no binding
- Squared edges
- PVC and vinyl free
- Price starts at $175

Not Useful for Judging Quality of Mattress

- Number of coils alone
- Brand name
- Warranty promises

The Brand Name Scam

Many consumers are relieved to find the quality brands they recognize from their own adult mattress purchases on crib mattresses as well. And the companies that paid the adult mattress manufacturers to "borrow" their names for this marketing scam are happy for it.

Don't blindly purchase a crib mattress based on brand name recognition. Chances are the wonderful mattress company you see on the label isn't the one who actually made the crib mattress.

How can you tell? We've found that the best crib mattress companies are the ones who proudly advertise on their corporate websites that they actually make crib mattresses. If you only see adult products on their site and can't even find a mention of their crib mattress line, it's probably because they aren't actually producing it themselves.

Price

One of the best ways to judge the quality of a mattress is by price. Unlike most baby product categories, there are no designer brands, so you're not paying a premium for name alone. More expensive mattresses are more expensive because they use better materials and are better constructed.

Because you're going to use it for at least three years and because it's such a key component of a safe nursery, we highly recommend purchasing the best crib mattress you can possibly afford.

How much is all this good quality going to cost? Brace yourself, because the price is a big percentage of how much most cribs cost. While cheap crib mattresses can be found for around $50, the best quality ones start at $100 and go all the way up to $300. We know, we were shocked, too. Somehow, before we had kids, we pictured this as a $30 purchase. But tempting as it may be, don't skimp on the crib mattress. There's just too much at risk, especially if you are going to use it for other babies.

Price Range

While it's easy to see that a higher-priced mattress is probably better quality than a lower-priced one, how can you compare the quality of mattresses that cost the same? Look at the entire price range of mattresses a company offers, and perhaps steer clear of manufacturers who make lower-end models at all. Confused? To clear things up and prove to my third grader that you really will use math someday, I wrote this completely unnecessary word problem to illuminate:

Jennifer has $100 to spend on a crib mattress. Company A offers mattresses that cost $40, $60, and $100. Company B offers mattresses that cost $100 and $200. Which company should she choose if she were on a train headed east at 75 miles per hour for 22 minutes at 11:32 a.m.?

Answer: We would choose Company B. We would rather take the lower end offering from a company that only makes high-end, quality goods than any product from a company that does a brisk business also selling crap.

Features to Consider
☆ Foam or innerspring

☆ Mattress weight

☆ Firmness

☆ Resiliency

☆ Fit

☆ Side rails

☆ Binding

☆ Multi-layered covers

☆ Convertibility

☆ Price

NOTES: *Crib Mattresses*

Model Name / Manufacturer	Store/Price	My Impressions	Grade

Thirteen

Crib Toys

rib toys make moms pretty. Here's how: they entertain your toddler in his own crib when he wakes up at the crack of dawn. He is distracted by the self-starting songs, sees his baby friend in the mirror, and babbles happily. While you sleep like a baby. The extra 15 minutes . . .OK, 30 . . . all right, we let our kids play alone for 45 minutes . . . of beauty sleep ranks right up there on our Favorite Things list with new shoes and a large frappuccino.

Don't get too excited; you can't use crib toys right away. Because the word "toy" denotes baby will actually touch it, crib toys aren't much use until baby can sit up. And even then, babies lack the coordination to really enjoy them.

Crib Toys

Age Range
6 to 36 months

Total Usage
2½-plus years

Recommendation
Must have

When to Buy
A great first birthday gift.

In fact, despite what the packaging promises, most babies don't care for crib toys until after their first birthday. The first crib toy we ever bought— early in eager anticipation of the joy it would bring—hung dormant and ignored for months. Just when we were ready to give it away, our kids turned 1 and the crib toy came to life. We have that day marked lovingly on our calendar. With a big heart.

What makes a "crib toy" different from a regular toy is the ability to be

163

attached to the side of the crib. Attaching a toy directly to the crib can make for a safer plaything because it reduces smothering risks for plush toys and stays out of baby's way when sleeping.

There are two types of crib toys: soft and hard.

Soft Crib Toys

Soft crib toys usually take the form of a thick, flat stuffed animal hanging from a closed hook. Lights, music, and sound effects are activated when baby pushes, pulls, or bats at it.

Why we love them: They are generally more attractive and obviously softer than hard crib toys. Better for clumsy toddlers.

Why we don't: They don't usually perform as many tricks as their harder cousins do.

Hard Crib Toys

Hard crib toys are made of molded plastic. They are generally larger than soft crib toys and hang from several loops rather than just one hook. Many hard crib toys balance on top of the crib railing and can't be used until you have a standing child. Hard crib toys usually offer more activities.

Why we love them: Didn't you hear? They make us pretty. We, like most moms, didn't stop at one soft crib toy. We bought a bunch of hard and soft, to see which ones worked, and then did a happy dance when the answer was "all of them." Obviously, don't go overboard and turn your baby's crib into a toy store, but a couple of toys on either end makes for a busy bed-bound baby.

Why we don't: Like all plastic things, they are large, ugly, and hard. And why can the manufacturers put motion-activated electronics inside, but not figure out how to paint straight eyeballs on the outside?

Favorite Features

While the variety of activities built into a crib toy are endless, some are more entertaining than others. Our babies' favorite feature without a doubt is music they can turn on and off by themselves. Look for big, easy-to-press buttons and nice melodies that don't offend the ear, as well as good sound quality and volume control.

Other favorites are mirrors, pages that turn, and colored lights.

Features to avoid? Music you can't turn off manually and motion-activated anything. Motion-activated sounds like a good idea, but considering babies move in their sleep, they are wont to activate things at the most inconvenient times. Think you'll always remember to turn that feature off when baby goes down? Think again.

Visual Toys

Some crib toys are meant to provide visual stimulation for smaller babies, such as soft wallpaper with patterns you hang from the inside side of the crib. However, because even crib bumpers are out now and you can't leave plush toys in the crib with small babies, these visual toys should be removed every time baby goes to sleep. For us that translates to "never going in."

Placement

Many developmental experts suggest you move a baby's crib toys around every couple of weeks to give them variety and exercise their neck muscles as they search for different things. We can see this working with younger babies, but we don't give them crib toys anyway, and we're not risking more scratches moving our mobile around. And for older kids, that's just mean.

Attachments

Unlike mobiles, which must hang off the crib side, crib toys can be attached numerous ways: with clamps, ties, Velcro, plastic tabs, or the big, giant plastic screw thing. However it is secured, check that it is secure. No strings over seven inches should be allowed in your baby's crib for strangulation hazards; this includes attachment ties.

Dangerous Crib Toy Shapes

Pay close attention to the shape of any crib toy and avoid any tall pieces that might be considered "posts." Federally mandated crib safety regulations require that cribs themselves not have posts, knobs, or protrusions higher than one-sixteenth of an inch because children have strangled to death when their clothes got caught on them. But no one regulates toys that are attached to a crib. This safety standard should apply to toys that attach to a crib as well.

We recently purchased a popular crib toy that featured a zebra on top holding open a book. The zebra is three inches tall, but only two inches wide, with pointy ears pointing even higher. It sits secured to the edge of the top crib rail and creates its own post. An escape artist scaling the side could easily get hooked on this crib toy. As much as we loved it, we put that zebra to pasture.

Look for a crib toy with a smooth, all-over rounded shape completely devoid of protrusions baby could get hung up on.

Safety Hazards

Check that the crib toy doesn't include any pieces that present a choking hazard, especially if they were pulled or sucked off. Remember your enterprising toddler will have quite a bit of alone time to try to figure out how to dismantle it. All crib toys need to be toddler proof.

If the toy uses batteries, check that the battery compartment is sealed securely with a permanent screw that cannot fall out. Watch for sharp edges, and routinely check for cracks, peeling stickers, and other wear and tear.

Many people suggest checking that the crib toy is securely fastened at all times, but for once, we disagree. If the crib toy could harm your baby in any way once it was unattached and free floating in the crib, then it is not a safe toy and shouldn't be anywhere near the crib.

Price

The price of crib toys varies depending on size and number of features. You can find simple ones for $10 and more complicated ones for $50. Most hover in the $25 to $30 range.

Music Boxes

As if you didn't have enough choices to hang off the side of your kid's crib, there are also crib music boxes that range from simple tunes a toddler can control to speaker systems for your iPod.

Music boxes that use an MP3 player let parents customize diverse—and maybe more importantly—longer playlists for baby that include musical selections outside of Mozart and "Three Blind Mice." Just remember that parent-operated music boxes should be removed by the time baby can reach them.

Music boxes that a baby can activate are one of the best inventions ever. As long as the music isn't too loud, repetitive, or annoying, your DJ baby will be thrilled at being able to spin his own tunes.

Why we love them: Music soothes the savage beast. It works on babies too.

Why we don't: We do! We do!

Crib Gyms

Crib gyms are like a clothesline of toys that straddle the entire crib allowing toys to hang from side to side. And they are just as dangerous a strangulation hazard as a clothesline. Their very design—long yet skinny to enable them to cross the whole width of the crib—makes them a hazardous shape.

Why we love them: We don't! We love all our other crib toys, but not these.

Why we don't: Several babies have died when they reached up, pulled their crib gyms down, and got entangled. We need no stronger reason to stay away.

Features to Consider

☆ Music

☆ Mirror, flip book, lights

☆ Smooth surfaces

☆ Method of attachment

☆ Safety hazards

NOTES: *Crib Toys*

Model Name / Manufacturer	Store/Price	My Impressions	Grade

Fourteen

Diaper Bags

Considering the price, fabric, and use range, and the fact that you'll carry it as much as you carry your baby, we recommend putting some serious thought into the perfect bag (especially before your mother-in-law makes a grand gift of a great, big teddy bear–covered tote).

Thankfully diaper bags have evolved from the vinyl monstrosities of our childhood. They now come in a variety of styles with hip, colorful fabrics and fabulous features.

There are as many different types of diaper bags as there are moms. There are backpacks for adventurers, slings for urban warriors, silk-covered confections for the well-heeled, hobo bags for the free-spirited, as well as messenger bags, weekenders, mini bags, and more.

Are you an all-of-the-above mom? Most moms are, and most moms have more than one diaper bag to prove it. Just as you have multiple purses for multiple places, having a different diaper bag for each major occasion can make your outings with baby a little less stressful. Many diaper bags are a good investment anyway, because the non-baby patterns and sturdy designs

Diaper Bag

Age Range
Birth to 36 months

Total Usage
3 years

Recommendation
Must have!

When to Buy
As soon as you find one you like. A great first gift for yourself when you're expecting.

make for non-baby use later (as toted items evolve from formula to juice boxes to half-time water bottles).

Diaper bag selection is very similar to buying a purse. Style, fabric, color, and price will all depend on your personal preference and lifestyle. So, what are your choices?

TRADITIONAL/STANDARD TOTES

The traditional diaper bag is carried over one shoulder like a large purse, which in effect, it is—a large waterproof purse with tons of pockets. These diaper bags can close with magnetic snaps, zippers, or flaps of fabric.

Why we love them: They're basically a purse. We love purses.

Why we don't: Most are quite a bit larger than a standard purse and less attractive. And they scream diaper bag. We don't always like to enter a room advertising we wipe butt.

BACKPACKS

Much like a regular backpack, the diaper bag backpack is carried via two shoulder straps and has a rugged design and large, deep main compartment. Side insulated pockets hold bottles.

Why we love them: They close securely, are easy to carry long distances, and free up both our hands. We can abuse them endlessly, and boys don't mind carrying them.

Why we don't: They're bulky and hard to stuff into a stroller basket and aren't a very stylish replacement for our purse (which, let's be honest, a diaper bag is. We don't know who can manage to carry a baby, a diaper bag, *and* a purse, but we can't).

MESSENGER BAGS

A flatter diaper bag in a range of flattering fabrics, the messenger bag is the hottest style now. It resembles a laptop case and for many moms makes for an easier transition from the workforce to the playground. Most messenger bags come with adjustable straps that allow it to be carried like a purse, slung across the body, or hung from the back of a stroller. Messenger bags feature a flap that holds contents inside, but we don't recommend turning them upside down.

Why we love them: A slave to fashion, we love the look. You also can't find a more easily accessible bag.

Why we don't: They don't hold as much as a traditional diaper bag, especially when stuffed. And our diaper bag does turn upside down. Often.

SLINGS

Just like a messenger bag, but slightly smaller and usually with no flap for closure. They just snap or zip shut.

Why we love them: The ones that zip shut are our messenger bag dreams come true.

Why we don't: They're smaller than a messenger and the flapless design is slightly less elegant.

WEEKENDERS

The largest diaper bag around, as the name implies, these are great for weekend trips. Weekender diaper bags are slightly smaller than traditional duffel bags, but instead of just empty space inside, they are constructed with pockets, pouches, and insulated places for all of baby's things.

Why we love them: A weekend away is a fabulous thing. A gorgeous bag built for baby's accessories is even better. Who wants to tote baby toys, extra clothes, and all those diapers in a dirty old gym bag?

Why we don't: There are no reasons we don't. We love-love-love weekender bags. We only wish more manufacturers made them!

Toddler Totes

Toddler totes are for the transitional period when you no longer need to lug as much stuff as a newborn requires, but, alas, do still need a few diapers and snacks. They are smaller than a traditional diaper bag and have fewer pockets and are mostly, mercifully, cartoon free. Some still have insulated compartments for juice boxes or sippy cups, but most are more geared toward carrying board books and big kid distractions.

Why we love them: The day you get to downsize is a great, great day. And even if you could squish a size 6 diaper or sippy cup into your regular purse, why would you want to?

Why we don't: It's really just a regular, small bag. Calling it a "toddler tote" doesn't change that.

Mini Diaper Bags

Basically a changing pad folded around an envelope that holds just three to four diapers, travel-size wipes, and a tube of ointment, the mini is a portable essentials-only diaper bag.

The mini can be thrown in a larger bag, strapped around your wrist or clipped to your stroller. Many feature removable changing pads, which we love.

Why we love them: Everything is adorable in miniature. Great for keeping in your car (for the inevitable day when you leave your real diaper bag at home) or if you like to take the occasional stroll around the block but don't dig the occasional diaper emergency.

Why we don't: Although it's the centerpiece of this product, most mini bag changing pads are heartbreakingly small, especially for our toddlers. Hold out for a larger pad; it's well worth the couple of extra inches.

DIAPERS AND WIPES POUCHES/PODS/CLUTCHES

The most Spartan diaper bag of all, the clutch is a simple envelope that holds just three to four diapers and a travel-size container of wipes. Period. No changing pad. No extra pockets. Designed to be thrown in your regular diaper bag or purse, it was invented to keep your diapers neatly together and easy to find. Some are made of water-resistant material, but most are just fabric. (And we might not remember our sixth grade sewing class, but even we could sew one of these. For way less than the $20 they charge.)

Why we love them: We really don't, but we have neat-freak friends who do.

Why we don't: They only hold a couple of diapers, and we have half a dozen stuffed in our diaper bag. They're cute, but they're the least essential diaper bag. We can live without them.

Emergency Diaper Bag

The first time you leave the house without your diaper bag is a rite of passage. The fourth time you do it, it's more like a nightmare.

We highly recommend you keep an emergency diaper bag in your car for the inevitable day (or days) when you find yourself out, about, and without everything you need for baby.

Here's what to pack in it:

- Three diapers
- Travel wipes
- An extra binky
- An extra outfit (we suggest the ugly one your aunt gave you because you may not use it before your baby outgrows it)
- Single-serving formula packets
- Clean baby bottle
- Bottle of water

Price

Price is an important determining factor in choosing a diaper bag. While most diaper bags fall in the $40 to $65 range, there are wonderful bags for under $30 and deluxe leather totes for over $2,000.

On a budget? No worries! The underlying design of diaper bags is the same: they carry stuff . . . like diapers. You'll get pretty much the same features in any bag, expensive or not. Designer bags don't have any magical extras: no voice-activated Starbucks locator or odor-neutralizing diaper disposal system. But more money will buy you better fabric and more durable construction.

Less expensive diaper bags do tend to rip, fray, and split more readily than their more expensive counterparts, but it also depends on how you treat them. If you know you won't be playing nice with your bag, it might make sense to spend an extra $40 for a sturdier brand. Then again, if you choose a cheaper bag, when it breaks down, you can just buy a whole new one for less than that $40.

Fabric

Diaper bags come in almost every fabric available, from microfiber and vinyl to corduroy, denim, silk, suede, and leather. You can bet that the more expensive the fabric, the more expensive the diaper bag.

While some bags are waterproof and others water resistant, many of the more stylish choices today are neither. Whatever you choose, we recommend a fabric that's at the very least spot-washable. (Honey, where are you going with that silk diaper bag? Has no one ever spit up on you?) Some manufacturers have started wrapping more exotic fabrics with clear plastic vinyl so the designer look is preserved throughout life with baby.

We've also found that light-colored interiors can be lifesavers. It sounds simple, but most diaper bags (especially backpacks!) become literal black holes. It's nice to actually be able to see what you've packed.

Straps

There are as many different types of straps as there are types of bag, and many bags come with multiple straps for different uses. Our favorites are the straps that convert to hang on the back of lightweight (and notoriously basket-deficient) strollers; just remember, weight on the handles can make a lighter stroller tip over easily!

Comfort

Choose a diaper bag that you're comfortable carrying. Backpacks and shoulder-strap messenger bags are popular for hands-free walking, but the straps should be wide enough, relatively slip-proof, and adequately padded. And remember, larger bags hold a ton of stuff, but can also weigh a ton.

Closure

How you access the various parts of your diaper bag and how it closes are two important functions. Most bags have outer pockets for easy access to accessories and/or zippers that allow access to secret inner sections. But how the bulk of the bag stays closed varies greatly. There are bags with zipper tops, flaps that fold over, magnetic snap closures, and even ties. If you prefer quick and easy access, a snap or tie might work best for you. If you anticipate the horror of an overturned diaper bag in a wet parking lot, you may prefer the security of a zipper. Regardless of the closure you choose, you need to be able to do it relatively easily, that is, with your pinkie finger and chin while holding a squirming baby.

CHANGING PADS

If not for the included, color-coordinated changing pad, you would be hard pressed to tell the difference between many of the trendier diaper bags and actual purses. We love the changing pads that aren't just basic black and (ew!) white, but feature bright and surprising colors and patterns. Although we draw the line at silk- and faux fur–covered ones. Pee and poo do not belong on silk or fake fur. Not only do they not belong, they're like mortal enemies. Of each other and of common sense.

But that's pure vanity. The crucial features of a changing pad are that it's at least slightly padded, fully washable, large enough, and removable. Changing pads that remain attached to larger diaper bags confound us, as they can lead to a disastrous balancing act at small public changing tables, especially the ones that hang off the wall.

Nothing is as critical as the size of the changing pad. Some diaper bag manufacturers seem to think the changing pad is just a cute accessory, but there's nothing cute about having to choose between placing your baby's bottom or head on a dirty public changing station. A too-short, too-small changing pad is a giant nightmare. Our own favorite diaper bag, practically perfect in every way, comes with a craptastic 21-inch changing pad. Twenty-one inches? Our baby was bigger than that in the womb! Thankfully, some companies are dedicated to just making changing pads—in great fabrics, beautiful colors, and even big, bold, new shapes. Our favorite? Circular changing pads. They fold up nicely to fit in any diaper bag or stroller and even offer small inner pockets for wipes or small lotions. And not only is baby's top and tushie covered, he can't reach for germs on any side. Genius!

So how can you tell if a changing pad is too small before you even have a baby? Take it out and wrap it around your head. No joke. The average head circumference of an adult woman is 21 to 23½ inches. Too short for a good coverage changing pad. If the changing pad in question doesn't wrap around your head and then some, find one that does.

Extra Features

Many diaper bags come with little accessory pouches or pockets to make life easier for the 21st century parent. Extras include bottle insulators, waterproof pouches for wipes or dirty objects, key clips, cell phone pockets, and even iPod compartments. If the diaper bag you desire doesn't come with the accessories you'd like, many places now sell separate diaper bag accessory items.

Features to Consider

- ☆ Style
- ☆ Price
- ☆ Size
- ☆ Fabric/color
- ☆ Comfort of strap
- ☆ Waterproof/washable
- ☆ Removable changing pad
- ☆ Included accessories

NOTES: *Diaper Bags*

Model Name / Manufacturer	Store/Price	My Impressions	Grade

Fifteen

DVDs and Videos

The experts say that children under age 2 should not watch television. Yet there it is, in all its big-screen glory, taunting you from the family room and promising you the ability to make dinner in peace. Keeping your toddler away from the TV is almost impossible if you have older children, and impractical if you want to take a shower before the year 2015.

So you let your toddler watch TV. You, me, and 30 million other moms. No, our kids aren't babysat by the television, but no matter how much time you spend on the floor playing with your child and no matter how many hugs you give, balls you throw, or books you read, eventually, every mom needs a break. (I'd like to see "the experts" entertain my child 24 hours a day, seven days a week.)

Those experts argue that television can be a negative influence on impressionable young minds because of early exposure to excessive violence,

DVDs and Videos

Also Known As
Baby videos, educational DVDs, little baby genius makers (just kidding!)

Age Range
1 to 4 years

Total Usage
3 years

Recommendation
Must have

When to Buy
A great gift for baby's first or second birthday.

inappropriate content, and unregulated advertising. We agree. Those things are bad for kids. Very, very bad. We don't want to show our children of any age any of those things. But we moms—who really were raised by the television, by the way—still stubbornly love our televisions and aren't willing to give them up completely.

The use of prerecorded content, such as an educational DVD, is a great compromise, giving moms a tiny infant intermission, while limiting a child's exposure to age-appropriate, noncommercialized content.

Besides your own common sense—is the program teaching your child anything?—you can be on the lookout for certain hallmarks to determine if your child is benefiting from an educational tape or just being mesmerized by an onscreen lava lamp.

High Production Quality

Simply put, how does the video look overall? Does it look like the production company spent time and money on the presentation, or does it look like something your brother-in-law shot in his basement?

If you wouldn't stand for lousy homemade production quality and cheap computer effects in your own programs, your baby shouldn't have to either. Good quality educational videos look like good quality educational videos. If the production quality is outstanding, chances are the company spent just as much time in preproduction, working with educators and medical professionals, researching the subject, and planning the best program possible.

Safe, Non-dangerous Content

This sounds obvious, but watch closely. Many so-called "educational" tapes are made by media professionals, not educators or physicians, and include unsafe content. Sure, a close-up of a candle onscreen is pretty, but do you want your baby lulled in real-life by *fire*? One popular baby tape shows characters digging a bottomless hole and then jumping into it, forever disappearing. Not exactly what I want my adventurous 2-year-old to see.

Soothing, Not Startling, Presentation

Many parents mistakenly believe that for a program to be effective, their child needs to be hypnotized by it. In actuality, the best educational programming allows your children to be their natural, active selves: they watch, wander, come back, get distracted by something right in front of them, eventually look up, and start watching again.

Small children have short attention spans. Good educational programming tailors its presentation to that attention span in nonabrasive ways—for example, with quicker editing and an interesting soundtrack.

Programming that purposefully demands a small child's undivided attention is actually incredibly harmful. One popular series uses startling sound effects—trash can lids dropping on concrete, balloons popping, tires screeching—to make sure babies don't dare look away from the screen. These sounds are not only the unnerving equivalent of snapping in an infant's face, they actually act as negative reinforcement, conditioning children, like tiny Pavlov's dogs, to never look away from a television for fear of punishment. No doctor or educator in the world would endorse this operant conditioning (and none has).

Fully Orchestrated Music

Almost every baby tape on the market uses classical music and cites the "Mozart effect"—the idea that compositions by Mozart and other classical composers can accelerate a young child's brain development—as proof of their educational worth. However, all classical music is not created equal. The merits of the Mozart effect exist because of the mathematical qualities and varying complications in the movements of fully scored orchestral music.

To save money on music licensing, many companies take classical music and run it through a computer, removing 90 percent of the instruments, variations, and musical richness. The result is a tinny melody that sounds as if it were played on a music box. Music boxes are fine, but educationally stimulating, they are not.

Realistic Promises

Don't be fooled by the hyperbolic marketing claims on the video box. The more outlandish the claim, the more unlikely it is that the program is truly educational. No single DVD can "raise your child's IQ" or turn her into a "genius." Look for programs that tout stimulation, creativity, and exposure to art and educational concepts.

Watch with Your Child

Like any educational resource, DVDs are most effective when used with an adult caregiver. One of the most important things for a child's healthy development is for you to hold them, hug them, talk to them, and interact with them. Watching television together can be a tremendous interactive experience. Hold your child on your lap or snuggle up next to him while you talk about the lessons you're viewing together. Ask questions about what you see, what might come next, and why he thinks things happened.

Of course, it's OK if you allow your child to watch without you sometimes (we grew up in the age of basic cable without lockboxes, after all, and we're just fine!). But you should *always* watch everything you play for your child at least once yourself first. There is unfortunately a lot of garbage on the market masquerading as "educational" videos. Don't just blindly trust the packaging. Watch for yourself.

Having watched just about every tape ever made for babies and toddlers, I can attest that it can be mind numbing to sit through some of them. But ask yourself, "Is this the best program for my child then?" The best children's programming is made with adult viewers in mind as well, to promote co-viewing and family bonding opportunities. If you find yourself wondering what in the world your baby could be learning from shabby puppet shows and annoying sound effects, you might be right in thinking, "nothing."

Used sensibly with the right content, television can enrich the life of viewers of any age. Just make sure the exposure is age appropriate, guided by you, and, most importantly, part of a loving learning environment you've created in your home.

Little Laureate: My Quest for the Ultimate Baby DVD (or, How I Almost Went Broke Following My Passion)

Like most entrepreneurs, I started my first business because I felt I could do something better than it was being done. A fan of any and all media, I was delighted when I heard about the very first "baby videos," but horrified when I actually bought one. In an age where you could watch slick programming at the gas pump, I was shocked that what the box advertised as a "celebration of the humanities" actually looked like a bad 1970s public access show filmed in someone's garage.

I tried to believe in it, I really did. I could live with the sock puppets, but couldn't for the life of me figure out how close-ups of cheap plastic toys and office desk accessories were doing anything beneficial for my baby. And watching along with my child was pure torture.

You know you've discovered your passion when you can't stop thinking about it, day and night, at your other job and on vacation. My quest for a better product soon turned into an obsession. So in 2001, I took out a second mortgage on my house and founded Little Laureate. My mission was to make a National Geographic–like tape for babies that would introduce them to the world beyond their backyards. A tool parents could share with their children that would inspire a viewer of any age.

I assembled a team of Montessori educators, the leading pediatric brain development experts in the country, and the best animators in the business. I licensed the music from Sony and the live footage from National Geographic and the BBC. I dragged my own children around the world to film their wonder at meeting new people and seeing new places.

Having worked at Disney myself for five years, I knew a thing or two about the importance of inserting magic. I think we succeeded, as the Little Laureate series was voted one of the "Best Videos for Babies of All Time" by the readers of *Parents* magazine, and our cheerful animated tour guide, Star, has an almost cult-like following among two-year-olds.

The company, like Baby Gizmo, is a family affair, and proof that one mom with a dream can do anything. It wasn't all wine and roses, of course. Raising children on a middle class income, we had no cash to spare. Raising them in the Midwest, we had no fancy connections or celebrity friends to help. I teetered on the edge of bankruptcy more than once and ate mac and cheese for dinner while my friends bought new cars.

But if you have enough passion for whatever you set out to create, you'll find a way to make it happen. For me, it was the idea of creating a product that not only helped raise world-conscious kids but also gave moms a small, happy, uplifting break. Because sometimes the constant crying/chaos/poo makes us forget we have the best job in the world.

Features to Consider
- ☆ Age appropriate
- ☆ High production quality
- ☆ Safe content
- ☆ Fully orchestrated music
- ☆ Soothing presentation
- ☆ Realistic promises
- ☆ Enjoyable for adults as well as children

NOTES: *DVDs and Videos*

Model Name / Manufacturer	Store/Price	My Impressions	Grade

Sixteen

High Chairs

Surprisingly, the high chair has changed very little in the last 200 years. The first high chairs were meant to be pushed right up to the table, then in the 19th century trays were added. Think modern design is so advanced? Some of the earliest surviving high chairs were clever convertible models that turned into a tiny table and chair for toddler . . . all the way back in the 1700s.

Of course today we have all the bells and whistles that built-in electronics and Microban bring, but you can find good, old-fashioned, stripped down, wooden varieties to choose from as well (see the next page for information on Microban). Modern-day high chair choices include full-size standard high chairs, compact high chairs, trayless table high chairs, booster high chairs, booster seats, and hook-on high chairs.

High Chair

Also Known As
Feeding chair, feeding seat, table chair, booster seat, booster high chair

Age Range
4 to 36 months

Total Usage
3-plus years

Recommendation
Must have

When to Buy
Wait until baby is ready to use it, otherwise you might end up storing a giant box for the better part of a year and might miss a pattern or design you like better.

186

What Is Microban?

Microban is an antibacterial protection technology that can be applied to plastics. It was developed in 1969 and first used in industrial and medical products. In 1994 it was introduced to more consumer products. Many baby products now have it built into their plastic components. It is now also the name of the company that makes most Microban additives.

While some critics doubt its effectiveness, the term has come to signify antibacterial, germ-fighting properties.

FULL-SIZE HIGH CHAIRS

The traditional full-size high chair has a tray and is made of wood, plastic, or metal. Styles vary wildly, however. The most common types look like seats perched on either four legs or two with curved bar legs, but a handful of new, round, pod-like chairs rise from a single foot and are designed to match more modern kitchens. While many fold for compact storage and have wheels, they are not considered portable outside your house. Features include reclining and height-adjustable seats, removable dishwasher-safe trays, and attachable toys.

Why we love them: We like giving baby his own space, especially when he's learning to feed himself. He can join us at the dinner table later, after he's stopped finger painting with spaghetti.

Why we don't: They're so big (and usually ugly), we can't wait for the day we can pack them up and ship them out of our kitchen!

COMPACT HIGH CHAIRS

Compact high chairs are full-featured high chairs minus the legs. Meant to be a kitchen-based space saver, they strap onto a regular dining chair, but still offer a large, usually reclining seat with five-point harness options for smaller babies, removable tray, and other full-size high chair conveniences such as dishwasher-safe trays and height-adjustable seats.

Why we love them: Back in the day when we actually had a free chair at our table, the compact high chair was a great way to save space but still give baby her own messing place.

Why we don't: We really do. Not having a giant high chair rolling around in our midst was wonderful.

TRAYLESS TABLE HIGH CHAIRS

While you can simply remove the tray and adjust the height on many standard, full-size high chairs, trayless table high chairs are specially designed to bring your tot tableside. Most resemble modern, wooden works of art with crazy angles and graceful bending curves. Meant for children that can sit up on their own (around 7 or 8 months), most table high chairs grow with your child and convert for use all the way to adulthood. Extra cushions are usually available for those who prefer a softer seat.

Why we love them: There's a giant swath of time between when our toddler refuses to be belted into a "baby" high chair and when he's big enough to sit on a regular kitchen chair. The trayless table high chairs fill that time beautifully (and so much better than a phone book!).

Why we don't: They're more modern looking than the rest of our house. Should we be embarrassed by this, or relieved?

Booster High Chairs

While booster high chairs are frequently called "booster seats" on the box, they really aren't just seats. In our mind, a booster seat is a simple seat that gives a toddler or bigger kid a boost. Booster high chairs are portable, usually foldable mini-high chairs that strap onto a regular chair and are meant for babies. Because they don't recline, they are meant for older babies with good head control, but they have the same age limit as most full-size high chairs. In other words, it's no boost for your preschooler. Booster high chairs are great travel chairs for babies who regularly use a full-size high chair. Perfect for vacation and Grandma's house and a wonderful alternative to oh-so-icky restaurant high chairs. We found a booster high chair with an electronic toy insert for the tray that has saved our lives in restaurants. We can actually leave the house again! Ah, small miracles!

Why we love them: It always bothered us that while we eat on plates in restaurants, our babies picked their food off the table. The disgusting, dirty table. And because our little Houdinis were all too adept at ripping table covers and tablecloths off—in fact, they delighted in it—a portable seat with a tray was the answer to our dine-out prayers.

Why we don't: The best ones—with a tray and attached toys—are a bit bulky to tote around. But well worth it!

Booster Seats

Like a fancy phone book, a booster seat is a simple, no-frills seat that raises the bums of older children. They are only seats: no trays and no toys. Some have safety straps, some are just free-floating seats, but all are meant for older toddlers to kindergartners. The beginning age range depends on the presence of safety straps.

Check the manufacturer's recommendation, but in general, a sturdy, solid booster with straps can be used at 12 months; less sturdy versions shouldn't be used until 18 months; those without straps are for 2 years and up. Booster seats are portable; some fold, some inflate, and others you just pick up and go. Many come with carrying totes. Booster seats range from solid-colored molded foam seats to patterned oilcloth seats that recall fun retro diners.

> *Why we love them:* A nice solid booster seat gives kids a prime place at the family table with a good view but the balance requirement that they sit relatively still. Kids on their knees don't learn good posture or good table manners.
>
> *Why we don't:* We don't like the flimsy, folding kind. They are a pain to assemble and don't work in restaurant booths. And the cutest solid boosters are pretty expensive, especially if you have more than one kid in that age range. But family dinnertime is important to us, so we pay. Begrudgingly, we pay.

P.S. Strapless seats made for *babies*, like the Bumbo, are not feeding chairs. While they are mistakenly labeled "booster seats" by some retailers, they are not ideal feeding solutions because they have no safety straps, should never be placed on a chair, and must stay on the floor. These "babysitters" are covered in Chapter 7, Bouncers, Rockers, and Infant Seats.

Hook-on High Chairs

A hook-on high chair is a small, portable seat that hooks or clamps onto the lip of a table-top. The hook-on high chair has no legs or tray; it is suspended entirely on the edge of the table. While some people profess to have good luck with these, we are not one of them. Hook-on high chairs only work for certain tables (firm, four-legged tables only) with a certain tabletop thickness (the perfect thickness, however, varies wildly for each hook-on high chair). They cannot be used on tables with extension flaps, slippery, uneven or glass tops, table with tablecloths, single pedestal tables, or those with wooden struts underneath—in other words, tables at more than half the restaurants we frequent. Other drawbacks to the hook-on high chair include metal pieces that can scratch a table, or rubber stoppers that prevent this but become choking hazards when they pop off. Some are hard to assemble; most are hard to clean. Hook-on high chairs are meant for older babies who can sit up unassisted but aren't too big to kick themselves free. And pay close attention to the weight limit of the chair, the weight of your baby, and the weight distribution of the table—a hook-on high chair could tip over an unsteady or too-light table.

Why we love them: We don't.

Why we don't: Babies can kick free? Flip entire tables over on themselves? Um, yeah, we're out.

Whichever type of high chair you choose—and if you're like us, you'll choose more than two—you'll want to be sure it passes muster for certain safety and convenience features.

Stability

Whether it's freestanding or meant to be clipped to a chair, and especially if it's to hold a younger baby, choose a solid, stable high chair. A good test? Try to knock it over. Give it a good shake. A good high chair will have a nice, wide base that doesn't tip easily.

Safety Straps and T-bars

Until babies can sit up on their own—about 7 or 8 months—they should be buckled into all gear, including high chairs, with a five-point, over-the-shoulder harness. A three-point harness is safer than a waist-only belt for older babies because of the extra strap that clips between the legs.

Regardless of how many points the strap has, the most important safety feature of any chair meant for babies under 3 is a T-bar. A T-bar is a piece of molded plastic that sits between baby's legs and prevents him from slipping out. T-bars are incredibly important because a baby that slips out from underneath the tray is at risk not just of falling but also of strangulation should he get stuck on the way down.

Most high chairs now come with T-bars, even portable boosters, but look for one with the T-bar attached to the seat, not the tray. T-bars protruding from the bottom of a tray will stop baby from sliding, but only when the tray is attached. You want the flexibility of being able to remove a tray for cleaning or loading and unloading baby without worrying about him falling out the second you turn your back. And an attached T-bar makes for a heavy, unwieldy, non-dishwasher-friendly tray.

All safety straps on your high chair should be thick, strong, and durable. Most are now made of webbed nylon for strength, but keeping all those tiny webbed holes clean is almost mission impossible. Our secret? Avoid snow-white straps. If you can, find straps that are an already dirty color like gray or off-white. In six months, you'll know why. Oh, you'll know why.

The Tray

We love trays because they provide a separate, sanitary eating space—vital for a baby, especially in restaurants. Some trays are dishwasher safe. Some come with covers to keep the tray clean until you use it. And some even come with a detachable tray of toys to entertain and distract baby.

What makes a good tray? It should be easy to get on and off, but not easy enough for babies to do it, especially when they kick like maniacs, as we promise, they will. One-handed release trays are a lifesaver, especially if you have your kid in the other hand, as we promise, you will. Look for a smooth surface with relatively few crevices that's easy to wipe down and has a bit of a lip to corral rolling Cheerios. And watch out for trays with big metal clamps or hinges that could pinch tiny fingers.

Try the tray release in the store. For a real world test, hold something large and breakable in one hand, have someone try to wrestle it from you while screaming and spitting in your face, and see how easily the tray releases with your free hand. Also note how heavy the tray is. A one-handed release tray is not helpful if the tray is so heavy it cracks your carpal tunnel–wracked wrist like a twig. A painful twig.

Attachable Toys

We suspect we love toys that distract our babies almost more than our babies do, but because they will be around food constantly, you want playthings that can be successfully cleaned and sanitized. As much as we loved the electronic flip book that attached to one of our trays, after three months of daily food fights, the speaker holes were full of crust, the paper stickers worn and peeling, and the on-off button almost caked shut. Yummy.

Just because the toys claim to be washable doesn't mean they are. It takes more than a little spit on a paper towel to remove dried banana (otherwise known as "baby glue"). Look for toys that can be scrubbed and disinfected without being destroyed. This means no paper stickers, no nooks and crannies, and for goodness sakes, no plush! What are manufacturers thinking, putting little stuffed creatures with yarn hair and felt bodies on baby high chairs? Soft fabric and baby food do not play well together. Also avoid those clear, plastic, hollow balls that spin and have little toys or mirrors inside, because they are most likely not waterproof. After we first washed ours, a couple of stray drops of water leaked in and never left. We simply got to watch in horror as the plastic ball became a little mold terrarium. Good for science. Bad for baby.

Cleaning

Considering how messy babies and toddlers are, how easy the entire high chair is to clean is of utmost importance. No one wants to cart around a crusty booster with Cheerios stuck in the crevices, and a green bean–covered high chair in your dining room is more than a little embarrassing when neighbors drop by unannounced (unless they bring dinner, and then we don't care what they see).

Give a high chair a common sense cleaning once-over: How easy is the entire thing to wipe down? Are all surfaces washable? How many cracks and crevices are there? Are any parts dishwasher safe? Note problem cleaning areas: metal hinges, joints of any kind, fabric, and straps.

If you can, avoid a hard-to-clean color palette. White fabric is an obvious nuisance—baby food and colored toddler drinks laugh at your "stain resistant" fabrics—but white plastic seems to also possess a spaghetti sauce–sucking

Must-have Accessory: High Chair Cover

We're not germ-a-phobes, but we do like to cover the public places our babies sit, especially during flu season and especially where babies are prone to slobber, put their hands in their mouths, and wipe their germ-filled spit all over the place (that is, where they eat).

That's why the high chair cover is our must-have accessory for dining out. It's a simple fabric cover that fastens over the entire top of a standard restaurant high chair and folds compactly for premium portability. Top features to look for include attached toys (nice), an easy-to-clean fabric (important), and slots that allow you to still use the high chair's safety straps (imperative).

property that leaves it mysteriously and permanently stained. Spending even five minutes scrubbing a baby product is four minutes more than we ever have.

Seat Comfort

There seems to be an inverse correlation between how comfortable a high chair seat is and how easy it is to clean. Bare wooden seats wipe clean in an instant, but don't provide much cushion to bony little bums. Plush fabric seats cradle baby, but even if the fabric is machine washable, products that create more laundry are not our friend. Vinyl seats seem to be the middle ground mainstay, offering a bit of cush and easy cleaning. Make sure the seams don't present sharp edges. Run your hand over any seat to check for scratchy surfaces, splinters, or super evil seams.

Height Adjustment

Because both babies and moms come in all sizes, many high chairs have height adjustment features that allow you to drop the seat farther below the tray, better align the seat next to a table, and even turn a full-size high chair into a closer-to-floor toddler seat.

Reclining Seats

It might not seem like a necessity because now pediatricians don't recommend solid foods until 6 months and by then baby can sit up just fine, but a reclining seat is great not just for babies who can hold their own bottle (finally!), but also for older babies who literally fall asleep on their grilled cheese. Believe us, it happens. And it's a wonderful, wonderful day. A few quiet clicks, baby is reclined, the napping is secured, and we're free for a solid 20 minutes to bask in our gossip magazine. Oh, heaven, thy name is *Us Weekly* . . .

Wheels

For in-house mobility, many high chairs now have wheels. Look for ones with locks to prevent accidents and runaway babies. And be careful with wheels on soft wood floors as the buggers do scratch! We learned the (sob!) hard way.

Locks

If the high chair folds for storage or portability, check that it locks well both in the closed and open position. Chairs that aren't tightly clamped into a folded position but flop all over are more than a small pain to deal with. And chairs that don't lock open securely are a giant safety hazard.

P.S. Stay on top of safety recalls for your high chair, as they are recalled frequently for nasty problems like folding in on seated babies.

Convertibility

Many high chairs and booster seats offer features that extend their age range. Seats for babies become toddler chairs. Seats for toddlers can be used for bigger kids. There are even high chairs that come apart and turn into child-size chairs and tiny tables.

Whether you choose a convertible model depends on how long you want to use your high chair, how many kids you plan on using it for, and, of course, your budget.

Just remember that a convertible model might follow one child as she grows, but is likely to be facing retirement by the time another baby comes along because it has been abused for more years than a regular high chair. If you plan on having more than one child, it's probably easier and cheaper to find new seating for your older child than it will be to buy a whole new high chair for the new baby.

Price

The price range on high chairs is great, from $29 budget picks to $600 designer works of art. The span on mid-range full-size high chairs is still pretty big: from $69 to $129. More money will get you more features, more durability, and sadly, nicer patterns. Ask yourself how long you want the high chair to last. If you have the budget and plan on more kids, you might want to invest in a nicer chair. We're not going to lie: a $50 model is not going to make it to your next baby, at least not aesthetically. Not by a long shot. We thought our first high chairs held up pretty well . . . until we had our husbands pull them out of storage. The scratches, the fading, the crumbs, oh my! Those high chairs made a quick one-way trip to the trash.

Age and Weight Limits

Every chair has them. Heed them.

Features to Consider

- ☆ Stability
- ☆ Five-point or three-point harness
- ☆ T-bar
- ☆ Tray
- ☆ Tray release and weight
- ☆ Attached toys
- ☆ Easy to clean
- ☆ Seat comfort
- ☆ Seat recline
- ☆ Height adjustment
- ☆ Age and weight limits

NOTES: *High Chairs*

Model Name / Manufacturer	Store/Price	My Impressions	Grade

Seventeen

Humidifiers and Air Purifiers

When we're sick, we want our mom. When our kids are sick, maybe because we're still in shock that we're "the mom," we want our mom. Lucky for us, our mom is a doctor, triple board-certified in pediatrics, neonatology, and pediatric emergency medicine. Really. (Yeah, you're jealous, but you wouldn't have been the day she found out we weren't going to be doctors. "Entrepreneur? Writer? Marvelous . . .")

Our doctor mom's advice on the most "must-have" item in this entire book is the humidifier. Because young children get an average of six to eight colds and upper respiratory tract infections each year, and because breathing humid air helps them breathe easier, we might have to agree. (On this. Not on the whole life choices thing.)

Simply put, humidifiers increase the humidity in a room. They add moisture to the air in all manners of ways: vaporizers boil the water into

Humidifier

Also Known As
Vaporizers

Age Range
Birth to 36 months

Total Usage
3-plus years

Recommendation
Must have

When to Buy
Before baby is born. Great registry item.

vapor, impellers run water through a rapidly turning disk, evaporative systems use a foam wick and a fan to draw water out of a reservoir, and ultrasonic humidifiers use vibration to create tiny droplets.

What about Adding Medicine to Humidifiers?

Proponents of warm mist humidifiers argue that you can only add medicine to warm mist models, thereby making them more effective. Dr. Mom assures us, however, that there are no prescription medications for humidifier dispersal.

What's more, over-the-counter humidifier-friendly add-ins can be harmful to small babies. Most contain camphor and menthol, which is highly poisonous to small children. If you use these products, read the label and age limits carefully and keep the product well out of your child's reach. Vapor products made just for babies are camphor- and menthol-free and usually just made of aromatic ingredients such as lavender oil.

Humidifier or Vaporizer?

Originally, the word "humidifier" was used to denote cool mist, and "vaporizer" hot steam, but the terms have become completely interchangeable. Because you can find both labels on both hot and cold moisture producers, we recommend ignoring these two words completely. Because they all make a room more humid, whatever you call them, they are "humidifiers."

Warm or Cool Mist?

Regardless of what the product is called or how it works, there is only one phrase you should be searching for on the box: "warm mist" or "cool mist." You want cool mist. Trust us.

The myth that warm air humidifiers work better has probably been propagated this long because we all have fond memories—or have been reminded by our parents as they recalled their years of sacrifice and toil on our behalf— of being holed up in a steamy hot bathroom when we were sick in the chest. The fact is our parents had no other way to make steam except from a hot showerhead. We now have cooler options.

Our medical mama assures us that while the biggest medical benefit of humidifiers comes from the moisture and not the temperature, cool mist is the most helpful for soothing inflamed membranes because cold contracts. Likewise, because a fever usually accompanies the illnesses that require a humidifier, choosing a model that heats up a child even more isn't a great idea. And of course, regardless of how "warm" the output is, the water inside a warm humidifier is hot . . . *boiling* hot. Boiling hot + nursery = bad idea. Especially if you have one of those toddling types.

It turns out the entire American Academy of Pediatrics agrees with our mom. Its official recommendation is a cool mist humidifier.

Of course, some packaging makes it difficult to discern which is which. If it doesn't explicitly advertise that it's "cool mist," it's probably warm. Other key words that denote a warm mist humidifier are "boil" and "steam." If a humidifier is "ultrasonic," it's cool mist.

Here are the other major differences between warm and cold mist models, along with their pros and cons.

WARM MIST HUMIDIFIERS/VAPORIZERS

Warm mist humidifiers boil water using a heating element and then send it out as either hot steam or slightly cooled warm mist. Because they use a heating element, they also use a lot of electricity and can be very expensive to operate. And while boiling the water first does cut down on the possibility of spraying germs that might have collected inside the tank, hot muggy rooms invite more bacteria growth in carpets, on drapes, and in bedding. Because electrical appliances with heating elements are also prone to become fire hazards when they fail, it's not surprising that tens of thousands of warm mist humidifiers have been recalled through the years.

Why we love them: We don't. We hate them. Can't you tell?

Why we don't: More than anything, we hate using electric plug-in things in the nursery. Especially hot things. Mechanical things fail all the time. And when they do, we'd rather they didn't have a white-hot electrical heating element next to a giant tank of water in our baby's bedroom.

COOL MIST HUMIDIFIERS/VAPORIZERS

Cool mist humidifiers use a fan or vibrations to break water down into tiny or even micro droplets. Because there is no boiling, many parents are afraid that cool mist humidifiers can become breeding grounds for mold and bacteria in their tanks. But with filter advancements, germ infestation should not be an issue as long as you empty and clean the humidifier frequently according to the manufacturer's instructions.

Why we love them: They bring almost instant relief. We'd give anything to help our poor sick babies. Yay, cool mist humidifiers!

Why we don't: It's a total pain in the butt cleaning them every day. But so is changing our kids' diapers and we do it anyway because we care about their well-being (and the way our house smells, of course).

Special Medical Conditions

No matter how you do it, adding moisture to a room can roll out the welcome mat for uninvited guests: mold and bacteria. This can be especially bad news for children with certain medical conditions, such as asthma. If your child has any chronic respiratory difficulties or special medical needs, consult your pediatrician before making any humidifier or air purifier purchase.

Ultrasonic Humidifiers

Ultrasonic humidifiers are cool mist humidifiers that use an ultrasonic vibration to break down water into its finest form, releasing a cool fog. These new humidifiers produce the most moisture with the least maintenance. Many high-end models have antibacterial features built in, such as ultraviolet lights to kill bacteria. They operate silently, which is nice, but we actually miss the white noise of our old units. However, we don't miss how they break down and mold up.

Which Water?

When you add water to a humidifier, minerals in the water can be left behind, collecting and coating the inside of the machine. This white dust can eventually build up and shorten the life span of your product, but it can also loosen and then be dispersed into the air via the humidifier's spray, potentially irritating small, sensitive lungs.

To avoid this, many manufacturers recommend filling the humidifier with low mineral water. Because the mineral content of tap water varies depending upon where you live, you might want to consider using distilled water or filtering your tap water with a faucet filter, such as Brita or Pur.

If you don't want to deal with special water, look for a humidifier with a demineralization cartridge. These cartridges stop limescale and mineral residue buildup, but they do need to be replaced, usually once a season.

If you already have a faucet filter, this is the cheapest and easiest option. Distilled water costs about $1 a gallon; replacement demineralization cartridges are usually between $6 and $12 each. The more expensive option depends on how often you use your humidifier, but we've found that keeping distilled water on hand for an unexpected illness is the bigger pain.

Filters

Filters help prevent dust, germs, and minerals from being sprayed into the air and should be considered the must-have accessory for any humidifier.

Of course, not all filters are the same. Choose a humidifier that can be easily accessed and easily cleaned or replaced, with replacement filters that aren't too hard to find or too expensive. We've had to retire more than a few humidifiers before their time because we could no longer find replacement filters. We usually buy two or three extra filters on the spot whenever we buy a new humidifier.

Our favorite humidifiers have built-in, permanent filters that never need replacing.

Humidifier Drying Tip

The humidifier has to be bone dry before you pack it away, and for most people that means having it sit upside down in the bathtub for three days while it air dries.

A great shortcut? After you've wiped the inside of your humidifier as dry as you can, use a hairdryer on the heat setting to blow dry the inner nooks and crannies. The heat is bad for germs and the quick dry is good for you and your nightly bubble baths.

Just make sure to keep the nozzle of the hair dryer at least six inches away from the humidifier's opening so you don't short out your hair's best friend. (We learned the hard way that if you completely restrict the air flow of a hair dryer by say sticking the nozzle completely in a wet shoe, you can burn out the motor, or worse, so use caution!)

Germ Protection

Germs love wet things, and your humidifier will likely get wet in places you can't even reach. Your first line of defense against microorganisms making a home in your humidifier is to follow the manufacturer's directions and clean and sanitize it regularly.

Many humidifiers offer even more germ protection built right in, from Microban protection to nano silver technology (a process that uses electrolytic silver nanoparticles to destroy bacteria), to prevent the growth of tiny bacteria beasties. All good.

Cleaning and Maintenance

No matter how "carefree" the humidifier might pretend to be, they all need regular cleaning. We know it's a total pain, but so are most of our household appliances. And unlike the crust in the bottom drawer of our fridge that doesn't hurt anybody, the germs in the humidifier are spraying into our already-sick kid's face. So we do make the time for this chore. The good news is that some units are easier to clean than others. Some have so many ridiculous, time-consuming, complicated steps that involve distilled white vinegar, bleach, and boiling water, you half expect to need "eye of newt and toe of frog." Others pop right into the dishwasher. Guess which we prefer?

How do you tell in the store which are easy to clean? You might have to open the box and dig out the directions. It embarrasses our husbands no end when we rip open packaging, but we firmly believe there's no shame in kicking the tires before you buy.

Price and Reliability

Humidifiers range in price from $30 to $300. More expensive models do come with better features and more convenient cleaning options, but look for the hidden costs of replacement parts and filters as well. We've found good, mid-range humidifiers generally cost about $60.

We're not going to lie; humidifiers don't last forever. In fact, many don't last long at all. We're heavy humidifier users and have one for each kid's room, and we still usually end up buying at least one new one every year. And that can be expensive.

We've tried it from both angles: cheap ones that don't last very long but are cheaper to replace, and more expensive models that will presumably hang around longer. We actually have both. The more expensive models do have better features and last longer . . . until the inevitable day we completely forget about it, leave it full somewhere, allow an entire mold colony to flourish, and have to pitch the whole giant expensive thing.

We've resigned ourselves to the yearly cost, and chalk it up to medical care. However, because it is an electrical appliance, don't push your luck. If your humidifier starts making noise or smelling funny, toss it out immediately. It's not worth the risk!

Humidity Control

Many humidifiers now give you the option of controlling or measuring their moisture output. Some include mechanical or digital humidistats and even offer timed humidifying.

Being able to control the output is nice, because you don't want to over-humidify a room and invite bacteria or mold growth. A warning sign that a room is too humid is water condensation on the windows, pictures, furniture, or walls.

Other Features

Humidifiers come in all shapes and sizes; some even look like licensed characters or zoo animals. While nice for grade school siblings, we personally don't want to draw toddlers' attention to electrical appliances, so we opt for serious-looking models. We can get our cute fix from hundreds of other products that don't plug in.

Other features include auto shut-off and filter cleaning indicator lights. Because we don't relish crashing into it in the dark of night, our absolute favorite humidifier feature is the night-light or glow-in-the-dark tank.

Whichever model you choose, the tank should be relatively easy to refill.

Placement

It's recommended that you place a humidifier at least three feet from your child, in a location where it's not easily knocked over.

And before you perch it on an expensive dresser, we'll let you in on a little secret about humidifiers: they leak. Frequently. Even the best, most expensive ones. We don't know why we're always surprised when they do, because they're not yachts—they're cheap plastic, removable tanks—but we've not only ruined dresser tops but actually permanently buckled the wood floor beneath carpet and needed quite costly renovations after a particularly insidious leaking event. (The unit leaked for weeks and we didn't notice. I claim severe sleep deprivation and sick-kid-induced stress.)

You might consider getting a drip pan, similar to the ones they make for washing machines or barbecues. We did.

P.S. A leak can also be quite dangerous because it wets the floor around an electrical appliance. When you're approaching a humidifier all stressed out and groggy, don't automatically grab for the plug. Check for leaks around your bare feet first.

WATERLESS VAPORIZERS

Don't be fooled. These units, also called "vapor plugs" or "aromatherapy diffusers" have nothing to do with adding humidity to a room. They are heater units that warm vapor pads to release their scent.

Why we love them: While we're not big on plugging anything into the nursery, this seemed like the safest way to disperse vapor products . . .

Why we don't: . . . until we learned that 15,000 waterless vaporizers were recalled in 2005 because, as stated by the official CPSC recall notice, a defective internal heater could cause "sparking and emit flames while in use." Yeah, we're going to stick with our no-plugs-in-the-nursery theory.

NURSERY AIR PURIFIERS

Air purifiers have been around for years, but they are suddenly being sold as ideal nursery accessories. We disagree. There's nothing ideal about plugging unnecessary products into your baby's nursery, and from what we can tell, nursery air purifiers are unnecessary.

There is debate as to whether they actually purify the air, and concern over the methods they use to do so. Some experts have warned against ionic air purifiers and ozone generators because they take in air and then release air with negative ions; others have said they're fine. Here's our rule of thumb: if the expert jury is still out, so are we.

A cheaper alternative is to simply change (or upgrade!) the filters on your house's furnace system regularly. Other clean air options include furnace add-ons that filter even more indoor particles, and individual register filters you can add to each room's vents.

Why we love them: Purer air is good.

Why we don't: You can get purer air for free from a plant, and plants don't accidentally set your nursery on fire.

Features to Consider
- ☆ Cool mist
- ☆ Ultrasonic
- ☆ Filter
- ☆ Filter replacements
- ☆ Easy to clean
- ☆ Price
- ☆ Humidity control
- ☆ Auto shut-off

NOTES: *Humidifers and Air Purifiers*

Model Name / Manufacturer	Store/Price	My Impressions	Grade

Eighteen

Layette, or Bitty Baby Clothes and Linens

"Layette" is one of those old-fashioned words steeped in historical mystery like "trousseau"— a magical combination of items you need to collect before you can be a proper bride or new mother.

Hearing the word when we were pregnant made us feel as domestic as Laura Ingalls Wilder or Meg March; we couldn't wait to learn the secret numbers of things we needed to join the mommy club. We were a little disappointed to learn that there is no perfect combination or set number of things. We perked up when we discovered the tiny treasures moms collect before their babies are born are indeed magical.

Layette

Age Range
Birth to 6 months

Total Usage
2 weeks to 6 months, depending on item

Recommendation
Must have

When to Buy
Before and even after your baby is born. Any day, every day. Great shopping for when you're having a bad day.

Today "layette" is used much more generically—even as section signs in department stores—to mean any soft fabric item you would dress or wrap a newborn in. It can refer to clothes, blankets, and socks just as easily as burp clothes and lap pads. Technically layette items are for birth to 3 months, but some retailers include items for use at up to 6 and even 12 months.

Because modern layette items are so varied, and because moms live in various climates, what you need and how many is totally up to you. It's a bit of a guessing game, of course, but every list with specific numbers we've ever seen was dead wrong (and ended up costing us beaucoup bucks because we bought six sleeping gowns, eight hats, and five receiving blankets six months out that we never used and couldn't return), so we're not going to presume to tell you how many you need of what. We *will* tell you what everything is and offer tips on what to look for in each category and general advice we've gleaned from the trash bags full of unused baby items we've donated to Goodwill.

ONESIES/BODYSUITS

Onesies are so named because they are one-piece outfits that have no legs, almost like a little swimsuit for baby. They can be short- or long-sleeved; they cover the belly and snap shut between the legs. Onesies are a staple of most baby wardrobes, worn alone in the summer or under pants in the winter, because they stay "tucked in." Babies can't wear onesies until their umbilical cord falls off (so don't get any too small) but can be used up to toddlerhood.

Why we love them: They keep baby all nice and neat, tucked in and warm.

Why we don't: Add pants and you've got a double-snapping hassle every diaper change.

DIAPER COVERS

Diaper covers look like granny underpants and are worn over the diaper for pretty much no reason other than to cover the diaper. While they used to be mainly for dress-wearing baby girls, they are now used for both genders, frequently paired with a onesie or baby tee, especially in the summer. They usually have designs on the butt, which sounds cute but isn't until they can crawl. Until then, babies are sitting on those designs. Diaper covers for girls often have frills or rows of lace that up their cuteness factor by five.

Why we love them: They are super cute and our diapers are not.

Why we don't: They pull on over the diaper, so they have to be pulled off every diaper change.

BABY TEES

Short- or long-sleeved, the thing to look for in a baby tee is a wide neck opening. Our babies always had giant noggins and having to force too-tight necks over their too-big heads wasn't fun for either of us. Some tees have little shoulder flaps that allow for the easiest dressing and undressing. Kimono or wrap-style tees have a snap or tie at the side so you can put them on like a coat rather than over the head. Great for fussy babies and those hanging onto their umbilical stumps for dear life.

Why we love them: They go with anything: skirts, shorts, pants, diaper covers, and naked butts that figured out how to undress themselves from the waist down and run around the house all hysterical-like.

Why we don't: They can ride up and expose the belly, unlike a more secure onesie. But they're still super cute.

ONE-PIECE SLEEPERS

Sleepers are technically one piece like a onesie, but the big difference is they have legs. Sleepers can be short- or long-sleeved, but they go all the way to the ankle and sometimes the toes. Some sleepers have attached feet, some don't. The little feet sections tend to run small and pinch babies with pudgy ankles; they also don't keep baby toes super warm, so in the winter we add socks inside as well. They are super great at keeping those socks on. Sleepers either snap all the way down the body or zip. (Don't accidentally buy one that zippers up the back, as they are physically impossible to deal with.) Some sleepers come with collars, which are cute, but collars do tend to flip up into baby's face quite frequently and become hard and crusty after a few hours of slobber.

Why we love them: Babies are all warm and cuddly in their sleepers. Perfect for snuggling.

Why we don't: Changing baby means exposing his entire body to cold air blasts, which he will not like.

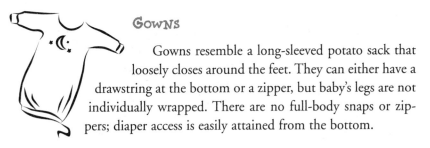

Gowns

Gowns resemble a long-sleeved potato sack that loosely closes around the feet. They can either have a drawstring at the bottom or a zipper, but baby's legs are not individually wrapped. There are no full-body snaps or zippers; diaper access is easily attained from the bottom.

Why we love them: While some people profess to love them, gowns are a mystery to us. Our babies always kicked like maniacs trying to get the weird blanket thing off their feet. And we don't blame them.

Why we don't: Babies' legs aren't tightly wrapped and drafts get in, so they are cold. If we have to layer other clothes inside, then our easy diaper-changing access is ruined, so what's the point?

Sleep Sacks/Sleeping Bags/ Wearable Blankets

Because loose bedding is thought to be a cause of SIDS, babies now wear their blankets in the form of sleep sacks, which look like a cross between a gown (on top) and a sleeping bag (on bottom). Meant to be worn over their pajamas, sleep sacks resemble gowns except they are usually thicker and warmer, and completely close around baby's feet. There are long-sleeved and no-sleeved tank-top versions, but the long sleeves raise worries of babies putting a fleecy arm to their face and having breathing issues. You want a snug sleep sack that doesn't have too much extra fabric that can ride up around baby's face, but watch out for too tight arm holes. Some have adjustable shoulder straps to accommodate all sizes. To aid in diaper changes, some have inverted zippers while others have a separate zipper that zips along the very bottom. There are thick fleece ones for cold nights and thinner cotton ones for warmer nights, but layer babies accordingly to avoid overheating them.

Why we love them: We love anything that helps prevent SIDS.

Why we don't: Prepare to pay. While we can find sleepers for $5, sleep sacks start at $20. And because they get just as dirty as pajamas and need to be washed frequently, we needed to buy quite a few. We'd pay anything for the safety of our babies, but something tells us we're the ones getting fleeced on sleep sack pricing.

BABY MITTENS

Baby mittens have nothing to do with the snow, and everything to do with scratches. Thin cotton mittens—usually with cute designs on them—are meant to cover baby's hands to keep them from scratching their cute little faces with their microscopic but razor-sharp nails. Because baby's hands sweat, don't get ones that are too thick. And because baby is still growing, don't get ones that are too small or leave them on too long at one time.

Why we love them: Aside from the scratch prevention, we love them for their germ protection. For some reason, complete strangers in public love to grab newborn baby hands. Baby hands go in baby mouth and germs have a field day. Baby mittens not only stop the germs, but for some reason, they usually stop the crazies from even attempting to touch our babies.

Why we don't: Just like socks, we seem to keep losing just one.

Socks

Buy socks one size bigger than you think you'll need, because they run very small, and in the wash they make like Shrinky Dinks. Also multiply how many you thought you might need by three. The trick is to get socks tight enough that they aren't kicked off every five seconds, but not too tight that they leave zigzag imprints in your baby's ankles. Nonslip designs on the soles are a must for tiny walkers, but can get in the way of shoes for non-walkers. Slipper socks are thicker than regular socks, but if you use them over bare feet, check for rough seams and scratchy bits inside.

Why we love them: Is anything cuter than little baby socks? We say no. They even have little socks that look like little Mary Janes or sneakers.

Why we don't: Most baby socks don't wash well. They snag and ball and sometimes look like crap after just a single wash. They also get sucked into that secret place in your washing machine at a ratio of one lost for every seven washed. Some socks now come with their own little wash bags, or you can just throw them into your lingerie bag for safekeeping.

Receiving Blankets

A receiving blanket is just like a regular blanket except that it's smaller and thinner. Usually square shaped, although that isn't a rule, receiving blankets can be made of any fabric, although breathable 100 percent cotton is best. Receiving blankets are especially useful around newborns because they can be used not just for warmth, but for swaddling, shielding the sun on strollers, impromptu playmates, changing, and more. Save your fluffy, satin-edged blankets for snuggling, but look for a stack of receiving blankets that you can abuse and that will wash well.

Why we love them: You can use a receiving blanket for anything and forever—a nursing cover today, a teepee tomorrow, a Halloween costume in five years.

Why we don't: The one thing they don't excel at is giving a lot of warmth because they are pretty thin.

SWADDLING BLANKETS

After being smushed in the womb for nine months, babies like to be as cozy as possible the first few weeks of their lives. And as seasoned moms will tell you, the secret to a good sleeper is in the swaddling! Of course you can swaddle a baby in any blanket, but swaddling blankets have an elongated shape, extra fabric, and special fastening systems to make it easier for mom to do and harder for baby to undo.

Choose a swaddling blanket free of scratchy patches or ill-placed Velcro that might nick baby. You can get unbleached, organic cotton swaddling blankets for extra sensitive skin.

Why we love them: The only thing better than a baby is a sleeping baby. And things that make it easier to get a sleeping baby are high on our list of favorites.

Why we don't: Swaddling blankets serve a special and limited purpose for just the first few months. Some babies get sick of swaddling after the first few weeks, so if you are going to invest in a swaddling blanket, we recommend just one until you discover your baby's unique desires.

BURP CLOTHS

Burp cloths are not so much for the burp, but for what the burp brings up. Burp cloths are simply pieces of fabric that parents throw over their shoulder when burping a baby to save their own clothes from spit-up. There are two kinds: pretty decorative ones shaped like a hot dog for shoulder use only, and generic white square ones that can be used as a baby rag for any mess. Burp cloths can be made of any fabric, as long as it's machine washable. Standard burp cloths are actually cloth diapers, but the fashion-conscious gal who even likes her rags to look nice can choose quilted, personalized, and ruffled-edged ones.

Why we love them: We hate what we ended up using them for, but we're glad to spare our kitchen and bath linen just the same.

Why we don't: We actually love these things. We have generic ones and decorative ones. Stacks and stacks. When they become too stained and embarrassing to be used around our babies, our husbands commandeer them for the garage.

LAP PADS

Lap pads are waterproof pads meant to be placed under baby to catch leaks. They are frequently used as changing pads, although some moms place them in car seats, swings, and strollers (you can also get customized waterproof pads to fit those products, but they are more expensive). Look for a lap pad with at least a small amount of cushion that can absorb some wetness. Lap pads aren't really useful if liquid yuck hits a piece of waterproof vinyl and just bounces off to somewhere else.

Why we love them: What's not to love about a cheap, waterproof rag?

Why we don't: They are usually ugly sherbet colors, and multipacks all too often include pink in every bag. Great if you have a girl; not so great if you have a boy and a super masculine husband.

BATH TOWELS AND ROBES

Baby bath towels and bath robes are just like regular towels and robes, except they're itty-bitty and usually have a hood. They come in all colors, fabrics, and sizes. Check for rough seams, especially on the back side of embroidery, which will be rubbed against baby's bare skin, and get the softest, plushest one you can possibly find.

Why we love them: We're suckers for anything baby size, and these are no exception.

Why we don't: You can actually just use a regular-size towel for your baby, and baby robes are equally optional. We loved our tiny robes, but our babies literally wore them for all of two minutes. You tend to dress babies after a bath rather quickly to keep them from getting cold, and putting them into a robe only to take them right back out again is more of a pain than anything.

WASHCLOTHS

There are two kinds of baby washcloths: nice ones for the bath, and crappy ones for the butt. The bath kind is self-explanatory and totally optional; you can use a regular washcloth just as easily. Baby washcloths are smaller, which is easier, but they aren't necessities in any way. (There are disposable baby washcloths meant for the bath, but we're going to have to call those out as one of the dumbest products ever. We're lazy, but even we aren't that shamefully wasteful.) The crappy kind of washcloths are for early diaper changes. To keep tiny bums irritation-free, pediatricians now recommend you don't start using diaper wipes until the second month to spare a new babe from the chemicals. This makes for more than a little inconvenience and a lot of mess. Most moms buy a couple of packs of thin, cheap washcloths to use with water for cleaning baby after each dirty diaper. We stocked up like it was the end of the world because some poopy just doesn't wash out of the little cloths, and some begged an immediate trip to the trash.

> *Why we love them:* OK, we take it back, we don't love every single baby-size thing. Tiny washcloths are useful, but we still have trouble managing them during the first month of diaper changes.
>
> *Why we don't:* You can only fold the tiny washcloth so many times to find a clean side. Some diaper changes required three washcloths! And then, where do you set them? On the changing table? In the trash? You can't leave baby unattended. We need a better system!

Quantity

While it can be tempting, don't buy too many of any one item before your baby is born unless you enjoy wasting money. Until you get in a groove with your newborn, you won't know what the perfect number of onesies, lap pads, and socks really is.

If you're worried about not having a well-stocked nursery the day you come home from the hospital, save the bulk of your purchases until just before your baby is born, shop at a store with a long return period, and save your receipts. Most importantly, resist tearing everything open as soon as you get home, washing them, and putting them away. Wash just the bare minimum until you get a better picture of your needs. While your neighbor might have scared you about how bedridden you'll be after birth, in most cases, you will definitely be up and doing laundry within a couple of weeks. Sadly, doing laundry. More laundry than you ever thought possible.

Machine Washable

Verify that everything you buy for a baby is machine washable. Regardless of what the tag says, we usually wash all baby clothes on the delicate cycle, as they are more prone to snags, tears, and shrinking. When you are washing baby clothes, zip all zippers, snap all snaps, and buckle overalls to keep pieces intact and from attacking each other.

We usually wash baby clothes separately for at least a year because they can be destroyed by the zippers and hooks on adult clothes and swallowed up by sheets and such.

Special Detergents

Because more and more babies are born with allergies, eczema, and other sensitivities, we believe in keeping chemicals away from our newborns as long as possible. We use specially formulated baby detergent for the first year.

Sizing

The sizing of baby layette items varies wildly. Some are "one size fits all," others are grouped into ages, and most also list weight. The labels are just best-guess estimates for a typical baby and should not be taken as gospel. The same baby might wear a 6-month onesie, a 3-month pair of pants, and a medium sleep sack. If possible, shop by the weight of your baby, not the age.

Scratchy Items

While embroidery is super cute on baby clothes and blankets, check that it's not scratchy on the inside. We've bought more than one adorable outfit we had to take back when we discovered the gorgeous decoration on the outside was a war zone on the inside.

Run your hand over all parts of baby layette items, both inside and out, to check for any spots that might scratch baby's thin, sensitive skin. Look for rough seams, knotted thread, and evil tags.

Diaper Friendly

Because you'll change diapers more than any other activity, every piece of baby clothing should be diaper-change friendly. If you have to fasten 22 snaps around the legs every change, you're not going to be a happy mama after the 14th diaper.

Snaps and Zippers

Speaking of snaps, test them in the store before you buy. Nothing is more aggravating than an entire outfit ruined because of the snap. There are good snaps and bad snaps. Some won't close securely and pop open too easily. Sometimes the snap-stamping machine in the factory gathered too much fabric around the snap to allow for a solid connection, but sometimes it's just a crappy snap. Some snaps are too tightly sealed, and the repeated yanking causes the fabric around them to tear.

Also test zippers for easy threading and sliding, but also for sharp edges. Some open zippers have razor-sharp teeth that are no good for new babies.

Features to Consider

☆ Machine washable

☆ Free of scratchy parts

☆ Diaper-change friendly

☆ Good snaps and zippers

NOTES: *Layette*

Model Name / Manufacturer	Store/Price	My Impressions	Grade

Nineteen

Mobiles

Every photo of a beautiful nursery we've ever seen includes a sweet mobile that neatly coordinates with the crib bedding and room décor. We killed ourselves trying to find that perfect mobile and have it all set up for the day baby came home from the hospital. What a waste of time and money!

For starters, most babies spend the first three months of life in a bassinet in their parents' room. By the time your baby is old enough to sleep in her own crib—and you're ready (deep breath!) to let her cry herself to sleep—you're going to want a serious mobile that helps you in the battle of tears. And stuffed pink bears just won't cut it.

We didn't know it at the time, but there are actually two types of mobile on the market: the sweet, but relatively useless, decorative mobile and the stimulating, but rather ugly, developmental mobile.

Mobile

Age Range
Birth to 5 months

Total Usage
5 months

Recommendation
Nice to have

When to Buy
Whenever you see one you like. Great registry item.

DECORATIVE MOBILES

Like a Hollywood starlet, the decorative mobile's main job is to just look cute. Yes, they do coordinate with our crib bedding, but that's about all they do. Decorative mobiles typically share the same design: white, plastic arms arch up from a simple music box to dangle stuffed things overhead. The music boxes are very basic; they operate by manual wind-up, play one simple tune (usually Brahms' Lullaby), and wind down after about three minutes. The stuffed things are usually animals, sports items, or things you'd find on a baby wallpaper border, such as boats. They are usually pastel colors your baby probably can't see and are usually not even pointed down toward your baby.

Why we love them: They match our dust ruffle.

Why we don't: They really just collect dust.

DEVELOPMENTAL MOBILES

Developmental mobiles are specially designed to provide various stimuli for a baby. And sadly, there's nothing decorative about them. Equipped with multiple songs, sound effects, remote controls, and visually stimulating colors and patterns, most convert to crib toys when your baby can sit up, extending their usefulness by several months. Some play light shows on the ceiling. Some even shake up the old circular orbit by sending the stuffed toys on sliding, more unexpected paths. "Unplugged" developmental mobiles without music or effects simply allow patterned objects to dangle from minimalist fishing line structures that blow in the slightest breeze.

Why we love them: If you can get past the fantasy of bears wearing tutus and can live with Technicolor creatures, we recommend a developmental, multiuse mobile. It's not going to be pretty. But then again, neither is a screaming baby at 2 a.m. . . .

Why we don't: Did we say "not pretty"? Try inexplicably, horribly ugly. We hate how the chunky plastic mobiles look, but we can't live without their music and distracting tricks.

What about White Noise?

White noise—which technically means random noise patterns, but which many parents use to refer to soft, continuous, background noise—has long been used as a fussy baby sleep aid. Until a single study with rats in 2003 got everyone all aflutter.

The media headlined the study's conclusion that white noise machines might impair a baby's hearing. And many popular baby "experts" jumped on the panic band wagon and warned parents against using white noise for their babies.

We've studied the study (published in the journal *Science* on April 18, 2003), and we don't think there's any cause for alarm. Here's why: the study showed that baby rats subjected to continuous white noise loud enough to drown out all other environmental noise had hearing delays. You don't say. The ears of any creature subjected to an audible assault would eventually adapt to block it out. And true enough, when the white noise torture tests were stopped, the baby rats' hearing was restored to regular levels.

As long as your baby is exposed to other normal environmental sounds throughout the day, we don't see any reason why you can't continue to use white noise machines, ceiling fans, humidifiers, or any other soothing background enhancements to help your baby sleep. Just don't overdo it, don't subject your baby to any noise too loud, and stop reading scary stories on the Internet. No, really, stop. It will make you crazy, and half of it's not true anyway. At least, that's what our avatar told us.

Baby's Point of View

Regardless of whether your style is more Calder or caterpillar, check that the mobile you choose is actually aimed at your baby. Be sure the images can be seen fully from directly underneath, not just the sides and seams. Testing for this is easy. Simply hold the mobile directly over your own head, employ some of your Pilates to angle a peek from the store's display crib, or look for a box with really good pictures and use your imagination.

Music

Because most of the time a baby spends in her crib is in the dark, what a mobile sounds like can be more important than how it looks. Pick music as rich and varied as possible. A single tune tinkling from a crappy speaker will drive your baby as bonkers as you. When shopping for a mobile, good music is one of our most important criteria.

Music is everything because it's the one part you can't replace. I once bought a mobile that featured scary—seriously scary—bird-like creatures because the music box was the best on the market. Because I couldn't let those birdie things give my baby nightmares, I bought another mobile with animals I liked but a stinky music system, cut some strings, tied some knots, and made my own mobile creation. It turned out to be the best mobile ever. Of course, if you're going to pull a Martha Stewart in your baby's nursery, always make sure to follow proper safety guidelines—no strings less than seven inches in length, no small pieces baby could choke on, no sharp edges or pointed posts, and so on.

What makes for good music? A big selection—think more than 10—of varied songs that are played well. Our favorite mobile had three different styles of music: classical, traditional nursery songs, and lullabies. Some even come with nature sounds, which is a nice extra.

Now that you've found good music, make sure you can keep the tunes cranking, indefinitely and remotely if possible. Many mobiles stop playing their music too early and tragically cause almost asleep babies to pop awake at the sudden silence. We've found the best length for continuous play is no less than seven minutes.

Volume Control

The best mobiles also have different volume levels, softer play for smaller babies and nighttime use, and louder settings for naptime parties.

Remote Controls

Many mobiles now come with parent remote controls; some even have hooks so you can hang them on the nursery doorknob. As remote-less parents who've had to tiptoe, skulk, freeze on one foot, and drop to the floor *Mission Impossible*–style, trying to reset the mobile without baby seeing us, we highly recommend this feature. However, because many great mobiles don't come with a remote and you can live without it, don't base your entire purchase on this.

Light Shows

Soft lights are nice, but beware, they can startle a baby awake should you accidentally hit the light button when you're fumbling for the music. We prefer our mobiles without lights, as we think babies fall asleep in the dark better. We want them to be stimulated, but not mesmerized.

Ceiling light shows, while they look neat on the box, are not so neat in person. Most of the time, instead of projecting clearly defined shapes, they beam fuzzy blobs like a flashlight that's just about out of battery power. And your baby, especially if under 4 months, probably can't even see the ceiling anyway.

Convertibility

Many mobiles allow you to remove the mobile part and leave an attached crib toy behind once baby can sit up (see Chapter 13, Crib Toys, to see what features make for a good one). We like convertible mobiles because they give us more for our money; however, your baby probably won't pay attention to the crib toy for a few more months. Don't base your entire purchase on convertibility unless the crib toy left behind is a really good one.

Durability

The more moving parts a product has, the more parts that can break. The same is true with mobiles. We've found that the number of features a mobile has is directly related to how quickly it will stop working. It's a sad fact of mobile shopping, but most mobiles are really poorly made and won't work half as long as you'd hoped. In fact, we think the reason manufacturers completely retire mobiles and release new designs every couple of months is because the old ones stop working right about then. Have a problem with our Wee Waterfall mobile? Sorry, we can't help you; that product's been discontinued.

We know this going in, so we look for a mobile without too many moving parts that has a great music box, try to buy it on sale, and don't get too attached.

Don't think mobiles with characters or brand names you recognize will necessarily be more durable either. Those are all just licensing gimmicks to convince you to trust and to buy. All mobiles are made as cheaply as possible overseas. Of course, some are more durable than others. Look for the best you can find. We wish you luck.

Safety

No matter which mobile you choose, you must remove the parts that swing, dangle, and circle overhead as soon as your baby is old enough to sit up, around 5 months, due to strangulation hazards (you can leave a crib-mounted music box behind, but check the manufacturer's instructions to be sure). When mounting a mobile, make sure it is securely fastened so it doesn't fall into the crib.

Also check that no pieces of the mobile are small enough to be considered a choking hazard should your little renegade somehow manage to get hold of it. This includes pieces that might be, say, bitten off stuffed animals, such as button eyes. (See Small Parts Choking Hazard in Chapter 27, Toys, for how to test if a piece is small enough to be considered a choking hazard.)

If the mobile is battery powered, the battery compartment should be sealed securely. The most secure way to keep batteries from babies is a compartment that closes with a permanent screw.

Mounting

Note how a mobile is supposed to be fastened to your crib, as many employ a giant plastic screw and washer system that will leave a giant round scratch on your expensive crib. We learned this the hard way and are still angry about it, three years later. Better systems have padded clamps or clips. Key word: padded.

Some mobiles are also designed to hook onto or sit on the side of the crib. However, this method will only work on cribs with straight sides and skinny enough rails. Curved or thick sides won't house many mobiles. You should try not to, but if you're forced to mount a mobile on the drop side of a crib, never leave the side down with the mobile attached as baby might reach it. Better yet, look for another mobile.

PORTABLE MOBILES

Tiny portable mobiles allow you to soothe baby with music and little circles of movement outside of the crib. Meant to be attached to infant car seat carriers, strollers, or swings, the portable mobiles can be manual or battery powered. Our favorite is a battery-powered model that plays classical music until infinity if we let it.

Few things actually capture a newborn's attention because they can barely see anything. Portable mobiles are one of those magical devices that do, because they hang just a few inches over baby's head. Instead of dangling toys, portable mobiles feature fan-like paddles printed with stimulating pictures and patterns. They're a must-have in my book, and my go-to baby shower present.

Why we love them: A portable mobile managed to engage my 2-month-old for an entire emergency room visit for his big sister one day. Thank heaven for small miracles!

Why we don't: We only wish they played more songs.

Price

Despite their poor workmanship, mobiles cost a pretty penny. Both decorative and developmental mobiles start at about $30 and run up to $60. Portable mobiles clock in at around $20.

Features to Consider
- ☆ Music
- ☆ Sound effects
- ☆ Light effects
- ☆ Remote control
- ☆ Converts to crib toy

NOTES: *Mobiles*

Model Name / Manufacturer	Store/Price	My Impressions	Grade

Twenty

Monitors

W e're going to warn you right away: this is one product category where there is no "perfect fit" for every person. The monitor that works great for your next door neighbor might be a nightmare for you. Prepare yourself for some serious shopping agony.

However, because unlike other baby gear categories the monitor is a must-have, and the pain comes not from flaws in the product design but from incompatibilities with the houses we live in, we're not going to complain. Too much.

Baby monitors are basically specialized walkie-talkies that allow you to hear (and sometimes see) the goings-on in your baby's nursery

Monitor

Also Known As
Nursery monitor, video monitor, wireless monitoring system, movement sensor

Age Range
Birth to 36 months

Total Usage
3 years

Recommendation
Must have

When to Buy
Anytime before baby is born. A great item for your registry!

from afar. Monitors are not only great for hearing baby down the hall before he wakens the rest of the house in the middle of the night, but also provide parents with a large tract of freedom during daytime naps. Modern monitors are electronic marvels—they are sensitive enough to broadcast baby's every rustle, compact enough to be carried in your pocket, and powerful enough to beam baby news up to 2,000 feet.

Monitors have two major components: a transmitter and a receiver. The transmitter is usually the larger of the two, and is placed near baby to record movements. The receiver is generally more portable, and is placed near or carried around by the caregiver.

There are three types of monitors: audio, video, and movement.

AUDIO MONITORS

The audio monitor is one of the most indispensable baby products made for the multitasking, modern mom. Audio monitors transmit sound only, but they can do so with crystal clear clarity. And they offer the most features, such as extra parent receivers, intercom ability, sound-and-light displays, and out-of-range warnings.

Why we love them: Three words: peace of mind.

Why we don't: Oh, but we do! There are so many sophisticated choices available, you should be able to find one you love. If not, keep trying.

VIDEO MONITORS

On video monitors, the transmitter has a small camera and the receiver unit features a screen that displays picture and plays sound. The advancements in video monitors in the last few years have been great: the picture is now full color, with infrared technology to deliver night vision, and instead of a small television set–like receiver parents have a portable, handheld screen. While they are expensive and your mom will tell you completely unnecessary (our mom talked us out of a video monitor for years—long years of sleepless nights spent praying our baby was still breathing), most of us find them a worthwhile investment. Priceless even.

Why we love them: Beyond breathing checks, they allow you to peek on your sleeping baby without a squeaky door giving you away, they enable you to determine that the crying you hear is due to tantrum and not injury, and with the magic of mute, they can actually help you get a better night's sleep while still monitoring your baby.

Why we don't: The picture's not HD-quality, of course, but it's far better than we expected and getting better every day.

MOVEMENT SENSOR MONITORS

Movement sensor monitors have three parts: an audio transmitter, a receiver, and a sensor pad that lies under baby's mattress. The sensor pad records movements and breathing, but not accurately enough to be considered a SIDS-prevention or an official, medical nonbreathing detection device. If baby hasn't moved at all for a set period of time—usually 20 seconds—an alarm will sound on the parent unit. Movement sensors operate on low frequencies and are susceptible to interference.

Why we love them: OK, we don't. Grandma was right on this one, it's a bit of overkill. And false alarms from this give us true panic attacks.

Why we don't: We're not the only ones. Pediatricians warn that these monitors give caregivers a false sense of security.

Frequency

Baby monitors are basically radio transmitters that operate on a fixed frequency. Theoretically, the higher the frequency, the better the sound clarity and signal range. The typical lowest cost monitors use lower frequencies such as 49 MHz, although most also have multichannel switches that allow you to adjust around that frequency to find the best signal.

Long-range monitors use a 900 MHz or 2.4 GHz frequency and do deliver better clarity and a bigger working radius.

Range

Every year, new monitors debut with even larger ranges. Of course, the bigger the range, the bigger the price tag.

Standard 49 MHz monitors typically give a range of 400 to 450 feet. "Long distance" or "long range" monitors (900 MHz, 2.4 GHz, and beyond) have an advertised range of 850 to 2,000 feet. We've found in our real-world tests that the advertised range is usually a quite hopeful overestimation. Our experience is that most monitors only deliver acceptable sound quality at about 75 percent of their promised range. So if the box says "800 feet," it's more likely 600.

But how far is 600 feet? And how much range do you really need? It's easy to get seduced by the numbers and confused because the square footage of your house is not a useful number for figuring out your required use radius. When we're in the store, we can barely remember our own names half the time, so trying to estimate how big our backyard is and if we need a 450- or 750-foot radius is nigh impossible. So we went home and measured.

And here's what we found. In our large 3,000-square-foot suburban house, the distance between baby and the farthest corner indoors is 70 feet. From our front door to the street is 100 feet. To the front door of our neighbor across the street is 150 feet. From sleeping baby to the corner of our backyard (yes, the corner with all the weeds—we have a baby, we don't have time for yardwork!) is 110 feet. Are you seeing the same pattern we are? Unless you're Richie Rich, a standard monitor will probably keep you more than covered.

P.S. A 2,000-foot range? That would be our neighbor's house *15 doors down.* We hope no one ever travels that far from their unattended baby! We're nervous just to be weeding. Ok, maybe not weeding, because we don't weed, but watching TV in the basement.

Performance and Interference

While most have multiple channels to minimize interference, a monitor's performance will depend largely on the setup of your own particular house. Some houses are minefields of interference, some have no issues. One trick is to limit the number of devices operating on the same frequency in your house. If you have a 900 MHz cordless phone, pick a different frequency for your baby monitor.

Sadly, no matter what you do, you still may run into performance problems due to the construction of your walls, the configuration of your house, interference from other electronic devices, the setup at your neighbor's place, local architecture, or even the weather.

And because the trial and error can be frustrating and quite noisy—bad interference or feedback from a competing wireless device can practically

Are Digital Baby Monitors Safe?

Unlike analog monitors, devices that use digital communication are actually sending tiny pulses of electromagnetic energy. There has been some debate recently about the safety of electromagnetic energy radiating constantly near babies, because their nervous systems are still developing and they are more vulnerable in every way.

Apparently, with the prevalence of wireless everything, our modern American houses are now chock-full of "electrosmog." Baby monitors are causing extra concern, because while mobile phones and microwaves, which use similar pulses, are frequently turned off, many baby monitors are permanently left on.

To date, there have been no studies concerning digital baby monitors and adverse health or developmental effects. And while some experts claim the amounts of electromagnetic energy transmitted are incredibly minute and positively safe, others warn against having any digital devices in the nursery.

The manufacturers of digital baby monitors assert that independent testing found their products to be electromagnetically safe—emitting in some cases 10,000 times less electrosmog than internationally accepted norms—but for total peace of mind, they themselves suggest placing the transmitter at least three and a half feet away from baby.

make your ears bleed—it's best to find the perfect monitor before your baby comes home.

How do you find the perfect monitor? Try a bunch, keep all your receipts, and then celebrate the one that works best.

Analog versus Digital

You can assume that most baby monitors—particularly if they don't say "digital" in giant letters on the box—are analog. Analog is the common method used for sending a signal through radio waves. It's also the cheapest and works just fine for most people. The downside is that it isn't the most secure signal—anyone with a radio scanner could "tune in"—and when you move too far from the base, you're rewarded with static.

New digital technology eliminates static altogether because once you are out of range, there is no connection at all, simply silence. More importantly, digital monitors also offer a stronger, clearer, more secure signal because they digitally encode sound before transmitting it and dynamically search for available channels repeatedly, selecting the one with the least interference.

Digital monitors are more expensive, but also more robust by the minute. The FCC recently approved a European cordless phone technology called Digital Enhanced Cordless Telecommunications, or DECT, for use in baby monitors. DECT can access exponentially more channels than regular digital signals, meaning users get virtually no interference ever.

Privacy

Because they are simple FM transmitters, some monitors, especially those that operate on common frequencies, can pick up and transmit other local signals. To keep the neighbors at bay, many monitors now offer "privacy" settings, which can mean a higher number of channels to use or actual signal encryption. Not being spies ourselves, we didn't think privacy settings mattered much, but random snippets of other people's conversations—and the surprising burst of static that usually accompanies them—can be quite annoying. Privacy settings are especially useful if you live in a densely populated area, such as an apartment building.

Price

Audio monitors can cost anywhere from $30 to $100, with digital monitors at more than twice that. Video monitors cost between $200 and $400. Movement monitors are typically around $65 to $80.

In terms of baby monitors, more money will buy you better sound quality and usually more reliable technology, but mid-range monitors suffice just fine for most folks. Cheaper monitors break more easily and more frequently, of course, but then again, when they do, they're cheaper to replace.

Battery Power

Because the parent receiver is meant to be portable, it is battery powered. And we really mean "powered." Those things suck batteries dry like nobody's business. Mercifully, many manufacturers now produce parent units with built-in rechargeable battery packs. And we'd like to thank them for it. This is an incredibly important feature in a monitor, so look for it.

We're also fans of rechargeable batteries in the baby transmitter, because you may not always be able to park your baby near a plug, especially when on the go. The ideal setup is a monitor with both plug-in and rechargeable battery options on both the transmitter and receiver.

And because the monitor is useless when dead, we also appreciate low battery indicator lights.

Light Alerts

The most useful monitors have light effects on the parent units that visually demonstrate sound so if you have the volume turned down, you can still see baby's calling. What we really love is the vibration feature, so when we're weed . . . I mean watching TV . . . we can feel baby's cries should we not be listening or, um, even looking.

Sound-Activated Features

Believe it or not, some monitors are actually "sound-activated," meaning they are in a stand-by "sleep" mode until a sound from baby awakens them. This is a great feature because it eliminates the white noise fuzz of a regular always-on monitor and conserves battery power.

Multiple Receivers

Whether you have multiple kids, want dad to carry a receiver as well, or like having little baby listening stations in different locations throughout your house, manufacturers have heeded your call and now offer multiple parent receivers with many models. Some even allow you to purchase extra receivers separately.

Intercom Function

Some monitors offer a two-way switch that allows you to talk back to the transmitter or communicate with other receivers. We have a multireceiver model and love the ability to talk to the other parental unit without baby hearing. However, every time we've tried to use the intercom feature to "soothe" baby and let him know "Mommy's coming," we found we had to peel our petrified kid off the wallpaper. Some babies just don't appreciate a scary synthesized voice. Who knew?

Other Great Features

Because we lose things a lot, we love the pager function that locates lost parent units. Lifesaver. We also like parent units that are as small as possible. Belt clips are good, neck lanyards even better. We like out-of-range warnings, but wish they weren't so loud and scary.

Some much-ballyhooed new monitor features are fun, but not necessary. We don't need to know the temperature in our baby's room, because we have a thermostat and we assume our AC works. Light and music shows aren't necessary because we have a mobile or music box for that, and we put the transmitter too far away from baby for her to see it anyway.

Features to Consider

☆ Audio or video

☆ Analog or digital

☆ Price

☆ Frequency

☆ Privacy

☆ Range

☆ Rechargeable battery system

☆ Multiple receivers

NOTES: *Monitors*

Model Name / Manufacturer	Store/Price	My Impressions	Grade

Twenty-one

Play Yards and Playpens

If you are lucky enough to have a night nurse, then you probably won't appreciate the genius that is the play yard. So go ahead and read a different chapter, while we talk about how much we hate you behind your back. (We don't really hate you. It's jealousy, pure and simple. We middle-class moms don't dream of unlimited shoe budgets or private jets; it's the night nurse we covet . . .)

While the benefits of a traveling baby bed are fairly obvious, the reason most American moms are in love with their play yards is because of the attached bassinet and changing table features.

A play yard's bassinet allows us to keep baby in our room the first couple of months for easy feeding, peace of mind, and safe sleeping.

Play Yard

Also Known As
Pack'n Play®, portacrib, travel yard, Superyard, baby den, play-den, travel cot, play zone, baby jail

Age Range
Birth to 18 months

Total Usage
18 months

Recommendation
Must have

When to Buy
Great registry item! Choose one before you bring baby home from the hospital.

Attached bassinet or not, play yards are a must-have for most moms because of their versatility, portability, and magical baby containment properties.

While the mesh-sided play yard is the most purchased, there are also slatted baby play pens for roomier daytime playing, and tent-like travel cots for
parkside naps.

PLAY YARDS

Play yards resemble small, rectangular cribs constructed with mesh sides and hollow metal poles at
the corners and beneath the mattress support. They
have a thin, padded mattress raised several inches off
the floor. Some come with bassinet and changing table
attachments that allow them to be used as newborn cribs or portable changing stations in rooms other than the nursery. Many come with additional
features such as attached toys, lights, music, canopies, and sunscreens. Play
yards are fairly easy to set up and fold down to the size of a golf bag, albeit
a heavy, heavy golf bag.

Why we love them: We couldn't live without them the first two
months. We personally don't want our newborns in bed with us, but
we do like to be roommates. And after we ban them from our
bedroom altogether, we still find the play yard to be invaluable as a
satellite changing station, portable nap center, and vacation bed.

Why we don't: They are h-e-a-v-y. Like 35 pounds heavy. Wheels are
a must. And some are too wide to easily fit through a standard house
doorway.

Age Range

While most play yards can be used from birth, they all have weight limits, so check the manufacturer's specific requirements. Many attached
bassinets have lower weight and age limits than the rest of the product, so
check those too. No matter what the packaging says, once babies can roll
over, they are too big for a bassinet, and once they even start thinking about
trying to climb out, they are too big for the entire play yard.

Bassinets

The play yard bassinet is our favorite feature because it gives us the opportunity to sleep near, but not with our babies. Bassinets on play yards are safer than freestanding bassinets and cradles because they have a wide, virtually tip-proof base. And they are safer than co-sleepers because while babies can be just an arm's length away, they are protected by their own four walls.

Play yard bassinets are generally a firm bottom that hangs on mini mesh sides hooked to the top of a fully assembled play yard. They basically raise the floor of the play yard for a tiny newborn who can't move very much, and form a higher plane for easy parent care. Some bassinets span the entire play yard, some only half. Some are rectangular, although newer play yards have oval-shaped bassinets that eliminate dangerous corners. There are even twin bassinet attachments so your multiples can snooze side by side in the same play yard.

Whatever the shape, the sides of the bassinet must have enough ventilation, should a baby skooch over to the side. We prefer the fully mesh-sided ones over the ones with more suffocating solid bumper sides. Bassinets usually have slightly padded little mattresses of their own, but they are generally covered in a scratchy, noisy fabric. When covering a bassinet mattress yourself, use a small, specially fitted sheet and nothing more. No plush bedding or pillows or even sleep positioners should be added to a bassinet.

Because bassinets are basically hanging, check the seams for loose stitching or wear and tear regularly. And we found many of them have that toxic new product smell at first, so we recommend setting it up a couple of weeks early to let it air out.

Bassinets usually have weight limits of around 15 pounds, which believe it or not is very close to our babies' birth weight, but having our babies nearby for even the first two weeks at home is worth the full price of admission.

Changing Tables

Some play yards now have attachable changing tables as well, and we love-love-love them. With a weight limit of 25 pounds, they can be used longer than bassinets, making our entire play yard a perfect portable nursery for various levels of our house.

Play yard changing tables either clip onto the top rails like a bassinet, or hinge off the corners and can be folded back and out of the way in between changes. Depending on the size of the bassinet, some changing tables hang side by side, but some hang over the bassinet below. If this is the case, always remove or fold away the changing table when baby is in the bassinet. The first play yards with changing tables neglected this safety warning, and several bassinet-bound babies got trapped between the side of the play yard and changing table.

Many newer changing tables are even raised over the play yard for further safety and to help a mom's back.

Most play yard changing tables offer storage for diapering accessories, ranging from a simple diaper stacker to compartments and even built-in wipes dispensers.

Parent Organizers

Most play yards have at least some form of storage, whether it's a simple side pocket or a big plastic parent organizer. Newer play yards even have storage shelves underneath the bassinet for when you're not using the bottom half of the play yard. If you think you'll only use the play yard occasionally, then parent organizers aren't that important, but if you're looking to use it as a portable nursery, the more pockets, shelves, and little cubbies, the better.

Mattress Pads

The mattress pad in the bassinet and in the bottom of the play yard is hard and thin for a reason. Babies need firm sleeping surfaces. Tempting as it is, don't soften it up by adding extra thickness or plush bedding.

Play Yard Sheets

While the mattress pads on play yards are thin, they are also usually scratchy and noisy and even cold. If you are going to use a sheet on the mattress pad, pick one that is specially made to your model's specific size. Most major manufacturers also sell branded sheets to fit their play yards. Even if you don't end up purchasing a play yard, or sometimes leave it at home when you travel, we highly recommend picking up a couple of play yard sheets for your suitcase. They come in handy in hotels, especially if you want to use a communal play yard but want to shield your baby from communal germs. Full-size sheets should never be used in a play yard.

Bells and Whistles

Like most baby products, play yards are getting more pimped out with accessories every year. Here's a rundown of the ones we love, like, and loathe.

☆ **Music boxes:** We love them, as long as the music is tolerable. As in a crib music box, look for variety of music, length of play, and volume control. Nature sounds are good, especially white noise/surf sounds.

☆ **iPod/MP3 docks:** Pure genius.

☆ **Night-lights:** Great feature for the fumbling, nocturnal, zombie mom who needs to find a lost binky in the deep recesses of the bassinet. Also makes midnight changes a little easier.

☆ **Electronic light shows:** As long as they aren't part of a dangerous overhead system or too loud and annoying, light effects and musical numbers are fine, but not necessary. We're actually of the school that most babies prefer low-key activities like communing with the ceiling fan to the overstimulation of a full Broadway production. At least, that's what our babies told us. From Harvard. In French. Draw your own conclusions.

☆ **Vibration:** Some play yards feature a vibration box that can shimmy a baby at varying speeds. We had colicky babies who loved the milkshake, so we're big fans of any vibration features. It's not a make-or-break feature, but when in doubt, we go with it.

☆ **Mobiles:** We like the idea of mobiles, but not the kind they put on play yards. See Chapter 19 on what makes a good mobile; these are not it.

☆ **Hanging toys:** Little toys that hang off the edge of the canopy are a completely useless accessory. They aren't very cute, your baby probably can't even see them, and they get in the way. We don't not buy a model because of hanging canopy toys, but we will happily prune it.

☆ **Toy gyms/toy bars:** In Chapter 13, Crib Toys, we mentioned how crib gyms are mortally dangerous because they are so long that when yanked down, they can cause gruesome strangling accidents. We're going to go ahead and toe the same line for toy gyms that crisscross over play yards. They may be shorter, but they are still bad. You can still buy a play yard with them, but instead of attaching the toy bars, introduce them to Mr. Trash Can.

☆ **Canopies:** Many play yards come with canopies to shade baby from sun or sleep-preventing light. Sometimes the canopy is attached to the bassinet only; sometimes it attaches to the play yard for use without a bassinet. We like canopies, as our little ones sleep better in the dark, but they aren't necessities.

☆ **Bug covers:** Some play yards have sporty screen attachments to allow you to zip a child completely in for protection from bugs when outside. Fully featured play yards with bassinets and other attachments are far too heavy to drag to the backyard, so keep that in mind when considering this accessory.

☆ **Wheels:** Most play yards have two wheels so you can lift one side of the unit and more easily move it without allowing baby to be fully locomotive. We highly recommend wheels so you can scoot your play yard around for premium placement, but they are an absolute necessity for lugging around a folded play yard. Inexplicably, some play yards fold into a travel bag without exposing their wheels, so avoid this type or you will rue the day you ever thought it was a clever idea to take it to the airport with you.

☆ **Carrying bag:** Many play yards have carrying bags for easier, cleaner, and more compact transport. Carrying bags are great; we highly recommend them. Just make sure the entire bag can be wheeled or again, you will engage in some serious rue-ing.

Play Yard Placement

Place play yards in a safe, level location, especially if you have a sitting or standing toddler inside. This means nowhere near fireplaces, window coverings, or open stairways.

Hotel Cribs and Play Yards

Although we prefer to travel with our play yard for the utmost in safety, lugging around an extra 35-pound piece of luggage isn't always ideal for vacations. If you're stuck using the hotel's crib or play yard, check the recall history at recalls.gov. Yes, this may be a pain, but most hotels these days do have an Internet connection. It's worth the extra ten minutes for peace of mind to make sure the unfamiliar play yard isn't one of the CPSC's Most Wanted. In addition, here are some tips for checking safety from the Consumer Product Safety Commission (CPSC):

Cribs

• Crib slats are not more than two and three-eighths inches apart, or you can't fit a soda can through them.

• No slats are loose, missing, or cracked.

• You can't fit more than one finger between any side and the mattress.

• No posts or corners higher than one-sixteenth of an inch.

• No decorative shape cutouts on the headboard or foot-board.

• No full-size sheets or pillows in the crib.

• No missing screws or hardware.

• Mattress platform is secure.

Play Yards

• Mesh does not have holes larger than one-fourth of an inch (or the diameter of a baby finger).

• There are no tears, holes, or loose threads in mesh.

• There are no tears or holes anywhere on the play yard.

• No full-size sheets or pillows in the play yard.

A History of Death

Now for the not fun part: exploring the tragic history of play yards. While we think they are one of the greatest baby products ever invented, you should know they have a sad, very unsafe history. As we detailed in the safety chapter, early play yards had a faulty design that caused them to collapse on helpless babies and led to the recall of *10 million* play yards. And by "early," we mean the 1990s. Not so long ago. But whether you were in college or still watching *Saved by the Bell* back then, you probably weren't up on baby gear. So we're here to tell you, don't use an old play yard. Pretty much ever.

The juvenile products industry got together and set new *voluntary* safety standards for play yards in 1999 and again in 2002. Because that was pretty recent, we're going to go ahead and strongly recommend you buy this product brand spanking new. That's not to say they won't discover some faulty design flaw in a few years, so use your common sense, check the product regularly, and consider investing in a nice one. Crappy is as crappy does.

We know it's expensive and your best friend has a like-new one. Too bad. Sure your mom found a great one at a garage sale. Good for her. Tell her she can probably recoup her investment (and maybe even make a little green if she's a hard bargainer) by turning it in to the original manufacturer, as many of them are still offering cash rewards for the destruction of the unsafe products.

Also, be very careful about the play yards you allow your baby to be put in outside your home. This includes the babysitter's house, day care, hotels and motels, the gym's children's center, and even Grandma's house. (If she tries to lay a guilt trip on you about wasting money and says the play yard was just fine for your older sister's kids and it's still fine for yours, simply start crying about how you spent your whole life with hand-me-downs and you hoped your children could have something brand new just once in their lives. We've found crying trumps guilt every time.)

Register Your Product

We hate junk mail like nobody's business, so we usually opt out of registration cards. But the frequency and seriousness of recalls in this product category means this is one of the products we really do register. You should too.

Price

Play yards range in price from $39 to $69 for stripped-down varieties all the way up to $200. You can find a good, feature-packed one with a bassinet and changer for around $100.

PLAYPENS

While the term "playpen" is sometimes used interchangeably with "play yard," in our opinion, a play yard is meant primarily for portable sleeping, and a playpen is for corralling awake babies. Playpens, also called "play zones," are constructed of gate units clipped together to form a pen, just like for baby animals. Some are square, but most are hexagonal to give baby more room. Most are made of thick, colorful, playground-like plastic with attached toys so babies don't know they are on lockdown, although some are still made of wooden slats (look out for splinters!). Most playpens do not have a bottom; they simply assemble right on the floor. You throw a bunch of toys in with baby (nothing they can use as a step to escape, however) and know they are safe from fireplaces, older siblings, and other in-room dangers. Some playpens do have bottoms, though they are very thinly padded and add much bulk to the whole system. Playpens are generally much larger than play yards, giving a baby a lot more room to play. The extra room does allow parents to climb inside to prove to baby that it isn't so bad. Playpens cost between $49 and $150, depending on the thickness of the walls and the inclusion, or not, of activities.

Why we love them: We can only baby proof our house so much. Eventually you just have to corral a baby (especially when your disapproving mother-in-law is over). And they are just as good for corralling things away from baby: Christmas trees, fireplaces, the new big-screen TV, and the like.

Why we don't: They are very big and don't usually fold for easy portability. You set it up and leave it up.

TRAVEL COTS/BABY TENTS

Travel cots resemble little baby tents and are used primarily outdoors, but can be used just as easily inside. Instead of hollow metal pole supports, they use tent stakes to set up mesh sides. They also have a flat or domed top to protect babies from the sun, bees, and other buggies. Most are rectangular, although there are hexagonal ones as well. They are about the same size as play yards, but weigh about one-fifth as much. Their light weight and extra screens make them an ideal park or backyard accessory. Because babies can sleep in them, they do have a bottom to protect baby from the ground, usually in the form of a self-inflating mattress. Check all seams for strength, and make sure that the mattress isn't too soft. Travel cots cost around $150.

Why we love them: At only six pounds, they're perfect for the park, the beach, and that multidestination vacation.

Why we don't: If you frequently visit the park or beach, or have a fabulous trip planned, get one. But if not, it is the least necessary play yard.

Features to Consider

☆ Bassinet

☆ Changing table

☆ Parent organizer

☆ Play yard sheets

☆ Music box

☆ Vibration feature

☆ Canopy

☆ Wheels

☆ Carrying bag

NOTES: *Play Yards and Playpens*

Model Name / Manufacturer	Store/Price	My Impressions	Grade

Twenty-two

Potties

We're going to let you in on a little secret: we love diapers. Yes, it sucks changing babies 15 times a day when they're first born, but by the time they're 18 months, it's a pretty convenient way to contain a toddler's mess. It's pretty much the only mess that we can contain on our toddler.

But because we don't want them to be made fun of in kindergarten, we do potty train. And we do hate every minute of it.

We hate it because it takes so long—months and months before they've mastered it. Sure, they can figure out how to use the potty pretty quickly, but the big problem is, they don't know how to hold it. And we looked into it because we thought

Potty

Also Known As
Toilet trainer, potty bench

Age Range
12 to 36 months

Total Usage
2-plus years

Recommendation
Must have

When to Buy
Start looking a month or two before you think you'll start potty training, because it may take a while to find the perfect potty and you don't want to rush into a bad choice.

they were doing it just to drive us crazy, but toddlers' bladders are really, really small. And unlike adults, toddlers actually pee tiny bits all day long into their diaper. Remove that diaper and multiply the number of trips to the potty you anticipated by 12.

Our Dirty Little Potty Training Secret: Preschool

With our first daughter, we went back and forth on the potty training for months and months. There were two big reasons for our repeated failures: we didn't have the perfect in-house potty (a permanent toddler-sized potty that flushed, like you see in grade schools) and being a busy gal, I didn't have the 24 hours a day to commit to it.

Our second daughter was completely potty trained in two weeks with no stress. The difference? Preschool. When her big sister started kindergarten, she was lonely, so I signed her up at the local Montessori the day she turned 2. They don't allow diapers, so she showed up in the thick, "big girl" panties they required us to purchase, toting 15 extra pairs.

The secret to their success: time, tiny potties, and tiny peer pressure. The wonderful teachers there had a set schedule that included hourly potty visits. Their bathroom had toddler-size, fully plumbed white porcelain potties that toddlers didn't need a stool for, couldn't fall into, and could flush. And going to the potty was a community affair. All the kids went together, and no one wanted to be the odd diaper man out.

If you're stressed out about potty training and afraid your kid will go to prom still wearing a diaper, you might consider signing up for a potty training program. Many city clubs, private gyms, and local preschools offer them. It's expensive, yes, but the months of diaper and dry cleaning savings help offset the cost. Well, well worth it for this multitasking, overextended mom!

As long as you've cleared your schedule, it's manageable at home, but once you leave the house, it can be a nightmare. You end up dropping everything and running like a lunatic to the nauseating store restroom for a bathroom emergency just so they can deliver three drops. And you do this three times per store. Oh, it's a party.

And once you've started, you can't go back. Try explaining to a kid who thinks diapers are for babies that they have to wear one again for the two-hour trip to somewhere that doesn't have bathrooms, such as a long drive at night or a gulf-crossing toll bridge.

Our first piece of advice is to wait until the child is good and ready. Don't let anyone talk you into jumping the gun on this one. There's no certificate of good parenting for having a potty trained 12-month-old. No one cares. In fact, while moms still compare how old their children were when they first walked at said child's college graduation, no one will ever ask you when your child was potty trained. And if they do, lie. We don't even begin thinking about it until the child turns 2 years old in our house, and then we put the whole thing off for another 3 months.

Our second piece of advice: don't plan any major family vacations during potty training. Especially to Disney World. The aggravation of losing your place in a two-hour line for the trickle emergency will make you lose your mind. We still can't talk about the Orlando trip of 2004.

Because children have to use the potty all day long and you're not under house arrest (at least, we hope you're not), you will need potty training equipment for at home and on the go. Here are product choices for home potty parties.

Potty Chairs

A potty chair is a separate little potty just for toddler that sits on the floor of your bathroom. There are two main types: those made of a single, solid, molded piece of plastic, and those that are not. The type that are not have removable cups, can come with trays, and some even fold for easy storage. Either type catches your child's achievement in an empty plastic bowl that must be dumped into the regular toilet and then cleaned every time. The single molded plastic potty chairs are bulkier to empty, because you have to pick up the whole thing, and can be harder to clean. The potty chairs with removable cups are easier to empty but more apt to allow leaks.

Why we love them: Your toddler can jump on them any time.

Why we don't: We hate emptying and cleaning them, and eventually you have to transition your child to the big potty anyway.

POTTY SEATS

A potty seat is a plastic or padded seat that sits over a regular toilet seat allowing your toddler to sit more securely on a regular-size toilet. Potty seats are just doughnut-shaped seats with a hole that either fit underneath the regular seat, or on top of it. Because the regular toilet is used, they don't require emptying. They should have rubber bottoms so they don't slip. Most potty seats can be removed each time and stored easily next to the potty (some even come with little hooks for the wall), but some attach permanently and can be lifted out of the way for adult visitors and lowered for toddler trainers. Our favorite potty seats come with little handles built onto the sides; they keep toddlers balanced and, more importantly, give their hands a place to rest. Believe us, when you're toilet training a toddler, you want their hands occupied at all times.

Why we love them: They're less messy and teach our toddlers regular big kid toilet etiquette.

Why we don't: Not all products will fit all toilets, and you have to get your toddler up onto them.

Potty Chairs versus Potty Seats

Each option has its own pros and cons, although most moms buy one of each kind and then figure out which system works best for their unique little guys and gals. We've tried them all, and each of our toddlers liked something different. Who cares about drawbacks when you find something that works!

Potty chairs are probably better for overachieving younger toddlers, because they can have their own seat, they are in control, and they can access it all by themselves. But potty chairs are a pain to clean and don't mimic the real toilet experience. We always thought going potty into an empty bucket was a little weird, so we added a couple of inches of water to more resemble a real toilet (and aid in cleanup), but it backfired when our kids figured out how easy it was to reach down and touch the water and then flick it into Mommy's face. (A word on emptying potty chairs: in your excitement, don't tip the little bowl's contents into the big bowl's basin from too high up or you will get a shower you will not appreciate.) Many moms use potty chairs first, and then have their little ones graduate to a potty seat.

Potty seats are generally easier to travel with and clean, and they give a toddler the sense of real toilet training, which is the point after all.

P.S. You can also train a toddler to use the regular toilet with no extra apparatus at all. It takes some balance, a brave kid, and a lot of adult supervision, but it saves some money, a lot of cleaning, and, for many moms, tons of time.

Convertible Potties

Some potties convert from a potty chair into a potty seat to give you the best of both worlds. This system works well as long as all the individual pieces are of good quality. If the chair is great, but the seat subpar, you and your wallet would be better served by purchasing separate products.

Painted Wooden Thrones

There are dozens of designer potty chairs, cut and painted to look like little prince or princess thrones. They are made of wood, have a removable catch basin, and don't work very well.

Why we love them: They are super cute.

Why we don't: They are also hard to clean and sanitize, they leak, and they really scream playtime rather than potty time. Save the $150 for real play chairs and get a good, disinfectable plastic potty.

FOR BOYS ONLY: TODDLER URINALS

There is a new toddler urinal on the market that is essentially a stand-alone potty chair in the shape of a small urinal. It can also be wall mounted. Although it advertises that you can flush it, the flushing is really for show. A top container is filled with water; "flushing" causes a stream of water to swish down the drain to a bucket at the bottom that you empty each night. Obviously, it's meant only for the bodily fluid of its namesake, so you will need another toilet training product to sort out the solids, but for little boys with aiming problems, it can cut down on the yellow mess we moms abhor. Never mind about the floor and the back of the toilet seat, it's the joy of no more pee stains on the wall, the trash can, the shower curtain, and the light switch (yes, the light switch), that has us celebrating.

Why we love them: Didn't you hear? No more pee stains on the wall!

Why we don't: They are rather big. And emptying them is no fun.

Urine Deflector (aka "The Hump")

Speaking of boys, many potty chairs and seats have an odd hump in the front called a urine deflector. It's meant to be used with little boys, to keep their stream headed downwards, but little girls must deal with it because standard potty products are unisex.

We don't like urine deflectors for a couple of reasons. First, they don't really work. They might deflect a pee stream, but in all kinds of directions besides down, and sometimes right back at our boys. This, they do not like. Second, they can be sharp edged and actually end up scraping little boys as they try to straddle the seat and sit around it. Third, they are in the way for both genders. In the case of an emergency approach—which is often—overly enthusiastic sitters can misjudge and seat themselves on quite a painful surprise. Even a small hump makes saddling up awkward for either gender. We look for potties with little or no hump at all.

That's not to say that both genders, especially when they have extra full bladders or are distracted, won't soak the front of the toilet, their own underpants, and in some tragic instances, you. Our trick? Have them look straight above their heads at the ceiling. They will arch their back, and gravity will work its magic. If you want to make up a nice little story about catching a glimpse of the Potty Fairy to remind them to look up, you are a much better parent than us.

Comfort

Sadly, considering how long little ones sometimes sit there waiting for a sign, not all potty seats and chairs are comfortable. Because there are plenty to choose from, do your tiny buddy a favor and get a comfortable one. Signs of comfort: contours, cushion, and smooth edges. You can spot an uncomfortable seat when your little one stands up and has a severe case of ring-around-the-butt.

Also, run your fingers around every inch of the product and check for sharp edges. Sharp edges are the enemy of tiny privates, especially boys'. Be on the lookout too for any part that might pinch. It sounds obvious, but many, many seats are poorly made. We have more than a few friends who've nursed their little boys through unspeakable injuries after the excited toddlers sat down or jumped up too quickly and sustained scratches, cuts, and stitches where stitches should never, ever be.

Size

Just as toddlers come in all shapes and sizes, so do potties. Get one that fits your child, now and for the next few months. Make sure the seat is big enough, as well as the hole. Make sure it's not too tall or, sometimes worse, too short.

To save you a few extra buy-return-try-again trips to the store, take your toddler potty shopping with you. This can not only help build excitement, but can help ensure you get the right size as well. Don't be shy. You can't tell if it's the right size from the picture on the box. Open it up, take it out, and let your toddler try it, right there in aisle 5. Fully clothed, that is.

Cleaning

All potty chairs and seats must be cleaned, some more often than others. Look for one that is easy to wipe down. The fewer cracks and crevices, the better. It can be hard to tell if a dark-colored potty is thoroughly clean, yet bright white potties do stain.

Toddler Disassembly

While versatility is nice, remember at this age, anything a toddler can remove, he will remove. Remove and turn into a weapon. If you don't want pieces of the potty thrown at you, fed to the dog, or flushed down the big toilet, look for a potty that is somewhat toddler proof.

Sound Effects and Toys

To provide extra encouragement, some potties offer lights, sound effects, songs, and even attached toys. We find these features do provide extra encouragement—extra encouragement to jump off the potty, dance around, push buttons over and over, and laugh. Laugh like a little maniac.

We've had the greatest success from potties that look like potties. No more, no less.

Elmo Goes Potty

There are many potty products covered with favorite cartoon characters, from Big Bird to Sponge Bob. We're all for bribery, and if this might help motivate your child, great, but don't settle for an inferior product because of the characters on it. You can always add your own fun with a pack of stickers, and letting your child participate in the potty decorating can even sweeten the deal.

STOOLS AND STEPS

If you use a potty seat, you'll most likely need a way to get your toddler up onto it. Dozens of stools and steps are available, from little plastic boxes to elaborate staircases with handrails. Some potty chairs even become stools, allowing you to close the lid and stand on them.

We're not big fans of the potty-turned-stool products because they aren't the right shape, they aren't very sturdy, and they aren't very attractive. The giant staircases are great, unless adults also use that particular bathroom, and then they are quite in the way. Simple stools that can be easily moved out of the way are best, but look for a nice wide top step because children will turn around on this to face backward. A step they can rest their feet on while sitting is also useful.

Most importantly, the step stool should have thick, nonslip material on both the bottom and every step. While we think they are more attractive, for this age, for this purpose, we don't recommend slippery wooden steps.

Why we love them: They help our little ones up on the toilet and up to the sink.

Why we don't: They also help our little ones up on the coffee table.

Potties-to-Go

Once you've become a citizen of Pottyville, you're a full-time resident, whether you're home or not. Thankfully, a number of products make excursions with an emergency tinkler a little easier. They range from throw-in-a-backpack-for-emergencies to keep-in-the-back-of-the-minivan-permanently.

PORTABLE POTTY CHAIRS

While any potty chair or seat is technically portable, some fold into nicer packages than others. Some portable potties zip into a tiny backpack and some turn into little briefcases. Portable potties all have a seat of some sort, but design varies wildly from there. Some portable potties are containers that pull apart, revealing a seat and catch basin. Some are simply inflatable rings attached to a plastic bag. The larger ones are bulkier to cart around, but they are also more durable and less likely to leak. Choose one that suits how often you feel you'll need it. Will you be taking quick trips to the mall or hiking the Adirondack Trail with your diaperless wonder? Some portable potties use disposable liners. This can make for an easier cleanup, but could be an added expense. Some use custom refills, while others will allow you to recycle some of your 2,000 saved plastic shopping bags, or even use actual diapers as catcher's mitts (great if you overbought and have dozens of extra diapers lying around, but expensive if you need to buy them new).

Why we love them: Side of the freeway, middle of the park, you'll never be caught unprepared.

Why we don't: Because our toddlers have thrown up in our purses, you'd think we'd be used to the less glamorous side of parenthood by now, but it really does gross us out to carry a potty around.

Must-Have Travel Potty Accessory Checklist

- Travel hand sanitizer or wipes
- Flushable toddler wipes
- Disposable toilet seat covers
- Car seat and stroller seat protectors

FOLDING POTTY SEATS

A folding potty seat is just that: a child-size toilet seat to cover a public adult-size toilet that folds for easy portability. We love the idea, but hate the design. Despite what the pictures advertise, they are actually much, much bigger and heavier than you would ever anticipate, so much so that we stopped carrying one after a single outing. They are usually very cheaply made, so check for sharp edges. They are also full of cracks

258 ☆ the **Baby Gizmo** buying guide

and crevices because they fold into fours, which creeps us out because it practically invites public restroom germs to hitchhike a ride home in our diaper bag. They are generally flat with no contours, so our children didn't fit on them well. And for some insane reason, instead of being a complete circle, they are U-shaped, with a big gap in the front. A big gap that leaves the sickest, hairiest part of the toilet bowl open, practically begging small hands to touch. Until you are squatting two inches from the edge of the public toilet, you have no idea how disgusting this opening really is. Trust us on this, open gap is a no go.

Why we love them: Um . . . well . . . there's . . . yeah, we don't.

Why we don't: While we know we need to get over our public bathroom phobia (the retailers could help us out by providing cleaner restrooms!), we prefer disposable toilet seat covers.

TRAVEL URINALS

Suitable for boys and girls—although admittedly easier for the boys—the travel urinal is a glorified plastic bag with a rubber lip around the opening that is simply held up against the body while the user pees. It only works for the liquids, but on the plus side, in a pinch, it can be used in the back seat of a moving car. Most are completely disposable, so you simply throw the entire full urinal away, although some are like little medical water bottles that can be dumped, rinsed, and reused.

Why we love them: They're better than the soda cans our mom used to pass around on long road trips (and much less dangerous!).

Why we don't: One word: gross.

Price

Thankfully, potties are pretty cheap. They're pretty cheaply made, usually, so don't expect them to last until your grandkids, but they're cheap to buy too. Both potty chairs and potty seats cost between $9 and $39, most around the $25 range. Plastic stools also start at $9, but wooden stools will cost more. Elaborate staircase systems can run up to $100 and more.

Potty Accessories

All manner of potty accessories are available: dolls that teach technique (good, if you can stick with it), timers for structure (great preschool technique), books and DVDs that sing poopy songs (can really help if it's your kid's favorite character singing it), floating targets that teach little boys aim and the alphabet, powders that magically change the color of the toilet bowl water upon delivery of a little urine (sick), and even, we kid you not, long plastic tubes that "extend" a little boy's reach (we're still having nightmares about that one).

Here's a list of the items worth checking out:

☆ **Flushable toddler wipes:** Sort of like diaper wipes, only slightly smaller, thinner, and (hooray!) flushable. These wipes are a welcome replacement to the cold, wet toilet paper our grandma used on us when we were kids. They help keep kids super clean and help the potty training process because the easy wiping builds their confidence. They're biodegradable, so they're also good for the environment. (Watch out, though, as some are more flushable than others. If the package says "not for ejector pumps," it's code for "not thin enough, might clog your pipes, so buy another brand.")

☆ **Disposable toilet seat covers:** Sort of like flushable tissue seat covers, only larger, thicker, and (sniff) not flushable. But still quite helpful for less-than-perfect public restrooms and tiny toilet trainees. They are quilted to be stronger than the tissue covers in stalls, have adhesive strips on the bottom so they stay in place (and don't stick to little bums as they stand up), cover a good portion of the seat including the nasty front hole, and while they can't be flushed, they can be simply thrown away.

☆ **Waterproof seat protectors:** Waterproof inserts that help protect your major baby gear, such as car seats and strollers, from major diaper blowouts, potty training accidents, and even leaky sippy cups and forgotten bottles. Anything that makes cleaning messy things a little easier is a great buy in our book.

☆ **Mattress protectors:** Waterproof pads or protectors for your child's mattress. If you don't already have these, consider them if you're potty training. Nothing will ruin a good crib mattress quicker than a nighttime drenching.

☆ **Potty training stickers:** Little stickers, given as a reward for potty accomplishments, to either stick on a chart or just elicit a smile. They work quite well because everyone likes a gold star.

☆ **Potty training dolls:** Interactive dolls or stuffed animals used for potty training that allow your toddler to feed the doll from a bottle, then position it on the doll's potty to watch it "go." They work well for some kids; some kids couldn't care less.

☆ **Toilet targets:** Flushable, floatable shapes you drop in the toilet to help little boys practice their aim. Nice to have, but Cheerios work just as well.

Features to Consider

☆ Potty chair or seat

☆ Stability

☆ Smooth edges

☆ Small contours

☆ Easy to clean

☆ Price

NOTES: *Potties*

Model Name / Manufacturer	Store/Price	My Impressions	Grade
_____	_____	_____	_____
_____	_____	_____	_____
_____	_____	_____	_____
_____	_____	_____	_____
_____	_____	_____	_____
_____	_____	_____	_____
_____	_____	_____	_____
_____	_____	_____	_____
_____	_____	_____	_____
_____	_____	_____	_____

Twenty-three

Safety Gates

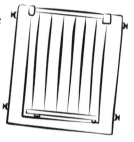

Our houses are pretty. Safety gates are not. We procrastinated like crazy about chopping up our gorgeous walls and gouging into our nice stairwells for ugly safety gates. And then 2-year-old Hadley fell down the stairs at a model home. Only four, well-padded, carpeted stairs. And cracked her cheekbone.

If you have a nice, baby-proofed, one-story ranch house, you might be able to get away without a single safety gate. (Although they are great for keeping toddlers out of offices, away from fireplaces, and in only certain areas of your house.) But if you have stairs, they are a necessity.

You actually need safety gates sooner and longer than you think. As soon as babies can move off their blanket, it's time to put gates up. And because clumsy can last through kindergarten, they should stay up for quite a few years.

Safety Gate

Age Range
5 months to 5 years

Total Usage
4-plus years

Recommendation
Must have for any home with stairs

When to Buy
When baby hits 3 months old, start looking.

Thankfully, safety gates have gotten more attractive. You can find wood ones with turned spindles stained to match your décor, sleek modern metal ones, and even mesh rolls that disappear like a horizontal window shade when not in use. While gates can be used many places for many purposes in your house, they are grouped into two main categories depending on how they are installed: pressure mounted or hardware mounted.

PRESSURE-MOUNTED GATES

A favorite of first-time moms who haven't yet relinquished their pristine homes to the ravages of savage children, pressure-mounted gates use a pressing force to stay put. Like a shower curtain rod, they have feet that screw or push open against the wall to tautly hold the gate in place. Pressure-mounted gates require almost no assembly and are easy to install. They are great for hallways, doorways, and the bottom of stairs, but should never be used at the top of steps. Pressure gates are usually one piece that you clamp open and close every time, or jump over, although there are more expensive versions that have a swinging gate cut in the middle. Swingers are much easier to operate and should be considered if you're going to use a pressure-mounted gate regularly.

> *Why we love them:* Like a moth to the flame, like a mom to chocolate, toddlers are uncontrollably drawn to stairs. You can block your own home stairs all you want, but dare to visit someone else's house and you'll spend your entire afternoon pulling your deliriously happy toddler off their stairs. We actually have a pressure-mounted gate we take with us on road trips to save our babies and our sanity.

> *Why we don't:* Even the tightest mounted ones aren't perfect. A toddler built or acting like a battering ram can eventually pull or bully it down. And you may suffer significant wall damage when that happens.

HARDWARE-MOUNTED GATES

Get out the tools! Hardware-mounted gates are screwed directly into your wall for maximum strength and security. An ideal mount is into a stud, but because that's not always possible, there are mounting kits available for drywall and stair post mounting as well. They are usually more durably constructed than pressure-mounted gates, but be warned, if your kid uses them like a swing set, they will break, buckle, or screw up your wall just the same.

Why we love them: Once they are up, they are up! And providing a gigantic relief.

Why we don't: Mounting these gates is a monumental nightmare. A break-out-the-divorce-papers nightmare. The instructions are usually written in another language, obscure, and sometimes just plain wrong.

A Special Note about Stairs

Only hardware-mounted gates should be used at the top of stairwells. If you only have a stairwell post on one or both sides, fear not, there are several kits on the market that consist of little panels of wood you either screw, clamp, or tie around the post for hardware mounting.

Gates at the top of the stairs should also only swing one way: toward the landing, not out over the stairs. Many gates are one-way only, but if not, look for one with a swing-stop mechanism that will prevent it from opening over the stairs.

Specialty Gates

Most people just need a rectangular gate to block a stairwell or hallway, but there are times when you need a special, bigger, badder gate. Since pressure-mounted gates only work in small spaces, and the following gates are closing off wild places, they are all either hardware-mounted or free-standing.

CONFIGURE GATES

Configure gates are individual gate panels that you either hook together to form a big shape to cordon off an area (like around a piano) or corral a baby (like a playpen), or mount to the wall and shape around a dangerous location such as a fireplace.

HEARTH GATES

Hearth gates are essentially configure gates that are sold specifically to block off your fireplace. They come in various sizes depending on how big your hearth is. The safest hearth gates permanently mount to your wall on either side of the fireplace.

RETRACTABLE GATES

Some gates retract like a giant window shade into a giant waiting box on the wall. Sounds good on paper, but in practice we find them to be a hassle. And the soft mesh gate material is easily destroyed by our naughty toddlers.

ACCORDION GATES

The ubiquitous safety gates of our childhood, the diamond-shaped accordion gates that retracted open caused so many injuries that they were all but banned. (We say "all but banned" because the CPSC never actually bans anything. *Lighter fluid filled teething ring? We'll think about how to modify it so the voluntary safety standards aren't too expensive for the manufacturers.*) Children not only strangled when their heads got caught in the openings, but when their clothes got hung up on the V-shaped open tops. Accordion gates manufactured today do have a plastic safety top to eliminate the open V's, but we're going to recommend against them. There are plenty of other wonderful alternatives on the market.

Swinging Doors-in-a-Gate

Some gates are one piece on a hinge that completely swing open, while others have a door within the gate that swings open (also called a "walk-through" gate). Gates with swinging doors sound great, and usually have the coolest features, but there is a hidden hazard. Because the door is cut out of the gate, there is a bottom piece left behind that you must step over. Or, more likely, trip over. Not a good option for a top-of-the-stairs mount.

Auto Close Feature

Some gates have an auto close feature that makes them swing shut after you walk through them. Because gates are only good safety devices when they're closed, we love this feature. Just make sure there aren't any little ones swimming in your wake who might get an auto pinched finger as you walk through.

Lights

Believe it or not, even safety gates have lights now. Some are simple night-lights, while some are motion activated. Very convenient for midnight and early morning stumblings.

Alarms

Some gates include a chirping alarm when the latch is opened. We don't find this particular feature very necessary. It annoys us when it's just us, older siblings who are allowed on the stairs will trip it constantly, and if your toddlers can open the gate and trip the alarm, you either don't need a gate anymore or you need to find a better one they can't open at all.

Hands-Free Features

Many gates offer a hands-free option that allows a busy, overburdened mom to open sesame without having a free hand. This engineering marvel is achieved by foot pedals and even voice activation.

Remote Control

Some gates offer remote controls. While we were worried that we had already hit the federal limit for number of remotes allowed in one house, we were relieved to discover the "remote" was actually a button mounted on the wall out of junior's reach, but easily employed by our elbow.

Easy to Open

Whatever gate you choose, look for one that's easy for you to operate 325 times a day. A gate with a three-step, hold-pinch-and-lift lock might keep your toddler off the stairs, but you'll be pulling out your hair in big fat chunks after about the 16th ascent each day.

Toddler Proof

That said, choose a gate that isn't too easy to open. Toddlers are great at patient, methodical, yet violent shaking. If this is enough to pop your gate open, find another. Quickly.

Gate Size

It didn't actually occur to us until we were in the store staring down the baby gates, but not all doorways are the same size, and neither are all baby gates. Avoid the frustrating second trip to the store by measuring your openings before you leave. Most gates come in multiple sizes and include extension options. Some gates are extra tall and extra wide and have angle mounts for uneven positions.

Slat Size

As on cribs and cradles, if your gate has slats, they should be less than two and three-eighths inches for baby safety. Get out another can of Diet Coke and see if it slides through. (We love Diet Coke and all, but we seriously need to think of a test that involves Snickers bars or something caramel . . .)

Material

Gates can be found in almost any material: wood, plastic, steel, even soft mesh. People generally choose to match the style and color of their house, but don't let that consideration lead you to an inferior gate.

Durability

While motion lights and hands-free options are fun, no single gate feature is as important as a strong, sturdy design. All the bells and whistles in the world on a flimsy gate will do you no good. When shopping for a gate, we look for the ones we think are the most solid and toddler proof and can be mounted successfully in our space, and then look for features afterward.

You will also get what you pay for in safety gates. While a $15 gate can be had, when it breaks (and takes off a chunk of your wall with it), it wasn't a great bargain. Because our gates are meant to last through thousands of openings and closings for several years, we get the nicest ones we can find.

Price

The price of gates varies wildly depending on quality of material and size. Small, thin, pressure-mounted wooden ones can be found for as little as $15. Fancy wooden ones will run up to $100. Most gates hover around the $50 range. Remember, you usually need more than one.

Features to Consider

☆ Gate size

☆ Pressure or hardware mounted

☆ Swings open

☆ Swing-stop mechanism for stairs

☆ Easy to open

☆ Toddler proof

☆ Durable

NOTES: *Safety Gates*

Model Name / Manufacturer	Store/Price	My Impressions	Grade

Twenty-four

Shoes

The only thing better than new shoes for us is tiny, leather, embroidered new shoes for our babies. Hands down our favorite category, baby shoes are pure heaven!

That's not to say we didn't completely screw up shoe shopping for our first babies. We got them hard-soled, synthetic shoes at a discount store on sale in a size we sort of guessed to be correct. We didn't think anything mattered beyond cuteness and cheapness—it's not like our babies were hitting the treadmill or anything. Turns out it matters a lot because you can actually hinder your child's mobile development with a poor shoe choice.

Because baby feet are filled with tiny bones that aren't fully fused together yet and are constantly growing, shoes that are too tight or too stiff can constrict growth, movement, and even circulation. Pediatricians actually recommend babies be shoeless as long and as often as possible. It's a fairly easy rule to follow inside, but out of the house, safety and climate rule out socks-only in many cases. The closest thing to barefoot is a soft-soled shoe. Here's what you need to know to shoe any size baby.

CRIB SHOES

More slipper than shoe, crib shoes provide extra warmth and loads of style to tiny nonwalkers, from newborns through cruisers. Made of soft, supple material, usually leather, they have tiny soles, but not much rigidity. You should be able to bend or twist them quite easily. Because babies don't walk yet, you don't need to worry about support or soles. Just look for crib shoes made of a breathable material that are as kick-proof as possible without cutting off a baby's circulation.

Why we love them: Crib shoes are just about the cutest baby accessory ever. Some babies don't have enough hair for barrettes, some look funny in hats, but all babies look adorable in shoes!

Why we don't: We can technically live without them. Technically. And fetching the errant shoe tossed here and there at the mall is far less fun for us than our babies.

Shoes

Age Range
Birth to 36 months

Total Usage
Generally 2 to 4 months per pair

Recommendation
Must have, for walkers anyway

When to Buy
When your baby needs them, not a day before. You can't guess the size ahead of time, and you'll end up wasting money and crying over the size 4 dinosaur or mermaid shoes they never wore because they jumped from a size 3 to a 5 seemingly overnight.

BABY/EARLY WALKER SHOES

Meant for babies who are almost ready to walk to those who toddle away from their diaper changes, walking shoes look like regular, structured shoes, but in miniature. While hard-soled options exist, you should only purchase super flexible, soft-soled shoes for this stage. Most of the better shoes have multilayered soles that offer enough protection from the sidewalk cracks and sticks a tiny tot will cross at this age.

Why we love them: Crib shoes and booties are adorable, but tiny penny loafers and Mary Janes are to die for!

Why we don't: We wish there were scuff-resistant tops because toddlers still like to drop to their knees and crawl around sometimes, scuffing the heck out of their shoes, usually on the day we bought them.

TODDLER SHOES

Once a child has mastered walking, usually around 2 years, when they no longer bobble from foot to foot but run in a straight line, you can graduate them to toddler shoes. Toddler shoes have thicker soles for extra protection from the naughty places your toddler will venture, but you should still be able to easily bend them in half. Instead of pure slip-ons, toddler shoes fasten with laces or Velcro straps. Laces are a pain for mom, but know that toddlers quickly discover how to undo Velcro, pull their shoes off, and throw them at you. Expect a shoe or two in the head when you're driving.

Why we love them: Sadly they aren't quite as cute as crib or baby shoes, but they're still pretty adorable.

Why we don't: Toddler shoes mean our little baby is (sob!) growing up. First this, then kindergarten, then before you know it, college and then a family . . .

Flexibility

The most important feature in any shoe is flexibility. Good shoes should be flexible enough that you can easily bend them in half with one hand. Shoes with solid soles, such as certain thick-soled tennis shoes or dress shoes, are not recommended. We were sad to lose the shiny, black patent leather shoes at holidays, too, but there are dozens of great soft-soled alternatives, and more on the market every day.

Low Profile

Shoes should also have a low profile, meaning they don't rise above the ankle, otherwise they restrict natural movement. So, cute as they are, mini high tops and hiking boots are out. Soft booties that rise above the ankle are just fine because they don't have a constrictive form.

Look for Leather

Ever wonder why your baby's feet really do smell stinky? It's not your imagination. Babies' feet actually sweat two to three times more than adults'. Put all that moisture in a nonbreathable shoe, and you can encourage bacteria growth that makes them smell even worse (á la your kindergartner's feet).

For any age baby, look for a shoe with a leather interior. A leather insole will wick the moisture away from baby's feet; synthetic soles will cook up smelly baby sweat stew. And high quality shoes have treated leather insoles that prevent bacteria growth.

Allergy alert: some people are allergic to the chemicals used in the leather tanning process. If your baby gets a red rash on the top of his feet after wearing leather shoes, chances are he is allergic, and you'll need to find synthetic shoes.

Nonslip Soles

Shoes with nonslip soles are essential for vertical babies. Even those cruising the furniture or standing for one nanosecond need a sticky bottom. Soft-soled leather shoes made with quality leather might look slippery on the bottom, but if you pull them out of the package and skid them across a slippery surface,

Successful Shoe Store Fitting Tips

- Go in the late afternoon or evening. Babies' feet swell throughout the day just like adults', and you want a pair that fits baby's most swollen size from the start.
- Make sure your baby is well rested and fed.
- Make sure baby is wearing socks.
- Take your baby out of the stroller or cart and have her stand in the shoes.
- Leave the shoes on for a few minutes. When you remove them, look for red marks or irritation. If you find any, pick a different pair or bigger size.

you'll see they don't slide. Cheaper leather shoes will have glassy bottoms, but you can scuff them up on your own by simply rubbing them on your concrete driveway.

Size Matters

When it comes to your baby's shoe size, don't guess. Every time we've taken our kids in for a measurement, we've been embarrassed to discover we had them in shoes two sizes too small! Take them to a shoe store and have their feet measured.

The rule of thumb for babies is that you should have a full thumb's width of space from the top of their toes to the top of the shoe to give their little piggies plenty of wiggle room and room to grow. If in doubt, go a half size bigger.

You should also have about a pinkie's width between the side of the shoe and the side of the foot. We've always had a problem with shoes being too narrow for our Barney Rubble–footed babes, but thankfully, many baby shoe manufacturers now make wide width shoes for baby.

Getting Baby Shoes On

Babies have solid, fat feet and don't know how to contort their foot to slide into a shoe, so save yourself some serious aggravation and look for a shoe that has a wide opening for easy dressing. The best shoes have ankle elastic systems or giant tongues that allow you to practically open the entire shoe, set baby's foot on the sole, and wrap the shoe closed around the foot. Just make sure any elastic bands or straps aren't so tight they leave a red indentation around the ankle.

Check Baby's Size Regularly

Because baby's feet can grow at light speed, check your baby's shoes for a perfect fit every couple of weeks. They grow in fits and starts, so while some shoes might last for four months, others might last only two.

Price

Baby shoes run anywhere from $10 to $150. Good quality shoes start around $25 to $35.

Worth the Extra Money

In the world of baby shoes, a higher price will get you much better quality. And because shoes play a daily role in development, we think the extra money is well worth it. Higher quality shoes fit better and last longer.

We know they can be a brutal blow to your budget, but because baby will most likely outgrow rather than outwear them, you can recoup some of your investment by reselling them. Quality, name brand baby shoes are a hot commodity on eBay, generally selling for half of their original retail price. So even if you paid twice as much for the better shoe, you can come out even, but your baby comes out several steps ahead.

Features to Consider

☆ Flexibility

☆ Low profile

☆ Leather insole

☆ Nonslip sole

☆ Sizing

☆ Easy dressing

☆ Quality

☆ Price

NOTES: *Shoes*

Model Name / Manufacturer	Store/Price	My Impressions	Grade

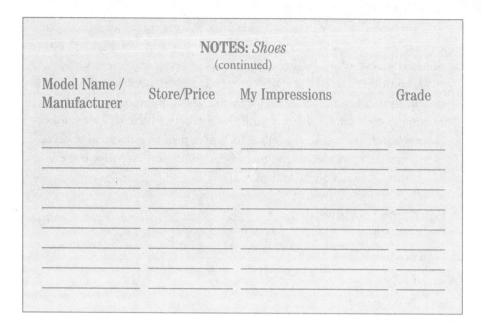

NOTES: *Shoes*
(continued)

Model Name / Manufacturer	Store/Price	My Impressions	Grade

Twenty-five

Strollers

M en have cars. Moms have strollers. Equal parts comfortable ride and fashion statement, no purchase is as fulfilling or personal to a mom as her stroller. And because you will use your stroller as often as you take your child out of the house, the perfect stroller purchase is one of the most important (and most fun!) baby gear purchases a mom will make.

While safety features dictate 90 percent of the decision-making of buying other baby gear, personal preference drives stroller buys. Yes, you still need to look for good straps and a safe ride, but a good part of choosing a stroller is all about color, fabric, design, budget, and pride.

For moms who just need a quick-wheeled contraption to push pokey kids, there are $15 umbrella strollers. For moms who want a complete luxury "system" that includes bassinets, rockers, and even toddler steering wheels, there are $1,500 options. For stroller junkies like us, there are is a whole bunch of heaven in between.

Design

Strollers have never looked so fine, thanks to a little designer company called Bugaboo and a little show called *Sex in the City.* Like Manolo Blahniks, Carrie Bradshaw and company introduced the middle class mom to luxury strollers when Miranda appeared onscreen in 2002 pushing a then-$700 Bugaboo. It was too rich for most of us, but oh, how we wanted one! And enough moms responded to the graceful lines and gorgeous fabrics—ditching their clunky, navy blue plaid strollers on the way—that the midrange stroller manufacturers sat up and took note.

The Bugaboo trickle-down design effect has hit almost every major stroller manufacturer. Graco hired Andrew Serbinski, an industrial designer who specialized in racing bikes and motorcycles, and designer Cynthia Rowley to give their strollers some visual appeal. The results: graceful arcs and more modern fabrics. Maclaren tapped designers Kate Spade, Philippe Starck, and Lulu Guinness to make their strollers more fashion-forward. Even Fisher-Price and Kolcraft have debuted new, minimalist-looking models.

We've noticed the consumers are footing the bill for these new design advancements, as prices have gone up, but we're willing to pay for it because they're all just so pretty.

Life Cycle of Strollers

As we've alluded, and as our in-garage stroller parking lots attest, most moms need more than one stroller. In truth, the average mom ends up with up to three strollers per kid because most strollers suit a particular age and particular function well, but don't meet all needs.

Here's the typical life cycle of the strolling mom:

☆ **Newborn:** This age demands the biggest stroller for new baby protection and stability. You need a sturdy stroller that either can support an infant car seat carrier, or sports an infant bed. Because new babies need the most stuff, the best strollers for this age double as portable nurseries, giving you the most basket room and accessories, and are able to accommodate the world's largest, most overstuffed diaper bag.

☆ **Older babies:** Once baby has outgrown the infant car seat carrier or infant bed, you strip the newborn parts off a stroller. You still need a pretty hefty diaper bag and still pack the kitchen sink on every outing, but you secretly wish the stroller you bought for your newborn wasn't so darn heavy.

☆ **Toddlers:** By now, you're completely over your giant, utilitarian stroller and ready to banish it to the attic because it's so big and heavy and you simply don't need that much room anymore. Toddlers like to walk sometimes anyway, so you purchase a convenient, lightweight, umbrella stroller.

☆ **Activity strollers:** As baby's first birthday approaches, you vow to shed the pregnancy weight once and for all, and take up jogging (or, more realistically, quick walking). You'll quickly discover the limitations of your standard or umbrella stroller, as even a brisk pace will send your front wheels aflutter. Now is when you purchase an all-terrain or jogging stroller.

☆ **Multiple-kid strollers:** As soon as baby number two starts kicking up the ultrasound, you realize all of your single strollers are for naught, as your first child is never going to make it if they have to walk full-time. There are double strollers in all categories: standard, lightweight, all-terrain, and jogging. There are even special strollers-and-a-half designed to fit one rider full-time and one part-time.

Primary Stroller Options

If you're looking for just one stroller to take you from birth through preschool, the following strollers are possibilities. You'll need the appropriate newborn accommodations, of course, and no small amount of durability, but it can be done with these types:

- Standard stroller
- Travel systems
- Lightweight-plus strollers
- Luxury stroller systems
- All-terrain strollers

Types of Strollers

To give you an idea of the scope of strollers (and better explain to our husbands why we really did need all 16 strollers parked in our garage), here's a quick summary of the types of strollers available in order of use, from birth to lazy kindergartner. Each stroller category below has its own special section in the following pages that will tell you what specific features to look for and more. (You can also find our Top Five picks and thousands of other moms' opinions on BabyGizmo.com.)

☆ **Carriages:** Giant baby baskets on wheels, carriages are traditional and usually luxurious rides for new babies. These strollers are usually bought for their heirloom qualities and don't typically travel very well.

☆ **Standard strollers:** The most common stroller, standard strollers are large, can accommodate newborns to preschoolers, and offer loads of convenient features. There are single and double standard strollers.

☆ **Travel systems:** This is a standard stroller that comes with an infant car seat carrier as part of a coordinating set.

☆ **Lightweight-plus strollers:** The perfect cross between a standard stroller and a lightweight stroller, they are technically a couple of pounds heavier than a true "lightweight" class, but are sturdier, can support an infant car seat carrier, and provide more features than their lighter cousins. Although most of the models are for single babies, there are a few doubles out there.

☆ **Lightweight/umbrella strollers:** A lightweight stroller weighs 15 pounds or less. "Umbrella" refers to the two curved handles and the way most lightweight strollers close like an umbrella, but some lightweight strollers fold flat as well. Lightweight strollers are not suitable for newborns, most have fixed seats, and they are great for travel—but stripped of many convenience features. You can choose single or double lightweight strollers.

☆ **Luxury stroller systems:** A new breed of stroller with advanced design and luxury fabrics, luxury stroller systems are lightweight frames that come with multiple seating arrangements you snap in as your child grows. Most come with bassinets and standard stroller seats; some also come with infant car seat carriers and even rockers for use indoors. While some do sport footboards, sadly, for now, they are only available in the single variety.

☆ **Strollers-and-a-half:** A standard stroller with a single seat for a primary rider, these strollers offer a rear footboard or tiny folding seat for hop-a-long bigger sibling to hitch a ride every once in a while.

☆ **All-terrain strollers:** These are rugged, outdoorsy strollers with special wheels and more flexible handling that allow you to tread over uneven, unpaved, and even unusual surfaces like sand. Some all-terrain strollers will allow you to walk at a brisk pace, but are not suitable for a full jog, because the front wheels swivel. There are both single and double versions.

☆ **Jogging strollers:** The only stroller designed for safe running, jogging strollers have a sturdy construction to withstand the speed, a fixed front wheel, hand brakes, and parent tethers so they can't get away from you. There are singles and doubles to be had.

☆ **Multiples strollers:** If you have triplets or more, there are special strollers designed just for you. With multiple seats to safely sit same-aged siblings, multiples strollers are large, but a lifesaver for moms born with only two arms.

Budget

How you slice up your stroller purchases depends primarily on your budget. If you're on a tight budget, you can certainly get away with a single standard stroller that you can use for up to four years. You can even score one for $70, or less if it's slightly used (and this is the one category we will give you our blessing to beg, borrow, and eBay to your heart's content).

However, because you will shove, slam, and drag your stroller, and because your child will kick, rip, and vomit on your stroller, there's a good chance many oft-used cheaper strollers won't last from sibling to sibling.

The average mom ends up with a standard, an umbrella, and an activity stroller. If you buy them separately, nice mid-range models from a discount store will mean you will likely spend a total of between $500 and $1,000. While most middle class moms think a luxury stroller system is out of reach, we did the math, and if you add up all the separate strolling and baby activity gear they offer in one package, the $500 to $800 price tag can actually save you a few hundred bucks. You do get a much nicer, strut-worthy system as well, but you do have to outlay the cash all at once rather than working it into your expenses every couple of months.

Universal Stroller Features

While the construction and function might vary, all strollers share some universal features. They all have seats. They all have wheels. And if they want us to like them, they all have cup holders. Here is an explanation of the key stroller features for all types, including our comments about what we adore and what we abhor.

Safety

Look for a stroller that is stable, well constructed, and has strong safety straps. Also, check that the stroller is locked open every single time you unfold it. Some may seem locked, when in fact they aren't. The most common accidents with small children in strollers occur when strollers collapse while a baby is inside (usually because they aren't snapped and locked open properly) and when babies slip out through the seat bottom but get tangled in the straps. Always strap your child in with a safety strap between the legs, each and every time.

Height Limits

While every stroller has a weight limit, there aren't really height limits on strollers. Even so, most kids will grow too tall for a stroller long before they grow too heavy for it.

Every stroller design is different, but if you have tall children, note how easily they could squeeze into the seat or where they might comfortably rest their legs. An immobile snack tray that gets in the way of an older toddler's knees might force you to retire your stroller earlier than you might like. Some straps will be too snug between the legs too soon. And some are built so low, your preschooler's ankles run the risk of being eaten by the stroller wheels.

Stroller Weight

Unless you live on the ground floor with no stairs in a flat state and walk everywhere, you're going to have to pick up your stroller from time to time. Suburban moms will be shoving them into the trunks of minivans, while urban moms will be dragging them down subway stairs or wrestling them into the backs of taxicabs.

While the best, sturdiest strollers used to be the heaviest, engineering advancements and the use of an aluminum chassis has cut the weight of many strollers by 10 pounds or more.

When stroller shopping, one of the first things we check is the weight of the stroller. Here's how those measurements translate into momspeak:

☆ **Under 10 pounds:** A dream. You can lift it with one finger. Like Superman.

☆ **10–15 pounds:** Still very light. You can lift it with one hand. Not forever, but you can.

☆ **15–18 pounds:** Light enough to easily swing up into a car's trunk by a single handle without throwing out your back. Light enough to carry through an airport without wanting to cry. But we wouldn't strap it to our backs and hike with this weight.

☆ **18–23 pounds:** Now you'll start to feel the stroller's weight. You're more lugging it around when it's folded than carrying it.

☆ **23–25 pounds:** See above. Now multiply the lugging by a factor of two.

☆ **25–30 pounds:** You had better really love the stroller, because you won't love this weight.

☆ **30+ pounds:** If you have this size stroller, you either have a carriage (and a bodyguard to carry it for you), or a double stroller that, heavy as it is, cannot be avoided. You will more pull this stroller out of your car and let it crash to the ground than actually lift it, and beg passing strangers to lift it back into your car for you (especially if you're still sporting stitches).

Folding

Equally as important as how sturdy and heavy a stroller is, is how it folds. You want a stroller that collapses easily, with one hand if at all possible, and folds into the most compact size. (On BabyGizmo.com you can find a wonderful chart listing all strollers' folded dimensions to help you determine which ones will actually fit in your trunk and which strollers would need to be strapped to your roof. We'd love to have included it in this book, but it would be outdated by the time you are reading this. Real-time information is one of the best by-products of the Internet. Only slightly better than online Scrabble.)

Most strollers fold well, but you'll hate a stroller that doesn't. Like really hate. Like balancing your checkbook hate. A bad fold isn't necessarily a complicated one. Even complicated systems can be quickly mastered and executed in a matter of seconds. In our opinion, bad folds are the ones that require you to wiggle, spit, and pray, and sometimes just don't happen. We've been stuck in the parking lot, cursing our fancy stroller, unable to get it to fold, but afraid we'll break something if we shove it too hard. Wanna know which ones suck to fold? Drop a few brand names and people will be quick to tell you.

We're also interested in a fold that results in the smallest, tightest bundle possible. If it also ends up standing upright, we ask it to marry us.

Folding lingo can be quite confusing, because some of it refers to the final, folded shape of the stroller, some refers to the method used to fold the strollers, and some is just terminology made up by manufacturers to sound cool. To add to the chaos, many strollers will claim several different folds in one or even make up new names that are a combination of old ones because they are trying to tell you both how the stroller folds and what it will look like folded. And maybe they're hoping we just get so blinded by the jabberwocky that we buy the one with the most words on the box. Which, sadly, has worked on us before.

Let's see if we can't slog through the terminology (remember, some strollers can have more than one of these folds):

☆ **Flat fold:** Basically folds forward or backward in half, so it remains just as wide as it was unfolded, but now twice as thick, only kind of flat. Kind of. This is the bulkiest of all folds. The sworn enemy of our small trunks.

☆ **Umbrella fold:** The stroller folds forward and inward into a thick bundle, log shaped rather than flat. While the motion is different from how you actually fold an umbrella, the end result is a tight, stroller bundle that resembles a thick, folded umbrella (the big, giant golf kind, not the cute, in-your-purse kind).

☆ **Three-dimensional fold:** Simply another name for the umbrella fold.

☆ **Two-piece fold:** Common for luxury stroller systems, this fold requires you to unclip a seat from its base, then fold the base and store the two pieces separately, usually stacked on top of one another. The most time-consuming fold, and rather large. Like twice as large as a regular flat fold.

☆ **Compact tri-fold:** A two-handed fold in which you lift folding levers on both sides of the handle. Result is similar to a finished umbrella fold.

☆ **One-hand fold:** The entire stroller can be collapsed using one hand, albeit with usually a couple of steps for the hand. You usually push a button, twist a handle, and pull on something to complete the collapse.

☆ **One-touch fold:** A fantastically easy, foolproof folding system that allows you to push a single button with your thumb while holding a handle; you pull said handle and the stroller collapses. Very close to the one-hand fold, but a little better. (It's no magic Jetsons fold, though. You don't just push a button and stand back; exertion is required.)

☆ **One-step fold:** "One step" literally refers to your stepping on something. You step on a rear bar or lever, and the entire stroller lurches forward into a flat fold. It's easy, but these folds do kind of scare us. We don't like the idea that our kid is sitting in a stroller that could fold should we stumble against a single bar near our feet.

☆ **Five-second fold:** A quick fold that can be completed in five seconds, but does require the use of one foot and one hand. You step on one lever, then another, then push the stroller closed with your hands. End result is an umbrella fold.

☆ **Quick fold system:** A patented system for certain all-terrain strollers that allows you to grab a strap in the seat and lift up, and the entire stroller then collapses into a bundle. Unlike the one-step fold, we actually do like this one because you can't accidentally fold it on the run.

☆ **Standing fold:** Our favorite fold! Any of the above folds—one-step, one-handed, and so on—can also use a standing fold. Instead of collapsing away from you onto the ground, a standing fold brings the stroller toward you and ends with it in a folded, but upright, self-standing position. Genius system that keeps us from having to bend over, allows for easy loading into our car, and keeps our nice strollers looking nicer longer.

Locking Mechanism

When strollers are folded, you want them to stay that way. Not all strollers lock closed, but most do. Look for an easy-to-operate lock that holds the stroller as tightly closed as possible. One of our biggest pet peeves is loosey-goosey locks, which make transporting a folded stroller a giant pain.

Construction and Durability

Some strollers are made of steel and built to last. Others are made of plastic and will fall apart before your first kid's first birthday. More durable strollers tend to be more expensive, of course, but are a wise investment if they last longer.

Whatever stroller you choose must be sturdy enough to hold your kid. A stroller that cracks or has wheels that fall off when you're in mid-stride is not good for you and not good for baby.

All brand new strollers seem nice and solid in the store on the flat, glossy floor. But we put them to the test by bringing along a 4-year-old who is guaranteed to test the top of the stroller's weight limit. We strap our little test subject in, and then try to hop a curb. If there's not a short shelf nearby that you can push the stroller up onto, tip the stroller back onto its back wheels and pretend you're about to jump a log. Make no mistake, the salespeople hate this, but you can tell tons about the solid construction of a stroller by the way it feels tipped up with 40 pounds inside. If the stroller feels like it's about to snap in half, we move on.

Five-Point Harness

While strollers come with three- and five-point harness straps, five-point is better, especially for younger babies. Many systems allow you to convert a five-point into a three-point—nice for older children who only need to be snapped in at the waist and hate to be held back at the shoulder.

Strap Covers

Straps covers are a very nice feature much appreciated by babies because the straps can actually be sharp enough to scratch tender skin, especially around the neck. Strap covers can be purchased separately, but they never match quite as well and tend to pop off and get lost far, far too easily. As Oprah says, "Love is in the details," and we look for strollers that offer strap covers as a sign of how much the manufacturers think about the little things.

Reclining Seat

While most stroller seats recline, some recline more than others. Many offer "multiposition" recline, but the only position we care about is a full recline. Tiny babies require a full recline, as does any sleeping passenger. While many strollers advertise a full recline, they don't always deliver it. Full recline means flat, not sort-of-leaning-backward.

We've overlooked the importance of this feature before and then hated how our children were slumped over in strollers that didn't recline enough.

How easy the seat back reclines is another important consideration. More often than not, you'll discover your child is nodding off, and you want to gently recline the seat to coax her into a permanent dreaming state. A smooth, easy recline is best.

Stroller Color and Pattern

Let's be honest, looks are important to all of us. We'd guess a full 80 percent of our final purchase decision is based on the stroller color and pattern. They could cover a roller skate in Burberry plaid and we'd want it. Thankfully, we have hundreds of choices from solid colors to plaids to graffiti-inspired to cartoons. There are bright reds, safety cone oranges, moss greens, and simple blacks. Many upscale strollers now offer the fabric separately, so you can even swap out the color for the next gender kid, or simply when you're sick of it.

For the most part, strollers are pretty safe, they share the same set of features, and so we give you permission to choose based on nothing else than the one you thought was prettiest. We have, and we still do.

Seat Fabric and Padding

More expensive strollers show their worth immediately in the seat fabric. Fancy strollers have fancy Italian fabrics and plush seats. Cheap strollers have scratchy polyester with hardly any padding at all. Nicer fabric will wear better and is easier to care for than cheaper fabric, so consider the fabric's contribution to the overall durability and worth of your stroller. And kids do appreciate a little extra padding, especially when we have them on mall duty for six hours at a time.

Washable Fabric

Many strollers have removable fabric for easy washing; just as many do not. But all should be at least spot cleanable.

We've found that how easy a fabric cleans is directly related to the price of the stroller. Cheap strollers stain easily, not helping their overall appearance of cheapness. Nice strollers usually clean up quite well.

Pay attention to how many seams and folds the seat has, and how deep the cracks are. Some baby food combinations—wet vanilla wafer comes to mind—will dry like mortar and you won't be able to chip it out with a jackhammer.

Seat Edge

Just like on a fancy ergonomic office chair, strollers that offer a waterfall edge are better for a small rider's leg circulation. Some seats offer a curved front, while others just dead-end in a taut line.

Many strollers now offer an adjustable edge that can be raised for small babies and lowered for older riders. Our favorites are the ones that completely lift to a 90-degree angle, closing off the foot space entirely, making a cozy infant bed.

Footrest

For good posture and development, strollers should have a footrest for their small riders. Some footrests are nice, big shelves, while some are simple straps. In this case, size doesn't matter. As long as a child has something to rest the feet on, anything will do. Besides, bigger footrests add unneeded bulk and weight to the stroller.

Stroller Basket

When it comes to the basket, size matters. The bigger, the better. While most strollers do deliver in the basket department in terms of size, not all baskets are easily accessible. Pay close attention to how a basket is accessed, especially when the seat is fully reclined for an infant car seat or a sleeping child. A big basket is useless if you can't actually reach into it.

Some of our favorite baskets actually have a lower and load function that allows you to always be able to get at them. Baskets you have to access from the front? Not our friend.

Canopy

Large canopies are important for small children, especially because they can't wear sunscreen for the first six months. While the sunshade is obvious, canopies can also help shield a baby from cold, wind, and rain. Like our friend the big basket, the big canopy is best. The very best canopies rotate 180 degrees forward until they hit the baby snack tray to completely protect your child.

We also like peekaboo windows and pockets on the back of the canopy for storing our car keys or cell phone.

We're not big fans of canopies that have locking bars on the side to keep them extended because we inevitably forget we've got them locked down, and almost break them when we fold the stroller. We know they're there to keep the canopy extended, but most good strollers have solid enough canopies that the lock isn't needed. Living in the Windy City, we've had our share of upturned umbrellas, but have never had a canopy flip open on us. We won't throw out a stroller for having canopy locks, but we will routinely refuse to lock them.

No matter what size the canopy, it should always provide adequate ventilation to your child. Stick your own head up under there and make sure it isn't too stuffy and you can still feel the breeze.

Stroller Handle

Stroller handles can be a single straight bar, a curved bar, two separate handles, or two curved hooks. Some are even ergonomic. While some moms prefer the single handle, others prefer two. It's really a matter of personal preference, and which handle you think will best accommodate your shopping bags.

When you're test-driving a stroller in the store, be sure to try it one-handed, as more often than not, you'll be lucky to have one of those free. For a complete real-world test, also try pushing the stroller with your belly, steering it with your elbow, or pulling it from the front so you can baby talk to your baby, hopefully shushing them enough so you can try on one more outfit before they kick you and your crying kid out of the store.

Some stroller handles are wonderfully padded, and some are not. Some are even inexplicably covered in a mean, ridged rubber that hurts a poor mom's hands. We like the most padded ones possible, but look for a quality covering. Foam chunks falling off the handle has prematurely aged more than one of our strollers. How can you tell if the padding is quality? Pinch at it in the store (and then blame your husband if anything actually falls off).

Height-Adjustable Handle

Many strollers offer a height adjustment setting that allows you to raise or lower the handles. This is not necessary for the average mom, but is an absolute lifesaver if you or your husband are super tall or super short, as it can save your back and keep you from kicking the stroller as you stroll.

The handle should be at a comfortable height, generally at waist level or slightly below.

While we do love to use our stroller handles to hang any and every thing, be careful never to overload a stroller from the back—especially lightweight strollers—as they can tip backward.

Reversible Handle

One of our favorite new stroller features is the reversible handle. With a few simple clicks, a reversible handle allows you flip the handle in the opposite direction and push your stroller with your baby facing you rather than out at the world. This is especially useful for smaller babies, whom we like to see at all times. In big strollers, sometimes tiny ones are hidden behind the canopies when they are front facing, and we appreciate the opportunity to remedy that.

Maneuverability

All strollers will wheel your baby from here to there, but the amount of effort it takes to push them varies greatly. Some strollers glide like a dream. Others you have to really shove. Check turning radius, remembering that more often than not, you'll be trying to squeeze your stroller down tight store aisles and into small spaces. Some strollers turn on a dime with one pinkie. Some you have to dig into so hard to take a corner that your wrists ache. When shopping for strollers, remind yourself that you're going to be pushing one for the next 1,460 days. A stroller that maneuvers well is the difference between loving those days and cursing your purchase.

Wheels

While the traditional stroller has four same-sized wheels, sometimes those wheels are doubles (for eight in all), sometimes they are double in the front only, and sometimes they are larger in the back. Some strollers now even rock the three-wheeled look.

The number of wheels is irrelevant; you're looking for a good turning radius, easy maneuverability, and quality wheels. Some wheels are rubber, some are air filled, some simple plastic. Avoid the plastic if you can. Like our old Big Wheels, crappy plastic wheels will wear unevenly and eventually you'll end up with flat spots. No good.

Rubber wheels are best. Some are sealed, and some allow you to fill with air accordingly; each stroller company has its own preference. Self-filled wheels have both advantages and drawbacks: filling them yourself means you can adjust for varied terrains, but it also means you can get a flat.

The bigger the wheels, the easier the stroller will be to push, but the larger it will be when folded.

Suspension

The best strollers offer suspension—a springing system over the wheels to help absorb some of the shock of bumps and potholes, giving baby a smoother ride. Some strollers have suspension only on the back wheels, but we like it in the front and the back. Note that full-wheel suspension can make a stroller seem extra "wobbly." A quality stroller will have a strong frame, even though the suspension wiggles when you shake it. A lower quality stroller will feel so rickety, you think it might fall apart (as, trust us, it eventually will).

Brakes

Any stroller you ever buy, even the $9 umbrella ones, should have a brake to prevent runaways. While some braking systems are hand operated off the stroller handle, most are levers you kick to engage. Some back wheels have individual brakes that must be set individually, but we prefer the ones with a single brake bar that locks both wheels at the same time.

You want solid brakes that will catch and hold; heavier strollers should have stronger brakes. And pay attention to the ease with which brakes are disengaged. Some are simple to undo, but others will darn near break your toe.

Cup Holders

The simple, lowly parent cup holder is the convenience feature we cannot live without. We've tried, and we truly almost died. And while there are universal, after-market cup holders available, they never work quite as well as ones built right in.

Not all cup holders are the same. Some hang off the side and get in the way when we're folding the stroller or shoving it into our trunk. Some are too shallow to hold a jumbo coffee. The best ones are nice and deep and positioned between the two handles.

Parent Consoles

Some strollers come with an entire parent console straddling the handles. Some are hard, molded plastic; others are soft, fabric pockets. We like multiple cup holders and carved-out spaces to throw our keys, but we find covered compartments, built-in glasses cases, and wipe containers to be overkill.

Sadly, most of the best strollers are sorely lacking in the parent console category. You can buy any number of pouches to hang off the back, but that's where we have our spectacular diaper bag. In many cases, we are forced to just make do with the cup holder.

Child Snack Tray

While most strollers come with a stroller bar in front of baby, many instead (or in addition) offer a snack tray. We love snack trays as they help us corral snacks. Snack trays don't have to be giant sized to be useful, and the larger ones do contribute to a bulkier fold size and end up scraping on the concrete every time we collapse our stroller.

Many child snack trays come with cup holders as well, but they are almost always too shallow, even for a sippy cup.

Look for a snack tray that can be swung open to one side so an older toddler can more easily climb in. Some snack trays remove completely for when you're looking to de-bulk your ride.

Snack Tray Toys

Some snack trays come with attached toys, which sounds good in theory, but in practice they end up in the way, extra grimy, and our kids are usually stimulated enough when they're on a roll not to care about batting at something in front of them.

Newborn Pillows

Many strollers offer extra headrest and body pillows for newborn use, which is a great feature because newborns need all the support they can get. You can buy pillows separately, but they look nicest and fit the best when they come with your stroller.

Rain Cover

A rain cover is an additional accessory that many stroller manufacturers now include for free. It's a specially designed plastic cover that shields your entire stroller from the rain, but still allows proper ventilation for your child (which is why we highly recommend it over your regular Hefty bag).

How important they are to you depends on where you live. If you're an urban mom and have to walk a lot, they are a must-have. If you're a suburban mom who lives in her car, rain covers are a nice-to-have. We love ours, but we frequently forget to bring it. When unexpectedly caught in a downpour, we just tend to run really fast and hide somewhere until it stops raining.

Foot Muff/Weather Boot

A foot muff, also called a "weather boot," is like a tiny, half sleeping bag attached to the bottom of the stroller seat that can help keep your baby's feet and legs warm in cold weather. They are a wonderful luxury addition, not entirely necessary, but a great alternative to the receiving blanket we used to use that inevitably ended up being dragged behind us through puddles in the parking lot.

Test Drive

Finally, before you purchase a stroller, take it for a test drive. You might be able to find the best prices online, and the pictures all look great on the Internet, but when it arrives and you find that you kick the basket when you walk, you'll be kicking yourself.

We've taken more than one day trip across town just to visit a baby boutique and test drive a certain stroller. In person, you can touch the seat, feel the fabric, pull on the canopy, push it around, test the brakes, check its turning radius, and of course, learn how it folds and unfolds. Stroller salespeople in specialty stores are notoriously well versed in not only the strollers they sell, but the strollers they don't (and they're more than happy to tell you why they don't sell certain brands).

CARRIAGES

Created in 1733 for an English duke, the first known baby stroller resembled a small horse-drawn carriage and was meant to be pulled by small dogs or ponies. Shaped like a shell with snake patterns painted on it, the carriage did include a comfortable seat for baby and even springs for shock absorption. The cumbersome design did not become parent operated until handles were added 50 years later. A luxury toy for the upper class, baby carriages were large, ornate, nonfolding, and a nuisance to pedestrians on crowded sidewalks.

The baby carriage, sometimes called a "pram," of today has changed very little. It is still a large, cumbersome basket on gigantic wheels that does not collapse and clears quite a path on the street. Meant for urban strolls or walks around "the grounds," carriages are still beloved by the metropolitan upper class, modern-day royalty, and celebrity moms. They offer baby a plush ride and many even sport ornate curtains to deter peeping paparazzi.

Carriages are bulky and far less portable than any other category of stroller. Most do not include big baskets or any other typical stroller features such as cup holders or adjustable handles. But what they lack in conveniences, they make up for in élan.

Carriage

Also Known As
Pram, baby buggy

Age Range
Birth to 9-plus months

Total Usage
9-plus months

Recommendation
Nice to have

When to Buy
Before baby is born, so you can enjoy it immediately.

Construction

The most famous carriage company in the world is Silver Cross, which has been hand finishing their prams since 1877. Each carriage is individually numbered and personally signed by the artisan, craftsmen who pass their skills down with each generation.

Most carriages are a study in historical nostalgia and evoke a feeling of a quieter, simpler life. The baby bed is roomy and plush, yet very open to the mom, who can take dreamy walks while actively bonding with her bouncing baby.

Snooty Vocabulary Lesson

Carriages are called "prams" in Britain and well-heeled American circles, but we bet most of them don't even know that "pram" is actually short for "perambulator." So what's a perambulator? It technically means a baby carriage, of course, but it's derived from the verb *perambulate*, which means to walk around and survey things, or to stroll.

Feeling smarter? Us too. Now if only we could figure out how to use our trivia superpowers to score one of those $2,000 prams . . .

Carriages are beloved for the protection they offer small babies thanks to their steel construction, and are known for their smooth suspension. The most exquisite carriages feature a hand-sprung chassis, leather suspension straps for extra cushioning, and even hand-spoked wheels.

Size

Traditional carriages are large, like four feet tall and 66 pounds large. Much like the Hummer, that much size may seem unnecessarily extravagant to some, but many people feel the point of a carriage is to give a baby a large, magical, traveling space.

In fact, the appeal of the carriage is mythical. Pushing it, you feel elegant, and somehow the extra space makes you feel like you've got an extra special baby. You need an extra special bank account, of course, and if you have it, we certainly don't fault you for perambulating with your baby in style.

Portability

While many carriages do not fold, more often these days, they do. In the 1970s, many manufacturers allowed for the bed portion of the carriage to be removed, and the "carry-cot" was born. The portable bassinet feature allows parents to carry their baby from the street into the house without the bulky frame and wheels.

Age Range

Most carriages have a weight limit of up to 30 pounds, although by the time babies attempt to climb out, they need to be transferred to a new stroller.

Most parents only use traditional carriages for the first few months, from birth to around 4 months. This limited age range makes them a nonnecessity, luxury purchase for most, but for many, they are quality heirlooms to be passed down from generation to generation.

Wheels

Most carriages have large, air-filled wheels that are fixed, although some modern models have added swivel capabilities, as even the toniest mom sometimes has to steer around dog poop.

There should be firm brakes on both back wheels that you can access easily.

Steering

Carriages are large, but most of them push like a dream. Look for one that steers smoothly and doesn't allow for too much give when turning corners or traversing uneven ground.

Stability

Look for a solid, durable carriage with a wide base that resists tipping over, even if baby should roll to the side (although when babies can roll over by themselves, for safety, you need to pick a new stroller).

Material

The fancier carriages have fancier fabrics, everything from brushed linen to silk to the finest combed cotton. Look for a durable, moisture-resistant fabric that can be spot cleaned.

Baby Bed

Typically, the baby carriage compartment features plush fabrics and a soft mattress, but make sure the fabric is not near baby's face and that the mattress is firm enough for safe infant sleeping. And just like any mattress in any baby sleeping space, the mattress should fit firmly in the frame, allowing no more than one finger width of space.

Mindful of the SIDS danger of soft bedding and tight sleeping quarters, many carriages now have special ventilated mattresses and even ventilation systems in the bed.

Price

While most carriages cost around $1,000, you can find $400 and $4,000 versions.

Why we love them: Carriages are the very embodiment of rich romance. And we love pretending we're famous.

Why we don't: They're giant, not very maneuverable, and for all the money, our babies outgrow them so very quickly. Sigh.

Features to Consider

☆ Portability

☆ Wheels

☆ Maneuverability

☆ Stability

☆ Fabric

☆ Mattress

NOTES: *Carriages*

Model Name / Manufacturer	Store/Price	My Impressions	Grade

SINGLE STANDARD STROLLERS

The workhorse of strollers, single standard strollers are the largest single stroller, the most common stroller, and for many families, the primary pick.

They usually have large, padded seats with multiple reclining options, roomy baskets, double wheels that swivel in front for a smooth ride, and tons of features. They are heavier than lightweight strollers, but still light enough to be pulled in and out of most trunks quite easily.

Price

We're going to start with the price range, because it affects so many aspects of the stroller. The more you spend, the more features you'll get, the longer the stroller will last, and the nicer it will look. Because this is the stroller most parents use the longest, we recommend investing in a good one that will actually outlast your kids. A crappy stroller will roll its way to the trash before your first kid is done with it. A well-built, well-maintained stroller can be sold on eBay or Craigslist for up to 70 percent of its original price.

Standard strollers range in price from $79 to $500. Real quality kicks in around the $120 to $200 range.

Single Standard Stroller

Also Known As
Full-size stroller, pushchair

Age Range
Birth to 4 years

Total Usage
4 years

Recommendation
Must have, unless you choose another option from birth

When to Buy
Before baby is born.

Age Range

Not all standard strollers can be used from birth because newborn babies, with no neck control, need an almost flat recline and special support.

Although the actual stroller seat might not be able to accommodate a newborn, most standard strollers do offer infant car seat carrier attachments to allow parents to snap newborns tucked into their car seats into the stroller from day one.

Ideally, with a high enough weight limit and durable enough stroller, you should be able to use a standard stroller from birth through the end of your stroller days. However, most strollers aren't that ideal, as they break down or wear out their welcome. Most likely you will be tired of lugging so much weight and room around by late toddlerhood, but in a pinch, if you're a one-stroller-only gal, the single standard stroller is for you.

Weight Limit

The weight limit of most standard strollers is generally higher than any kid you'll care to keep pushing around. Most top out at 40 pounds, although some models do go all the way to 50 pounds.

Weight of Stroller

Standard strollers are the heaviest single strollers. They range in weight from 20 to 28 pounds. Every year, manufacturers try to shave a bit of weight off their strollers without sacrificing too much sturdiness, and oh, how we appreciate it!

Folding

Due to their weight and bulk, standard strollers are all flat fold. Look for one with the easiest fold, one-handed if possible.

Reclining Seat

Especially if you're going to use this stroller with a newborn, find a seat that fully reclines. And make sure the reclining function is smooth and easy to operate.

Portability

While they are heavy, they aren't too heavy to travel with. It's not the most fun trip, but it can be done.

302 ☆ the **Baby Gizmo** buying guide

Why we love them: We love strollers and standard strollers are the standard. The workhorse of strollers, they fit most purposes, most children, and most budgets.

Why we don't: We don't don't.

Features to Consider

☆ Fully reclining seat

☆ Shock-absorbing wheels

☆ Large, easily accessible basket

☆ Snack tray

☆ Sun canopy

☆ Footrest

☆ Parent console

☆ Harness type

☆ Brakes

☆ Ease of fold

☆ Weight

☆ Suspension

☆ Locking mechanism

☆ Pattern

☆ Infant car seat carrier adapter

NOTES: *Single Standard Strollers*

Model Name / Manufacturer	Store/Price	My Impressions	Grade

TRAVEL SYSTEMS

A travel system is a single standard stroller packaged with a complementary infant car seat carrier designed to be clipped to said stroller. Like peanut butter and jelly, the stroller and car seat in a travel system set are made for each other—with matching color, matching fabric, and guaranteed mechanical compatibility. It's the most popular pick for the new mom who likes all her gear to match, and for those seeking peace of mind that their infant car seat will work with their stroller.

Only a handful of stroller manufacturers make car seats as well, and many moms consider the ability to clip the infant carrier into the stroller a necessity for the first six months of baby's life. Most strollers have adapter pieces that allow the most popular infant car seat carriers to work with their model, but travel system sets guarantee a perfect match.

The Components

The infant car seat carrier and the standard stroller in the travel system set are not special models made just for a travel system. They are regular models, sold separately most everywhere, just packaged together by color and pattern, with hopefully a break in price. Don't be blinded by the pairing; each component should be evaluated individually. Read our sections on infant car seat carriers and single standard strollers to know which features to look for.

Travel System

Also Known As
Stroller system, car seat/stroller system, pram system, car seat–compatible stroller

Age Range
Birth to 4 years

Total Usage
4 years

Recommendation
Nice to have

When to Buy
Before baby is born.

Err toward the Better Car Seat

Because the combinations of which model car seat comes with which model stroller are endless, you'll have quite a decision to pick the best match. Our advice is to research all car seat carrier and stroller models individually as if they never came in a set at all, decide which models you like best, and then see if you can find them as a travel system set. Too many moms think the planning is all done when they are presented with a travel system and just choose based on color, but not all travel systems offer the safest car seats or the best strollers.

If in doubt—you love the stroller but aren't crazy about the car seat that comes with it or vice versa—err on the side of the better infant car seat carrier, as the perfect car seat is more important for your baby.

To better prepare yourself for picking the perfect infant car seat (and to learn when to safely use and not use it), check out our detailed section on infant car seats (pages 98–106).

Beware the Bad Stroller

While we recommend you concentrate on the car seat portion, don't forget about the stroller entirely. Many travel systems are put together not for the convenience of parents, but for a manufacturer to unload unpopular strollers that aren't selling well singly. In the blush of first baby gear purchases, it's easy to think all the strollers rolling along under the car seat carriers are the same, but six months down the line, when you unclip the seat and discover you're left with an unwieldy, monstrous stroller that doesn't maneuver well and folds like a nightmare, you will not be a happy mama. And when mama's not happy, nobody's happy!

Travel Systems Sold Separately

Because some of the best stroller makers don't make car seats, those of us in love with those strollers were stuck using infant car seat carriers that didn't color coordinate. Doesn't sound like a big deal, but pushing a bright red stroller with a blue plaid car seat is hardly ideal. Thankfully, some of the car seat makers and stroller experts started working together and have released their respective products in matching fabrics and colors. You usually have to buy the pieces separately, but they look great together.

Price

Travel systems range in price from $100 to $400. Most are in the $200 range.

Why we love them: We love "matchy-matchy."

Why we don't: We love it to a fault. And sometimes get stuck with a subpar stroller because of it.

Features to Consider

☆ Car seat quality

☆ Stroller features

☆ Car seat attachment to stroller

NOTES: *Travel Systems*

Model Name / Manufacturer	Store/Price	My Impressions	Grade

LIGHTWEIGHT-PLUS STROLLERS

A relatively new type of stroller on the market falls right between a standard stroller and a lightweight stroller: the lightweight-plus. Lightweight-plus strollers offer the strength and stability to carry your newborn or infant car seat carrier, but at half the weight.

Lightweight-plus strollers are a little bigger and a lot more stable than a lightweight stroller. An infant car seat carrier rides securely on top, but the stroller you're left with after your baby grows up is nimble, light, and easy to travel with.

Hard to Spot

Lightweight-plus strollers can be hard to find in a crowd because they are usually miscategorized—either thrown in with standard strollers or mixed with the lightweights. Most online stores don't differentiate either, but on BabyGizmo.com we give them their own, special category (because we think they are such a special stroller).

The way to spot a lightweight-plus stroller is by stroller weight and infant car seat compatibility. True lightweight strollers weigh less than 15 pounds and are not meant for newborns. (While a few lightweights do advertise they can accept an infant car seat carrier, we personally wouldn't put our newborn in a stroller that weighed less than 15

Lightweight-Plus Stroller

Also Known As
Buggy, lightweight stroller, standard stroller, midweight stroller

Age Range
Birth to 4 years

Total Usage
4 years

Recommendation
Must have, unless you choose another option from birth

When to Buy
Before baby is born.

pounds.) Standard strollers weigh over 20 pounds. Lightweight-plus strollers are between 16 and 19 pounds and can accommodate a newborn or an infant car seat carrier.

Longest Age Range

While standard strollers can be used from birth to about 4 years, they are large and heavy enough to make you regret them before your child turns 18 months. Many parents, desperate to lighten their load, turn to a lightweight stroller. Lightweight strollers, however, offer smaller baskets, fewer convenience features, and stiffer seats that can be a shocking downgrade to a mom used to having a place to pile everyone's winter coats, 12 shopping bags, two Cokes, and a diaper bag.

Lightweight-plus strollers are genius because they give you much of the room and features of a standard stroller, but in a tinier, lighter package. We actually found we never wanted to retire our lightweight-plus stroller because we didn't want to lose the big basket, the stability, and the cup holder. And because it was only two pounds heavier than a lightweight stroller, we never had to.

Maneuverability

In our opinion, due to their smaller but superior design, lightweight-plus strollers handle much better than standard strollers. Like a lightweight stroller, they fit in tight places and can turn corners more easily, but unlike lightweights, they won't tip over in a stiff breeze.

Reclining Seat

Because they are safe for newborns, lightweight-plus strollers should have a fully reclining seat. Make sure it reclines smoothly and easily.

Carry-Cots

A few lightweight-plus strollers actually make carry-cots, also called bassinets, that attach to their strollers. They are very beautiful, and allow a mom to stroll carriage-style with her newborn, but also take baby into the house to sleep. The bassinets are usually around $200 extra, not cheap, but cheaper than a carriage or luxury stroller system.

If you choose a carry-cot, verify that the fabric is breathable, the baby has proper ventilation, the mattress is firm, and you cannot fit more than one finger between the mattress and any side.

Price

Because they weigh less, many mid-range lightweight-plus models are cheaper than their standard counterparts. Some upscale lightweight-plus strollers cost considerably more than a typical standard stroller, but not more than a comparable quality standard and lightweight stroller purchase together. And because the lightweight-plus stroller serves as both, we think you come out ahead. Lightweight-plus strollers range from $59 to $350.

Why we love them: Pound-for-pound, they are the best single stroller purchase you can make. They last the longest, can be used for the most varied functions, and would be our pick if we could only pick one.

Why we don't: We know it defies the laws of science, but we still wish we could stuff a few more parent conveniences and a bigger basket on them without adding to the size or weight.

Features to Consider
- ☆ Carry-cot option
- ☆ Fully reclining seat
- ☆ Shock-absorbing wheels
- ☆ Large, easily accessible basket
- ☆ Snack tray
- ☆ Sun canopy
- ☆ Parent cup holders
- ☆ Harness type

☆ Handle

☆ Footrest

☆ Locking mechanism

☆ Brakes

☆ Ease of fold

☆ Weight

☆ Suspension

☆ Pattern

NOTES: *Lightweight-Plus Strollers*

Model Name / Manufacturer	Store/Price	My Impressions	Grade

LIGHTWEIGHT/UMBRELLA STROLLERS

Lightweight strollers earn entry into this category because they are *(drum roll, please)* light in weight. Weighing 15 pounds and less, they are not only a necessity, but also a lifesaver for short trips with tired toddlers. Their ability to fold compactly makes them a great, trunk-saving choice, and their small size makes maneuvering in tight spaces a breeze.

Not meant as a replacement for a full-size, standard stroller, most lightweight strollers are too light to accommodate infant car seat carriers; even a shopping bag hung from the back handles can tip them over. Unless they have a reclining seat, they are not to be used with infants under 6 months old.

Technically a stroller is labeled "umbrella" if it has two U-shaped handles and folds in on itself like an umbrella. A "lightweight" stroller folds flat.

Because this is the only category of stroller (and perhaps baby gear!) where $9 models are available, it might seem like a great place to give your wallet a break. However, we recommend investing in a good, feature-packed lightweight stroller because you'll use it longer and more often than any other stroller (you'll be sick of your full-size one by age 1, we promise!). The extra durability, nicer fabric, and ease of steering are well worth the extra money. Don't believe us? Try pushing a cheap one through Disneyland all day. Your wrists, back,

Lightweight/ Umbrella Stroller

Also Known As
Buggy

Age Range
6 months to 4 years, unless it has a flat recline, and can be used from birth

Total Usage
3½ to 4 years

Recommendation
Nice to have

When to Buy
When you are tired of lugging around your full-size stroller.

and shoulders will not thank you. In fact, they may light torches, rile the villagers, and come after you.

Maclaren: The Umbrella Stroller That Changed History

For more than two hundred years, parents only had one choice of stroller—the heavy, unwieldy baby carriage. It's hard to believe, but the modern, folding stroller wasn't invented until 1965.

Owen Maclaren, a British test pilot and aeronautical designer, decided to try something new after a visit from his daughter, who flew from America with her baby and cumbersome baby carriage. In converted stables at his country farmhouse, he formed an ingenious frame out of aluminum that weighed just six pounds and folded compactly. And thus the umbrella stroller was born.

We love Maclarens, and we're so grateful for the superior handling and styling, we feel like sending them a small donation. And then we found out that they are releasing a black leather and gold umbrella stroller for $4,000, and we changed our minds. They seem to be doing all right on their own.

Maneuverability

We used to think all umbrella strollers were the same—hard to maneuver, flimsy little things that strained and tilted when you tried to shove them around a corner. And then we pushed our first high-quality umbrella stroller. With our breath. Unbelievable, life-altering difference. We'd wept through a trip to an amusement park because pushing our umbrella stroller was like hiking through waist-deep snow uphill, but we assumed they were all like that.

Perhaps because we grew up going to the Dollar Store with a mom who'd never dream of dropping $100 on a stroller when you could get one for $10, we never touched one until our second children. We thought the only difference between higher-priced umbrella strollers was in the fancy fabric. Yeah, the fabric is nice, but the real difference is in the design. Cheap umbrella strollers are crisscrossed, hollow steel tubes with a sling of fabric buttoned on them. Nice umbrella strollers are feats of engineering that carefully balance their load over the back wheels for maximum stability and mobility. You can push a good umbrella stroller with a fifth grader in it with your thumb. If you are even slightly interested and can possibly afford it, do yourself a favor and get a good one—early.

The Seat

Lightweight stroller seats are generally quite stiff, quite unpadded, and quite uncomfortable for riders. Rather than a supported seat with a stiff, reinforced frame, many lightweight seats are simple slings of fabric. Some are barely even fabric, but a ventilated mesh. Because you will use this stroller for years, and your children will spend days of their life in it, we do recommend getting a nice padded one.

Reclining Seat

Many umbrella stroller seats are fixed in position and do not recline. Make sure that if you buy one of those, it's what you want. We've grabbed one by mistake before and what a mistake it was! The only thing better than a happy toddler is a sleeping toddler, and yours will be neither in a fixed frame seat.

Plenty of umbrella strollers do have reclining seats now, even fully reclining for a newborn (although we wouldn't put a newborn in a lightweight stroller). While some offer various levels of recline, others only offer two positions: up and down. The method of recline for umbrella strollers is quite different from the mechanical methods on standard strollers. Seats on lightweights recline using zippers, hooks, drawstrings, straps, buckles, and sometimes levers.

Handles

The handles on cheaper lightweight strollers are notoriously uncomfortable; the nicer strollers have nicer handles. Some are hard plastic, but some are padded. We like the padded ones.

Be careful of anything you hang on the back of your umbrella stroller, as they are lightweight enough to tip backward quite easily. We're always extremely careful when our toddler is in one, but somehow we always forget about unloading the back first, and when we lift our child out, the stroller crashes backward to the ground. While our child is safe in our arms, our purse and the stroller take a beating.

Basket

Seriously scaled-down umbrella strollers will not have a basket at all. Some nicer ones do, and we seek those out. However, prepare for a much smaller basket than on standard strollers.

Extra Features

Lightweight strollers are lightweight because they don't offer much extra. No snack trays, no parent consoles, no cup holders. You can add some of these things with universal accessories, which we do. Oh, we do.

Stroller Weight

Under 15 pounds, they are all pretty light. So light, you won't really feel a difference between an 11- and a 13-pounder. The lightest ones weigh in at 7 pounds, but most are around 12.

Price

There are two basic types of umbrella stroller: cheap and not. The cheap ones range from $9 to $39. The higher you go on the pay scale, the better your stroller will maneuver. Period.

The not-cheap umbrella strollers range from $50 to $200. Too steep? Look online for last year's model; you can usually score a brand new one for $100 less and the only difference is generally the color.

Why we love them: They are lightweight and easy to travel with.

Why we don't: They are lightweight and easy to tip over.

Features to Consider
☆ Maneuverability

☆ Seat

☆ Seat recline

☆ Handles

☆ Basket

NOTES: *Lightweight/Umbrella Strollers*

Model Name / Manufacturer	Store/Price	My Impressions	Grade

LUXURY STROLLER SYSTEMS

In 1999, Max Barenbrug, a design student from The Netherlands, set out to make a new kind of stroller that offered more functionality and a sleeker form. He pitched his concept to every major manufacturer and was turned down. He decided to make them anyway, so he and his brother started their own company, a little outfit called Bugaboo. And a new era was born.

Loved by the very starriest of celebrities—think Madonna and Gwyneth—the stroller crashed through price barriers, selling for a full $400 more than the next priciest brands.

Who would pay that much for a stroller?

A lot of people, apparently, as sales tripled from 2003 to 2004. Now almost a dozen new manufacturers are producing luxury stroller systems. Owners swear by them, reviewers swoon over them, and magazine editors can't print their photos enough.

So, are they really worth all the croaking? In a word, yes.

When we first started testing them, we were prepared to push through the hype and were even a little biased against them. We're middle-class moms, after all, and proud of it.

And while it was lust at first sight (the delicious solid-colored fabrics against the cool gray aluminum is such a relief from the 6,000 muted plaid variations of other strollers), it was true love at first push. A luxury

Luxury Stroller System

Also Known As
Designer stroller, pram system, infant stroller system

Age Range
Birth to 4 years

Total Usage
4 years

Recommendation
Really nice to have

When to Buy
If you're going to pull the trigger, do it before your baby is born, so you can enjoy the benefits of this stroller system from day one.

stroller system surpasses every stroller we've ever laid hands on in terms of mobility, maneuverability, and just plain modern marvelousness. It responds with the slightest touch. Drives as if on clouds. And offers flexibility the likes of which we've never seen.

Only having viewed them (jealously) from afar, we were surprised to learn that luxury stroller systems are more than just a designer stroller. They are, in fact, full systems, good from birth through preschool, for use in the car, in the park, and even in the house.

They are three strollers in one: a carriage, a toddler stroller, and an all-terrain stroller. They come with detachable carry-cots that can be carried into the house and used as a Moses basket. And many now come with baby rockers and infant car seat carriers.

The core of the system is the chassis—the metal frame of the stroller—and it includes the luscious handlebar and wonderful, giant, air-filled, shock-absorbing wheels. The seats are separate pieces you attach depending on your need: a carry-cot for an infant, a regular stroller seat for a toddler, even "fun seats" for big kids with little steering wheels.

They are very sleek and modern, and sadly lacking parent convenience features. Most have started adding cup holders, but that's about all.

However, they do offer tons of accessories, many included: sun canopies, rain covers, mosquito nets, foot muffs, wheeled boards so toddler can hitch a ride, travel bags, and infant car seat adapters.

Weight

Unbelievably, all that stroller goodness weighs very little. Most luxury stroller systems weigh less than 20 pounds.

Price

Luxury stroller systems range in price from $500 to $1,000; most fall in the $700 range. Sounds like a bomb, but we added up the price of all the individual buys a luxury stroller system would save us from having to purchase:

Travel system:	$300
All-terrain stroller:	$350
Umbrella stroller:	$160
Rain guard:	$20
Moses basket:	$100
Baby seat:	$40
TOTAL:	$970

Yeah, we were shocked too. In fact, we managed to spin it to our husbands that a luxury stroller system was actually going to save us money!

We can't afford the Hermès Birkin bag. We'll never drive a Bentley. But to discover that the most beautiful, most versatile, designer strollers on the planet actually cost the same price we're spending anyway on lesser quality products was a great, great day for us middle class moms. It's not for everyone, sure. But if you can swing it, you won't regret it.

Special Features

So what special features should you look for in a luxury stroller system?

Fabric

Plush is king, but not always easy to clean. And some fabrics that look good actually turn out to be too hot. Pick a nice, breathable fabric that you can at least spot clean. Or, in the case of a diaper explosion, replace.

Easy-to-Use Clips

Because most systems require you to clip the bassinet or stroller seat onto the frame—and sometimes unclip them every time you want to fold it— look for a system that makes this easy. Some are foolproof; some make us feel like fools.

Folding

Luxury stroller systems have been notoriously difficult to fold, but they are getting better. Look for an easy one to save time and save face.

A stand-up fold is a good, good thing on an expensive stroller, because it brings the frame up to you rather than crashing to the pavement.

Wheels

Part of the secret to their superior handling is in the wheels, which are generally air filled. However, some are puncture proof, and some are not. There's nothing worse than sporting a flat on your luxury stroller. Annoying, embarrassing, and in our opinion, inexcusable for such an expensive product.

Handle Height Adjustment

Most luxury stroller system handles are adjustable, but some move more easily than others. Especially if you're trading off with a taller dad, a single push-button adjustment is much easier than one that requires a screwdriver.

Caché

Let's be honest, part of the appeal of luxury strollers is snob appeal, and that declines dramatically if a hundred other moms are pushing the same stroller at the mall. To avoid this, you might consider looking into the hottest, newest releases. New designers, most coming from Europe, debut their American lines every day. See if you can't score one of the first. You'll definitely score points with the paparazzi.

> *Why we love them:* Luxury strollers are like Christmas morning, full of gifts. Carry-cots and toddler seats and foot muffs, hooray!
>
> *Why we don't:* They cost a wad of cash, up front. Even though we know we'll spend the same amount on each accessory separately, somehow spreading those purchases out makes them easier to swallow (and explain to our mother!).

Features to Consider

- ☆ Fabric
- ☆ Attachments
- ☆ Fold
- ☆ Tires
- ☆ Handle
- ☆ Caché

NOTES: *Luxury Stroller Systems*

Model Name / Manufacturer	Store/Price	My Impressions	Grade

All-Terrain Strollers

The SUVs of strollers, all-terrain strollers are sportier and sturdier than their standard stroller counterparts, but are more maneuverable than joggers. The main feature of an all-terrain stroller is that it sports a triangular design with larger, air-filled wheels in back, a more durable frame, and true suspension, so it can go over "all terrains." They have large sun canopies because presumably you'll be using them primarily outdoors.

Many standard strollers look sporty these days, but take them off the sidewalk and they threaten to shake apart and they overshake the baby. The wheels on all-terrain strollers are large, pneumatic, and well-shocked, giving baby a better ride and parents an easier push through uneven terrain.

Most all-terrain strollers are not meant to be used as jogging or running strollers, however. Jogging strollers have fixed front wheels, hand brakes, and parent wrist tethers. They are constructed to withstand a great amount of rock and roll. All-terrain strollers are great for off-roading excursions: hikes, beaches, and even the uneven urban jungle.

Hard to Spot

Like lightweight-plus strollers, all-terrain strollers are frequently hard to

All-Terrain Stroller

Also Known As
Sport stroller, sport utility stroller, terrain stroller, urban stroller

Age Range
6 months to 5 years, unless it has a flat recline seat and can be used from birth

Total Usage
4 1/2-plus years

Recommendation
Nice to have

When to Buy
Before baby is born if you plan on using it from day one. Or as you find you need it because you're off-roading more than you expected.

find because they are miscategorized in stores and mislabeled, sometimes even by the manufacturers themselves, as "jogging strollers." The surefire way to spot an all-terrain is to look at the front wheels. True jogging strollers have a fixed front wheel that is 16 inches or larger; all-terrain front wheels swivel and are usually around 12 inches in diameter.

To Jog or Not to Jog?

Their bigger wheels, suspension, and sturdier frame mean you can take most all-terrain strollers for a jog around the block. They are great for power walks too. But if you're a serious runner, you should get a true jogging stroller.

Also, while many all-terrain strollers can hold newborns, you shouldn't jog with babies under 6 months old, as they don't have the neck muscles to withstand the jostling.

Age Range

Unlike more serious-minded jogging strollers, all-terrain strollers want to be your primary ride, not just a single-use activity stroller. To achieve this, many of them are packed with features and can actually accommodate newborns. If you are considering using an all-terrain stroller from day one, look for one with a fully reclining seat and infant car seat carrier adapters. Some more upscale models even offer bassinets.

Their extra durability means all-terrain strollers are almost guaranteed to last through your baby's kindergarten days, so you can get quite a lot of use out of them.

Carry-Cots

Many all-terrain strollers come with an optionally purchased carry-cot, or bassinet. If you're considering an all-terrain stroller carry-cot, you have a lucky, lucky baby. Most of them are dreamy. As with any baby bed, however, check that the fabric is breathable and washable, the interior is well ventilated, the mattress is firm, and you can't fit more than one finger between the mattress and any inside side.

Features

Some of the parent-friendly features (sorely lacking on jogging strollers) include storage baskets, parent consoles, height-adjustable handles, all-weather boots, and even reversible seating for newborns.

Color and Fabric

If strollers were Spice Girls, the all-terrain would be Sporty Spice—a tomboy with outdoorsy qualities but girly flair. You can see this immediately in the color and fabric options. The material on all-terrain strollers is more durable and weatherproof, and mostly solid colors—more fun than the somber grays and navy blues of joggers. You will find light greens and pink trim, but never a teddy bear pattern. Many moms make the all-terrain their stroller of choice for this very reason.

The Seat

While many all-terrain strollers do have reclining seats, just as many do not. If you choose one with a fixed sling seat, realize that it is an inappropriate choice for babies under 6 months old.

Folding

All-terrain strollers do fold, but not as compactly as their standard cousins, and many require you to remove the front wheel before folding.

Size

All that all-terrain durability and feature-packed goodness will cost you in size and price. All-terrain strollers are much, much larger than standard strollers, usually as big as double strollers when folded, and they only hold one kid.

Weight

Amazingly, all-terrain strollers aren't all that heavy. Thanks to their innovative aluminum frames, they are generally as weighty as standard strollers: between 21 and 30 pounds. Not nearly as light as luxury or lightweight strollers, but completely manageable.

Price

Their superior styling and construction does lead to a higher price tag than a standard or lightweight stroller. The price range on all-terrain strollers is from $200 to $450. The most durable strollers start at around the $350 mark. Past that, they are very similar in construction and quality; you'll start to pay extra for brand appeal.

Why we love them: They allow us to leave the pavement. Sometimes a mom has to drive over the mulch at the playground or across the grass.

Why we don't: They are very big and that removing-the-front-wheel-when-folding thing is a real pain.

Features to Consider

☆ Weight
☆ Bassinet option
☆ Basket
☆ Parent console
☆ Handle

☆ Boot
☆ Reversible seating
☆ Seat recline
☆ Fold
☆ Canopy

NOTES: *All-Terrain Strollers*

Model Name / Manufacturer	Store/Price	My Impressions	Grade

JOGGING STROLLERS

If you plan to run with your child, you should purchase only a true jogging stroller. Other strollers don't have the construction or safety features required to protect your little one. Jogging strollers have running-specific safety features built in, including parking brakes, hand brakes, and an emergency parent wrist tether for runaway strollers. However, it is important to note that pediatricians recommend not running with babies under 6 months old because they lack the proper neck strength and head control to safely manage the motion.

Jogging strollers are well-known for their size, large inflatable tires, three-wheel setup, and brightly colored fabric. Most also feature giant sun canopies for shade, although some are canopy-less.

Jogging strollers are constructed with a sturdy chassis to withstand vibration. With an aluminum frame, they are easier to push than most other strollers, but because of the fixed front wheel and considerable bulk, difficult to navigate around corners. Most feature shock absorbers and plush suspension, offering baby a very smooth ride. However, they have limited storage space and usually no convenience features—cup holders and tray toys would get in the way and add to the weight of the stroller, making it harder to push while running.

Jogging Stroller

Also Known As
Jogger, runner

Age Range
6 months to 5 years

Total Usage
4 1/2-plus years

Recommendation
Must have if you ever plan on jogging or running with your baby; don't need, if you don't

When to Buy
Start looking just before your baby turns 6 months old, so you'll be ready to use it.

History of the Jogging Stroller

You can thank Jane Fonda for the jogging stroller. The fitness revolution of the 1980s brought about the very first jogger.

Actually, you should thank Phil Baechler, a journalist and long-distance runner who tried bonding with his new baby during runs, but instead ending up trashing his standard strollers. So he invented one specifically designed for jogging with baby. And named it, appropriately, Baby Jogger.

Baby Jogger is still happily in business, and unlike Maclaren, actually offers some of the more reasonably priced jogging strollers to this day. No bling need apply.

Wheels

With jogging strollers, it's all about the size of the wheel. A serious jogger doesn't have wheels less than 16 inches in diameter, although a couple of 12-inchers are out there.

The larger the wheel, the easier the stroller will be to push, especially on more jagged terrain. If you plan on light jogging on mostly flat surfaces, 12-inch wheels should suffice. Serious jogging should be done with nothing less than 16-inch wheels, while serious runners will take nothing less than 20 inches.

Swivel Wheels

While traditional jogging strollers have a fixed front wheel, it does make them a bear to push around corners. Some models have started offering a swivel wheel that can be locked into place. For safety, when you are running or even jogging, the front wheel should always be fixed to not swivel. Why? Ever ride down a big hill in a wagon like Calvin & Hobbes? Ever lose control of the handle, and when the front wheels turned suddenly, you and the wagon flipped over? That's why. A fixed front stroller wheel is necessary when jogging or running because it won't abruptly turn at high speeds, sending you, the stroller, and its precious contents flying.

But being able to flip a lever and have swivel capabilities when you are just moseying is an attractive feature to many.

Suspension

While not all joggers come with suspension, we highly recommend it to help absorb the shocks of the road so your baby's brain doesn't have to.

Brakes

Most jogging strollers come with both hand and foot brakes. We're big fans of having both. Just make sure they aren't so tight that you have to be a carnival champ to squeeze them.

Wrist Tether

A tether is a strap that goes around your wrist to keep the stroller from getting out of your reach, just in case you stumble or get so tired you lose your grasp on the handle. Because we're almost delirious near the end of even a short run and can sometimes barely manage to stay upright ourselves, we highly recommend this feature.

Aluminum versus Steel Frame

While steel frames are less expensive, they do eventually rust. They are also easily tortured by climate changes, marine environments, and mountain weather. It might cost a bit more at first, but an aluminum frame will add years to the life of your stroller, which could save you money if you plan on using it for more than one kid.

Seating

For safety, most jogging stroller seats are set to a permanent deep recline that your child might not like. Instead of facing forward, they face the sky. Younger kids probably won't mind, but older kids are apt to complain. At least, ours do.

Safety Straps

For reasons beyond our comprehension, the highest speed strollers in the world also have the worst safety straps. Many models have straps that are too loose, even when tightened as far as possible, to adequately restrain a small child. A 2-year-old being able to eject herself at any time is not something we want to worry about when we're sprinting down a hill.

Know this is a liability of many models, and check diligently for it in the store, as you can't really home sew a safe alternative.

Features

You won't find many convenience features on a jogging stroller. Many don't even have baskets, but do offer a pocket or two. We couldn't figure out why they couldn't at least stick a cup holder or something on them, but then our personal trainer aunt reminded us that you're not guzzling Starbucks when you're running. Touché, Miss Fitness, touché. (Although we are running with a water bottle and we would like a place to put that.)

Canopy

We like sun canopies to shade our babies, but they can add drag to a jogging stroller, and when you're running, you frequently run in directions that make the sun shine directly onto your rider anyway. Just be sure to use lots of sunscreen, a hat, and maybe even lightweight long pants on your little guy.

Size and Weight

Jogging strollers are big, like leave-in-your-garage-unfolded big. They aren't too heavy—about the same as standard strollers, thanks to their light frames and lack of extras. Jogging strollers typically weigh between 20 and 30 pounds.

Fold

Jogging strollers don't fold very compactly, and many require you to remove the front wheel before folding. Not an issue if you're constantly running around your own neighborhood, but if you ever plan on hauling it to the local park, find one that folds.

Price

Unlike all-terrain strollers, many discount joggers are available. Prices range from $99 to $400. Cheaper joggers near the $100 range will not handle well or last long, but can be a good choice for the casual exerciser. Good quality models for serious athletes start at around $200.

Why we love them: They allow us to continue our pre-baby jogs with baby.

Why we don't: They allow us to continue our pre-baby jogs with baby.

Features to Consider

☆ Weight   ☆ Frame

☆ Canopy   ☆ Seat recline

☆ Pockets   ☆ Safety straps

☆ Wheels   ☆ Fold

☆ Brakes

NOTES: *Jogging Strollers*

Model Name / Manufacturer	Store/Price	My Impressions	Grade

DOUBLE STANDARD STROLLERS

They're big, they're bulky, and they're expensive. But if you're having twins or expecting your next baby before your first is able to walk long distances (like through the mall), you're going to need one. Standard double strollers weigh anywhere from 24 to a whopping 47 pounds, but they're chock-full of features, offer comfortable seating for both babes, and they get the job done.

Most double strollers are unwieldy to steer, but they do offer large baskets, double sun canopies, and parent-friendly features such as cup holders, adjustable handles, and shock-absorbing wheels.

Double Standard Stroller

Also Known As
Full-size double, double stroller, twin pushchair, double pushchair, double buggy, twin buggy, twin stroller, tandem double, side-by-side double

Age Range
Birth to 4 years

Total Usage
4 years

Recommendation
Must have, if you have more than one non-full-time walker

When to Buy
Just before your twins or next baby is born.

Seating

There are actually two different types of double standard strollers based on how they stack the seats: tandem or side by side.

Tandem Seating

The most popular seating arrangement in double strollers is the tandem, where one seat sits in front of the other. Many tandems go one step further and offer stadium seating, giving the little guy in back a view from the top. Tandem strollers are usually very stable, but can be a nightmare to maneuver. To make things easier, you should load the heaviest weight in the back seat, over the

back wheels. While many manufacturers recommend placing an infant car seat carrier in the rear seat for safety (presumably so you can be closer to your baby), if you have a heavier toddler, this arrangement can be almost impossible to push. Many tandems only offer a full recline on the back seat, which is a total pain, because everyone wants to kick back sometimes. We look for tandems that allow both seats to recline. Many newer tandem strollers allow you to reverse the direction each seat faces independently, so your children can see where they're going, look at you, or even face each other.

> *Why we love them:* Tandems are easier to fit through the door, and are more car seat compatible.

> *Why we don't:* Tandems are the heaviest and hardest to push stroller in the free world. And if you have same-aged children, prepare for fights about who gets to sit in the front (we don't know about you, but we prepare by packing M&M's).

Side-by-Side Seating

Side-by-side seats sit, well, we think you can guess. They offer a more democratic view, although they pose a challenge for many doorways, elevators, and small aisles. While each seat reclines, more often than not, neither accepts an infant car seat. If you have same-sized kids, it's much easier to push them in a side-by-side than in a tandem, but if one kid is significantly heavier, these strollers tend to veer to the side, all crazy-like. They are a little lighter than a tandem stroller, but much bigger when folded. Make sure the side-by-side stroller isn't too wide to fit through a standard doorway; less than 30 inches wide is recommended.

> *Why we love them:* They allow our children to play with each other.

> *Why we don't:* They allow our children to punch each other.

Seats

Look for seats that both recline. You'll need a full recline for infant use.

Basket

Double strollers offer them, but they can be nearly impossible to access, what with four little legs in the way. Also see if you can access the basket when the seats are reclined, as it's no good trying to grab a blanket to cover a sleeping child if you have to wake that child to get to it.

Canopy

Look for a large one that adequately covers both riders.

Wheels and Suspension

Look for good wheels, as the extra weight of two riders will crack little plastic ones in no time. Also suspension on the wheels is not just nice for the rider, but can aid the pusher as well.

Handling

They are all pretty bad, but some are worse than others. No matter how big it is or how much it costs, you'll hate your double stroller if it pains you to push it. Keep test-driving until you find an adequate model.

The Handle

Because you're shoving so much weight down the sidewalk, you need a good, solid handle. A single bar is best. Ergonomically padded is even better. Just make sure it doesn't shake or wiggle too easily in the store when you're not even pushing the stroller, or when you actually try to push you'll end up wanting to push it off a cliff.

Folding

Many double strollers fold quite easily—too easily in fact. Thousands of the most popular models were recently recalled because they kept folding in on tiny riders. Check that the stroller has a foolproof locking mechanism to keep the stroller open when it's in use.

Stroller Weight

Pay careful attention to how heavy a stroller you are committing to, because you might consider committing hari-kari on a large one after you have loaded and unloaded it about three times. Double standard strollers weigh anywhere from 24 to an upsetting 47 pounds. We're just going to go on record as saying that after you leave the 20 to 30 pound range, you leave all good sense behind.

Features

Most double standard strollers come packed with parent convenience features—thank goodness for small miracles! We highly recommend getting as many as you can, without adding too much to the weight, because being able to walk with your drink of choice can make any walk more pleasant.

Price

Double standard strollers range in price from $99 to (are you ready?) $899. Most are firmly in the $150 range.

Other Alternatives

If you have a wide enough range in the age of your children, you might not need a full double standard stroller. You can find much smaller, easier to manage products designed for the older child, think 3 and up, who like to walk but can't make it all the way through a day at Disneyland. You might also consider a toddler footboard attachment to your standard stroller (some luxury stroller systems offer them), or a stroller-and-a-half, which offers a little half seat for your bigger hitchhikers.

Features to Consider

☆ Tandem or side-by-side

☆ Seat reclines

☆ Car seat adaptable

☆ Basket

☆ Canopy

☆ Suspension

☆ Wheels

☆ Maneuverability

☆ Handle

☆ Fold

☆ Weight

☆ Parent console

NOTES: *Double Standard Strollers*

Model Name / Manufacturer	Store/Price	My Impressions	Grade

DOUBLE LIGHTWEIGHT/UMBRELLA STROLLERS

About the time your twins or your second baby turns 1, you'll start looking for a lighter stroller to ease your double pushing duties. Double lightweight or umbrella strollers are the lightest double strollers available, but they are still twice as heavy as a single umbrella stroller, weighing roughly the same as a single standard stroller, anywhere from 18 to 28 pounds. While they are the ultimate in convenience (especially important for the mom of multiple children who doesn't need to be weighed down by anything else), the double lightweight stroller you choose should be sturdy enough to carry two children.

Double lightweight strollers share many of the same features and options as single lightweight strollers, so take a peek at that section so you know what to look for. Just know that everything—wheels, handles, and even the folding mechanism—will take double the pressure under double the weight. Here are the features that are specific only to double versions.

Age Range

Most double lightweight strollers are meant for children over 6 months in age. Some do have newborn capabilities, and if you are willing to trust your tiny one in a tiny stroller, look for newborn head pillows, body padding, and secure straps. Babies under 6 months old also require a fully reclined seat.

Double umbrella strollers are the go-to choice for moms with older toddlers who no longer need to tote quite so much stuff. A good one should last you into the preschool years.

Seating

Due to their light construction, double lightweight strollers only offer side-by-side seating and are not able to safely hold infant car seat carriers. (Some claim to be able to hold an infant car seat carrier, but we wouldn't trust them with our newborn baskets.) The side-by-side seating arrangement makes for equal viewing—great for twins—but does make the stroller quite wide, a nuisance in narrow store aisles.

Cheaper double umbrella strollers will have only a single-stop recline, while nicer models will give you more recline positions. Look for seats that offer at least one position of recline, as the rhythmic motion of strolling could put even the most stubborn insomniac to sleep.

Sun Canopies

Make sure canopies are adequately sized to cover both little passengers. And because your riders are sitting side by side, peekaboo windows on the canopy can be especially helpful to see who really "started it."

Features

Many double lightweight strollers do have a few convenience features like moderately sized baskets and parent cup holders, but not nearly as many as a double standard. We're all about convenience, so we look for strollers with the most we can get.

Double Lightweight/ Umbrella Stroller

Also Known As
Double umbrella, twin umbrella, double umbrella buggy, double umbrella pushchair

Age Range
6 months to 4 years

Total Usage
3½ years

Recommendation
Nice to have

When to Buy
Start looking just before your twins or youngest baby turns 6 months old.

Handling

Because they are wide and weighed down with two kids, double lightweight strollers don't handle nearly as dreamily as single lightweights, but they do steer much, much better than double standard strollers. Nicer, more expensive strollers will push much, much easier and actually allow you to turn corners, unlike some of the cheaper models.

Look for a handle that is at least slightly padded, because you'll be pushing twice the weight. Handles that adjust can save your life, especially as many double lightweight strollers are awkward and can get in the way of your natural stride. Kicking the stroller every three steps does not make for a fun stroll.

Also, if you thought suspension over the wheels was important for an easy pushing experience, double that thought.

Size

Check that the double lightweight stroller you choose can actually fit through a standard door; in other words, it should be 29 inches or less in width. This size can lead to a rather snug fit for wider kids, but you can't exactly park your kids outside while you shop because their stroller doesn't fit through the front door. (We've heard moms do routinely leave their kids outside stores in Iceland, but we're pretty sure that won't fly here. They also get a nine-month maternity leave with 80 percent of their pay in Iceland. We're thinking about moving to Iceland.)

Folding

There are still clever, one-handed folds to be had on double lightweight strollers, but they do require some amount of parent patience. You are collapsing more supports and more fabric, so give yourself some time to perfect it. Seem too complicated or time consuming? Find one that isn't.

One of the biggest advantages of a double lightweight stroller over any other double stroller is how much smaller it is when folded. While other doubles take up the entire trunk on our SUV (Geo Metro? forget about it), double lightweight strollers do collapse into a pretty small size. Not as small as a single umbrella, but comparable to a single standard.

Weight

Surprisingly, double lightweight strollers aren't as light as we'd hoped, but they do have to safely support two kids. They actually weigh as much as single standard, and even some double standard, strollers. Double lightweight strollers weigh between 18 and 30 pounds.

Price

Just as with single umbrellas, double lightweight strollers have two price groups: cheap and not. Cheaper strollers cost between $59 and $139. More expensive varieties range from $150 to $350. More money will buy you a sturdier stroller, better maneuverability, more durability, and more options. For this type of stroller, we have found that great, long-lasting success starts at the $200 range.

> *Why we love them:* Bringing two kids everywhere means bringing a lot of stuff. We appreciate not having to bring it all in a giant, heavy stroller.
>
> *Why we don't:* We wish they better accommodated newborns. But then, of course, they'd have to be bigger and heavier. We can't win.

Features to Consider

☆ Reclines

☆ Canopies

☆ Basket

☆ Parent cup holder

☆ Handle

☆ Suspension

☆ Width

☆ Weight

☆ Fold

NOTES: *Double Lightweight/Umbrella Strollers*

Model Name / Manufacturer	Store/Price	My Impressions	Grade

DOUBLE ALL-TERRAIN STROLLERS

Just as the right all-terrain stroller can be used as your primary single stroller, you can use a double all-terrain stroller for more than just casual jogs—it can be your primary double stroller, period.

The features to consider when choosing a double all-terrain are very similar to single choices, so flip back to that section and read all about it.

The specific concerns for double all-terrain strollers include the extra size, weight, folded dimensions, and unique seating arrangements.

Seating

Double all-terrains typically offer two types of seat—side-by-side or tandem. There is, however, a weird new breed: the tandem basket seat, also sometimes called a "second seat."

Side-by-Side Seating

Side-by-side seating is the most popular arrangement for double all-terrains. It gives each child an equal view, although for better or worse, they can easily touch each other. Side-by-side seating makes for the widest stroller, both fully assembled and folded.

Double All-Terrain Stroller

Also Known As
Sport double, twin sport, sport utility double stroller, terrain double, all-terrain double, urban double, twin terrain

Age Range
6 months to 5 years, unless it can accommodate a newborn, and then it can be used from birth

Total Usage
4 1/2 years

Recommendation
Nice to have

When to Buy
Just before your twins or next baby is born.

Why we love them: We like it for jogging.

Why we don't: We hate it for shopping.

Tandem Seating

You won't find as many tandem seats with double all-terrains, generally because it's a harder engineering feat to pull off in a triangular shaped stroller. If you're looking at this type, choose one that is nice and stable and can't tip over easily like a tricycle.

Why we love them: They are much easier to shop with, because we can actually fit into the shops.

Why we don't: The stability thing bugs us. Especially when an overexcited front passenger unexpectedly decides to dismount.

Tandem Basket Seating

As strange as it sounds, this new seating design puts one child literally underneath the other. The front rider sits in a seat that resembles a single all-terrain setup. The second child sits in a sling seat mounted underneath and slightly behind, where the stroller basket would be (and now, most definitely is not). They have room for their legs and all, and there is a high seat back and safety straps. But we still hate it. The kid is inches off the ground. They stare at the back of the seat in front of them. And the wheels are right there, just begging to be touched. Yes, there are parents who love them and kids who swear they love to ride in them. And the manufacturers have finally started adding wheel guards. We're still not sold.

Why we love them: We really don't.

Why we don't: No matter what you say, the kid is riding in the basket and looks like an unsafe afterthought to us.

Reclining Seats

Look for a recline capability on both seats, or else you run the risk of revealing who really is your favorite kid.

Weight

Of course, double all-terrain strollers are heavier than singles. They range in weight from 28 to 35 pounds.

Price

Double all-terrains are more expensive, too. Price ranges from $300 to $700.

Features to Consider

☆ Stroller seat setup

☆ Reclines

☆ Weight

NOTES: *Double All-Terrain Strollers*

Model Name / Manufacturer	Store/Price	My Impressions	Grade

DOUBLE JOGGING STROLLERS

If you are a serious runner and have two children you want to take with you, you'll need a double jogging stroller.

Read our entry on jogging strollers to learn about which features make a good one, but here are the specific specifications for doubles.

Seating

Jogging strollers only offer one seating arrangement for double riders: side by side. The positioning makes the entire stroller much wider, of course, and can make pushing more difficult, but you're guaranteed a better workout.

Look for seats that are wide enough to comfortably seat your children. As with single joggers, seats are typically very deep and tend to force riders to look up rather than out.

Safety Straps

As on single joggers, the safety straps are decidedly loose and lacking on double joggers. Check their adjustability in the store and see if you can actually strap younger children in tightly enough.

Double Jogging Stroller

Also Known As
Double jogger, runner double, Duallie, Twinner, twin jogger

Age Range
6 months to 5 years

Total Usage
4 1/2 years

Recommendation
Nice to have

When to Buy
Just before your twins or next baby turns 6 months old.

Canopy

Because the seats are side by side, double jogging strollers have one giant canopy that shades both passengers. Look for one that provides adequate shade, but beware. Some are so large, a big gust of wind, and poof, you're Mary Poppins.

Size

The largest of all strollers on Earth, the double jogging stroller is wide as a house. Forget about being able to push it through a single, standard door. Seriously, forget about it.

Folding

Most do fold, with more steps than most strollers. And you'll still need an extra parking spot for it when it's folded.

Price

Double jogging strollers range in price from $200 to over $400.

Why we love them: Because we've never needed to continue our jogs more than after we've had our second kid.

Why we don't: Because we still hate jogging.

Features to Consider

☆ Seat width   ☆ Canopy

☆ Safety straps   ☆ Fold

NOTES: *Double Jogging Strollers*

Model Name / Manufacturer	Store/Price	My Impressions	Grade

Strollers-and-a-Half

If you have two children but are worried about the size, weight, and price of double strollers, you might consider a stroller-and-a-half. Meant for moms with children of different ages, they are a great option if you have an older child who likes to walk sometimes and would leave her seat in a full double empty more often than not.

A stroller-and-a-half is a single standard stroller with a regular stroller seat and an additional area behind that seat for the occasional older hitchhiker.

When shopping for a stroller-and-a-half, employ the same tactics and look for the same features found on a single standard stroller, but also consider the following.

Age Range

While the standard stroller's seat can be used on most models from birth up (with an infant car seat carrier only, unless the seat fully reclines and is specifically suited for a newborn), the minimum age for a back passenger is around 2½ years, or when your child is old enough to not just throw himself off the little platform on a whim.

This is not a suitable stroller choice for twins, as they can't be in the back when they're younger, and they'll fight for the back when they're older.

Stroller-and-a-Half

Also Known As
Sit-N-Stand, baby-toddler ride-along stroller, Caboose stroller

Age Range
6 months to 4 years, unless you attach an infant car seat carrier, and then it can be used from birth

Total Usage
4 years

Recommendation
Nice to have

When to Buy
If you have an older toddler (2½-plus years old), buy this stroller before your second baby is born.

Front Seat

The front seat is a standard stroller seat, although with much less recline than we like. Look for adequate padding and appropriate safety straps. Many models also offer a child snack tray, which we like.

Back Board and Bench

Behind the front seat is extra space with a little board and bench seat for the older child. The back rider can either stand on the board or sit on a little bench. The bench is usually quite small and backless and resembles a tiny camping table. There is usually a strap that hooks between the stroller handles, however, that can give back support to a child when she is standing. We prefer models that have a sliding rather than fixed bench, so it can be moved out of the way when the rider stands.

While some back seats do have a little lap strap, children can easily free themselves, so let only mature kids ride in the back.

Finally, look for a stroller that doesn't allow easy, tempting access to the back wheels. Another reason to not let your 18-month-old ride in the back, no matter how smart he might be.

Basket

The stroller-and-a-half does come with a nice large basket, but it can be difficult to access when the back rider is onboard.

Canopy

The canopy on the stroller-and-a-half only covers the front seat. Back riders are left to their own hat and sunscreen devices.

Size and Weight

The size and weight of a stroller-and-a-half is comparable to a lighter standard stroller. They usually weigh between 21 and 25 pounds. They are much easier to manage, steer, and store than double standard strollers and feel much sturdier than double umbrellas.

Price

The price ranges from $130 to $250. More money will get you a more durable, easier-to-drive stroller with more parent convenience features.

Why we love them: Because they're bigger than a single, but smaller than a double. Perfect for our baby/older toddler combination.

Why we don't: Because our older toddler sure does think it's funny to jump off midstride. We, however, don't.

Other Toddler Seats

Some standard single and all-terrain single strollers actually have their own "stroller-and-a-half" versions with the addition of attachable toddler seats. These tiny seats usually resemble little grocery cart seats and attach directly to the single stroller. The seats have no recline and are meant for older children, up to 35 pounds, but we found that kids over 2½ actually didn't like sitting in them for very long. However, they are a great option to see you through the stage of an older sibling from age 18 months to 2½ years.

Features to Consider

☆ Front seat padding

☆ Harnesses

☆ Snack tray

☆ Basket

☆ Bench padding

☆ Bench slide

NOTES: *Strollers-and-a-Half*

Model Name / Manufacturer	Store/Price	My Impressions	Grade

MULTIPLES STROLLERS

You can get a multiples seat setup on almost any type of stroller, but your options will be very limited beyond that. There is usually only one or two on the market of each style. You'll have to decide which type of stroller you most prefer, and then everything about that stroller will basically be picked for you. What kind of multiples mom are you? There are carriages for city walkers, standard strollers for the budget-minded, minimalist designs for car seat ferrying, all-terrain strollers for the active mom, and even joggers.

Most multiples strollers accommodate triplets, but there are strollers for quads, and even a company that makes six-seaters, called minibuses.

Seating

You can find side-by-side-by-side options, as well as inline (tandem for triplets) arrangements, even those with stadium seating. Look for seats with nice padding and as much recline as possible. A flat recline or infant car seat carrier connection is required for newborns, and we're guessing you are going to want to leave the house at some point during the first six months.

Multiples Stroller

Also Known As
Triplet stroller, Triplette stroller, triple stroller, quad stroller, Minibus, Trio

Age Range
Birth to 4 years

Total Usage
4 years

Recommendation
Must have, for those with marvelous multiples

When to Buy
When you find out you're expecting twins or more, start shopping!

Handling

Inline strollers feel like you're pushing a semitruck, but they do fit through doorways. Side-by-side-by-sides, not so much. Most multiples strollers will get you from point A to point B, but some require a Herculean effort. Don't expect the maneuverability of an umbrella stroller, but some models made by ex-automobile engineers are modern marvels of mobility.

Size and Weight

Did we say double jogging strollers were the largest strollers around? Multiples strollers laugh at little double joggers—*ha ha ha ha!* They are heavy behemoths, weighing anywhere from 30 to 60 pounds. But they are heavy for a reason. You have lots of babies to protect!

Folding

Remember these strollers are large and bulky and will not be the easiest to fold. Some are definitely easier than others, and some are more compact when folded than others. So if size is an issue, consider the folded dimensions. Also consider if any or all the seats have to be removed to fold it.

Handles

Most have telescoping handles for easier adjustment. Because you won't know how the weight distributes until you start pushing it fully loaded, an adjustable handle is key—but choose a solid one.

Brakes

All strollers need brakes; none more so than one with the extra momentum of multiple little bodies. Most multiples strollers have hand and foot brakes. They should be solid, but not so sticky as to be hard to disengage.

Canopies

Most multiples strollers either come with canopies or offer them separately. We're big fans of big amounts of shade.

Fabric and Color

Don't expect fabulous fabric choices. Sadly, the choice in the style department is much more limited than for other types. You can find pretty nice options, especially if you're only looking for triplets. Got six? The very name "minibus" should tell you it's not going to be that pretty.

Stroller Basket

With multiples, you have multiple diaper bags and more stuff, so look for the biggest basket you can possibly find. And make sure it's easily accessible.

Price

Prices vary according to the number of seats you require and the type of stroller you want. Carriages, jogging, and all-terrain strollers are the most expensive. As with most strollers, the more expensive models will last much longer than the cheaper versions.

Multiples strollers range from $250 to $1,500. Most good ones are in the $600 to $900 range.

Availability

Multiples strollers are hard to find in retail stores. We would drive a good two hours to test-drive one. All can easily be ordered on the Internet.

EBay, Craigslist, and multiples message boards are great resources for secondhand models at giant savings.

Why we love them: Being a product of one, we love any product made especially for large families.

Why we don't: We're not a freak show, people! Triplets are not that amazing. Quit staring! Move along, move along!

Features to Consider

☆ Seat padding

☆ Seat reclines

☆ Car-seat adaptable

☆ Fold

☆ Handle

☆ Canopy

☆ Brakes

☆ Basket

NOTES: *Multiples Strollers*

Model Name / Manufacturer	Store/Price	My Impressions	Grade

Twenty-six

Swings

The most famous American lullaby is "Rock-a-Bye Baby" for a reason. Babies love to rock. And because cradles aren't very safe, an indoor baby swing is as close to treetop heaven as your infant can get.

Our babies adored their swings. Raised up from the floor, ensconced behind metal poles, plastic trays, and wide-winged seats, our babies had a great view of the family room and yet were protected from most of the hubbub of our house. If they felt like nodding off, they did so. Our babies practically lived in their swings for the first couple of months.

Swing

Age Range
Birth to 5 months

Total Usage
5 months

Recommendation
Must have, for most

When to Buy
Any time before your baby is born. Great for your registry.

We've heard people warn against swings, christening them "veg-o-matics" and claiming they are surrogate parents. We want to punch those people in the face. No one can hold her baby all day long. We tried and our arms got very, very tired. (And our mother-in-law snarked that we were spoiling the baby anyway.)

History of the Swing

The very first automatic baby swing was invented in 1953 by David Saint, an engineer and father of nine who worked for Graco.

He noticed that on nice days, his wife used a backyard swing to calm fussy babies and decided to make an indoor version. The Swyngomatic debuted in 1955.

Product design talent must run in the family (or maybe, just maybe, swings make babies geniuses), but 32 years later, David's son, Nate Saint, invented the first portable play yard, the Pack 'n Play.

We salute you, Saints. Without you, we'd all still be setting our babies on the washing machine to calm them on cloudy days and letting them sleep in our suitcases.

That's not to say that every baby in the whole world loves swings. Some babies don't like swinging at all. But if you're one of the lucky moms with a baby that likes to rock out, you've got three main swing choices.

STANDARD SWINGS

A standard swing includes a padded seat into which baby is strapped, which hangs from a metal frame, usually A-shaped, although variations exist. The main attraction is of course, swinging, although many models throw in even more excitement in the form of music, lights, sound effects, toys, and even mobiles. Buttons on the top allow parents to start, stop, and change the speed of the swinging; play music; and even set timers. Standard swings are space hogs, but they need to be to provide stability and safety, so we don't really mind.

Why we love them: Everything about them is soothing. They even make a rhythmic noise when they're in motion that makes us calm and sleepy.

Why we don't: Everything about them is soothing except for their color scheme. For some reason, most swings are garish and overly cartoonish. We get it, babies can only see big, bold patterns. But our babies are *sitting* on this bold, patterned fabric. And when they're not, *we* can see it. Oh, how we can see it. From the Grand Canyon, we can see it.

CRADLE SWINGS

Today, the term "cradle swing" is used to refer to a full-size standard swing with a standard seat into which baby is strapped, which has a special side-to-side swinging motion like a cradle. Many also swing back and forth as well. The metal frame is a slightly different shape to accommodate the new direction, and cradle swing seats are usually a little rounder than standard seats. Cradle swings are chock-full of as many features as standard swings, although some models are tricked out with canopies and glow-in-the dark stuff to make them more nest-like.

Why we love them: Many of those swing-hating babies actually dig cradle swings because of the different motion. And cradle swings are usually more muted and attractive.

Why we don't: They are more expensive than standard swings—in some cases, twice as much.

TRAVEL SWINGS

A travel swing is a swing with a full-size seat on shorter legs. They fold for easy portability, and most contain a good number of the same bells and whistles as the big boys, such as music, lights, and toys.

Why we love them: It means we can have a happy, sleepy baby anywhere we go.

Why we don't: When they chopped off the legs, we wish they would have chopped off more of the price.

Age Range

While all seats have height and weight limits that must be obeyed, they are usually far greater than your children will ever be when they are swingers. Instead of using these as a guideline for when your baby is too big, use your child's personal development as a signal. Swings are dangerous places for babies who can crawl out of them. Don't wait that long, however. We say, once babies can stick their hand out and try to stop themselves from swinging by grabbing the poles, it's time to retire the swing.

Stability

As with any product that lifts a baby off the floor, stability is one of the most important features of a swing. Look for one with a nice wide base that is super sturdy. We would recommend giving the store models a good shake, but frequently, they're tied down. You can still get a feel for how solid they are, however—and don't forget to jiggle the seat.

The Seat

The seat on a swing is where it's at. Look for one that's adequately padded, but also has soft fabric. Some are covered in cheap, scratchy stuff that can chafe little cheeks.

A reclining seat is a must, because babies ride before they have good head and neck control. Use the most reclined option for the littlest ones.

Safety Straps

Safety straps are extremely important because they are the glue that keeps your baby safely put. Do not rely on any other measure to keep your baby in—such as a tray—and always, always strap them in every time.

Five-point harnesses are superior to three-point harnesses because they hold the shoulders back and keep baby from lurching forward, but three-points are acceptable as long as baby is securely fastened between the legs.

Babies have been known to get tangled and strangled in their straps, however, so always check that you haven't left too much slack, look for solid straps that aren't too loosey-goosey in how they are attached to each other, and pack that swing away before baby even looks like he's ready to climb out.

Trays

Most seats have a tray you must lift or unlatch to get baby in and out of the seat. Many trays have attached T-bars underneath (the plastic "leg" that rests between your baby's legs) for extra security against baby slipping out. The tray should be your last line of defense for keeping baby safely in the swing, but make sure the tray is snapped closed every time. Some trays are tricky; some are sticky. Test them all in the store; open and close until you find one that's not so loose baby could kick it open, but not so tight you'll bust a fingernail every time you open it.

While swing trays look like the snack trays on high chairs and strollers, they are not. No snacking will ever be had in a swing, because once babies have the dexterity to lean forward and pick up Cheerios with their forefinger and thumb, they are too big for the swing anyway.

Tray Toys

Tray toys scare us. Mounting things for baby to just look at on the tray is fine, but a toy that baby must touch to activate—whether it's a rattle or a fancy electronic toy with buttons—is pointless and dangerous.

Pointless because safe swing riders are tiny blobs of baby that can't even reach the tray. Even if your baby is within the weight limit of the swing and still enjoys it, if she has the dexterity to play with tray toys, she's too big for a swing. Physically advanced babies try to climb out of their swings and get seriously injured, and sometimes killed, doing so.

Tray toys are also dangerous because they trick parents into waiting around until the day baby will actually play with them. And because that day is the day a baby is too big for a swing, encouraging parents to leave their older babies in swings past when they should is a bad, bad thing. Boo, to tray toys. *Boooooo!*

Other Toys

The best toys for swings are visually interesting things for baby to look at, because at this age, they can't do much else. Some swings have little light shows and even mobiles, but they should be positioned so that your baby can actually see them but aren't tortured and overwhelmed by them.

Some swings have teething toys on little tethers and things a baby can bat at from the sides of the seat, but our children were never motivated enough to even attempt touching them. We don't blame them, as it's pretty hard to grab something, hold onto something, or focus on anything when you're mid-swing.

Baby Loading

Many swings have an overhead arch for support (and to hold lights and toys in many cases), but others have an open-top design to allow for easier baby loading and unloading. As moms who have boinked their baby's heads on the top bar more times than we can count, we hail the genius of the open top.

What we'd really like is a lock feature that would stop the darn swing from swinging when we put our babies in and take them out.

Speed Control

Most swings have a minimum of two speeds; some offer many more. Start your babies on the lowest setting and graduate them as they gain more neck control and more weight.

You should test the swing's slowest setting with a doll before you throw your receipt away, especially if you plan on using the swing with a newborn. Some swings are crazy fast, even on the slowest setting. If Patty Peepants flops around or flies out of the seat, you need to find a different model.

Swing Power

Gone are the days of the manual crank. Today all swings are battery powered, albeit battery vampires. Almost all swings use the most expensive, giant D-sized batteries—one popular model requires 10! And they suck, suck, suck them dry. We highly recommend having a warehouse store–sized stash somewhere in your house for the inevitable day when your swing stops . . . guaranteed to be at 2 a.m. the night your croupy baby has to sit up to sleep. The purchase of a baby swing alone might be worth the investment of rechargeable batteries, if you don't already have a set.

To help offset all that battery buying, some swings now also use electricity. We would love a rechargeable battery pack from the manufacturer we could pop out and pop into an AC charger, like the ones on our digital cameras, but these swings actually plug into an outlet full-time. They do also operate on batteries, but crazily enough, just regular alkaline ones, not a battery pack that's recharged by all that plugging in.

The swing itself has wires running through the metal frame. We have a rule about not plugging things in around baby, let alone plugging baby in. Even though we've probably helped finance the Energizer bunny's private jet by now, we're going to stick with regular batteries. We're not happy about it, but we're still going to stick with batteries.

Music and Sound Effects

Most swings come with music, but what kind can make or break the whole product. Because babies shouldn't be left unattended, you'll be hearing the swing's music more than you've ever heard any melody in your life. Choose one you love, or if you can't find that, at least one you can stand.

Some swings come with sound effects and nature sounds. All a matter of personal preference. Personally, we like water noises, but cricket chirps give us the creeps.

Convertible Swings

Products that have multiple uses are a great purchasing motivator for moms, and manufacturers know it. They love to package and advertise four-in-one products, even if one of those uses is "collects dust." We like products that are truly versatile, as long as each use is as high quality, long-lasting, and as safe as similar products purchased individually. Sadly, that is often not the case.

Many swings now offer multiple products in one. The seat of the swing is detached and turned into something else: a rocker, a bouncer, or just a plain seat. We don't like these because we don't think a swing seat should be detached ever. We're not convinced a seat that can be removed is the safest, most secure seat. We're worried about the wear and tear from all that attaching and detaching. And we're positive the possibility of user error is great. Parents have enough to worry about just getting a baby safely snapped into straps and trays. Having to deal with an entire seat reattachment that must be perfect every time is too much hassle and leaves too much room for error.

Dangerous Swing Designs

A few years ago, there was another product called a "cradle swing" that employed a mini flat bed that hooked onto a swinging mechanism on a swing frame. The "cradle" was a true cradle with no straps, meant to gently rock a sleeping baby. However, as with all cradles and bassinets, babies who rocked unsecured could roll into corners, get caught by gravity, and suffocate. After enough babies died in these types of cradle swings, they were finally recalled.

That's not to say they won't reappear in another permutation someday or that your neighbor won't pull one out of her attic for you. Don't ever let a baby swing in a basket, bed, or anything else that is not a proper seat with proper straps.

Swing Frames for Infant Seats

Swing frames for infant seats are exactly that, frames meant to be used with your own infant car seat carrier. We don't like these not only because of the possibility of user error hooking and rehooking the seat, but also because infant car seat carriers don't recline. Not all infant car seats will naturally allow a baby to have the correct amount of recline for optimal breathing when swinging. We'd rather not mess around trying to guess if ours does.

Price

Swings aren't cheap. Standard swings range in price from $49 to $129. Cradle swings cost $109 to $159. And portable swings are $35 to $69.

Features to Consider

☆ Direction of swinging motion

☆ Stability

☆ Seat

☆ Safety straps

☆ Tray

☆ Toys

☆ Open or high top

☆ Speed settings

☆ Music

NOTES: *Swings*

Model Name / Manufacturer	Store/Price	My Impressions	Grade
_____	_____	_____	_____
_____	_____	_____	_____
_____	_____	_____	_____
_____	_____	_____	_____
_____	_____	_____	_____
_____	_____	_____	_____
_____	_____	_____	_____
_____	_____	_____	_____
_____	_____	_____	_____

Twenty-seven

Toys

While being a grown-up is fun and all, we missed toys. Having kids means having a reason to visit the toy section every time we go into a store. Having kids we spoil means buying at least a little something every time too.

But buying the right toy for the right age isn't as easy as just looking at the packaging. Either toy manufacturers are testing the spawn of Einstein (who, by the way, doctors thought was mentally disabled when he was a boy), or they are just plain lying. There is no way a 3-month-old can sort shapes into a box. Our 8-year-olds can barely get those blocks to fit!

Purchasing the wrong toy is not only a waste of money, but can be frustrating for baby and parent alike. Parents worry that babies aren't accomplishing the simple tasks illustrated by the model babies on the box, completely unaware that even the baby on the box can't really do it either. (We know this for a fact, because one of our babies was the model on the box of many fancy, electronic toys she basically just drooled on.)

Here's the skinny on what a real, healthy normal baby can actually enjoy and when.

0—3 Months

We're not going to sugarcoat it, at this age, your baby won't be doing much. If you consider pooping, burping, and cooing activities, then it's a party. Otherwise, most every toy you dreamed of them playing with will continue to sit, untouched and unloved, until your baby is almost ready to sit up—like 3 months from now.

As little back-laying lumps, they can't hold a toy, rattle, or teether, or even bat at something purposefully for cause and effect. They can, however, gaze at objects, track things with their eyes, and respond to music, motion, and your voice.

They startle easily, so loud noises and surprising effects should be avoided. Simple patterns and bold, contrasting colors are best. The best toys for this age are the 3 Ms: mobiles, music boxes, and mirrors. Activity gyms and bouncers are perfect for this age as well. And activity mats are great because they provide a clean floor covering and can give you an interesting narrative while you practice tummy time.

You can buy little rattles, soft toys, art cards, and books for newborns, but realize that they will require 100 percent adult operation. Many parents attach soft wrist or ankle rattles to babies at this age, but our kids always hated them and couldn't figure out why an involuntary jerk of their arm led to a strange sound.

Don't kill yourself trying to stimulate newborns. They are growing and learning so much every day just by breathing, feeding, and stretching their muscles, they really don't need to process much more. Besides, you'll both spend so much energy on all the changing, calming, and burping, that there won't be loads of time for play anyway.

Good Toy Choices for 0–3 Months

☆ Mobile

☆ Mirror

☆ Activity gym

☆ Activity mat

☆ For parent play: small plush toys, rattles, books, art cards

3–6 Months

At the end of month 3, babies blossom from a gelatinous glob to a grabbing, kicking, rolling, even sitting-up wonder. They have head and neck control and some gross motor skills. They can focus better and actually concentrate on items for a short period of time. They can hold and shake objects. They start to put things in their mouths. And they are beginning to learn about cause and effect.

The best toys for this age are still visually appealing with bright, bold colors and patterns, but also offer tactile stimulation. Interesting textures that can be rubbed, gummed, and even smashed into one's own little face help baby learn about the world. Different, simple sounds also provide stimulation.

Things that chime, crinkle, and rattle are great. Soft toys with teething attachments are too. Our babies particularly like the soft books and blankets that have multisensory teething attachments at the corners.

Some of the best, most stimulating toys for this age are soft, multicolored blocks that have different textures and different sounds in each one. Baby can see, touch, and hear them, while also learning that each one does something different. Soft balls are also fabulous toys, as babies can start to push them around, and mom can play catch with them (although don't expect your baby to develop throwing or catching ability until 9 to 12 months or maybe even later).

Babies 3 to 6 months old won't appreciate anything beyond color, texture, and sound. Printed words, numbers, and the alphabet mean nothing to your baby. Seek instead shapes, animals, and happy, smiling faces.

Babies this age also can't yet stack or sort shapes, so save yourself and your baby the frustration and don't buy any toys that require either. You know what babies this age love more than anything? Parents who make big fools of themselves dancing, singing, pratfalling, and imitating Scooby Doo. Puppets can help you.

As soon as your baby can start sitting up and has good neck control, you can introduce her to the wonder that is the activity center. Babies can bounce and turn in the sling seat, and a myriad of toys are at their fingertips. We've found activity centers are lifesavers at this age, because frankly, we can only do the same puppet show five times a day before we're sick of ourselves.

Good Toy Choices for 3–6 Months:

- ☆ Activity centers
- ☆ Soft blocks
- ☆ Soft balls
- ☆ Rattles
- ☆ Teethers
- ☆ Plush toys
- ☆ Hand puppets
- ☆ Books
- ☆ Mobile
- ☆ Mirror
- ☆ Activity gym
- ☆ Activity mat

6–12 MONTHS

Finally, baby can move, which means baby can play! Babies will start sitting up, scooting, crawling, pulling up, standing, and in some cases even walking during this time frame. They'll still put everything in their mouths and will love most of the same toys they liked three months earlier.

Babies this age have a longer attention span and will actually spend several minutes on a single toy. They'll examine it, taste it, throw it, crawl after it, even switch it from hand to hand.

They will not care for their activity gyms anymore, and you'll actually have to retire their swings and bouncer now too. But you can introduce activity tables. Many activity tables have removable tops that allow for floor play, but once babies start to stand, they'll enjoy standing upright at their table. (See Chapter 3, Activity Toy Systems, for what makes a good activity table.) Activity walls are also good near the end of this stage; many have toys near the floor that will entertain a nonwalking baby as well as little toddlers.

Babies will now start to stack their soft blocks or at least relish knocking down the stacks you build. Babies will also be able to actually activate toys with simple lever pulls, trigger bars, and big buttons. Lights and sounds that are activated by a baby's action will cause squeals of delight and teach baby about cause and effect.

Babies can now also push and pull toys, and they love to crawl after motorized things. Large soft vehicles, animals that roll, and basically anything with big wheels is a big hit (just make sure the wheeled toy isn't too big or it might run away with your baby).

Musical instruments are also a baby favorite at this age, but they're not our favorite, so our kids never even knew they existed. The drum set from Grandma? Yeah, we somehow lost that in "the move" . . .

Even at this age, try not to overstimulate babies, and remember, they still can't read. Won't be able to for quite a long time. Or speak French. At least not fluently.

Good Toy Choices for 6–12 Months:

☆ Soft blocks

☆ Soft balls

☆ Soft vehicles

☆ Activity tables

☆ Activity walls

☆ Hand puppets

☆ Books

12–18 Months

You now officially have a toddler—Magellan, Marie Curie, and Mario Andretti all in one. Toddlers like to explore, find out how things work, and run, run, run at full speed. Even right into walls.

Because toddlers can get around the house, everything is fair game. Your glass casserole dishes are more fun than some stupid blocks. And they make a much better sound when they crash.

Fueling a toddler's desire for motion is key to keeping them off the kitchen counters or from riding the cat. Toys for this age should also be a little more complicated to engage them. We're all about simple, use-your-imagination stripped-down toys for preschoolers, but toddlers will have none of it. You might get a toddler to play with a doll for a few minutes . . . before she tosses it heartlessly in the trash can. You might get a toddler to push cars around . . . for a few minutes before he decides to flush them down the toilet. This is not the age for quiet introspection. This is the age of out loud, right now, and *how far can I throw it?*

For obvious reasons, we recommend toys that focus on physical play. Ride-on toys, such as little cars, especially ones with electronic buttons and musical songs, are big hits. Small slides and climbing frames can be introduced, as well as outdoor toys such as water tables (we do shy away from sandboxes at this age because toddlers are little creatures of passion who will rub sand-covered fists of fury into their own eyes when you tell them play time is over).

Toddlers like to stack things immensely at this age, and fill toys with other toys. Sets of stacking cups and nesting boxes are great. Dump trucks, shopping carts, and even shoeboxes are much appreciated as well.

They still don't have the ability to role play at this age, so don't expect them to make dinosaurs stomp or play with little pirates. They will certainly crash toys into one another, but not because they are pretending the creatures are alive.

They will start to shake their own little booty at just about any sound, so give them plenty of opportunity to do so with music boxes and musical toys. (Bring out the drum set at your own risk.)

Activity tables and activity walls are still a big hit at this age, but be on the lookout, because now your toddler will enjoy climbing on top of it as much as playing with it.

We will finally allow you to break out the flash cards and start teaching numbers and letters, but don't expect much more than *"How old are you?" "One!"*

Children do finally enjoying being read to at this age and will climb into your lap and eagerly turn the pages for you. Board books are great. Ones with texture patches even better. Save the lavish, heirloom, leather-bound tomes for when they aren't as likely to rip the pages just to laugh at your horrified reaction.

Good Toy Choices for 12–18 Months:

☆ Activity tables

☆ Activity walls

☆ Ride-ons

☆ Water tables

☆ Blocks

☆ Balls

☆ Dump trucks

☆ Shopping carts

☆ Stacking cups

☆ Nesting boxes

☆ Board books

☆ Music boxes

☆ Electronic and musical toys

18–24 Months

Older toddlers are still just as rough-and-tumble as younger ones, but they do develop a role-playing, more imaginative mind-set that enables them to calm down and makes it easier to buy toys to occupy them.

Toddlers at this age are finally ready to pretend and love to mimic their parents with play food, kitchen sets, and little shopping carts. Nothing is more fun than tiny pots and pans, dishes, cups, and plastic steaks. The more you buy of this sort of thing, the more likely your toddler will actually leave your real stuff alone.

They will also start tending to dolls and stuffed animals, somewhat lovingly.

Doll accessories, such as small strollers and high chairs are great, but look out for parts that could pinch small fingers.

Older toddlers can also finally begin to draw, so break out the big, fat crayons and butcher paper. Doodle pads are also great for this age, and more portable.

Toddlers will also start to build stuff, so cardboard bricks, multishaped blocks, and big LEGO blocks are great presents. They can also attempt large puzzles; look for ones with knobs on the pieces that will develop their thumb and forefinger grasp, readying them for correct pencil grip.

Children this age actually start to like repeating the alphabet song, singing nursery rhymes, and counting to 10. But don't pressure them or stress yourself out. They don't really need to know any of that by now—that's what kindergarten is for.

Outdoor toys are still popular. You can now add a crazy expensive play house to the mix, but steer clear of the motorized vehicles until preschool. You are kidding yourself if you think your 2-year-old can control a little motorcycle. This is the child who yesterday pooped behind your couch and ate a roly-poly.

When toddlers are outside, watch them closely, especially anywhere near the street, even the street you call a driveway. Toddlers, like puppies, will run hells-bells into the street if you let them. Laughing all the way. Now is the time to invest in a "Slow Children Playing" sign for your street. Or some big, teenager-hating speed bumps. (You can find inexpensive, temporary versions of both at dozens of online stores and kid catalogs.)

Good Toy Choices for 18–24 Months:

☆ Large crayons

☆ Doodle pads

☆ Large LEGO blocks

☆ Dolls and doll accessories

☆ Pretend food

☆ Play kitchen and accessories

- ☆ Play house
- ☆ Activity tables
- ☆ Activity walls
- ☆ Ride-ons
- ☆ Water tables
- ☆ Blocks
- ☆ Balls
- ☆ Dump trucks
- ☆ Shopping carts
- ☆ Board books
- ☆ Music boxes
- ☆ Electronic and musical toys

Toy Boxes

Now that you've bought all these toys, where are you going to put them? While many moms today (count us in!) swear by train tables—low-lying tables with wheeled storage drawers underneath—because they are toddler height and you can store toys under and on top of them, most houses do have a toy box or two.

Most parents don't know how dangerous a toy box can be, and that little kids die every year trapped inside them or when lids come crashing down on their tiny heads.

A safe toy box has the following:

- ☆ Lightweight lid
- ☆ Hinges that hold the lid open and prevent it from slamming down, or no lid at all
- ☆ A way for the lid to be lifted from the inside

☆ Plenty of ventilation inside

☆ Gaps between the lid and the sides to keep little fingers from getting pinched

☆ No locks whatsoever

☆ Smooth, rounded edges

☆ No splinters or peeling paint

Toy Sterilizers

As you may have gathered by now, we don't like to plug in unnecessary appliances. And we passed on the bottle sterilizer. But because our kids get sick every time their germy cousins visit and you can't boil plush toys, we've become big fans of the toy sterilizer. Also called a nursery sanitizer because it's good not just for toys but bottles and binkies as well, the toy sterilizer is a big, humidifier-sized appliance that you bring out once a month, place on your counter, and fill with toys. Plug it in and 30 minutes later you have clean toys.

There are microwave versions, but we don't like to zap anything plastic. Our favorite sterilizer uses dry heat to reportedly kill 99.9 percent of germs without any chemicals and without melting anything. We only wish it was bigger so we could sterilize bigger toys. (We find they're even good for toothbrushes after a family sickness.)

Quality

Look for quality construction and solid design in all toys you buy for your baby. While we're not saying you have to spend a small fortune to get safe toys, we can tell you the number of dollar-store toys recalled is exponentially higher than the number of toys that don't cost a dollar. And remember, most toy testing is voluntary. Well-known manufacturers care about their reputation so they pretest things. Unknown, unnamed, third-world toy makers? Not so much.

Taste Test

Ah yes, we alluded to our disgusting in-store habit in the preface, but we're big believers in tasting our baby's toys. Right up until preschool, it's a guarantee that kids will put anything and everything in their mouth. It amazes us, then, that so many baby toys taste so bad. Even plush sometimes leaves a nasty aftertaste. There's no way something that tastes bad to an adult can be good for a baby. If we don't dig it, the toy certainly never reaches our babies.

Don't Let Your Guard Down for Older Toddlers

Most parents dutifully baby proof their house when baby starts crawling, but decrease their vigilance as toddlers grow older. This is a tragic mistake.

While kids seem super vulnerable at 6 months, it's actually older toddlers who more often swallow and aspirate (suck into their lungs) small pieces. Toddlers have died aspirating a single bead just one-fourth of an inch in diameter.

We have a friend who let her 2-year-old walk around with pennies. When we objected (occupational hazard of being friends with a baby gear expert—we'll object, frequently), she assured us that her daughter liked small coins, was very careful with them, and never put them in her mouth.

We're not child development specialists, but we can almost guarantee a 2-year-old is not that smart. Toddlers are passionate, impulsive, and by and large do not know better when it comes to their own safety.

Don't gamble your children's lives by ever giving them the benefit of the doubt when it comes to their own well-being. Remove all doubt and remove the small objects and other safety hazards.

Softness

For babies under 2 years old, soft and plush is always better than hard and plastic. Babies this age don't have the motor control or the good sense not to smack themselves in the face with anything you might hand them. Don't fall for packaging that promises an appropriate age range, but sports anything long, hard, and sharp. This means no plastic keys, and for heaven's sake, no metal ones! We know babies like to play with mom's keys, so manufacturers like to make "realistic" toys, but metal keys are a bad, bad toy.

Here's an idea, before you hand your under-2-year-old baby anything, poke yourself in the eye with it first. If it hurts, it's not good for your baby.

Toy Safety

Because it wouldn't be a complete chapter without safety information that scares the pants off you (we've been having nightmares from the day we started researching this book), here are the most common safety concerns for baby toy purchases.

Small Parts Choking Hazard

The most common toy-related injury comes from small parts that either start too small or break off larger toys. Any piece of anything is considered a choking hazard if it is less than 1¼ inches in diameter. Balls, however, are choking hazards if they have a diameter less than 1¾ inches.

Confused? So were we. So we bought a small parts cylinder tester (also called a choke test cylinder) from a toy catalog; this tiny, hollow, hard plastic tube is used to test whether an item is a choking hazard. But apparently it isn't good for balls, because the tester is based on the 1¼-inch safety parameter— and balls are unsafe at that size. Who knew? Not us. We discovered the trickery when my daughters dutifully tested a rubber ball. It didn't fit into the small parts tester, so I let them play with it. We found it later in my son's mouth. What good is a small parts tester if it only tests nonround objects?

Upon further investigation, we discovered more flaws in this testing method, as the cylinders claim items are safe if they are longer than 2¼ inches. In 2005, researchers at RAM, a company specializing in product safety information and solutions, found that 28 percent of children that aspirated or choked on small parts did so on objects that would have passed the small cylinder safety test. Apparently, pen caps are a common item that passes but are the cause of frequent choking accidents. We say *Boooooo* to the small parts cylinder: *Booooo!!!!*

Another common at-home test for small parts safety is that if an item is smaller than a golf ball or can fit inside a toilet paper tube, it's too small for your under-3-year-old. This test works, sort of. Both a golf ball and a toilet paper tube are slightly smaller in diameter than 1¾ inches, so if the item in question is smaller than the ball and fits in the tube, it's definitely too small, but if it's on the cusp, you need to measure it. We actually just pulled a golf ball out of 18-month-old Gavin's mouth, so we're even questioning the 1¾-inch rule . . .

Even if the toy itself is large, look at the smaller pieces on the toys—such as plastic eyes, noses, and buttons—and determine if children could choke not if but when they chew the pieces off.

Magnets = Death

There have been several scary and fatal accidents lately when small children ingested small magnets that fell off or out of larger toys. Apparently magnets aren't just choking hazards. According to the CPSC's recall notices, which read like a gruesome storyline from *CSI*, if a child swallows more than one magnet, they can attract each other in the intestines and cause perforations and blockages that can lead to death.

Because you never know when a tiny eraser-sized magnet is going to detach itself from a toy, we've even banned toys with small magnets from our older kids' collections.

Strangulation Hazards

No cord or tie or string anywhere near a child under 3 should be more than seven inches long. That's just about the length of your hand. Measure anything suspect and trim it if you have to.

Lead Paint

Believe it or not, toys are recalled every single month for being coated in lead paint. We used to think lead paint meant paint on metal surfaces, but it turns out that any paint can have lead in it. Toys that have been recalled for lead paint include cars and metal toys of course, but also rubber balls, wood blocks, and other nonmetal items.

We've learned to just be suspicious of anything painted, especially painted in Asia, especially sold by a manufacturer we've never heard of.

While lead paint was officially banned from toys and furniture in 1977 by the CPSC, it wasn't banned in Asia. And even though American companies are supposed to test products made overseas for lead paint, the number of reputable American brand name toys recalled for lead paint every year makes us wonder.

Be on the lookout for paint of any kind that is cracking or peeling (as that poses an additional choking or aspiration risk), and consider a home lead testing kit. They can be had for under $12.

Balloons

We know they're fun. They're fun for us too. And our babies freak out in pure joy when they see one. But balloons are the leading cause of toy asphyxiation in small children—kids up to 11 years old have died when they sucked down a balloon. The danger is that even a tiny piece inhaled in surprise (when the balloon unexpectedly bursts as they are wont to do, especially in the grasp of small, sticky hands) can block the air passages and is very hard to remove. Remove latex balloons from your party. If you must, choose mylar. They are shiny and don't tend to explode into a million pieces.

P.S. The strings on most balloons are over the seven-inch safety rule, so cut them down.

Features to Consider
- ☆ Age appropriate
- ☆ Color
- ☆ Pattern
- ☆ Softness
- ☆ Texture
- ☆ Taste

☆ High quality

☆ Durable

☆ No small parts

☆ No long pieces

☆ No magnets

NOTES: *Toys*

Model Name / Manufacturer	Store/Price	My Impressions	Grade
_____	_____	_____	_____
_____	_____	_____	_____
_____	_____	_____	_____
_____	_____	_____	_____
_____	_____	_____	_____
_____	_____	_____	_____
_____	_____	_____	_____
_____	_____	_____	_____
_____	_____	_____	_____

Twenty-eight

The Ultimate, No-Nonsense Registry List

We've seen the lists. We've used the lists. And we've ended up with 15 green onesies, three bathtubs, 200 pairs of socks, and diaper pail refills for a diaper pail we didn't get. We're not saying everyone else's registry list is bad, we're just saying that ours is better. Much, much better.

Before we give you our list, however, we want to teach you how to make your own list.

Big Stuff

Register for all your big items, even the nursery furniture and fancy stroller. While we know many of your shower attendees aren't going to spring for a new $200 play yard or $600 dresser, knowing which model, brand, and color you chose helps your guests buy coordinating sheets, stroller bags, and nursery décor.

Small Stuff

Don't go overboard registering for every single little thing you'll need. This isn't your grocery list; it's a gift suggestion list for your friends and family. You can buy your own baby shampoo. Ditto for diaper cream and pacifiers.

Personal Stuff

Leave personal hygiene stuff off your registry, especially because your dad might look at it. The guys at your husband's office don't need to know which breast pads you prefer.

Product + Refills = Refills Only

Be careful about signing up for even one refill-type item, as you are bound to get more than you'll ever use in your lifetime. Want a diaper pail? Just register for that, not that and the refills, or we guarantee which one you'll receive 15 of.

No Diapers

We know they're expensive, but some babies are born too big for the first size. And no matter which size you register for, people love to buy the little ones. Giving away 144 of them to your next-door neighbor's sister is a sad waste of a good shower gift.

Cut Your True Layette Wishes in Half

If you give guests an inch in layette, they'll take a mile. Sure, people love to buy the cute little baby clothes, but so will you! If you register for what you really want, you'll get it all—with extras. And your remaining shopping days will be spent buying boring burp cloths instead of frilly dresses.

Don't Overstuff Your List

While it can't hurt to list the big stuff—who knows, Grandma might actually spring for some of it—don't overwhelm people with every tiny little item that catches your eye, or all you'll end up with is every little item. If you really want the nursing pillow, make sure people can find the nursing pillow without slogging through 20 pages of lap pads, fitted sheets, and washcloths.

Timing of Shower

Take into account when your shower will be in relation to when your baby will be born. You won't know the true usefulness (or not) of many items until your baby uses them. If that's five months from now, you'll have a harder time exchanging items. Retail stores are getting meaner and meaner about returns, and having a $45 bathtub that didn't fit in your sink cluttering up your closet will drive you insane.

The best time to have a baby shower? Too early is too weird; you need a big belly to satisfy all those curious rubbers. Better also to have it after you know the gender of the baby (for those of you finding out ahead of time), but before you're too big and uncomfortable to really enjoy it. And we always went into preterm labor or were unexpectedly put on bed rest six weeks out, so to be safe, we had ours at the beginning of our seventh month.

Have Fun with the Gun

We must have been cashiers in a previous life, because nothing is more fun than scanning things with the price checker gun. So that everyone is as perky as you the day you register, warn your partner that it's going to be a long day, and feed him his favorite things before you go.

Here is a list, by category—because that's how we shop—of what you should put on your registry, what you should wait for, and what you really don't need. Remember to pick and choose wisely. Instead of just SKU-ing up everything, select the things you really want.

Gear

Activity
Activity gym
Activity mat
Backseat mirror
Bouncer seat
Car seat (infant or convertible seat)
Car seat base for second car
Play yard
Play yard sheets
Sling or soft carrier
Stroller (look for one with full recline)
Swing
Travel swing

Health and Safety

Baby monitor
Brush and comb
Cool mist humidifier
First aid kit
Medicine lock box
Thermometer

Diapering

Diaper bag
Diaper pail

Clothing and Layette

Baby tees
Booties or socks
Crib shoes
Hats
Layette sets
Onesies
Receiving blankets
Sleepers
Sleepsacks
Sweaters

Nursery

Changing pad and covers
Changing table
Crib
Crib bedding set
Dresser/armoire
Fitted sheets, cotton and/or flannel
Glider and ottoman or rocker
Hamper
Lamp
Mattress
Mattress pad
Mobile
Nursery accessories (wall hangings, shelves, etc.)
Nursery storage
Rug
Window treatments

Toys, Rattles, and More

Car seat and stroller toys
Crib mirror
Rattles/teethers
Stuffed animals
Toys for 0–12 months

Feeding

Bibs
Burp cloths and lap pads
Nursery sterilizer
Nursing pillow
Nursing stool

Bath

Bath accessories
Bathtub or bath sponge
Bath toys
Washcloths and hooded towels

Travel and Weather

Stroller blanket bag
Travel blanket

Products to Purchase Yourself

Baby shampoo
Breast pads
Diapers
Diaper cream
Diaper pail refills
Gas relief drops
Nail scissors

Products to Wait For

Baby backpack
Baby wipes
Booster high chair
Bottles and nipples
Breast pump
Corner guards and tot locks
Crib toys
Feeding sets
High chair
Infant spoons
Restaurant high chair cover
Safety gates
Shopping cart cover
Snowsuit or bunting and warm hat
Stationary entertainer
Stroller rain shield
Stroller sunshade

Products You Don't Need—Now or Ever

Baby powder
Bassinet or cradle
Bath seat
Bottle organizer
Crib blankets
Gowns
Jumper
Sleep positioner
Walker
Wipes warmer

Twenty-nine

Major Product Recommendations Recap

You've read this book. We've read this book. And still sometimes we can't remember if a travel blanket is a good idea or a bad one.

So, we've recapped all our product recommendations into three handy lists: "must haves," "nice to haves," and "don't need." Of course, these are only two women's humble opinions. Feel free to use this as a starting point, and mix and match your own lists.

Must-Have Products

Activity
Activity center
Activity gym
Activity table
Board books
Bouncer
Swing

Feeding
Bottles
Bibs
Bottle brush
Burp cloths
High chair
Sippy cups

Nursing
Breast pads
Breast pump
Nursing bra
Nursing pillow

Safety
Backseat car mirror
Blind cord windup (safety)
Cabinet locks
Outlet covers (plugs)
Safety gates

381

Bath and Potty
Baby lotion
Washcloths

Baby Care
Baby detergent
Cool mist humidifier
First aid kit
Nail clippers
Nasal aspirator
Thermometer

Nursery/Sleeping
Crib
Crib mattress
Mattress pad
Monitor
Play yard
Sheet protectors
Sheets (fitted, play yard, bassinet)
Sleepsacks

Baby Gear
Car seats
 Convertible
 Full size
 Booster
Diaper bag
Seat protector
 Seat bottom
 Seat back
Stroller
 Standard, lightweight-plus,
  all-terrain, or luxury system

Changing/Diapers
Changing pads (changing mat)
Changing table cover
Changing table
Rash ointment

Nice-to-Have Products

Activity
Activity mat
Rattles and teethers
Travel swing
Tummy time mat

Nursing
Breast shells
Breast therapy relief packs
Nursing milk organizer
Nursing privacy wrap
Nursing stool

Feeding
Baby food organizer
Booster high chair
Bottle organizer
Formula dispenser

Safety
Corner guards
Doorknob covers (safety)
Door lever handle lock (safety)
DVD guard
Finger pinch guard (for doors)

Safety (continued)
Fireplace guard
Safety harness
Step stool
Stove guard
Toilet locks
Tot locks
VCR guard
Wire guard

Bath and Potty
Bath toys
Bathtub spout covers
Hooded towels
Potties

Changing/Diapers
Diaper pail
Hamper

Baby Care
Mittens
Rattles
Receiving blankets
Travel blanket

Nursery/Sleeping
Crib bedding sets
Glider chair
Swaddler
Video monitor

Baby Gear
Baby carrier
Car seat base for second car
Car seat accessories
   Insert
   Organizer
   Protector
   Toys
Stroller accessories
   Blanket bag
   Cup holders
   Rain shield
   Sunshade
   Toys
Sling
Shopping cart cover
Restaurant chair cover

Don't-Need Products

Baby powder
Bath seat
Bathtub
Bicycle seat
Bottle sterilizer
Bottle warmer
Co-sleepers
Cradles
Crib blankets

Crib bumper
Crib gym
Gowns
Jumper
Sleep positioner
Walker
Warm mist humidifier/vaporizer
Wipes warmer

Thirty

Contents of
the Perfectly Packed Diaper Bag

We're not saying we're experts, but we have now spent 3,246 consecutive days with a packed diaper bag. We've learned a thing or two about what's necessary and what just takes up space. Below you'll find the ultimate list that will cover you in almost any situation. Want to travel lighter? Remove items at will.

Diapering and Clothing

☆ 6 to 8 diapers, depending on how long you'll be out; a good rule of thumb is one diaper for every two hours.

☆ Travel-size wipes container

☆ Changing pad

☆ Diaper rash ointment

☆ Small receiving blanket

☆ Seasonal change of clothing; the smallest, ugliest emergency outfit you have. Pack a onesie, not overalls.

☆ Extra pair of socks

☆ Plastic bags for soiled clothing and diaper disposal; we love the ones that come on a roll, ready to use.

☆ Hat appropriate for shade or warmth

Feeding

☆ Bottles and formula or baby food and plastic spoons

☆ Bib

☆ Burp cloth

☆ Bottle of spring/filtered water (for you, for cleanups, for baby . . .)

☆ Small can of formula or 6 packets of premeasured formula

☆ Emergency snacks for you, such as a couple of granola bars

Toys and Soothing Items

☆ 2 pacifiers

☆ Small toy, rattle, or teether

Safety and Emergencies

☆ Small, portable first aid kit with minimum 3 to 5 adhesive bandages, gauze, and antibiotic ointment

☆ 2 to 3 safety pins

☆ Nasal aspirator

☆ Travel-size hand sanitizer

☆ Cell phone, charged up

☆ Tissues

☆ Small tube of sun block

☆ Small tube of moisturizing ointment (for emergency chapping)

☆ Infant/toddler fever reducer/pain reliever

☆ $20 bill and some quarters

Thirty-one

Registration Card Reminders

Of course, you should always send in the registration card for any baby product, but because of historical recalls and the huge potential for babies to get injured, these are the products we insist you do. Commit them to memory. Fill out the little postcard as soon as you open the box. And relax, knowing if there's ever a problem, you'll be the first to know.

- ☆ Baby carriers
- ☆ Bassinets
- ☆ Car seats
- ☆ Changing tables
- ☆ Cribs
- ☆ High chairs
- ☆ Play yards
- ☆ Strollers
- ☆ Swings

Thirty-two

Baby Brand Pronunciation Guide

We have no problem shopping in the snootiest baby stores around. We love the designer brands. But we still get all sweaty palmed when we're asked to refer to some of the fanciest, usually foreign, brands by name. No one wants to pull a Pretty Woman and get laughed out of the store for calling the modernist high chair dream a "Stow-key."

So to spare other moms out there, we present the definitive Baby Brand Pronunciation Guide. Impress your friends! Educate your playgroup! And maybe, just maybe, you'll actually get to correct one of those uppity store clerks when she mispronounces something. Ah, the joy . . .

Ameda: uh-**MEE**-duh (*breastfeeding products from Sweden*)

Aveda: uh-**VAY**-duh (*skin care from Minnesota*)

BabyBjorn: baby bee-**YORN** (*front carriers from Sweden*)

Britax: **BRY**-tex (*car seats from Britain*)

Chicco: **KEY**-co (*strollers and baby products from Italy*)

Combi: **COM**-bee; rhymes with mom, not comb (*strollers and baby products from Italy*)

Isabooties: **IS**-uh-booties (*crib shoes from Virginia*)

Little Laureate: little **LAR**-ree-it; rhymes with car, not care (*our fancy children's educational media company from Chicago*)

Medela: muh-**DEE**-luh *(breastfeeding products from Switzerland)*

Mia Bossi: **MEE**-uh bossy *(diaper bags from Chicago)*

Mobi: **MOE**-bee *(monitors and baby products from Beverly Hills)*

Mustela: muss-**TAH**-lah *(skin care from France)*

Mutsy: **MOOT**-see; rhymes with boot *(strollers from The Netherlands)*

OiOi: oy-oy; rhymes with boy-boy *(diaper bags from Australia)*

Pediped: **PEED**-ee-ped; like pediatrician *(baby shoes from Las Vegas)*

Peg-Pérego: peg **PEAR**-rah-go *(strollers from Italy)*

Picci: **PEATCH**-ee; sorry, it's very Italian, sounds like peachy with a *t* thrown in the middle *(crib bedding from Italy)*

Primo: **PREE**-mo; rhymes with we *(bathtubs from Europe)*

Robeez: **ROB**-bees; rhymes with Bobby's *(shoes from Canada)*

Stokke: **STOW**-kuh *(high chairs, strollers, and cribs from The Netherlands)*

Thirty-three

The Secret Money-Saving Rules of Baby Shopping

We promised you a bargain book without the saving-the-last-drops-of-baby-shampoo-in-a-plastic-sandwich-baggie-and-then-making-a-new-bottle-later advice. We hope we gave you enough budget-friendly tips throughout, but in case you're a skip-to-the-end-first kind of person (we are too!), here is a summary of the best money-saving secrets when buying baby gear.

☆ If your first instinct is that a product is ugly, don't buy it. It will only get uglier.

☆ Buy new, but buy last year's model car seat and stroller. Hardly anything changes year to year but the pattern, and you can literally save hundreds of dollars.

☆ Whenever you can, buy on the Internet with free shipping. Online stores have less overhead and usually offer steep, steep discounts. Great for items you've already test-driven and know you want, such as strollers, or items you're sure not to return, such as diapers.

☆ Right before you check out online, do a search with the name of the store and the word "coupon." You can unexpectedly save some serious cash.

☆ All those free formula coupons you receive in the mail but don't use? You can exchange them for ones you do on special coupon swapping message boards. They also routinely publish the addresses of military families that could use the help.

☆ Products that force babies to develop faster than they would naturally are unnatural and could be dangerous. Your baby doesn't sit up at 2 months for a reason. Save your money and stay away from these products.

☆ No product will teach babies what nature has always programmed them to do. Products that promise to help—such as early walking aids—are usually wastes of money and should be looked upon with suspicion.

Thirty-four

Ten Things We Wish We Knew When We Were First-Time Moms

1. You don't teach a baby to sit up, crawl, walk, or talk. They are born to figure it out. Your real job is to cheer.

2. Your kids never see you as fat. Only full of love.

3. No one cares that you didn't dust your house for all of 2008.

4. You will rediscover the joys of grilled cheese.

5. You will accidentally use the word "potty" to excuse yourself from a group of adults.

6. Your lack of time will lead to new, creative multitasking: you will master the art of cleaning the shower while actually taking a shower.

7. Babies are super addicts. They will make a habit out of something after exactly 10 minutes or 2.1 times. Be careful that the rituals you begin are something you can continue ad infinitum. It sounds sweet, rocking your child to sleep in your arms, but three and a half years later, you will sincerely regret having formed this habit.

8. Babies have super powers. There's The Blob (the ability to revert to an invertebrate to slip out of mom's arms) and his twin, Stiff-as-a-Board. Super Glue Baby has the ability to grip doorways with superior force with only the tips of her fingers. And Self-Destructo sure is scary. We all knew kids could hold their breath, but we didn't know they could

391

do so until they passed out. Self-Destructo can also puke at will, knock himself unconscious, and will intentionally stick something in his own eye. All to spite you, just to spite you . . .

9. You will love this little creature more than it can even be defined. More than you've ever loved anything. You, who can't handle a splinter, would let a Mack truck back over you for two weeks straight for your baby. Gladly.

10. C-section scars and stretch marks are not horrible. They are badges of honor, proof of membership in the best club in the world: Motherhood.

Appendix

In-Store Buying Guide Reminders

More often than not, when we're in public, we can barely remember our middle name, let alone which features were important for an all-terrain versus a jogging stroller. So here is a complete reference, presented alphabetically, to remind you what you need to be looking for when you are in the store.

Activity Mats and Gyms
☆ Do you like the design and color?

☆ Does it set the scene for storytelling?

☆ Do the toys have a variety of color, texture, and use?

☆ Does it have any baby favorites, such as mirrors or mobiles?

☆ Do you like the music?

☆ Are the toys positioned well for your baby?

☆ Is it big enough for your baby, but not too big?

☆ Does it fold up and travel or store easily?

☆ Does it convert into another baby activity toy?

☆ Is the fabric baby soft? Are there any sharp angles or bits?

Activity Centers
☆ Is it the right size for your house?

☆ Does the seat slide or bounce?

☆ Does the seat spin easily?

☆ Does it convert into other toys or activities?

☆ Does it have height adjustment capability?

☆ Are the toys age appropriate and not overstimulating?

☆ Can baby reach all the toys?

☆ Are the toys soft and chew friendly?

☆ Do you like the music?

Activity Tables, Cubes, and Walls

☆ Do you want an electronic or unplugged table?

☆ Is it sturdy?

☆ Are there any sharp edges or loose pieces?

☆ Do you have room for it?

☆ Do you like the music and/or voice?

Baby Carriers, Slings, and Backpacks

☆ What is the minimum age?

☆ What is the weight limit?

☆ Is it a good size for you?

☆ Is it comfortable for you?

☆ Can you get baby in and out by yourself?

☆ Is the carrier durable and well made?

☆ Are there safety straps for baby?

☆ Is there adequate padding for you and for baby?

☆ Are the leg openings adjustable yet secure?

☆ Does the fabric have any stretch?

☆ Is the material breathable?

☆ Is the baby carrier machine washable?

☆ Can baby breathe in the carrier?

☆ Does it come with any cool accessories?

☆ What's your budget?

☆ Are there snaps or hinges that might pinch?

Bassinets, Cradles, Moses Baskets, and Carry-Cots

☆ Are all slats, if any, less than a soda can width apart?

☆ Are there any protruding posts or knobs?

☆ Does it have a wide base?

☆ Is it sturdy and well constructed?

☆ Is the sleeping surface or mattress firm?

☆ Can you easily remove any excess decorative bedding?

☆ Can you stop it from rocking?

☆ Does it have a canopy that retracts?

Baby Bathtubs

☆ Is it big enough for your baby, but not too big to store?

☆ Is it sturdy?

☆ Does it have nonslip feet?

☆ Is the baby seat nonslip and appropriately inclined?

☆ Is it easy to dry out?

☆ Are there any rough edges?

☆ Is it *not* a bath seat?

Bouncers, Rockers, and Infant Seats

☆ Do you want baby to bounce or rock?

☆ When can baby start using the seat? From birth?

☆ Is the fabric comfortable?

☆ Is the seat portable?

☆ Does the seat vibrate?

☆ Does it have music? If so, do you like it?

☆ How does the vibration and music turn on and off?

☆ Does it have a detachable, visually but not overly stimulating toy bar?

Breast Pumps

☆ Hospital grade, personal electric, or manual?

☆ Does it have adjustable suction control?

☆ Does it suck only or have massaging methods?

☆ How many sucks per minute does it deliver (48 per minute is very efficient)?

☆ Can you pump both breasts at once?

☆ Is it easy to use?

☆ Is it easy to clean?

☆ Are there multisize breast shields?

☆ What kind of storage bottles or bags does it use?

☆ Are the storage bottles/bags wide and stable with a good seal?

☆ Does it have a roomy carrying case?

Bottles

☆ Do you want standard or wide neck?

☆ Do you want a bottle system?

☆ If so, how many pieces does it have?

☆ How easy is it to clean?

☆ Do you want latex or silicone nipples?

☆ Did you buy one of every shape?

Car Seat: Infant Car Seat Carrier

☆ Is it from a reputable manufacturer?

☆ Does the seat have a good safety reputation?

☆ Does it fit your specific vehicle?

☆ Does it have Side Impact Protection (SIP)?

☆ Does it have an anti-rebound bar?

☆ How much does the actual seat weigh? Will it be too heavy to carry?

☆ What are the rider height and weight limits?

☆ Is it easy for you to install correctly every time?

☆ Is it easy and comfortable for you to carry?

☆ Does it have an ergonomic handle? Is the handle solid? Is the handle slightly padded?

☆ Does it have metal in the seat-to-base attachment or only plastic?

☆ Does it have a five-point harness?

☆ Does it have wide, thick, twist-resistant straps?

☆ Does it have strap covers?

☆ Does it have a two-piece chest clip that snaps together?

☆ Does it have easy-to-access front harness adjustment?

☆ Is there a height adjustment dial?

☆ Does it have a level indicator?

☆ Does it have a large canopy? Peekaboo window?

☆ Is the fabric easily removable? Breathable?

Car Seat: Convertible

☆ Safety reputation? (#1 feature)

☆ Vehicular fit? What is the size of seat? Does it fit your specific vehicle?

☆ Does it have Side Impact Protection (SIP)?

☆ Does it have a top tether? Can it be top tethered when rear facing?

☆ Weight and height limit?

☆ Rear-facing weight and height limit?

☆ Does it have a five-point (safer) or a three-point harness?

☆ Does it have wide, thick, twist-resistant straps?

☆ Does it have front adjustable straps?

☆ Does it have a crotch strap adjustment?

☆ What kind of chest clip?

☆ Will it be comfortable for your child?

Car Seat: Full-size

☆ Safety reputation? (#1 feature)

☆ Vehicular fit? What is the size of seat? Does it fit your specific vehicle?

☆ Does it have Side Impact Protection (SIP)?

☆ Does it have a top tether?

☆ Weight and height limit?

☆ Five-point harness weight limit?

☆ Does it have wide, thick, twist-resistant straps?

☆ What kind of chest clip?

☆ Front harness adjustment?

Car Seat: Booster

☆ Safety reputation? (#1 feature)

☆ Backless or high back booster?

☆ Does it have side impact protection (SIP)?

☆ If it has a five-point harness, what is the harness weight limit?

☆ Is it a comfortable fit for your child? Does the seat belt hit in the right places?

☆ Will it be easy for your child to use?

☆ Does it have armrests?

☆ Does it have cup holders?

Changing Table

☆ Freestanding or attached to a dresser?

☆ If attached to a dresser, is it securely attached?

☆ Is it stable? Not easy to tip over?

☆ Is it durable and well constructed?

☆ Does it have safety straps?

☆ Are there guardrails on all four sides?

☆ Are the guardrails at least two inches tall?

☆ Do you need a changing pad?

☆ Is the changing pad waterproof?

☆ Is there easy access to diapering accessories?

☆ Is it a comfortable height?

Cribs

☆ What style of crib do you want? Standard or round?

☆ How sturdy is the crib? Is it made of quality materials?

☆ How is the mattress supported? How safe would it be if a single piece failed?

☆ Does the mattress height adjust? If so, can it only be adjusted by an adult?

☆ Are there any drop sides?

☆ Do you want a convertible crib? If so, do you need to buy extra accessories?

☆ Does it have wheels? Are they metal?

☆ Is the crib free of dangerous decorative cutouts and posts?

Crib Mattresses

☆ Do you want a foam or innerspring crib mattress?

☆ Is the mattress heavy?

☆ Is it dense?

☆ Is it firm?

☆ Is it resilient? (Does it spring back quickly?)

☆ If it's innerspring, how many coils does it have? (Look for a minimum of 150.) What gauge steel and how many turns? (The lower the gauge number, the thicker—and better!—the steel; the more turns, the better.)

☆ Does it fit your crib with less than two finger widths of space between the mattress and all crib sides?

☆ Is the surface not too plush?

☆ Is it convertible for toddlers?

☆ Are there internal side rails?

☆ What fabric is used for the ticking?

☆ Is it bound with cloth or vinyl?

☆ How many layers make up the ticking?

☆ Is the stitching tight, tiny, and well done?

☆ How much does it cost?

☆ How much do the other mattresses made by this manufacturer cost?

Crib Toys

☆ Does it have music? Good music?

☆ Can baby turn the music on and off?

☆ Does the music have a volume control?

☆ Can you manually turn the music off?

☆ Does it have a mirror? Pages to turn? Lights?

☆ How does it attach to the crib? Will it attach to your crib?

☆ Is it a smooth shape overall with no protruding pieces?

☆ Any sharp edges?

☆ Are there any pieces that could break off and present a choking hazard?

☆ Is the battery sealed securely?

Diaper Bag

☆ Does the bag match your lifestyle?

☆ Is the fabric washable? Spot cleanable?

☆ Are the straps comfortable?

☆ How does the bag close? Will it stay closed?

☆ Is the changing pad washable and removable? Is it big enough?

☆ Does the bag have a place for your accessories?

DVDs

☆ Is the content age appropriate?

☆ Does the video have high production quality?

☆ Does it feature safe content?

☆ Is the presentation engaging without being overstimulating or startling?

☆ Is the music fully orchestrated?

☆ Are the sounds and sound effects annoying?

☆ Does the packaging make unrealistic promises?

☆ Do you enjoy watching it yourself?

High Chairs

☆ Is the chair stable? How hard is it to tip over?

☆ Does it have a five-point harness (safer), three-point harness, or just a lap belt?

☆ Does it have a T-bar so baby doesn't slip out? Is the T-bar on the seat (good) or the tray (not so good)?

☆ Are the straps strong and durable? What color are they? (Avoid white and really light colors if you can.)

☆ Does it have a tray? Do you want one?

☆ Is the tray smooth and easy to clean?

☆ Does the tray release easily? One-handed? How heavy is it?

☆ Any attached toys? How will they hold up to daily food fights?

☆ Are the toys easy to clean?

☆ Is the seat comfortable? No sharp edges?

☆ How washable is the seat? The whole high chair?

☆ Does it recline?

☆ Does it have height adjustment?

☆ Does it have wheels? Do they lock?

☆ If the chair folds, does it lock closed?

☆ What are the age and weight limits?

☆ How long do you want the high chair to last?

Humidifiers

☆ Is it warm or cold mist? (Cold mist is highly recommended!)

☆ Is it ultrasonic?

☆ Does it have a filter?

☆ Is the filter replaceable? How much do they cost?

☆ How do you clean the unit?

☆ Does it have humidity control?

☆ Does it have auto shut-off?

☆ Does it have a filter change indicator light?

☆ Does it have a night-light or glow in the dark?

☆ Is the tank easy to refill?

Layette Items

☆ Is it machine washable?

☆ Are there any scratchy bits?

☆ Is it diaper-change friendly?

☆ Do the snaps close securely, but not too securely?

☆ Are the zippers easy to slide and not too sharp?

Mobiles

☆ Does it have good, long-playing music?

☆ Does it have volume control?

☆ Does it have a remote control?

☆ Does it convert to a crib toy?

☆ How does it mount to the crib?

☆ Will it fit your crib?

☆ Are there any small pieces that could break off and become a choking hazard?

Monitors

☆ Audio only or video too?

☆ What frequency does it use? Do you have other devices already using the same frequency?

☆ Does it have privacy features?

☆ Analog or digital?

☆ What is the range? How much do you need?

☆ Does it have a rechargeable battery system? On both receiver and transmitter?

☆ Is it sound activated?

☆ Are there signal lights or vibration?

☆ Do they offer multiple receivers?

☆ Does it have an intercom function? Do you need it?

☆ Is the parent unit compact and easy to carry?

☆ Does the parent unit have a pager?

Play Yards, Playpens, and Travel Cots

☆ What is the weight limit?

☆ Does it have a bassinet?

☆ Does it have a changing table?

☆ Does it have a parent organizer?

☆ Is the mattress pad slightly padded but not too soft?

☆ Are there special sheets to fit the play yard?

☆ Does it have a music box or MP3 connection?

☆ Does it have vibration?

☆ Does it have a canopy?

☆ Does it have wheels? Can you use the wheels for transporting it folded?

☆ Does it have a carrying bag?

Potties

☆ Potty chair or potty seat?

☆ For a potty chair, is it a single piece or does it have a removable cup?

☆ If it fits over the toilet, how secure is it?

☆ Does it convert?

☆ Does it have a urine deflector? Is it too large? Can it be removed?

☆ Is the potty comfortable?

☆ Is it free from sharp edges?

☆ Any pieces that might pinch?

☆ Is it the right size for your toddler?

☆ How easy is it to clean?

☆ Does it have many crevices?

☆ Is the potty too dark or too light?

☆ Are there many removable pieces toddler can use as a weapon?

☆ If you need a stool, is it sturdy? Easily removable?

☆ Does the stool have nonslip bottoms and surfaces?

☆ Do you need a portable potty?

Safety Gates

☆ What size gate do you need?

☆ Is it pressure- or hardware-mounted?

☆ Does it swing open?

☆ If it's for the top of the stairs, will it not swing over the stairs?

☆ Are there any thresholds you could trip over?

☆ Is there an auto-close feature?

☆ How easy is it to open?

☆ Is the locking mechanism and operation toddler proof?

☆ Are the slats less than 2⅜ inches wide?

☆ Is the gate durable?

Shoes

☆ Are they flexible? Can you bend them in half with one hand?

☆ Do they have a low profile around the ankle?

☆ Do they have a leather insole? Any bacteria protection?

☆ Are the soles nonslip?

☆ Are they the right size: a thumb space in the front and pinkie on the side?

☆ Do they open wide enough for easy baby dressing?

Strollers: Universal

☆ How much does it weigh?

☆ What fold does it have?

☆ Is the fold easy? One-handed? Standing?

☆ Does it lock when folded?

☆ Is it well constructed and durable?

☆ Is there a five-point harness?

☆ Does the harness have strap covers?

☆ Does the seat recline?

☆ Do you like the color and pattern?

☆ Is the seat padded?

☆ Does the seat have a waterfall or adjustable edge?

☆ Is there a footrest?

☆ Is the stroller basket large and easily accessible, even when the seat is reclined?

☆ Is there a large canopy? Peekaboo window?

☆ Is the handle comfortable?

☆ Is the handle height adjustable?

☆ Is the stroller easy to handle?

☆ Are the wheels solid? Have suspension?

☆ Are the brakes solid? Easy to engage and disengage?

☆ Is there a cup holder? Parent console?

☆ Is there a child snack tray?

☆ Are there newborn headrests or body pillows?

☆ Does it come with a rain cover? Foot muff?

Strollers: Carriages

☆ Does it fold for portability?

☆ Does it have brakes on the back wheels?

☆ Are the wheels fixed or do they have swivel capability?

☆ Does it steer smoothly?

☆ Is it a solid, durable carriage?

☆ Does it have durable, spot-cleanable fabric?

☆ Is the mattress firm and fit properly?

Strollers: Single Standard

☆ What is the weight limit?

☆ How much does it weigh?

☆ What kind of fold does it have? One-handed? Easy to do?

☆ Does it have a fully reclining seat? Is it smooth and easy to operate?

☆ Does it have shock-absorbing wheels?

☆ Does it have a large, easy-to-access basket?

☆ Is it easy to maneuver?

☆ Does it have a snack tray?

☆ Does it have parent cup holders?

☆ Does it have a parent console?

☆ Does it have a height adjustable handle? Does it have a reversible handle?

☆ Does it have a five-point harness (safer) or three-point harness?

☆ Does it have an adjustable footrest?

☆ Is the sun canopy large enough to adequately shade your child? Peekaboo window?

☆ Does it accept an infant car seat?

☆ Does it stay locked when folded?

☆ Does it have dual rear brakes?

☆ Does it have good suspension?

Strollers: Travel System

☆ Review questions for Single Standard Stroller and Car Seat: Infant Carrier.

☆ Does the car seat snap in and out of the stroller easily?

☆ Is the car seat a quality, safe infant car seat?

☆ Is the stroller your first choice as a stand-alone stroller with all the features you desire?

Strollers: Lightweight-Plus

☆ Is it easy to maneuver?

☆ Does it have a fully reclining seat? Does it recline smoothly and easily?

☆ Does it have a carry-cot option?

☆ What is the weight limit?

☆ What kind of fold does it have? One-handed? Easy to do?

☆ Does it have shock-absorbing wheels?

☆ Does it have a large, easy-to-access basket?

☆ Does it have a snack tray?

☆ Does it have a five-point harness (safer) or a three-point harness?

☆ Does it have an adjustable footrest?

☆ Does it stay locked when folded?

☆ Does it have dual rear brakes?

☆ Is the sun canopy large enough to adequately shade your child? Peekaboo window?

☆ Does it have parent cup holders?

☆ Does it have good suspension?

Strollers: Lightweight/Umbrella

☆ Is it easy to maneuver?

☆ Is the seat padded?

☆ Does the seat recline? How many positions? Is it easy to do?

☆ Are the handles padded and comfortable?

☆ Does it have a basket? How big?

Strollers: Luxury Stroller System

☆ Is the fabric breathable and spot cleanable?

☆ Is it easy to attach/detach the bassinet and stroller seat?

☆ Is it easy to fold? Does it have a stand-up fold?

☆ Are the tires puncture-proof?

☆ Is the handle height adjustable? Easy to do?

☆ Will you be one of the only ones with it or does everyone seem to have it now? Do you care?

Strollers: All-Terrain

☆ What is the weight limit?

☆ How much does the stroller weigh?

☆ Does it have a bassinet option?

☆ How big is the basket?

☆ Does it have a parent console?

☆ Does it have a height-adjustable handle?

☆ Does it come with an all-weather boot?

☆ Does it offer reversible seating?

☆ Does the seat recline? If so, how many positions?

☆ Is it easy to fold? Do you have to remove the front wheel first?

☆ Does it have a large canopy that will adequately shade your child?

Strollers: Jogging

☆ Are you a serious runner who needs larger wheels?

☆ What is the weight limit?

☆ Does it have a canopy? If so, will it adequately shade your child?

☆ Does it have suspension?

☆ Does it have hand and foot brakes?

☆ Does it have a wrist tether?

☆ Does it have an aluminum or steel frame?

☆ What kind of recline does it have?

☆ Does it have good safety straps that will fit your child?

☆ If you plan on transporting it in your car, does it fold?

☆ Does it have at least pockets to hold little things?

☆ Does it have a lockable swivel wheel if you plan on using it other than just jogging?

Strollers: Double Standard

☆ Tandem or side-by-side?

☆ Do both seats recline?

☆ Does it accept an infant car seat?

☆ What is the basket size? Is it easy to access even if the seats are fully reclined?

☆ How big is the canopy? Will it adequately shade both children?

☆ Does it have good wheels and suspension?

☆ Does it maneuver well?

☆ Does it have a good, solid handle?

☆ Is it easy to fold? Does it have a good locking mechanism?

☆ What is the stroller weight?

☆ Does it have a parent console and cup holder?

Strollers: Double Lightweight/Umbrella
☆ Review questions for Stroller: Single Lightweight.

☆ Do the seats recline? How many positions?

☆ Will the sun canopies adequately shade both children? Peekaboo windows?

☆ How big is the basket?

☆ Are there parent cup holders?

☆ Is the handle padded? Adjustable?

☆ Does it have good suspension?

☆ Does it fit through a standard doorway (29 inches or less)?

☆ Is it easy to fold?

☆ How much does the stroller weigh?

Strollers: Double All-Terrain
☆ Review questions for Stroller: All-Terrain.

☆ Side-by-side, tandem, or tandem basket seating?

☆ Do both seats recline?

☆ What is the stroller weight?

Strollers: Double Jogging
☆ Review questions for Stroller: Jogging.

☆ Are the seats wide enough?

☆ Do the safety straps fit your children?

☆ Does the canopy adequately shade both children?

☆ Does it fold? How many folding steps?

Strollers: Stroller-and-a-Half
☆ Is the front seat nicely padded?

☆ Does the front seat have a five-point harness?

☆ Does the front seat have a snack tray?

☆ How large is the basket? Is it easily accessible?

☆ Is the bench padded?

☆ Does the bench have a strap or harness?

☆ Does the bench slide?

Strollers: Multiples

☆ Does it have adequate padding on the seats?

☆ Do all the seats recline? Flat recline?

☆ Car-seat adaptable?

☆ What are the folded dimensions?

☆ Do the seats have to be removed to fold it?

☆ Does it have a telescoping handle?

☆ Does it have hand and foot brakes?

☆ Does the canopy or canopies adequately shade all the children?

☆ Does it have a big basket? Is it easily accessible?

Swings

☆ Do you want standard swinging motion or back-and-forth cradle motion?

☆ Does it have a wide, stable base?

☆ Is the seat relatively soft?

☆ Does the seat recline? Enough for a newborn?

☆ Is there a five-point harness?

☆ Are the straps strong?

☆ Does it have a tray with a T-bar?

☆ Is the tray easy to open and lock closed?

☆ Are there toys or lights to look at?

☆ Is the top open or high enough for easy loading and unloading?

☆ Are there multiple speed settings?

☆ Is the slowest speed slow enough?

☆ Do you like the music?

Toys

☆ Is it truly age appropriate?

☆ Will it cause you or your baby frustration if baby can't operate it?

☆ Does it have bold colors and patterns?

☆ Is it soft?

☆ Does it have texture?

☆ Is it safe for babies to put in their mouth?

☆ Does it taste good?

☆ Is it good quality and durable?

☆ Does it have small parts that could be a choking hazard?

☆ Does it have magnets?

☆ Does it have any strings over seven inches long?

Every Baby Product on the Planet

All right, maybe we don't have every single solitary product on the planet listed here—who knows what they've got going on in Kathmandu—but we promise you won't find a more complete list of baby products anywhere on the planet.

Here they are, alphabetically, with definitions and advice, if we've got it. As you know, the major items have detailed reviews in the book; refer to the index for page numbers. If you see a product we missed (or invented something new yourself), let us know at BabyGizmo.com. We are pretty sure we do love baby gear more than just about anyone, well, you know where.

Acetaminophen-infant strength: An infant strength pain reliever, such as Infants' Tylenol®. This is a must-have in our diaper bags, because you never know when you will need it when you are away from home. Some moms swear by ibuprofen (or Children's Motrin®), but it is more likely to upset the tummy.

Activity center: A plastic base, usually circular, with a fabric seat with two leg holes for baby to sit and partake in an abundance of activities and noises. These centers have lights, toys, songs, noises, and many more activities to keep baby busy. A miracle for babies who can sit up, but can't yet crawl or otherwise entertain themselves.

Activity gym: An arch of toys that baby lies under, usually packed with features such as hanging toys, music, lights, and textured patterns.

Activity jumper: A round plastic chair with a sling seat and built-in toys that hangs from a large metal frame by four long, covered springs. It almost looks like a cross between an activity center and a giant swing.

Activity mat: A play quilt with attached toys, usually designed with bright colors and contrasting textures to make tummy time more interesting. Also great for sensory stimulation, motor skills, learning about cause and effect, and keeping baby off your dirty floor.

Activity seat: See *Stationary infant seat.*

Activity table: A small toddler-size table packed with toys. Some activity tables introduce all manner of educational lessons like colors, shapes, and first words. Others are just plain fun. A great toy for walkers; some even have removable tops for floor play.

Angle adjuster: See *Car seat accessories.*

Angle-neck bottles: Bottles that have a 45-degree angle near the top to help cut down on air and allow for baby to sit more upright when feeding. Harder to wash, store, and tote in your diaper bag.

Antibiotic ointment: First aid ointment, such as Neosporin®, used to prevent infection in minor scrapes, burns, and cuts. Also known as "magic cream."

Antibiotic ointment with pain reliever: Same as above, but includes a little pain relief to boot. Works wonders on stinging cuts and burns.

Appliance lock: A lock to keep little ones out of your refrigerator or other nonheating appliance; not for use on ovens.

Aquaphor®: Brand of healing ointment that protects dry, cracked, or irritated skin and can actually help enhance the natural healing process and restore smooth, healthy skin. Very gentle and great for use on baby's face to help with irritation caused by sucking on her binky.

Asian-style sling: A baby carrier made of a wide rectangle of fabric with very long fabric straps that wrap around the baby and mom's bodies and is then tied. These slings can be worn either on mom's front or back.

Baby backpack: See *Baby carrier: Backpack.*

Baby B'Air Flight Vest®: See *Flight vest travel harness.*

Baby bath: See *Bathtub.*

Baby bath cradle: A sling of mesh-like fabric stretched on a metal frame, resembling a small baby bouncer and meant to be set in a (very large) sink or in a larger bathtub.

Baby bath soap: A very gentle soap for the bath created for baby's delicate skin.

Baby bottle: A bottle, typically plastic or glass, with a nipple used to feed an infant.

Baby bouncy: Also called "delivery ball." A large exercise ball that comes with a stability stand to keep it in place; used to sit on and easily bounce a fussy baby.

Baby care cart: A rolling organizing container or cart used to store and organize baby care items such as diapers, shampoos, blankets, clothes, and so forth.

Baby care timer: A device used for keeping track of baby-care details such as the last diaper change, feeding, or nap. Usually also has a great feature that lets breastfeeding moms record which side they fed from last.

Baby carrier

Backpack: A large carrier, usually with a lightweight metal frame and made of tough, often waterproof material. It provides a seat for babies to ride on your back and is designed for prolonged baby-carrying outings. Baby backpacks are used for older babies who can sit up on their own.

Infant carrier: A hands-free soft carrier that straps over your shoulders and allows you to carry your baby on your front, side, or back; also provides close physical connection between mom and baby.

Sling: A hands-free infant carrier consisting of a wide piece of fabric that is supported by one shoulder strap and lies across mom's waist like a sash, with baby snuggled inside the sash.

Baby cubes: A tray of 10, snap-lid, one-ounce containers, used to freeze individual portions of homemade baby food.

Baby detergent: A specially formulated laundry detergent that contains no harsh chemicals; used for washing baby's clothes without leaving a residue that may irritate baby's delicate skin. We use this type of detergent on baby's clothes for at least the first year.

Baby exerciser: See *Jumper.*

Baby food mill: A small food grinder used to make homemade baby food. Usually cranked by hand.

Baby food organizer: A plastic, multilevel shelf for baby food containers that rotates for easy visibility and selection. This organizing shelf is either stored in your pantry or on your countertop.

Baby food processor: A mini food processor that allows you to prepare fresh baby food. These processors chop and blend fruits, meats, and veggies into easily digestible, baby-size portions. Usually electric.

BabyGizmo.com™: In our opinion, the world's best baby product resource site! Completely unbiased news, reviews, and price comparisons for more than 25,000 baby products. It's our baby, so of course, we love it!

Baby jogger: See *Stroller.*

BabyLegs®: See *Baby leg warmers.*

Baby leg warmers: Little leg warmers made especially for babies and toddlers that help keep little legs warm, especially the often exposed skin between the sock and the bottom of the pants or skirt. They can also pad knees during the learning-to-crawl stage.

Baby lotion: Moisturizing lotion made especially for baby's delicate skin, containing mild and gentle ingredients to moisturize, soften, and protect baby's skin.

Baby Orajel® Teething Pain Medication: See *Teething gel.*

Baby Orajel® Tooth and Gum Cleanser: See *Baby toothpaste.*

Baby pod: A soft, round, fabric playpen with one-foot-high walls to keep a tiny baby corralled. They are made with nice patterns, so we'll say "corralled in style."

Baby powder: A powder that our parents used to prevent diaper chafing—no longer recommended because of the high risk of baby inhaling the fine powder, which could cause potentially life-threatening problems and even death. We've never bought a single bottle.

Baby rocker: See *Rocker*.

Baby Safe Feeder™: A specially made small mesh bag attached to a retainer ring that allows your baby to enjoy fruit and vegetables without the hazard of choking. The mesh bag ensures that the food is chewed up in small enough pieces before it is swallowed by baby, helping eliminate choking risk.

Baby scale: A special scale that measures the weight of babies in pounds and ounces so you can better track their healthy development (and fill in their baby book) at home.

Baby shield: See *Car seat accessories*.

Baby toothbrush: A mini-size toothbrush perfect for baby's new teeth. You will need one of these from the time the first tooth appears.

Baby toothpaste: Toothpaste designed specifically for baby that is usually nonfoaming, nonabrasive, fluoride-free, and safe for swallowing. Many dentists, however, do *not* recommend the use of any baby toothpaste, as it encourages babies to suck, rather than just allow you to brush their teeth. Water only is preferred.

Babyview mirror: Also called "backseat mirror." A mirror that attaches to the rearview mirror or windshield to allow mom to see her baby in the backseat without having to turn around or move her rearview mirror. Be careful, as anything not seriously secured in your car can become a projectile in an accident.

Baby wipe alternative: A gentle hypoallergenic spray used in place of a standard baby wipe. You spray it on and gently wipe it off with a tissue to clean, soothe, and moisturize.

Backseat mirror: See *Babyview mirror*.

Back sleeper: See *Sleep system*.

Back-up sensor: A sensor for the back of your vehicle to alert you of anything behind you for up to six feet. These sensors attach to your rear license plate and have a digital dashboard display.

Balmex®: See *Diaper rash cream*.

Banister guard: A clear plastic shield to block your banister from little legs and arms getting stuck or from toys being thrown over the edge.

Bassinet: A first bed for your newborn that is smaller and cozier than a crib. Bassinets are designed only for a baby up to 4 or 5 months. Look for one with a sturdy base that isn't easily tipped over. (Mom tip: Many play yards come with bassinets.)

Bassinet sheets: Small fitted sheets designed exclusively for a bassinet.

Bath accessories

> **Bath appliqués:** Textured, nonslip surface decals for the bottom of the bathtub to prevent slipping.
>
> **Bath drain valve cover:** A rounded cover that suctions over the bath drain to prevent bumps and pinches from the drain valve.
>
> **Bath mat (cushioned):** A cushioned mat for the bottom of the bathtub to prevent baby from slipping around.
>
> **Bath ring:** See *Bath seat.*
>
> **Bath safety duck:** A floating rubber ducky that also takes the temperature of the bath water.
>
> **Bath seat:** Also called "bath ring." A suctioned seat that is used in the bathtub to bathe your baby. We do not recommend this product and it's on our Unsafe Baby Products You Should *Not* Buy list—so don't buy it!
>
> **Bath shower:** A press-and-pump plastic showerhead that suctions to the tub wall to prepare kids for taking real showers.
>
> **Bath splash guard:** Heavy-duty clear vinyl shield protects your bathroom floor from messy spills and splashes during bath time and helps prevent dangerous slips or water damage.
>
> **Bath thermometer:** A bath toy and floatable bath thermometer in one. It helps safely gauge and monitor the temperature of bath water.
>
> **Bath toy:** Special waterproof toy designed for bath time play; usually floats, and if baby is lucky, it squirts.
>
> **Bath toy organizer:** A container made of mesh or plastic that attaches to the bathtub/shower wall or hooks over the side of the bathtub, designed to organize bath toys and accessories. Most organizers allow toys to dry out quickly with draining holes.
>
> **Bathtub rail:** A rail that securely attaches to the side of the bathtub with no tools, designed to give your child a sure grip when getting in and out of the slippery bathtub.
>
> **Bathtub spout cover:** A soft, protective bathtub faucet cover designed to prevent bumps and bruises from babies and toddlers bumping into the spout.
>
> **Tub guard set:** A set of two foam, nonslip cushions, one for your elbows on the side of the tub and one for your knees on the floor, to make bathing your child more comfortable for you.

Bathtub: A large, plastic tub used for bathing baby that is usually contoured for little behinds. Some even have comfort and nonslip pads, footrests, and detachable showerheads. Many bathtubs are designed for use on the counter, but some fit into kitchen or other big sinks or can be placed on the floor of your regular bathtub.

Bedding sets: See *Crib accessories: Crib bedding sets.*

Bed rail: A long rail for the side of a bed that attaches under the mattress to keep a child from falling out of the bed. These can be dangerous if a child gets caught between the rail and the bed.

Bedside sleeper: See *Co-sleeper.*

Bedwetting alarm: An alarm activated by moisture that can help your older, potty training child learn to awaken in time to go to the bathroom.

Bell blocker: A plastic box to cover your doorbell, directing visitors to knock, while your children are sleeping. This box screws into your door frame and has a sliding panel to allow access to the doorbell after naptime.

Belt covers: See *Car seat accessories.*

Belt positioning device: See *Car seat belts.*

Belt tightener: See *Car seat belts.*

Bib: A piece of cloth or plastic that is secured under a child's chin and worn to protect clothing while eating.

Bib clips: Two clips attached together by a string, rope, or ribbon that allow you to make anything, such as a napkin, cloth diaper, or kitchen towel a bib.

Bicycle trailer: A motorless wheeled frame with a hitch system designed for transporting cargo or children by bicycle. They are very dangerous because their large width makes them vulnerable to off-the-trail spills and motor vehicle accidents. Due to their profuse shaking, they should *never* be used for children under 1 year.

Bike seat: A child seat that attaches to the back of an adult bike so that baby can take a ride with mom or dad. This is an extremely dangerous product we do not recommend; in fact, it's one of our Seven Deadly Sinners: Unsafe Baby Products You Should *Not* Buy!

Binky: Another name for a pacifier. See *Pacifier.*

Blanket bag: See *Stroller accessories.*

Blanket sleepers: See *Wearable blanket.*

Blind cord windup: A safety device that winds up the cord of a window blind to get it out of a child's reach.

Board book: A baby book with pages made out of very thick, virtually unbendable cardboard so baby can play with the book without having mom worry about ripped pages.

Booties: Soft, usually knitted shoes for a baby.

Boppy® pillow: See *Nursing pillow.*

Bottle brush: A long, round brush with bristles and a sponge piece designed to wash baby bottles. Many bottle brushes come with a nipple brush stored in the handle.

Bottle keeper: See *Bottle strap.*

Bottle organizer/dryer: A plastic rack that holds and organizes bottles and all their accessories for convenient drying.

Bottle sealer: A small, round, plastic disc that covers the mouth of the bottle to seal it for storage without the nipple in place.

Bottle sterilizer: A device used to sterilize baby bottles with steam, killing live, household bacteria and keeping the bottles clean and sanitary. Many sterilizers have room for nipples, rings, covers, and even breast pumps. Can be electric or activated in microwave.

Bottle strap: A simple strap (usually with Velcro tabs) that wraps around a bottle or sippy cup and then around your stroller, car seat, high chair, etc. Acts as a tether to prevent baby from being able to throw the bottle on the ground. Also, great for tethering toys (especially in restaurants!).

Bottle tamer: See *Bottle strap.*

Bottle tether: See *Bottle strap.*

Bottle (and baby food) warmer: A quick-steam warming device for evenly heating any single bottle of formula or milk or jar of baby food.

Bouncer: A sling of fabric mounted in a metal frame that allows baby to sit at an incline. The metal frame is a sideways V shape, allowing for a bouncing motion at baby's slightest movement. The bouncing is manual, however, and not an automatic motion as in a swing, although some come equipped with a vibration feature that soothes the baby similarly to a ride in the car.

Bouncy seat: See *Bouncer.*

Breastbottle Nurser®: A breast-shaped bottle with collapsible walls and a pressure-equalizing valve that minimizes air ingestion to mimic the breastfeeding experience.

Breast milk bag: Presterilized bag designed for expressed breast milk, which makes storing and transporting breast milk convenient and easy.

Breast moisturizing balm: Used to moisturize and soothe chapped, tender nipples from breastfeeding. The only safe creams for breastfeeding babies contain 100 percent lanolin and nothing else.

Breast pad: See *Nursing pad.*

Breast pillow: A wedge of memory foam, with softly textured stay-in-place covers, that lifts the breast up for breastfeeding, while leaving your hands free to hold the baby.

Breast pump: See *Nursing pump.*

Breast shells: Plastic shells worn under the bra to cradle sore nipples (from breastfeeding) and help prevent the nipples from rubbing against clothing and becoming chafed and further irritated. It looks like a dome with a hole in the center for your nipple to go in. It gives the nipple a protective shield and may help with inverted nipples.

Breast shields: Also called "flanges." The flexible, plastic cup you press your breast against on a breast pump.

Breast therapy relief packs: Warm or cool relief packs that provide immediate and effective warming or cooling relief to help ease the discomfort of engorgement, blocked ducts, and mastitis (breast inflammation) for woman who are breastfeeding.

Breathable crib bumper: See *Crib accessories.*

Brush and comb: A mini brush and comb used to comb baby's hair.

Buggy Bagg®: A combination shopping cart seat cover, high chair cover, and diaper bag in one. See *Shopping cart cover* and *High chair cover.*

Bug netting: See *Stroller accessories: Bug canopy.*

Bumbo®: See *Stationary infant seat.*

Bumper Bonnet®: A baby-size helmet to shield and protect a delicate little head from bumps and bruises.

Bumper pad: See *Crib bumper.*

BundleMe®: See *Blanket bag.*

Bunting bag: See *Blanket bag.*

Burp cloth: Burp cloths are simply pieces of fabric that moms throw over their shoulder when burping a baby to save their own clothes from spit-up.

Butt paste: See *Diaper rash cream.*

Cabinet latches: See *Cabinet locks.*

Cabinet locks: Safety locks designed for the inside of cabinets to prevent toddlers from simply pulling them open.

Calibrated medicine dropper: A soft plastic tube marked with dosage amounts for home-administered liquid medicine.

Car bed: A special-needs car seat for babies with low birth weight that positions baby in either the supine or prone position. Basically, babies lie down in it to give them a better breathing position. Your hospital will tell you if you need this (and usually help you procure it).

Car mirror: See *Babyview mirror.*

Carriage/pram: See *Stroller.*

Carrier toy bar: See *Car seat accessories: Toy bar for infant seat.*

Carry-Cot: See *Stroller accessories.*

Car seat: A removable safety seat for children that is equipped with a restraining device meant to be strapped to a seat in a vehicle.

    Booster car seat: A seat, with or without a back, that "boosts" children up to properly place them so that the lap and shoulder belt fits safely. The last car seat your child will ever use.

    Convertible car seat: A car seat that can be installed and used in both rear-facing and forward-facing positions. Convertible seats have higher weight limits than infant-only seats, so they are ideal for bigger babies. Many can be used from birth.

Full-size car seat: Also called "toddler car seat." Essentially a giant, high-back car seat that can be used in a forward-facing position only. These seats are typically used when a child has outgrown an infant carrier and convertible seat but is too small for a booster.

Infant car seat carrier: A small, rear-facing-only car seat meant for babies from birth through 7 or 8 months, typically with a removable base and a carrying handle. These seats can be clipped in and out of a stay-in-the-car base, allowing mom to remove the entire car seat easily from the car and tote baby and seat along with her (although experts strongly recommend installing a car seat correctly and then leaving the car seat in the car at all times). Infant car seats often come with a stroller as part of a travel system.

Toddler car seat: See *Full-size car seat.*

Car seat accessories

Angle adjuster: A built-in indicator on a car seat that can help you get the proper recline when installing.

Baby shield: A protective infant car seat carrier cover that provides a shield from sun, wind, insects, rain, or curious pets. The shields come in two styles: summer and winter. The summer shield is a mesh material that allows baby to see out and mom to see baby, while the winter shield is closed material to protect from harsher elements such as cold and snow.

Base: A plastic support that installs in your car either by LATCH or using the seatbelt to hold an infant car seat. The base stays installed in your car while you take the infant car seat in and out.

Clip-on basket: A small container that clips onto the side of a car seat to hold toys, pacifiers, or anything else that a child needs access to in the car.

Cover: Similar to a sun shade for your windshield, it's a reflective sun cover for the car seat to keep the seat cool in a hot car when not in use.

Dashboard: A soft, fabric panel of activities for baby riding in the car seat. Baby dashboards typically include music, lights, and toys such as teething toys and buttons.

Detachable base: See *Car seat accessories: Base.*

Insert: A padded support piece that gives baby the right head and neck support and allows smaller babies to fit more comfortably in a car seat.

Organizer: A container or bag to store and organize all your child's things, such as toys and snacks in the car.

Positioner: A device that properly positions a shoulder belt for a child.

Protector (in car seat): A mat that fits into your child's car seat to protect it from diaper blowouts and potty training mishaps.

Protector (under car seat): A mat for under the car seat that protects upholstery from spills and indent damage.

Seat back protector: A mat that hangs on the back of the front seats to protect the back of car seats from shoe prints and marks.

Shade: See-through film meant to protect young car riders from the glare and heat of the sun. A cling shade is a vinyl window shade that adheres to the car windows by static cling. A roller shade is a pull down shade that attaches to the rear car windows with suction cups.

Strap covers: Soft covers used to cover car seat straps next to the child's head to prevent rubbing and chafing.

Top tether: A safety belt attached to the top of a good car seat that clips over the back of the seat it's sitting on and onto a car's top tether anchor. They are very important safety devices as they keep a seat from lunging forward in a crash; we wouldn't buy a car seat without one.

Tote: A heavy-duty, waterproof, and rip-resistant bag to protect your car seat, making traveling or storing the seat easier and cleaner.

Toy bar for infant car seat: A tiny line of toys, either plastic or plush, meant to be hung from an infant car seat carrier's handle to entertain baby on the go. This item should *not* be used in the car, however, as it can turn into a dangerous projectile in a collision.

Travel bag: A bag that attaches to the back of the car's front seat to hold and organize baby's travel essentials.

Travel tray: A portable tray that sits on your child's lap for snacking, playing, or reading in the car. The tray folds up when not in use.

Car seat base for second car: A second base that works with your particular car seat; bought for a second car so that you don't have to move the securely attached base in your main car. If you get a second base, it should be specifically made for your car seat brand and model.

Car seat belt

Seat belt locking clip: A flat, H-shaped, two-by-three-inch metal clip that locks the car's seat belt tightly in position. It is intended to fasten together belt webbing (lap and shoulder portion) at a sliding latch plate, to prevent the webbing from sliding through.

Seat belt positioner: A device that is used to keep a car seat belt's shoulder sash from pulling dangerously across child's neck. Because children are shorter than adults and seat belts are designed for an adult height, positioners allow for the shoulder belt to be adjusted down for a child.

Seat belt tightener: A device that's meant to make installing a car seat easier by allowing you to tighten the car seat belts to eliminate slack and hold the car seat securely in place. These have not been tested for safety and are known to damage seat belts. *Safety experts do not recommend seat belt tighteners!*

Cart cover: See *Shopping cart wrap.*

Changing mat: A small, plastic mat that allows you to change diapers on the go without worrying about the floor, ground, or table beneath your baby.

Changing pad: See *Changing table pad.*

Changing pad (portable): See *Changing mat.*

Changing table: A raised table at mom's waist height to allow for easy, non-back-breaking diaper changes. Since we don't like broken backs, we really like our changing tables.

Changing table cover: A cover for a changing table pad that usually comes in terry cloth in a variety of colors to match your nursery. Covers are machine washable and great for those occasional diaper mishaps.

Changing table organizer: An organizer that attaches to a changing table that gives you compartments and shelves to help store diapering accessories at baby level, rather than on shelves below. They are usually clear plastic to match any nursery décor.

Changing table pad: A thick foam pad that turns any dresser top or flat surface into a changing table. Changing pads can be disposable, waterproof, flat, or contoured. Most changing pads come with a safety strap to keep baby in place and have a slip-resistant surface. We recommend never using an attachable changing table pad on a regular dresser.

Clip-on basket: See *Car seat accessories.*

Collection kit: A personal kit that you purchase for use with an electric breast pump. Collection kits usually include breast shields, tubes, gaskets, rings, disks, filters, bottles, and caps.

Contoured pad: See *Changing table pad.*

Convertible car seat: See *Car seats.*

Cooling dish: A specially designed plate that you fill with water and store in the freezer; used to quick-cool "too hot" food items for your little one.

Cool mist humidifier: See *Humidifier.*

Corner guard: Cushioned guard for coffee table corners or other furniture with sharp corners to help protect little heads or other body parts. These guards attach to the corners with double-sided tape.

Co-sleeper: A product that allows babies to sleep either in or next to an adult's bed. Co-sleepers can either be a soft-sided minibed for placement in a parent's bed, or a separate piece of furniture, similar to a play yard, with an open side that is placed next to a parent's bed. Because of suffocation hazards, co-sleepers are not recommended.

Cradle: A small, low-to-the-ground bed for a newborn, usually with rockers.

Crib: A bed with high sides made of slats and adjustable rails for a baby.

Crib accessories

    Breathable crib bumper: A safer alternative to standard crib bumpers, but still not recommended by experts (no bumpers are best). It's a mesh bumper that allows better air flow (important because babies can suffocate against a standard bumper because they can't breathe quashed up against it) but prevents baby from sticking arms or legs through the slats of the crib.

Crib bedding set: Coordinating crib bedding that comes in a set, usually three pieces: a crib quilt or blanket, a crib sheet, and a crib bumper.

Crib bumpers: Cushioned pads designed to decorate a crib; they were used in the past to help prevent baby from bumping into and sliding through crib bars. Now cribs have a narrower distance between slats, and experts recommend against crib bumpers because they can prevent optimal air flow to babies.

Crib CD player: A CD player designed to attach to the side of the crib. It usually has a night-light.

Crib gate alarm: A device that plays music or sounds a soft alarm if the side of the crib goes down unexpectedly.

Crib gym: A toy that hangs across the crib, attaching to each side of the crib railing and hanging within the baby's reach. This is a very dangerous toy; we do not recommend it!

Crib light: A soft night-light that attaches to a crib.

Crib mirror: An unbreakable mirror that attaches to the inside railing of the crib for baby to gaze in, make out with, and otherwise befriend. Usually bordered by plush designs and may include lights and attached toys.

Crib mobile: See *Mobile.*

Crib rail teether: A plastic piece that fits over the crib rail to protect the crib from little teeth when your child chews on it. Beware, as if they break, they can become quite sharp choking hazards.

Crib safety sheet: A crib sheet that is designed to stay in place to prevent it from coming loose and becoming a suffocation and strangulation hazard. Some crib safety sheets have extra material for a safer fit, while others encase the entire mattress like a pillow case.

Crib sheet: A fitted sheet made specifically for a crib mattress. The crib sheet should be tight and secure on all corners.

Crib sheet security clips: Clips that secure crib sheets at the corners so they stay safely put. A loose crib sheet can become a strangulation hazard.

Crib shield: A breathable, mesh shield that attaches to the inside of a crib, usually with Velcro, covering the slats to prevent baby from sticking arms and legs through the crib slats and getting them stuck.

Crib soother: A device that attaches to the baby's crib to simulate taking your baby for a car ride by gently vibrating the crib mattress, while playing soft music or nature sounds. Whenever you attach anything mechanical and large to a crib, make sure you are not compromising the crib's structural safety.

Crib spacer: A foam block to make a smaller space in the crib for your newborn or to divide the crib into sections for twins. Because bumpers are not a good idea, we think this foam block is not a good idea either, because it's not breathable.

Crib tent: A mesh tent that is designed to cover the top of the crib to help protect a baby from pets and older siblings, and also to prevent adventurous toddlers from climbing out. They aren't always very durable (small fingers picking at small holes might have something to do with this), and they are very expensive (like $80), but if you have a toddler who won't stay put or a naughty kitty, they can be a lifesaver.

Crib toy: A toy designed to hang from or tie to the side of a crib.

Crib wedge: A foam wedge covered in fabric used under a crib sheet or the entire crib mattress to gently elevate your infant's head and upper body for easier breathing, better digestion, and improved overall sleeping. We haven't had much luck with these, as baby tends to roll to the bottom anyway.

Dust ruffle: A decorative crib bed skirt.

Quick zip crib sheet: A two-piece crib sheet that completely covers a crib mattress and has a zip-off top piece to make cleaning easier.

Crib mattress: See *Mattress.*

Crib mobile: See *Mobile.*

Crib pad: See *Mattress pad.*

Crib shoe: An itty-bitty shoe made for newborns.

Cup holder: See *Stroller accessories.*

Dashboard: See *Car seat accessories.*

DaysAgo™ Digital Days Counter: A digital counter that attaches to refrigerated baby food jars with a magnet or suction cup to count how many days the jar has been open. Nice idea. Nice design.

Deck guard: A mesh guard to cover the rails of decks, porches, or balconies to prevent little ones from wedging themselves between open rails.

Desitin®: See *Diaper rash cream.*

Detachable base: See *Car seat accessories: Detachable base.*

Detergent: Mild and gentle baby detergents made especially for baby's delicate skin that can prevent irritation caused by regular detergents. We're not taking any chances on a full body rash for our babies (they cry enough as it is), so we use baby detergents faithfully for at least the first 12 months. Some do still have chemicals, while others are completely organic.

Diapees & wipees®: See *Diapers and wipes pouch.*

Diaper backpack: Much like a regular backpack, the diaper bag backpack is carried via two shoulder straps and has a rugged design and a large, deep main compartment. Insulated side pockets hold bottles.

Diaper bag: A handy bag for a parent on the go that has space for all baby's essentials. These bags have multiple pockets for items such as diapers, bottles, toys, wipes, and pacifiers and even a few pockets for adult things such as keys, cell phones, and wallets.

Diaper balm: A thick ointment you rub on baby's bottom to provide a moisture barrier and protect baby from diaper rash and chafing.

Diaper Champ®: See *Diaper pail.*

Diaper clutch: See *Diapers and wipes pouch.*

Diaper cover: A garment that looks like granny underpants and is worn over the diaper for pretty much no reason other than to cover the diaper. Plastic ones will help stop leaks, but fabric ones are just cute.

Diaper daypack: A backpack-style diaper bag that is good for hiking, camping, and the active outdoor lifestyle. One style of a diaper daypack zips onto a child carrier, making travel even easier.

Diaper day pouch: A compact diaper bag that is great for quick outings.

Diaper Dékor®: See *Diaper pail.*

Diaper Depot™: See *Changing table organizer.*

Diaper disposal system: See *Diaper pail.*

Diaper Genie®: See *Diaper pail.*

Diaper organizers: Also called "diaper stackers." Fabric bags that resemble clothes storage bags with a flat bottom and a hanger or ties on the top. They are meant to be hung from the side of a changing table and store loads of diapers out of sight. You access the diapers through a slit in the fabric.

Diaper pail: A dirty diaper holder that seals off the odors until the diapers can be disposed of properly.

Diaper pail deodorizer: A scented disc to toss into your diaper pail to help it smell fresh and clean for up to 30 days.

Diaper pins: Pins with safety lock heads designed to attach the sides of cloth diapers.

Diaper rash cream: A cream for baby's bottom to soothe, heal, and help prevent diaper rash. It acts as a barrier between your baby's sensitive skin and diaper and will also contain some soothing or healing ingredients. Cream is thinner than ointment and applies more easily, but also wipes off into the diaper more easily, leaving baby's skin less protected.

Diaper rash ointment: An ointment for baby's bottom to soothe, heal, and help prevent diaper rash. Ointment is thicker than cream, due to its higher lipid (fat) content. It goes on thick and can be nearly impossible to get off.

Diaper rash spray: A hands-free spray to soothe and heal diaper rash.

Diapers and wipes pouch: A small pouch designed specifically to hold a travel pack of wipes and two to four diapers.

428 ☆ the **Baby Gizmo** buying guide

Diaper stacker: See *Diaper organizer.*

Diaper tote: An open tote-style diaper bag.

Diaper wrap: A diaper cover that wraps around from the back to the front to keep moisture in.

Dishwasher baby bottle holder: A round, plastic piece that snaps to the dish rack in your dishwasher, holding a baby bottle upright for optimum cleaning.

Dishwasher basket: A plastic basket designed for use in the dishwasher to hold all the small pieces that come with bottles and sippy cups, as well as pacifiers, teethers, and small dishwasher-safe toys.

Dispenser for dry formula: A small, covered container, usually plastic, divided into sections to hold a premeasured amount of dry formula for on the go. The lid usually spins and has a covered hole to make dispensing the formula into the bottle easy. We always have one of these in our diaper bag when formula feeding. Look for one with a tight lid, or your premeasured contents will spill over into other compartments.

Disposable diapers: Diapers that you throw away after each use. The opposite of reusable cloth diapers.

Disposable feeding kit: A disposable kit of essentials for a meal away including a bib, tabletopper, fork, spoon, and sippy cup.

Disposable place mat: See *Place mat.*

Disposable toilet seat cover: A specially designed toilet seat cover that is kept in place by adhesive strips used to protect your little ones from germs from public toilets. We adore these! However, note that many of them cannot be flushed and must be thrown away in the trash. We'll take the tiny inconvenience for the thicker, stay-put covers any day.

Doorknob cover (safety): A plastic piece, easily operated by an adult but not a child, that fits over the doorknob to prevent toddlers from opening doors.

Door lever handle lock (safety): A plastic piece, easily operated by an adult but not a child, that fits over the door lever handle to prevent toddlers from opening doors.

Doorway jumper: Usually a seat (similar to an outdoor baby swing) that is suspended from the top of a doorframe with a metal or plastic clamp that is attached to a bungee cord. We do not recommend doorway jumpers.

Double stroller, all-terrain: See *Stroller.*

Double stroller, jogging: See *Stroller.*

Double stroller, standard: See *Stroller.*

Double stroller, travel system: See *Stroller.*

Double stroller, umbrella/lightweight: See *Stroller.*

Drawer latches: Plastic or metal safety latches to keep toddlers from opening drawers and accessing their contents.

Drawer stops: A stopper for a drawer to prevent the entire drawer from coming out and possibly falling on your toddler.

Dreft®: See *Baby detergent.*

Dry formula: See *Formula.*

Dry formula dispenser: See *Dispenser for dry formula.*

Drying rack: See *Bottle organizer/dryer.*

Dummy: Don't be offended! It's just another name for a pacifier, often used in Great Britain. See *Pacifier.*

Dust ruffles: See *Crib accessories.*

DVD guard: A plastic shield that covers the front of a DVD player to prevent babies and toddlers from pushing the buttons. The shield is made of clear plastic so that the remote will still work from a distance.

EarPlanes®: Soft, hypoallergenic filters that insert in the ears to regulate changing air pressure while flying, eliminating discomfort and reducing noise. Genius product! We highly recommend!

Ear and throat illuminator: See *Otoscope.*

EuroTote™: A five-in-one soft baby carrier that transforms into a bunting bag, stroller bag, play quilt, travel bed, and ergonomic Moses-style baby carrier. Unlike a Moses basket, though, you can carry this while baby is in it. They are brand new, so they have no safety record in the U.S., but we like what we see so far.

Exam kit: See *Otoscope.*

Exercise mat: See *Play mat.*

Exerciser: See *Activity center.*

ExerSaucer ®: See *Activity center.*

Feeding booster: See *High chairs.*

Fever monitor: A small, wearable baby thermometer that clips to baby's diaper to continuously measure baby's skin temperature to monitor a fever. The monitor softly beeps when temperature goes up one degree.

FingerGuard™: A dentist-invented rubber guard that wraps around the child's wrist and covers the two middle fingers to help break the habit of finger sucking. They also make a version for thumb sucking, called the ThumbGuard™.

Finger pinch guard (for doors): A small, U-shaped piece of foam material that fits on the side of a door to prevent it from closing completely and possibly slamming on little fingers. It also prevents children from accidentally locking themselves in a room.

Fire escape ladder: A fold-up ladder that attaches to your windowsill to escape a second story during a fire.

Fireplace guard: Cushioned foam strips designed to fit around the sharp edges of the fireplace to absorb impact and help prevent injuries to a toddler falling against it. The guard sticks to the brick or stone with provided double-sided tape.

First aid kit: A pre-assembled container of bandages and medicines for giving emergency care.

Fitted sheets (crib): A sheet tailored with gathered, usually elastic, edges made specifically for a crib mattress.

Flanges: See *Breast shields.*

Flight vest travel harness: FAA-tested infant safety garment worn during flight that attaches to your seat belt to keep your child under 2 years old securely on your lap. Note: These flight vests are designed exclusively for aircraft and should *never* be used in an automobile.

Foot rattles: See *Rattles.*

Formula: An artificially created milk product based on cow or soy milk designed to nourish new infants who are not receiving breast milk or not receiving it full-time.

> **Dry/powdered formula:** Formula in its powdered form that needs water added before its ready to be fed to a baby.

> **Ready-to-use formula:** Formula in liquid form that is ready to serve right from the can or jar.

Formula dispenser: See *Dispenser for dry formula*

Formula one-shot bags: Small, funnel-shaped, zip-closed plastic bags used to make your own single servings of dry formula. These disposable bags with a tear-off bottom take up less room than formula dispensers in your diaper bag and cost less than manufacturer prepackaged servings.

Formula pitcher: A pitcher for mixing powdered formula and storing in the refrigerator.

Furniture wall straps: Straps used to secure tall pieces of furniture, such as bookcases, to a wall to prevent a child from accidentally tipping it over trying to crawl up it.

Gate

> **Auto-close gate:** A safety gate that swings shut automatically after you walk through it.

> **Configure gate:** A gating system consisting of multiple segments to allow you to barricade different areas, such as a dining room or computer desk or stairwell.

> **Hands-free gate:** A pressure-mounted safety gate that opens with a step on the foot pedal. Not recommended for the top of stairs!

> **Hardware-mounted gate:** A safety gate that is mounted to the wall using hardware to secure it properly. Because the gate is screwed into the wall, it is the type of gate that you should buy for the top of stairs.

> **Hearth gate:** A multisegment gate that adjusts so that you can angle the pieces together to block off your fireplace from your children.

> **Kiddy guard:** A sturdy, laminated mesh barrier mounted to each side of the door or stair opening that rolls up discreetly in one end when not in use.

> **Pressure-mounted gate:** A wood, metal, or plastic gate that is mounted to the wall using pressure and no hardware. These types of gates are not usually recommended for use at the top of stairs.

Gate alarm: A loud alarm for the gate to the pool to alert that the gate has been opened.

Genie: See *Diaper pail.*

Glider: Similar to a rocking chair, but instead of the rocking motion, the chair gently glides back and forth.

Gown: Baby nightgown that resembles a long-sleeved potato sack that loosely closes around the feet. They can either have a drawstring at the bottom or a zipper, but baby's legs are not individually covered.

HALO SleepSack™: See *Wearable blanket.*

Hamper: A large basket usually with a cover used for dirty clothes.

Hands-free gate: See *Gate: Hands-free gate.*

Hanger: Mini hanger perfect for baby clothes.

Happi Tummi™: See *Tummy pack.*

Harness: See *Toddler harness.*

Harness Buddy®: Our favorite type of toddler harness that has a little stuffed animal backpack that peeks over the child's shoulder. It's a cute alternative to the standard tether toddler harness. See *Toddler harness.*

Head support cushion: See *Head support pillow.*

Head support pillow: A soft U-shaped pillow that surrounds the top and sides of a baby's head in a car seat or stroller to properly support the neck and head.

High chair

    Feeding booster: A portable and usually adjustable booster seat that allows your child to eat safely and conveniently when away from home. A feeding booster is used for babies that sit up on their own through toddlerhood. Boosters can come with multiple trays and are designed to secure to a stable chair.

    Full-size: A very young child's feeding chair that has long legs, a footrest, and usually a detachable tray.

    Space saver: Similar to a full-size high chair without the long legs. It's the top part of a high chair that is designed to strap to a dining chair to save room in the kitchen. A space saver is not a portable high chair but meant to save floor space in your kitchen.

    Hook-on: A travel high chair that hooks onto the side of a table. These chairs usually fold compactly for easy travel.

High chair accessories

    Mess mat: A large plastic mat that fits under a high chair to protect floors from mealtime spills.

    Toys: Toys that are either attached by suction or fastened to a high chair tray to keep baby entertained before, during, and after mealtime.

Hip hammock: See *Baby carrier.*

Hooded towel: A small bath towel for baby complete with a hood to wrap and keep baby warm right out of the tub.

Hook-on chair: See *High chair.*

Humidifier: Also called "vaporizer." A device for increasing the humidity in a room. There are cool mist and warm mist humidifiers, although cool mist humidifiers are recommended by pediatricians as the only type of humidifier to be safely used in a baby's room because of burn hazards. Humidifiers improve the air quality and moisturize the air, which can prevent stuffiness, making it easier for babies to breathe, especially when they have colds. Humidifiers are also good in dry climates to prevent baby's nasal passage from getting dry.

Ibuprofen: A nonsteroidal, anti-inflammatory drug such as Infants' Motrin® used for the management of mild to moderate pain, fever, and inflammation. Many moms swear by ibuprofen, but it is more likely to upset the tummy than acetaminophen (Infants' Tylenol®).

Infant car seat: See *Car seat.*

Infant car seat toy bar: See *Car seat accessories: Toy bar for infant car seat.*

Infant-only seat: See *Car seat: Infant car seat carrier.*

Infant support pillow: See *Head support pillow.*

Infant travel bed: A compact, lightweight, and foldable bed used for traveling with baby. This bed is designed to be folded up and carried with you.

Inflatable potty: Portable potty that inflates to give a convenient and sanitary solution when restrooms are unsanitary or not available.

Insert: See *Car seat accessories.*

Ionic freshener: A device that claims to cleanse the air of pollen, dust, mold, bacteria—even odors. Ionic technology circulates air without a motor, so it's silent and energy efficient.

Itzbeen™: A baby care timer to help new parents keep track of the overwhelming number of baby care details. Itzbeen™ has four timers that count up with the touch of a button, and a host of other helpful features, all designed with the needs of a new parent in mind.

Jar holder: A plastic device that holds a jar of baby food and suctions to a table or high chair tray to keep the jar in place.

Jar pac: A padded tote designed to carry three jars of baby food (any size) safely without worrying about the loose jars breaking in your diaper bag.

Jogging stroller: See *Stroller: Single jogging.*

Juice box holder: A hard, plastic container with open top and handles that holds a juice box to allow toddlers to hold their juice box without squeezing the juice everywhere.

Juice Pal™: See *Juice box holder.*

Jumper: Usually a seat (similar to an outdoor baby swing) suspended with bungee cords to allow baby to jump. Jumpers come in two types: doorway jumper and stationary jumper. A doorway jumper is attached to a doorframe, while a stationary jumper is attached to a frame, similar to a baby swing. We do not recommend doorway jumpers.

Jumperoo®: See *Jumper.*

Kangaroo carrier: See *Baby carrier.*

Kid's Switch™: A light switch extender that allows children to turn the light on and off by themselves.

Knee pads: See *Knee protectors.*

Knee protectors: Baby-size knee pads to protect little knees from rug burn and discomfort from crawling on carpet and hard surfaces.

Lanolin: See *Breast moisturizing balm.*

Lansinoh®: See *Breast moisturizing balm.*

Lap pad: An absorbent pad to soak up accidents; can be used to protect a surface, keeping it dry and sanitary, while changing baby.

LATCH: Stands for Lower Anchors and Tethers for Children. LATCH is an alternative to securing a car seat instead of using the vehicle seat belts. Special car seat LATCH straps are easily clipped onto permanent anchors installed in all cars sold in the United States after 2002.

Layette: Any soft fabric item you would dress or wrap a newborn in. It can refer to clothes, blankets, and socks just as easily as burp clothes and lap pads.

Lightweight stroller: See *Stroller.*

LilyPadz®: Silicon breast pads for nursing moms that cling to the skin and not the bra, which exert gentle pressure to your breasts, to prevent leaks.

Link-a-Doos™: See *Links.*

Links: Plastic, teethable rings and loops that link together to form a chain of toys by themselves or can be used to attach other favorite toys to a stroller, car seat, high chair, or swing. Very useful. Our babies love them.

Link set: See *Links.*

Link toys: See *Links.*

Lounger: A reclined sling chair for baby that resembles a very small camping chair folding up for travel and storage into a bag. These chairs usually have a three-point harness and soft toy bar.

Mattress: A small mattress designed specifically for the dimensions of a standard crib: 52 x 28 x 5.5 inches (132 x 71 x 14 cm). There are also round crib mattresses made specifically for round cribs.

Mattress cover: A pad (usually waterproof or highly absorbent) that goes on a crib mattress like a sheet. It is designed to protect the mattress from diaper leaks.

Mattress pad: A pad (usually waterproof or highly absorbent) that just lies on a crib mattress under the sheet. It is designed to protect the mattress from diaper leaks.

Medicine dispenser pacifier: A silicon pacifier that gently dispenses medicine from the attached reservoir, with built-in measuring indicator, as baby sucks. We've never had good luck with these. They are harder than a regular pacifier and our kids would not be tricked into sucking for more than one second.

434 ☆ the **Baby Gizmo** buying guide

Medicine dropper: A short plastic tube with a rubber bulb on top used to measure medicine by drops and dispense medicine to a baby.

Medicine safe: A box with a lock or kid-proof locking mechanism to keep medicines away from children. This is a must-have for parents because accidental poisoning remains a leading cause of death for kids! All medicines, vitamins, and other supplements should always be locked in a medicine safe. (P.S. Your prenatal vitamins and iron pills are especially poisonous to small children.)

Messenger bag: A diaper bag that resembles a laptop case, making it for many moms an easier transition from the workforce to the playground. Most messenger bags come with adjustable straps that allow them to be carried like a purse, slung across the body, or hung from the back of a stroller.

Mittens: Baby mittens prevent babies from accidentally scratching themselves. These are also great to use for newborns when going out in public to keep strangers from touching baby's hands and spreading germs.

Mobile: An arrangement of small toys or objects that hangs over a crib to provide visual stimulation for a baby. Most include movement and music.

Monitor: A compact, two-part gadget, including a transmitter and a receiver, that allows you to keep an ear or eye on your little one when you're not in the same room.

Moses basket: A small, portable newborn bassinet that is usually made of wicker and sits on the floor.

Motrin® (Infants'): A popular type of ibuprofen. See *Ibuprofen.*

Multiples stroller: See *Stroller.*

Nail clippers: A small device used to trim baby's fingernails and toenails.

Nasal aspirator: A rubber device that provides gentle suction to remove excess mucus.

Nasal syringe: A washable, durable, soft PVC bulb used to suck nasal mucus from the nose of babies when they are congested.

Neck pillow: A small U-shaped pillow that fits around baby's neck, with the opening in the front, to provide extra support to baby's head and neck in car seats, strollers, swings, and bouncers.

Neck wings: See *Car seat accessories.*

Nipple: See *Bottle nipple.*

Nipple shield: Also called "nursing shield." Nipple shields look like a hollow breast cast in silicone with a hole in the nipple. You wear them over your own breast and nipple to aid in breastfeeding while your baby is actually sucking.

Nuk®: A brand name for a pacifier. See *Pacifier.*

Nurser: Another name for a baby bottle.

Nursery air purifier: A machine that purports to clean the air and help eliminate odors in the nursery by releasing negative ions into the air, which are then supposed to remove positively charged allergens, bacteria, dust, and odors.

Nursery cart organizer: An organizing cart to keep all baby essentials in one convenient location in the nursery.

Nursery sanitizer: Automatic sanitizer for toys, pacifiers, and bottles that kills the germs that cause colds, flu, earache, diarrhea, and more by using dry heat.

Nursery storage: Wood, plastic, or fabric containers in which to store baby supplies and clothes to keep things organized.

Nursing bra: A specially designed bra to make access to the breasts for breastfeeding easier. Many nursing bras come with "flaps" or material that covers the breast that can be detached without having to undo the bra. Other nursing bras without flaps are made to be easily pulled to one side for nursing, but one drawback is that they don't provide great support.

Nursing footrest: A footrest used when nursing to help eliminate stress on the legs, back, shoulders, and arms. The footrest or stool also elevates your lap to help position the baby better for breastfeeding. Great for shorter people!

Nursing milk organizer: A plastic container that is used to organize bags of expressed breast milk by keeping them in order of date. This container also keeps breast milk away from other food in your refrigerator or freezer.

Nursing pads: Pads (either disposable or reusable cotton) designed to wear inside the bra to protect clothes and avoid embarrassment from leaking breast milk.

Nursing pillow: A firm pillow intended to help mother and baby position correctly for breastfeeding. The baby lies on this pillow during nursing to help maintain a proper position for latching on. A nursing pillow can wrap around mom or sit comfortably in her lap.

Nursing privacy wrap: Material, usually similar to a shawl, worn by a mother to cover a nursing baby for privacy.

Nursing pump: A manual or electrical device used for expressing milk from the breasts of a woman who is breastfeeding.

Nursing shield: See *Nipple shield.*

Nursing shirt: A shirt specially designed with slits, hidden pockets, or flaps on the front to allow easy nursing bra access.

Nursing stool: See *Nursing footrest.*

Nursing tank: A tank top with a nursing bra built in.

Onesie: A short- or long-sleeved one-piece outfit that has no legs, almost like a little swimsuit for baby.

Organizer: See *Stroller accessories.*

Otoscope: Also called "ear and throat illuminator." A medical device used to look in the ear and throat. The head of this device contains an electric light source and a low-power magnifying lens. It sounds neat, but we have no idea what we're looking for, and it does worry us that people will injure their baby's eardrums or self-diagnose at home incorrectly. Aren't we not even supposed to use Q-tips in our baby's ears? Somehow this seems much more intrusive.

Ottoman: A low seat or stool used to rest your feet on when seated. Gliders have matching ottomans (usually sold separately) that glide back and forth with the motion of the chair.

Outlet cover: A safety cover for an electrical outlet to prevent baby from getting electrocuted. Outlet covers are available as plastic plugs that plug into each socket or an over-the-outlet cover plate/box.

Outlet plug: See *Outlet cover.*

Oven lock: A heat-resistant lock made specifically for oven doors.

Pacifier: A nipple-like device given to a baby to suck to provide oral stimulation or to soothe. Much like bottle nipples, they are available in either rubber (the yellowish ones) or silicone (clear). Rubber is softer and many babies prefer it, but it will break down over time, and chunks could pose a choking hazard, so check your rubber pacifiers regularly. Silicone nipples are harder and some babies resist them, but they will never break down. Recent reports suggest pacifier use helps combat SIDS, although using one for too long can disrupt normal tooth development. Our secret? We never move past the smallest newborn size. No big size 3 binkies for us. Our kids only know that binkies are tiny, they use them perfectly when they are babies, and when they hit about 2 years old, the tiny nipple ceases to soothe them well because it is so tiny, and they happily abandon it.

Pacifier pod: A small carrying case, much like a cell phone case, that holds a pacifier and clips to the outside of your diaper bag or purse for easy access. Helps keep pacifiers clean as well. They're usually pretty stylish, and we love 'em.

Pacifier rinser: A device to rinse a dirty pacifier when no sink is available.

Pacifier thermometer: A pacifier that is a digital thermometer used to take baby's temperature. It's nice in theory but even though all our kids have taken pacifiers, none of them were willing to suck on this pacifier for more than 10 seconds before refusing it, therefore preventing a temperature reading.

Pack 'n Play®: See *Play yard.*

PC Guard® Tower Protector: A shield for the face of your hard drive that attaches with Velcro straps, preventing baby from touching it, turning your computer off without warning, and sticking things into your drives.

Pee-Pee Teepee®: A brand name for a baby pee shield. See *Pee shield.*

Pee shield: A cone-shaped, slightly stiff piece of cloth designed to make changing baby boys' diapers a drier experience for all. You place the product over the boy's exposed privates to keep cold drafts at bay, and urine from flying. Pee shields are machine washable and reusable.

Peter Potty®: A toddler urinal designed to make potty training a boy easier and fun.

Piddle Pad®: See *Waterproof pad for stroller/car seat.*

Place mat: A disposable or reusable mat used on a table in front of children during mealtime to protect them from germs on a public table as well as to protect tables at home from mess.

Plate cover: A device that seals off electrical outlets from curious toddlers.

Play center: See *Activity center.*

Playground: Another name for an activity mat. See *Activity mat.*

Play gym: See *Activity gym.*

Play mat: See *Activity mat.*

Playpen: Also called "play zones." An enclosure consisting of gate units clipped together to form a pen, just like for baby animals. Some are square, but most are hexagonal to give baby more room. Used primarily for corralling babies.

Play yard: A compact sleeping or playing enclosure that folds up, travels, and stores easily. Most have mesh sides and a metal frame. Many play yards come with features such as changing tables, bassinets, mobiles, music, and lights.

Play yard accessories

> **Canopy:** A removable shade or dome cover on a play yard to protect baby from the harmful rays and heat of the sun.

> **Changing table pad cover:** An absorbent cloth cover made specially for the dimensions of a play yard changing table.

Portable crib: A wooden or metal crib with slatted sides that resembles a standard rectangular crib, only slightly smaller and cheaper. Portable cribs have wheels for easy transport.

Portable feeding seat: See *High chair.*

Portable place mat: See *Place mat.*

Portable play yard: See *Play yard.*

Portacrib: Another name for play yard. See *Play yard.*

Positioner: See *Car seat accessories.*

Potty: A small plastic portable toilet used for toilet training a toddler. Potties are low to the ground so that toddlers can easily sit on them on their own.

Potty chair: See *Potty.*

Potty doll: An interactive doll or stuffed animal used for potty training to help children transition from diapers to underwear in a fun, encouraging way.

Potty Monkey®: A brand of potty doll. See *Potty doll.*

Potty seat: A toddler-size seat that is designed to fit right on top of your toilet seat to make potty time more comfortable and relaxing for your little one.

Potty stool: A stool to help children safely and easily get onto an adult toilet.

Potty Topper®: See *Disposable toilet seat cover.*

Pouch sling: A baby sling that is a continuous loop of fabric that makes a pouch seat for baby.

Powdered formula: See *Dry formula.*

Power strip safety cover: A plastic box that completely covers your power strip except for a long thin opening for the cords.

Pram: Another name for baby carriage. See *Stroller.*

Prenatal listening system: A device used to listen to your unborn baby's heartbeat. We've never had any success with the ones we bought, but if you're going to give it a go, you're supposed to wait until the second half of your second trimester, when baby has a stronger heartbeat. (Although all we ever heard was our own. And gas. Lots of gas.)

Protector: See *Seat protector.*

Puddle Pad®: A long, antibacterial, foam piece covered in machine washable terry cloth and in the shape of an animal such as a duck, used to soak up bathwater puddles next to the tub.

Rain shield: See *Stroller accessories.*

Rash ointment and powder: A cream or powder used to treat and prevent diaper rash. Most ointments are made with zinc oxide, which pediatricians recommend to protect, relieve, and soothe your baby's tender skin from diaper rash.

Rattle

> **Foot rattle:** A soft rattle that is either sewn onto a sock or attaches around the ankle with Velcro that makes noise when the baby kicks her feet.

> **Teething rattle:** A small toy rattle that makes a sound when baby shakes it, but is also good for chewing on when baby is teething.

> **Toy rattle:** A small toy that makes a sound when baby shakes it.

> **Wrist rattle:** A soft rattle that attaches to the wrist with Velcro.

Ready-to-use formula: See *Formula.*

Receiving blanket: A very soft, lightweight blanket used to wrap a newborn.

Rectal thermometer: See *Thermometer: Rectal thermometer.*

Ring sling: A baby sling that uses fabric threaded through two rings.

Rocker: A bouncer seat on rockers or a curved support that allows a parent to manually rock the seat back and forth.

Safe plate: A safety outlet cover plate that replaces a standard plate cover to keep the outlets closed when not in use with spring-loaded sliding doors.

Safety bed rail: See *Bed rail.*

Safety gate: A gate that either screws to the wall or suctions to a door frame to keep baby out of any room or away from stairs.

Safety harness: A safety restraint used for walking with children in crowds. It typically consists of a shoulder harness worn across the chest and over the shoulder that attaches to a strap in the back that the parent holds or attaches to his or her wrist. Safety harnesses prevent child separation from parents in a crowd.

Safety latches: Latches used on drawers, cabinets, and appliances to keep them closed and locked to prevent toddlers from accessing their contents.

Safety night-light: A cool-to-the-touch night-light that prevents children from getting burned from a hot light bulb.

Safety scissors: Scissors with a blunt point used to trim baby's fingernails and toenails.

Safety sheet: A crib sheet designed to stay in place to prevent it from coming loose from the mattress and becoming a suffocation and strangulation hazard. Some crib safety sheets go on the mattress like a pillowcase, so they cannot come loose.

Safety tap: A plastic box that applies to the shower wall, covering the hot water tap to prevent your child from turning up the hot water and scalding himself.

Scale: See *Baby scale.*

Sealing clip (for milk bags): Plastic clasp used to seal a bag of breast milk for storage.

Sealing disk: See *Bottle sealer.*

Seat belt adjuster: See *Car seat belt.*

Seat belt locking clip: See *Car seat belt.*

Seat belt positioner: See *Car seat belt.*

Seat belt tightener: See *Car seat belt.*

Seat protector

    Seat back: A plastic or vinyl protector for the back of a car seat to protect it from dirty shoes and scuff marks.

    Seat bottom: A seat mat, usually made of foam, fleece, or water-resistant material, for under a car seat to protect your car seat interior from dents, scratches, and spills.

Shade: See *Stroller accessories.*

Shampoo goggles: Plastic lenses that shield sensitive eyes; attached with a neoprene strap that creates a seal on the forehead, blocking out water and suds.

Shampoo rinse cup: A pitcher with one flat side that has a soft, rubbery panel used for rinsing baby's hair, while shielding face and eyes from soap and water.

Shampoo visor: A foam rubber visor for children to keep shampoo out of their eyes during hair washing.

Sheet protector: See *Sheet saver.*

Sheets (fitted, play yard, bassinet): Small bed linens designed to snugly fit onto crib, play yard, or bassinet mattresses.

Sheet saver: An absorbent pad with a waterproof layer so that baby leaks will not dirty the crib sheets. Usually has four ties to attach to the crib rails to keep in place.

Shopping cart cover: A protective overlay created with an elastic casing to easily expand to completely cover the entire seating area of unsanitary shopping carts. We love these. They are a must-have for our shopping trips.

Shoulder strap adjuster: A device that allows proper placement of a car seat shoulder strap, making the seat belt safer and more comfortable for a child.

Shower mat: A slip-proof, rubber mat for the floor of the shower to prevent slips and falls.

Side-snap shirt: A baby shirt that overlaps in front and snaps on the front side. These shirts are great for easy clothes changing because the shirt doesn't have to be pulled over the head.

Single stroller, all-terrain: See *Stroller.*

Single stroller, jogging: See *Stroller.*

Single stroller, standard: See *Stroller.*

Single stroller, travel system: See *Stroller.*

Single stroller, umbrella/lightweight: See *Stroller.*

Sippy cup: Spill-proof cup designed for toddlers. Well, more spill-resistant. They can certainly shake liquid out of these things.

Sippy cup tether: See *Bottle strap.*

Sit 'n Secure®: A triangle of fabric covering the chest and hip area of your child while it Velcros them to a chair, shopping cart, or stroller in a secure sitting position.

Sit and stand stroller: Also called "stroller-and-a-half." A stroller designed with one full stroller seat in front with a small bench and stand-on platform for an older child in back.

Sleeper: Technically a one-piece like a onesie, but the big difference is they have legs. Sleepers can be short or long sleeved, but they go all the way to the ankle and sometimes the toes.

Sleep positioner: A product made up of two soft rolls and a pad, designed to keep babies from rolling on their stomachs while sleeping. While positioners were initially intended to help keep babies on their backs to prevent SIDS, experts have discovered that babies placed on their backs stay on their backs and don't need positioners. And since the positioners themselves present suffocation risks, they are *not* recommended anymore.

Sleep sack: See *Wearable blanket.*

Sliding door lock: A plastic lock that attaches to most surfaces with heavy-duty adhesive. Helps prevent child's access to patio, balcony, closets, and more.

Sling: See *Baby carrier.*

Slumber Bear ®: See *Womb sounds bear.*

Snack Trap®: A plastic cup/bowl with handles to hold dry snacks for a toddler with a rubber lid, sporting a star-shaped slotted hole to prevent the contents from spilling, yet giving children access to snacks.

Snugli®: See *Baby carrier.*

Spill mat: An oversize plastic sheet for under the high chair that catches spills and protects floors.

Spill-proof cup: See *Sippy cup.*

Sport utility stroller: Also called an "all-terrain stroller." See *Stroller.*

Spout cover: See *Bath accessories.*

Static eliminator dryer sheets: Hypoallergenic, antistatic dryer sheets that soften fabric and smooth wrinkles without chemicals for kids with allergies and sensitive skin.

Stationary entertainer: See *Activity center.*

Stationary infant seat: An infant seat resembling a small, round restaurant booster. These seats are not ideal for feeding, as they have no straps for the seat or the baby, and can only be used flat on the floor. They should never, *never* be placed on chairs, counters, or any raised surface. They allow new babies to sit upright long before they can on their own, but should not be used with babies with poor head and neck control, or babies that can crawl or climb out of them.

Stay-Put Cutlery: Plastic utensils attached to a stretchy coil then suctioned to a table or tray to prevent utensils from being tossed or dropped on the floor.

Step stool: Typically, a portable set of two steps to allow children to reach higher objects such as a faucet that they wouldn't normally be able to reach.

Sterilizer: A machine to kill germs on bottles, toys, and other washable baby gear with high temperatures from steam, dry heat, or boiling liquid.

Stove guard: A sturdy, heat-resistant shield to protect children from reaching the hot burners, pots, and pans on a stovetop.

Stove knob covers: Plastic, hinged locking covers for your stove knobs. These are great for stove knobs in front of the burners because curious toddlers can't help themselves from the temptation of turning those knobs.

Strap covers: See *Car seat accessories.*

Stroller

> **Carriage/pram:** A giant baby basket on wheels, providing a traditional and usually luxurious ride for new babies.
>
> **Single stroller, all-terrain:** A rugged, outdoorsy stroller with special wheels and more flexible handling that allows you to tread over uneven, unpaved, and even unusual surfaces like sand.
>
> **Single stroller, jogging:** The only stroller designed for safe running, featuring sturdy construction to withstand the speed, a fixed front wheel, hand brakes, and parent tethers so it can't get away from you.
>
> **Single stroller, luxury travel system:** An expensive but lightweight designer stroller that comes with all manner of extras, including removable carry-cots, reversible handles, and toddler seats.
>
> **Single stroller, standard:** The most common stroller; a large stroller that can accommodate newborns to preschoolers and provides loads of convenient features.
>
> **Single stroller, travel system:** A standard stroller that comes with an infant car seat carrier as part of a coordinating set.

Single stroller, umbrella/lightweight: A stroller weighing 15 pounds or less that folds compactly for easy portability.

Double stroller, all-terrain: A rugged, outdoorsy stroller for two children, with special wheels and more flexible handling that allows you to tread over uneven, unpaved, and even unusual surfaces like sand.

Double stroller, jogging: The only stroller designed for safe running with two children, featuring sturdy construction to withstand the speed, a fixed front wheel, hand brakes, and parent tethers so your two riders can't get away from you.

Double stroller, standard: The most common double stroller; a large stroller than can accommodate two newborns to preschoolers and provides loads of convenient features. But they are heavy. And big.

Double stroller, umbrella/lightweight: A lightweight stroller with room for two.

Multiples stroller: A stroller designed to hold triples, quads, or even up to six babies.

Stroller accessories

Blanket bag: A cozy pouch or bunting to keep baby warm that fits into a car seat, stroller, jogger, or bicycle trailer.

Bug canopy: Also called "bug netting." A finely woven mesh protector that completely encloses the front and sides of the stroller while providing ventilation. This helps keep flying insects and bugs out of your stroller and away from your child.

Carry-cot: Sometimes called a "bassinet," this is actually a detachable Moses basket made of fabric that comes with or can be purchased for many upscale strollers. Meant for tiny babies only, they are indeed wonderful extras.

Car seat adapter: A device that allows you to snap your infant car seat into your stroller to make it a travel system.

Cup holder: A plastic device to hold a cup or bottle that is attached to a stroller.

Organizer: A hanging bag, usually attached with Velcro to the back of the stroller, that keeps essentials such as bottles, car keys, cell phones, and diapers organized and accessible.

Parasol: An umbrella that attaches to your stroller for extra shade or protection from rain.

Rain shield: A shield that protects baby from rain, snow, or wind while riding in the stroller.

Safety flag: A tall orange flag that attaches to your stroller to allow more visibility to motorists.

Snack tray: A tray attached to a stroller in front for baby and/or across the handles for mom to carry and make snacks accessible.

Sunshade: A protective covering that attaches to a stroller to protect baby from the harmful rays and heat of the sun.

Toys: Toys designed to attach to the side or front of a stroller to keep baby occupied while riding.

Strollometer®: A speedometer and odometer designed to help moms track the workout benefits of walking with baby; fits right on a baby stroller.

Suctionware® babyware: Bowls and divided plates that suction to the table or high chair tray to try to prevent baby from spilling or throwing dishware.

Sun block (baby): A substance (cream, lotion or spray) used to protect a baby's sensitive skin from the harmful ultraviolet rays of the sun. Parents should check with their pediatricians before using sun block on the littlest infants because most baby sun blocks are not suggested for infants under 6 months. Because babies don't sweat like adults, too much sun block could interfere with their natural cooling mechanism. According to the Academy of Pediatrics, babies under 6 months of age should be kept out of direct sunlight. Move your baby to the shade under a tree, umbrella, or stroller canopy.

Sunshade: See *Stroller accessories: Sunshade.*

Superyard: A large hexagon of plastic gates attached together to form an enclosed, safe, and portable play area for toddlers.

Swaddler: A blanket designed to make it easier to wrap (swaddle) your baby.

Swing: A seat suspended from a metal frame in which baby rides to an automatic push, supplied by battery or electrical power (no one makes manual, windup swings anymore). Many swings have multiple speed settings, as well as music, mobiles, and attached toys.

    Travel swing: Also called a "take-along swing" or "portable swing." A compact swing with shorter legs that folds for easier travel.

Talcum powder: Also called "baby powder." A powder made up of various combinations of zinc stearate, magnesium silicates, and other silicates that are finely ground; used in the past to try to keep the diaper area dry to prevent and treat diaper rash. Talcum powder use on babies is *not* recommended because baby's nose and butt are close together; babies are at risk of inhaling the fine powder, which could cause life-threatening problems and even death.

Tandem stroller: Another name for a double stroller. See *Stroller.*

Teether: An object made with different textures and softness for baby to bite or chew on during teething.

Teething gel: Baby teething pain medication that comes in gel, liquid, or swab form and is applied directly to baby's gums. Most dentists do not recommend the use of these products, as they essentially just numb the baby's mouth. We prefer Infants Tylenol®.

Teething rattle: See *Rattle.*

Teething tablets: Natural teething analgesic (painkiller) made of botanicals used to ease swollen gums, drooling, fever, irritability, and pain caused by cutting teeth.

Tether strap: A strap (material similar to a seat belt) that attaches to a child car seat on one end and the vehicle's tether-anchor hardware on the other.

Thermal tote: A bag that maintains the correct temperature for cold or warm items, such as cold bottles of breast milk or formula, for a few hours for feedings on the go.

Thermometer: An instrument for measuring baby's body temperature.

    Ear thermometer: A digital thermometer designed to take temperature when properly inserted into the ear canal. These are very popular because many of these thermometers take a very quick reading at the push of a button.

    Pacifier thermometer: A pacifier that is a digital thermometer, used to take baby's temperature. It's nice in theory but even though all our kids have taken pacifiers, none of them was willing to suck on this pacifier for more than 10 seconds before refusing it, therefore preventing a temperature reading.

    Rectal thermometer: A special thermometer with a short stubby tip, used for measuring a small child's temperature by inserting it into the rectum. A rectal thermometer is the most accurate way to take a baby's temperature.

    Temporal artery thermometer: A device that uses infrared technology to measure temperature with a wipe across the forehead.

ThumbGuard®: A dentist-invented rubber guard that wraps around the child's wrist and covers the thumb to help break the habit of thumbsucking.

Tinkle Targets™: This flushable, floating product encourages little boys to stand at the potty and helps teach them to aim.

Tinkle Tube™: See *Travel urinal.*

Toddler harness: See *Safety harness.*

Toddler tote: A bag, smaller than the traditional diaper bag, for the transitional period when you no longer need to lug as much stuff as a newborn requires but you do still need a few diapers and snacks.

Toddler tracker: A device that includes a child-tracking unit that clips to your child's clothes and a parent activator that can clip on your key chain. If you get separated, you push the button for an audible beep to lead you to your child.

Toddler wipes: Small, moistened, flushable wipes designed for toddler's little hands. Great for potty training.

Toilet lock: A safety lock that keeps a toilet closed so that toddlers cannot open it, because a toilet can be a drowning hazard.

Toilet paper saver: An easy-for-you, hard-for-your-child elastic band lock for your toilet paper roll to prevent unwanted unrolling.

Toilet trainer: A toddler-size toilet seat, designed to fit onto a regular toilet seat to make using the bathroom easier for your little one.

Toothbrush: A miniature toothbrush made especially for baby teeth.

Top tether: See *Car seat accessories: Top tether.*

Tot lock: A safety lock that is made to keep things closed and inaccessible to toddlers. Tot locks are available for doors, cabinets, toilets, stoves, drawers, and windows.

Towel: An absorbent cloth used to dry baby.

Toy bag: Any bag used for storing toys.

Toy bar: A cloth, plastic, or even wire bar with small toys attached that stretches in front of baby and is part of a stroller, bouncer, or swing. You can also buy toy bars separately to add them to many baby gear items that need additional toys.

Toy rattle: See *Rattle.*

Training pants: Very thick, absorbent, cotton underwear often used during potty training to transition from diapers to regular underwear.

Travel bed: See *Infant travel bed.*

Travel blanket: A large, usually waterproof, blanket designed for outdoor use. These blankets are meant for using on the ground and pack up for easy travel.

Travel cot: Another term for a play yard or small, portable bed.

Travel high chair cover: See *High chair accessories.*

Travel mat: See *Travel blanket.*

Travel system: See *Stroller.*

Travel tray: See *Car seat accessories.*

Travel urinal: A plastic container to assist potty training boys in out-of-the-house bathroom emergencies.

Triplet stroller: Also called "multiples stroller." See *Stroller.*

Triplette™ stroller: Also called "multiples stroller." See *Stroller.*

Tub guard set: See *Bath accessories.*

Tub toy organizer: See *Bath accessories.*

Tummy pack: An herbal pack you heat up in the microwave and then wrap around baby's torso. It uses gentle warmth and the natural aromatherapy of lavender, chamomile, and lemongrass to try to calm upset tummies without using drugs or drops.

Tummy time mat: A small mat that entertains babies while laying on their tummy, helping build essential head control and trunk strength with "tummy time."

Umbrella stroller: See *Stroller.*

Vaporizer: See *Humidifier.*

VCR guard: A plastic shield that covers the front of a VCR player to prevent babies and toddlers from pushing the buttons. The shield is made of clear plastic so that the remote will still work from a distance.

Walker: A plastic base with a fabric seat and wheeled frame that allows your child to "walk" around. Walkers are dangerous and should *never* be used!

Walking Wings™: A support vest that fastens around the chest of the baby with two adjustable straps and padded handles for mom or dad. These vests are used to assist baby with learning to walk without bending over. We're not buying it. Literally, we're not buying it.

Warmer (bottle): See *Bottle warmer.*

Warmer (wipes): See *Wipe warmer.*

Warm mist humidifier: See *Humidifier.*

Washcloth: Miniature cloth used for cleaning baby. There are two types of baby washcloths: thicker cloths used for bathing and thinner, cheaper washcloths used in place of baby wipes for diaper changes.

Water bottle nipple adaptor: Water bottle adaptor that actually screws a baby bottle nipple onto any standard water bottle.

Waterproof pad for stroller/car seat: A soft, absorbent waterproof insert for a car seat or stroller seat that eliminates the need to remove the whole seat cover after a diaper leak or complete blowout.

Wearable blanket: A long sleeping bag-type blanket that a baby wears over regular sleepwear that is closed at the bottom, zips up the center, and snaps over each shoulder. It's wide at the bottom to allow freedom of movement of baby's legs and once zipped cannot slip off a child's body. It is a safe way by eliminating loose blankets in the crib to give your baby warmth while sleeping.

Wee Block®: See *Pee shield.*

Weekender bag: The largest diaper bag around; a bag slightly smaller than traditional duffel bags, with pockets, pouches, and insulated places for all of baby's things, instead of empty space inside.

White Hot® infant spoon: A spoon with a heat-sensitive tip that turns white when food is too hot.

Wide-neck bottles: Just like a standard bottle, only shorter and fatter.

Window alert: An alarm for the window that sounds when the window has been opened.

Window guard: Window guards secure into the sides of a window frame and have bars spaced no more than four inches apart to prevent a child from falling out.

Window wedge: A safety device to prevent curious toddlers from opening windows and falling out. The wedge allows you to control the height and width of the window opening.

Wipes: Premoistened, disposable small towels used for cleaning during diaper changes. Wipes are also used to clean hands and faces when a wet cloth is not available.

Wipe warmer: A device that warms baby wipes so that the cold wipes don't startle baby. Definitely an unsafe product you don't need!

Wire guard: A safety device that looks like molding that encases electrical cords to keep them out of sight and out of reach.

Womb Sounds Bear: Soft, plush toy that plays in-utero sound recordings to soothe and comfort a newborn.

Wrist rattle: See *Rattle: Wrist rattle.*

Index

About the Authors

Heather Maclean, mother of three, is the founder of Little Laureate, an award-winning educational children's media company, and cofounder of BabyGizmo.com. Named one of the "16 Best Entrepreneurs in America" by Sir Richard Branson, she accompanied the adventurous business legend on a 50,000-mile trip around the world, alternately helping improve the life of others (designing sustainable development initiatives in South Africa) and fearing for her own (rappelling out of a Black Hawk helicopter in a Moroccan sandstorm). Heather began her career at Disney, where she had the distinction of being the first person ever to answer Mickey Mouse's e-mail. When not castle hunting in her husband's native Scotland, she happily resides in Chicago.

Hollie Schultz knows firsthand the ups and downs of trying to find the perfect baby gear purchase, as she just had her second (but hopefully not last!) baby. Hollie is a cofounder of BabyGizmo.com and a certified CPS (Child Passenger Safety) technician. She lives in Chicago.